Routledge Handbook
of Corporate Law

The *Routledge Handbook of Corporate Law* provides an accessible overview of current research in the field, from an international and comparative perspective.

In recent years there has been an explosion of corporate law research, as this area of law continues to develop rapidly throughout the world. Traditionally, Anglo–American corporate law theory has dominated debates and publications; however, this handbook readdresses the balance by exploring the treatment of corporate law in both Europe and Asia, as well as developments in the US and UK. Bringing together a wide range of key thinkers in the field, this volume is divided into three main parts:

- Thinking about corporate law
- Corporate law principles and governance
- Some cross-cultural comparisons

Providing up-to-date and authoritative articles covering all the key aspects of corporate law, this reference work is essential reading for advanced students, scholars and practitioners in the field.

Roman Tomasic is Professor of Law at the University of South Australia and, until 2012, held a continuing appointment as the Chair in Company Law in Durham Law School at Durham University. He has been the Chair of the Australasian Law Teachers' Association and has also been active in legal research and the development of legal education in Australia, the United Kingdom and East Asia.

Routledge Handbook of Corporate Law

Edited by
Roman Tomasic

Routledge
Taylor & Francis Group

LONDON AND NEW YORK

First published 2017
by Routledge
2 Park Square, Milton Park, Abingdon, Oxon OX14 4RN

and by Routledge
52 Vanderbilt Avenue, New York, NY 10017

First issued in paperback 2020

Routledge is an imprint of the Taylor & Francis Group, an informa business

British Library Cataloguing in Publication Data
A catalogue record for this book is available from the British Library

Library of Congress Cataloging in Publication Data
Names: Tomasic, Roman, editor.
Title: Routledge handbook of corporate law / edited by Roman Tomasic.
Other titles: Corporate law
Description: Abingdon, Oxon [UK]; New York: Routledge, 2017. | Includes bibliographical references and index.
Identifiers: LCCN 2016029625 | ISBN 9781138786899 (hbk) | ISBN 9781315767017 (ebk)
Subjects: LCSH: Corporation law—Handbooks, manuals, etc. | Business enterprises—Law and legislation—Handbooks, manuals, etc. | Corporate governance—Law and legislation—Handbooks, manuals, etc. | Corporate veil—Handbooks, manuals, etc.
Classification: LCC K1315 .R68 2017 | DDC 346/.066—dc23
LC record available at https://lccn.loc.gov/2016029625

ISBN 13: 978-0-367-58146-6 (pbk)
ISBN 13: 978-1-138-78689-9 (hbk)

Typeset in Bembo
by Keystroke, Neville Lodge, Tettenhall, Wolverhampton

Contents

Notes on contributors

Folarin Akinbami: Dr Folarin Akinbami has been a Lecturer in Commercial Law at Durham University, where he taught and researched financial regulation and corporate governance. He was seconded to the Law Commission of England and Wales, as Team Lawyer, between October 2013 and June 2014, where he worked on the Fiduciary Duties of the Investment Intermediaries project. Prior to his appointment as lecturer he was a Post-Doctoral Research Associate in Durham Law School and the Institute of Hazard, Risk and Resilience at Durham University, where he worked on the Leverhulme Trust-funded 'Tipping Point' project; this led to his co-editing of *Complexity and Crisis in the Financial System: Critical Perspectives on the Evolution of American and British Banking* by M Hollow, F Akinbami and R Michie (eds), which was published by Edward Elgar in 2016.

Helen Anderson: Professor Helen Anderson holds a teaching and research position at the Melbourne Law School. Her current research looks at the prevention and deterrence of fraudulent phoenix activity. She is the author of many scholarly publications, including the 2014 book *The Protection of Employee Entitlements in Insolvency: An Australian Perspective*, published by Melbourne University Publishing in 2014.

Stephen Bottomley: Professor Stephen Bottomley is Dean of the ANU College of Law, Australian National University. His main areas of research interest are corporate governance and law and regulation. His book *The Constitutional Corporation: Rethinking Corporate Governance*, first published by Ashgate Publishing in 2007, was awarded the 2008 Hart Socio-Legal Book Prize.

Jenny Fu: Dr Jenny Fu (PhD, Australian National University; MLeg, LLB, University of Canberra; BA Beijing Foreign Studies University) is an Assistant Professor at the School of Law and Justice at the University of Canberra. She teaches corporations law and conducts research in the area of corporate governance, particularly the governance of state-owned enterprises in China. Prior to her academic career in Australia, Jenny worked as a legal researcher in the Legislative Affairs Commission of the Chinese National People's Congress.

Bo Gong: Bo Gong is Reader in the Law School of Central South University, China. She received her Masters degree and PhD from the Law School of Durham University, UK. Her principal area of research concerns company law and corporate governance. She has published a number of articles, book chapters and a book on these topics. This chapter is funded by the Humanities and Social Sciences Foundation of the Ministry of Education of China in 2013 – 'The Relief of Shareholders' Dividend Rights' (No.13YJC820022) and the Philosophy and Social Science Foundation of Hunan Province in 2012 – 'The Mandatory Dividend System in listed companies' (No.12YBA319).

Philipp Kanzow: Dr W Philipp Kanzow (LL.M Durham, *Europajurist* Würzburg) is currently working as a trainee lawyer in Kassel (Germany). He specialised in comparative law and European law with studies abroad in Leuven (Belgium) and Durham (UK). His doctoral thesis focused on comparative corporate governance. This field and European law form his current research interests.

Harpreet Kaur: Professor (Dr) Harpreet Kaur is Professor of Law and Research Director for the Center for Corporate Law and Governance at NLU Delhi. She is the faculty-in-charge for certificate and diploma courses on Competition Policy and Law. She has authored a book on Business and Corporate Laws and co-authored eight books with Dr Avtar Singh.

Alex Lau: Dr K L Alex Lau was Associate Professor at the Department of Accountancy and Law, Hong Kong Baptist University, Consultant Solicitor at Haldanes, and Visiting Scholar at Oxford, Peking and Washington Universities. At the Law Society of Hong Kong, he was a member of the Guidance Committee, a Risk Management Tutor as well as an Examiner of the Overseas Lawyers Qualifications Examination. Sadly, Dr Alex Lau died while this book was in production.

Rob McQueen: Before retiring from Monash Law School in January 2013, Dr McQueen had previously been Professor and Head of the Law School, Victoria University, Melbourne from 2000–2005 and Professor in the Griffith Law School from 2005–2009, of which he was both Head of School and Dean during this period. Dr McQueen is currently a Senior Fellow in the Melbourne Law School, and continues his academic engagement as a member of the Editorial Board of the Griffith Law Review and the Executive Committee of the Australian & NZ Law & Society Association, of which he is a former President. Dr McQueen's research has principally focused on the history of corporations law in the common law world, culminating in his book, *A Social History of Company Law: Great Britain and the Australian Colonies 1854–1920*, published by Ashgate Publishing in 2009.

Marc T Moore: Dr Marc Moore is a Reader in Corporate Law and Director of the Centre for Corporate and Commercial Law (3CL) at the University of Cambridge, UK. He is a Fellow of Murray Edwards College, Cambridge, an Honorary Reader in the Faculty of Laws, University College London and Deputy Chief Examiner for Company Law on the University of London's external LLB programme. Marc has previously held teaching positions at University College London (2009–2014), the University of Bristol (2004–2009) and Seattle University (2011). Marc has written extensively in the field of company law, with particular regard to Anglo–American corporate governance and theory. In 2012 he was awarded a prestigious Philip Leverhulme Prize, which is awarded to outstanding scholars who have made a substantial and acknowledged contribution to their field of study. In 2013 his book, *Corporate Governance in the Shadow of the State* (Hart Publishing 2013), was shortlisted for the SLS Peter Birks Prize for Outstanding Legal Scholarship.

Jose Maria Lezcano Navarro: Dr Jose Maria Lezcano Navarro is a Panamanian lawyer who graduated from the University of Panama in 2008. He has an LLM in International Commercial Law, awarded by the University of Westminster in 2009. Furthermore, he was awarded a PhD by City University London in 2014. He currently lectures at the University of Panama and is the author of *Sistema Bancario* (published by *Editorial Portobelo*) and *Piercing the Corporate Veil in Latin American Jurisprudence* (published by Routledge). His immediate research interests are international commercial arbitration and the role of the corporate entity in the maritime industry.

Shanthy Rachagan: Dr Shanthy Rachagan is an Associate Professor with the School of Business, Monash University, Malaysia. She is the Head of Discipline for Business Law and Taxation. Her principal teaching is in corporate law, corporate governance, corporate social responsibility and banking and finance law. She has researched and published in high-ranking refereed journals and presented papers at conferences, including being invited as panel speaker for academic and industry seminars in corporate law, corporate governance, corporate social responsibility and banking and finance law, including Islamic finance. Shanthy is also the referee for certain prestigious journals such as the *Journal of Business Ethics* and *Oxford University's Commonwealth Law Journal*. She has also co-authored the books *Principles of Company Law in Malaysia* and *Concise Principles of Malaysian Company Law*, first and second editions, published by LexisNexis.

Mathias M Siems: Professor Mathias Siems is a Professor of Commercial Law at Durham University. He is also a Research Associate at the Centre for Business Research, University of Cambridge, a Research Associate at the London Centre for Corporate Governance and Ethics, Birkbeck, University of London and an Invited Fellow at the Maastricht European Law Institute. He was previously a professor at the University of East Anglia, a reader at the University of Edinburgh, an associate professor at the Riga Graduate School of Law, a Fulbright Scholar at Harvard Law School and a Jean Monnet Fellow at the European University Institute in Florence. He has also held various visiting positions at universities in Europe, Asia and North America. Mathias Siems is a graduate of the Universities of Munich and Edinburgh.

Aiman Nariman Mohd-Sulaiman: Professor Dr Aiman Nariman Mohd-Sulaiman is currently attached to the Faculty of Law at the International Islamic University Malaysia (IIUM). She obtained her doctoral degree (SJD) from Bond University, Australia in 2000 with a thesis on the public enforcement of corporate law. Her research interest is in regulatory techniques and enforcement strategies in corporate law, corporate governance and finance. She has undertaken large-scale research in corporate law, corporate governance and financial services law. Her recent publications include the book *Malaysian Company Law: Principles and Practices* (2015), co-author of *Commercial Applications of Company Law in Malaysia* (1st, 2nd and 3rd editions) and journal articles in international refereed journals including the *International Journal of Disclosure and Governance* and the *Journal of Financial Crime*.

Roman Tomasic: Dr Roman Tomasic is Professor of Law in the School of Law at the University of South Australia; he is also Visiting Professor of Company Law at Durham Law School and Emeritus Professor of Law at the University of Canberra. He was previously Professor of Corporate Law at Durham University. He is a former editor of the *Australian Journal of Corporate Law* and co-editor of a number of collections published by Ashgate Publishing, including *Commercial Law in East Asia* (2014), *Law and Society in East Asia* (2013) and *Insolvency Law in East Asia* (2006). He has undertaken many empirical studies on corporate law and corporate insolvency topics and has a particular interest in comparative corporate law and governance.

Jiangyu Wang: Professor Wang Jiangyu is an Associate Professor at the NUS Faculty of Law. His teaching and research interests include international economic law, corporate and securities law, and law and development. He practised in the Legal Department of the Bank of China and in Chinese and American law firms. Jiangyu served as a member of the Chinese delegation at the annual conference of the UNCITRAL Conference in 1999. He is qualified to practise in China and New York. He is also an Executive Member on the Governing Council of the WTO Institute of the China Law Society, an executive editor of the *Asian Journal of Comparative Law* and deputy editor-in-chief of the *Chinese Journal of Comparative Law*.

Sally Wheeler: Professor Sally Wheeler is Professor of Law, Business and Society in the School of Law at Queen's University Belfast. Her research focuses on corporate governance, business ethics and contract law from a socio-legal perspective. Her articles have appeared in the *Journal of Law and Society*, *Social and Legal Studies* and *Legal Studies*. She is the author of several monographs and numerous contributions to edited collections. Her current interest is in the intersection between corporate social responsibility, human rights and corporate law.

Angus Young: Dr Angus Young is Senior Lecturer at Hong Kong Baptist University and Distinguished Research Fellow at the German-Sino Institute of Legal Studies, Nanjing University. He is also a Fellow of CPA Australia, Fellow of FINSIA, Member of HKSI and a Certified Compliance Professional as well as a Certified Risk Professional accredited with the GRC Institute.

Introduction

Corporate law in transition

Roman Tomasic

Corporate law has developed considerably as a field of law and practice since the corporate law statutes of the early nineteenth century. There has also been an explosion in the range of corporate law scholarship; this development has often drawn upon other traditions, such as history, economics, politics and sociology.

This volume seeks to provide an understanding of a range of contemporary intellectual concerns that has preoccupied corporate law scholars. Not only has it sought to encourage the use of comparative law methods in the analysis of corporate law issues, but it has also sought to move away from a narrow Anglo–American focus and discuss global developments in this field. This is important as the nature and meaning of corporate law will be affected by local political and social factors. As a result, it is a field that is likely to develop further by drawing upon other areas of law and cultural traditions.

In its present form, corporate law has become a relatively extensive area of law covering core company law principles and extending to corporate finance, takeovers, corporate securities law and corporate insolvency law; it also extends further to cover areas of soft law such as principles of corporate governance and even corporate social responsibility. As corporate law ideas have expanded globally, similar company law principles and statutes can be found in many countries, especially in those that are more involved in international trade and commerce. This has been paralleled by a movement towards the globalisation of large corporations and the emergence of transnational corporate groups, presenting a challenge for state-based corporate law systems and their regulation (see Blumberg 1996; Hadden 2012; de Jonge 2011). The emergence of a globalised market has inevitably created a challenge for national systems of corporate law and corporate regulation as they move to respond to this multinational challenge (see generally Milman 2009).

Although there has been a considerable degree of convergence in core corporate law ideas, principles and regulatory practices in well developed capitalist markets (Kraakman and others 2009), even here there remain substantial differences in approach between corporate law principles and practice in Western countries such as the USA, the UK and Western Europe. Whilst the corporate form has been widely adopted, the operation of its internal mechanisms has varied considerably between developed and developing countries, between countries where companies have widely dispersed shareholdings and those in which shareholdings are more concentrated; between countries in which the market for corporate control operates through active stock markets and those where these markets play a less important role in corporate control battles.

These differences are most evident when a contrast is made between hegemonic market-based societies, such as the USA, and more state controlled or concentrated markets, such as China and other parts of East Asia. Not surprisingly, the structure and form of corporate law mechanisms, such as the institutions of corporate governance, have been shown to have been politically determined, reflecting different political traditions and accommodations in their respective countries (Roe 1994, 2003). Despite some important superficial similarities between different national bodies of corporate law, there remain important points of difference between them. For example, although much progress has been achieved in seeking to harmonise EU company law principles, the goal of a single private company law for the Member States of the EU remains elusive (see generally Andenas and Wooldridge 2009). This fragmentation of corporate law is also evident within individual large nation states, such as the USA and China.

Although corporate law has tended to be based on the nation state, much is to be learnt from the use of comparative law methods in the study of patterns of corporate law that are to be found in different parts of the world (see generally Siems 2014 and Chapter 1 in this volume). To some extent, basic comparative law methods have been widely used in the borrowing or transplantation of company laws from other jurisdictions. Further harmonisation efforts in regard to corporate law in part depend upon the use of more nuanced comparative law methods (see generally Siems and Cabrelli 2013; Cahn and Donald 2010; and Fleckner and Hopt 2013). However, the track record in building reliable models for the purposes of comparison has been mixed, as can be seen from the heated debate surrounding the legal origins approach to comparative corporate law that was pioneered by Raphael La Porta and his colleagues (La Porta and others 1998). This is a theme discussed further in Chapter 4 of this volume.

It could thus be said that corporate law has now assumed a level of maturity, but it is far from being uniform or close to having reached 'the end of history' in its development, as some have suggested (Hansmann and Kraakman 2001). This is not to say that corporate law has reached the end of the road in terms of developing a general model of such law, if indeed this is possible. There remain many pressures for further adaptation and change, but corporate law has often been slow to change, for example in its insistence upon the doctrine of the separate legal identity of the body corporate and a reluctance to lift the veil of incorporation. This has now become a major issue in the context of the regulation and control of corporate groups.

Pressures from other areas of law, such as from human rights law, labour law, consumer law, criminal law and environmental law are challenging some well entrenched corporate law ideas. Not surprisingly, some have even argued that in its current form, corporate law has failed (Greenberg 2006). Recent financial crises have questioned the effectiveness of corporate law gatekeepers and corporate regulation (see e.g. Coffee 2006, 2009) and seen calls for a review of many well established ideas regarding the capacity of companies and markets to be self-regulating.

Whilst it is tempting to argue that corporate law has now evolved into a more mature form, along lines found in the most modernised societies, even here there remains some diversity in view of the varieties of capitalism that can be identified in different countries; these differences have helped to shape national bodies of corporate law and have made the harmonisation of corporate law more difficult. The failure of many once highly regarded

Western companies, such as Enron, led to a reassessment of pre-existing views (see generally Armour and McCahery 2006; Gilson and Kraakman 2006). This also occurred following the catastrophic damage caused by the Global Financial Crisis (GFC), which damaged the reputations of major corporate entities and undermined the idea of self-correcting markets, in the process challenging the perceived superiority of Western corporate law and market models; this has seen a reassessment of the presumed superiority of Western corporate governance models (see generally Ferran and others 2012).

Historically, crises such as the collapse of Enron and the GFC have always provided an opportunity to review and reform corporate law practices. The world is currently within such a period of review and reform as a result of the loss of trust in banks and corporate management in many developed countries due to this ongoing crisis (see Tomasic and Akinbami 2011). This challenge has been attributed to failed corporate cultures, short-termism and opportunistic behaviour by corporate controllers. The central role of corporate culture in understanding corporate behaviour and its impact on corporate law has long been understood, but corporate law has often been ill-equipped to deal with it, unlike other areas of law, such as criminal law (see example Stone 1975; O'Brien and Gilligan 2013).

The impact of short-termism upon the governance of listed companies has also been much criticised by commentators and regulators, but it remains very difficult to deal with this problem through corporate law mechanism (see generally Kay 2013; and Keay 2011). Also, scandal and opportunism are important features of capitalist markets, but what has been described as 'looting' and the abuse of the corporate form remain key patterns of corporate behaviour in market-based societies (see generally Partnoy 2003; Mitchell 2001; Will and others 2013; Akerlof and Romer 2005). In financial markets this has been encouraged by what Maynard Keynes described as 'animal spirits' and by what Alan Greenspan saw as the 'irrational exuberance' of market actors that drove markets during the market bubble prior to the GFC (see generally Akerlof and Shiller 2009: 11–56; Shiller 2005).

These behavioural features of markets (see generally Langevoort 2006) have seen the acceleration of arguments advocating a greater role for stakeholder models of the corporation and the abandonment of narrow shareholder primacy models, which have focused upon shareholder wealth maximisation (see generally Stout 2012; Martin 2011). The development of a large academic literature dealing with stakeholder theory has been important, reflecting the influence of business school corporate governance scholars such as Edward Freeman (2010), but with a lesser impact upon legal education.

In contrast to the narrow view of the corporation as merely a 'nexus of contracts' (Easterbrook and Fischel 1991; for a critical view see Bratton 1992), stakeholder models of corporate law have relied upon the existence of higher levels of trust between stakeholders within corporate entities (Blair and Stout 1999, 2001; Tomasic and Akinbami 2013). Arguments have been made that not only must other stakeholders, such as institutional shareholders and large shareholders, take a more active role in monitoring governance within the corporation, as occurred in the Walker Review in the UK (Walker 2009), it has also been suggested that there is room for the imposition of greater responsibility upon such stakeholders, especially where they hold dominant positions of control within the corporation.

Although some legislative endorsement of a more stakeholder-oriented approach to corporate governance has occurred, such as in the United Kingdom's enlightened shareholder value approach to corporate governance (see generally Keay 2013), director primacy has created its own problems or distortions that stakeholders, such as institutional investors and employees, have been ill-equipped to manage. Similarly, there has been little enthusiasm among corporate lawyers for imposing greater duties or responsibilities upon controlling shareholders, although in cases of major environmental damage courts have sometimes sought to attach liability upon controlling or dominant shareholders, as occurred following the breach of a tailings dam operated by Samarco in Brazil: Samarco's two major shareholders were the multinational companies BHP-Billiton and Vale – Brazilian courts sought to impose liability upon its two controlling shareholders, for the damage caused by Samarco to the environment (Macdonald and others 2015).

Whilst directors of companies have often sought greater protection from prosecution in the context of business failure, there has been a counter-movement calling for greater director or agency accountability, such as renewed scrutiny of executive compensation in public companies. This has once again focused attention upon corporate cultures as a key factor explaining failures in corporate governance, even where the letter of the law has been complied with by agents of the corporation. The problem of 'toxic' culture dominated by 'perverse incentives' was frequently highlighted in the reviews of corporate failures after the GFC. This has seen a renewed focus upon the connection between corporate performance and executive compensation in companies (see generally Bebchuk and Fried 2006; Chapter 8 in this volume).

Governments and regulators were often complicit as they frequently encouraged, protected and sometimes lionised corporate leaders who were prepared to assume enormous risks, such as the former chief executive of the Royal Bank of Scotland in the UK. Of course, prevailing neo-liberal values have assumed that markets would be self-regulating and that governments should take a minimal role in companies, and that managers could be trusted to protect the interests of the corporation as a whole and not to prioritise self-serving behaviour. It is not surprising that after the GFC government regulators have become more active in seeking to emphasise the public dimensions of corporate law and the obligation of banks and financial institutions to a wider range of stakeholders, such as consumers of banking and financial services.

The relative rigidity of corporate law as a discipline has often meant that new corporate governance ideas have emerged slowly or have been the product of a crisis. Often they have been externally derived, which has seen the influence of ethical principles in shaping governance and investment practices, such as in the rise of ethical investing and the activity of civil society groups, such as NGOs concerned with corporate corrupt practices including the payment of bribes by corporations and labour practices of large domestic and globally active corporations. It is clear that a broader stakeholder approach to corporate governance will progressively reshape corporate law and public corporations particularly; however, the pace of change in this area has usually been slow. This is an inevitable consequence of the public law dimensions of corporate law and the role of corporations as private governments, which has seen a revival in recent times.

The research handbook contributions

This volume can only provide a limited overview of some of the major debates and research issues currently found in the literature on corporate law. Inevitably, the boundaries and nature of the field will be affected by the global rise of the network society and by the proliferation of information technology (see generally Castells 2010) and diverse forms of business (see generally Ribstein 2010). Inevitably, books of this kind are a reflection of the times during which they were written and will provide an introduction to some of the key developments in the three broad areas covered by contributors.

The four chapters in Part I seek to review some of the major contemporary debates and issues that have affected thinking in regard to corporate law. Professor Mathias Siems takes us through the various methods of undertaking comparative corporate law research and urges corporate lawyers to overcome the disconnection between comparative and corporate law research, as well as between legal and interdisciplinary approaches to comparative corporate law. In Chapter 2, Dr Marc Moore looks at Anglo–American corporate law and argues that the private law approach to looking at corporate law has drawn our attention away from the inherently public nature of corporate law; this distortion has been influenced by the somewhat artificial separation of corporate and securities law in the United States as a result of the distribution of corporate law-making between state and federal legislatures in the US. The increasing federalisation of US corporate law has drawn this separation into question.

In Chapter 3, Professor Stephen Bottomley brings us back to the key issue of defining the nature of corporate law, noting that the expansion of corporate law has produced a hybrid discipline. Finally in this part, in Chapter 4, Dr Rob McQueen reviews the legal origins debate that has been provoked by Rafael La Porta and his colleagues; as the model developed by La Porta and others drew heavily upon corporate law issues, it could have been characterised as a debate over how corporate law matters. McQueen points out that the conclusions reached by the legal origins research can be seen as leading to conclusions that are unwarranted and that different legal origins do not explain the differences in the economic performance of post-colonial societies.

Part II contains seven chapters that are broadly categorised as being concerned with corporate law principles and corporate governance. In Chapter 5, Professor Sally Wheeler examines issues relating to independence and diversity in the composition of corporate boards. The assumption that the mere appointment of independent directors will enhance board performance has long been challenged. After each crisis there has been a reworking of definitions of independence. Professor Wheeler notes that in recent times this has seen efforts to promote increasing diversity in the composition of company boards. In Chapter 6, Dr Folarin Akinbami draws upon his work with the Law Commission of England and Wales to examine the fiduciary duties of institutional investors in companies. This was promoted by concerns about short-termism and the decline in trust in financial investment intermediaries. He goes on to discuss the recommendations found in the Law Commission's report.

The problem of phoenix companies has been a growing concern that corporate regulators have had difficulties in grappling with. In Chapter 7, Professor Helen Anderson examines legal issues that have emerged from the separation of ownership and control, which has led to abusive use of the phoenix company. In making international comparisons, she urges caution in developing ill-targeted mechanisms for the control of phoenix companies as these may cause more harm than good. An equally contentious issue in corporate law has concerned the issue of executive remuneration and its governance. In Chapter 8, Dr Philipp Kanzow compares approaches to executive remuneration taken in Germany and the United Kingdom. The key issues in this area revolve around the setting of remuneration by the board, the disclosure of executive remuneration and shareholder voting on executive remuneration. Kanzow critically examines the strengths and weaknesses of the systems of executive remuneration found in these two countries.

In Chapter 9, Dr Jenny Fu turns to examine the emergence of corporate law in the context of state capitalism, which leads on to a case study of the governance of state-owned enterprises in China. Taking issue with the convergence of corporate law models that was proposed by Hansmann and Kraakman, Dr Fu provides further insights into the state-led model of corporate law and notes that, in the period since the passage of the new Company Law in 2005, China has adopted a more market-based regime, but one in which the party-state remains dominant. China is also discussed in Chapter 10; Dr Bo Gong compares institutional shareholder activism in the United Kingdom and China. She is critical of the nature and extent of institutional shareholder activism in both countries and argues that greater shareholder activism may help to lower the incidence of fraud and governance failures in both countries.

Finally, Part III of the volume contains five chapters that allow us to make some cross-cultural comparisons of corporate law. These five chapters deal with China, India, Malaysia, Hong Kong and Latin America. Chapter 11 provides a critical overview of corporate governance in China by reference to recent legislative reforms. Professor Jiangyu Wang seeks to examine China's corporate governance institutions from their political, economic and social contexts, illustrating that some transplanted corporate law ideas have operated differently in China from what had originally been intended by reformers.

India is also a country that has been engaged in massive corporate reform efforts in recent years. In Chapter 12, Professor Harpreet Kaur examines India's new Companies Act of 2013 (as amended in 2015), which seeks to improve corporate governance by placing more powers into the hands of shareholders, thereby creating enhanced shareholder democracy. These reforms have sought to be synchronised with the regulations of the Securities and Exchange Board of India. The failure of Satyam in 2009, often portrayed as India's Enron, was a crisis that has helped to promote further corporate law reforms in India.

Chapter 13 examines efforts to harmonise Malaysia's British-inspired company law tradition with Islamic *Shariah* law. Professor Aiman Mohd-Sulaiman and Dr Shanthy Rachagan provide a case study of the interaction that is occurring between these two traditions and identifies some of the challenges that this will create for regulators, practitioners and investors in Malaysia. In an era of increasing legal pluralism, Malaysia provides an important case study of efforts to harmonise Western-derived corporate law with increasingly important religious and legal traditions arising from Islam.

The use of the corporate form to support family enterprises and wealth management has seen the widespread growth of the family company, which is an area where traditional corporate law ideas regarding the relationship between a company's directors and share-holders has been challenged. In contrast to the discussion of Malaysian company law, in Chapter 14 Dr Angus Young and Professor Alex Lau once again examine how a Western derived common law system has adjusted in the face of local cultural forces. By examining Chinese family companies in Hong Kong, Young and Lau note that Confucian ideals of governance have had a significant impact on the ways in which company law rules have been used by these family companies, often leading to judicial criticism.

Finally, Chapter 15 returns to what has been one of the most heated debates in academic writing on corporate law, namely the circumstances in which the veil of incorporation will be lifted to attach liability to controllers. Dr Jose Navarro examines the manner in which doctrines regarding piercing the corporate veil have been developed in Latin America, with a focus upon the civil law jurisdictions of Argentina, Brazil and Columbia.

Bibliography

Akerlof, GA and PM Romer (2005), 'Looting: The Economic Underworld of Bankruptcy for Profit' (pp 232–75) in *Explorations in Pragmatic Economics: Selected Papers of George A Akerlof*, Oxford, Oxford University Press.

Akerlof, GA and RJ Shiller (2009), *Animal Spirits*, Princeton, Princeton University Press.

Andenas, M and F Wooldridge (2009), *European Comparative Company Law*, Cambridge, Cambridge University Press.

Armour, J and JA McCahery (eds) (2006), *After Enron: Improving Corporate Law and Modernising Securities Regulation in Europe and the US*, Oxford, Hart Publishing.

Bebchuk, L and J Fried (2006), *Pay Without Performance: The Unfulfilled Promise of Executive Compensation*, Cambridge, Harvard University Press.

Blair, MM and LA Stout (1999), 'A Team Production Theory of Corporate Law', 85 *Virginia Law Review* 248.

Blair, MM and LA Stout (2001), 'Trust, Trustworthiness, and the Behavioral Foundations of Corporate Law', 149 *University of Pennsylvania Law Review* 1735.

Blumberg, PI (1996), *The Multinational Challenge of Corporate Law*, Oxford, Oxford University Press.

Bratton, WW (1992), 'The Economic Structure of the Post-Contractual Corporation', 87 *Northwestern University Law Review* 180–215.

Cahn, A and DC Donald (2010), *Comparative Company Law*, Cambridge, Cambridge University Press.

Castells, M (2010), *The Rise of the Network Society, Volume 1, The Information Age*, 2nd edn, Chichester, Wiley-Blackwell.

Coffee, JC (2006), *Gatekeepers: The Professions and Corporate Governance*, Oxford, Oxford University Press.

Coffee, JC (2009), 'What went wrong? An Initial Inquiry into the Causes of the 2008 Financial Crisis', 9 *Journal of Corporate Law Studies* 1–22.

de Jonge, A (2001), 'Transnational Corporations and International Law: Bringing TNCs out of the Accountability Vacuum', 7(1) *Critical Perspectives on International Business* 66–89.

Easterbrook FH and DR Fischel (1991), *The Economic Structure of Corporate Law*, Cambridge, Harvard University Press.

Ferran, E, N Moloney and JC Coffee (2012), *The Regulatory Aftermath of the Global Financial Crisis*, Cambridge, Cambridge University Press.

Fleckner, AM and KJ Hopt (eds) (2013), *Comparative Corporate Governance: A Functional and International Analysis*, Cambridge, Cambridge University Press.

Freeman, RE (2010), *Strategic Management: A Stakeholder Approach*, Cambridge, Cambridge University Press.

Gilson, RJ and R Kraakman (2006), 'The Mechanism of Market Efficiency Twenty Years Later – The Hindsight Bias' (pp. 29–64) in Armour, J and JA McCahery (2006).

Greenberg, K (2006), *The Failure of Corporate Law – Fundamental Flaws and Progressive Possibilities*, Chicago, Chicago University Press.

Hadden, T (2012), 'Accountable Governance in Corporate Groups: The Interrelationship of Law and Accounting', 61 *Australian Accounting Review* 117–28.

Hansmann, H and R Kraakman (2001), 'The End of History for Corporate Law', 89(2) *Georgetown Law Journal* 439–68.

Kay, J (2013), *The Kay Review of UK Equity Markets and Long-term Decision-making*; House of Commons Business, Innovation and Skills Committee, London: The Stationery Office Limited.

Keay, A (2011), *The Corporate Objective*, Cheltenham, Edward Elgar.

Keay, A (2013), *The Enlightened Shareholder Value Principle and Corporate Governance*, Abingdon, Routledge.

Kraakman, R and others (2009), *The Anatomy of Corporate Law: A Comparative and Functional Approach*, 2nd edn, Oxford, Oxford University Press.

La Porta, R, F Lopez-de-Silanes and A Shleifer (1998), 'Law and Finance', 106 *Journal of Political Economy* 1113–55.

Langevoort, DC (2006), 'Taming the Animal Spirits of the Stock Markets: A Behavioural Approach to Securities Regulation' (pp 65–126) in Armour, J and JA McCahery (2006).

Macdonald, A, J Scheck and R Hoyle (2015), 'Samarco may not Shield BHP, Vale from Brazil Dam-Breach Repercussions', *The Wall Street Journal*, 11 November 2015.

Martin, RL (2011), *Fixing the Game – How Runaway Expectations Broke the Economy, and How to Get Back to Reality*, Boston, Harvard Business Review Press.

Milman, D (2009), *National Corporate Law in a Globalised Market*, Cheltenham, Edward Elgar.

Mitchell, LE (2001), *Corporate Irresponsibility – America's Newest Export*, New Haven, Yale University Press.

O'Brien, J and G Gilligan (eds) (2013), *Integrity, Risk and Accountability in Capital Markets: Regulating Culture*, Oxford, Hart Publishing.

Partnoy, F (2003), *Infectious Greed – How Deceit and Risk Corrupted Financial Markets*, New York, Times Books.

Ribstein, LE (2010), *The Rise of the Uncorporation*, Oxford, Oxford University Press.

Roe, MJ (1994), *Strong Managers, Weak Owners*, Princeton, Princeton University Press.

Roe, MJ (2003), *Political Determinants of Corporate Governance – Political Context, Corporate Impact*, New York, Oxford University Press.

Shiller, RJ (2005), *Irrational Exuberance*, 2nd edn, New York, Currency Doubleday.

Siems, M (2014), *Comparative Law*, Cambridge, Cambridge University Press.

Siems, M and D Cabrelli (2013), *Comparative Company Law: A Case-based Approach*, Oxford, Hart Publishing.

Stone, CD (1975), *Where the Law Ends – The Social Control of Corporate Behavior*, New York, Harper & Row.

Stout, L (2012), *The Shareholder Value Myth*, San Francisco, Berrett-Koehler Publishers, Inc.

Tomasic, R and F Akinbami (2011), 'The Role of Trust in Maintaining the Resilience of Financial Markets', 11(2) *Journal of Corporate Law Studies* 369–94.

Tomasic, R and F Akinbami (2013), 'Trust and Public Companies: Beginning to Reconceptualise Corporate Law in a Networked World', 27 *Australian Journal of Corporate Law* 233–61.

Walker, D (2009), *A review of corporate governance in UK banks and other financial industry entities: Final recommendations*, 29 November 2009, https://www.governance.co.uk/resources/item/256-the-walker-report-review-of-corporate-governance-in-uk-banks-and-other-financial-industry-entities-final-recommendations (last accessed 10 June 2016).

Will, S, S Handelman and DC Brotherton (eds) (2013), *How They Got Away With It: White Collar Criminals and the Financial Meltdown*, New York, Columbia University Press.

Part I
Thinking about corporate law

1

The methods of comparative corporate law

Mathias M Siems

Introduction

In the 1990s, it was said that there was 'very little systematic writing about the methods of comparative law' (Merryman 1999: 3) and that the comparative methodology was 'still at the experimental stage' (Zweigert and Kötz 1998: 33). However, this has changed to a significant degree: recent years have seen the publication of a number of new books about the comparative method of law (Husa 2015; Siems 2014; Samuel 2014) with a common core of themes emerging that most of these books discuss.

Comparative corporate law has also seen a rise in popularity, here too, with many books published recently (Ventoruzzo and others 2015; Roth and Kindler 2014; Siems and Cabrelli 2013; Cahn and Donald 2010; Kraakman and others 2009; Andenas and Wooldridge 2009). This line of research has made important contributions to the, traditionally, rather parochial scholarship on corporate law. However, in the comparative corporate law literature there is often a lack of consideration given to the recent advances made in the general field of comparative law.

This chapter aims to fill this gap: it will outline a conceptual framework that shows how seven core themes of comparative law can be linked to research on comparative corporate law. Subsequently, it will explain these seven topics in more detail, also distinguishing between research approaches that have a legal focus and those that follow a more interdisciplinary perspective. The conclusion will then suggest that there is a need to overcome not only the disconnection between comparative and corporate law research but also between legal and interdisciplinary perspectives of comparative corporate law.

Conceptual linkages between comparative and corporate law

The central idea of having a field of research called 'comparative law' is that there are certain themes that can apply to the legal comparison with any area of law. However, this general approach does not deny that variations may be necessary according to the area of law in question, for instance, since some areas may invite a closer link to the social sciences (e.g. to economics for research on comparative competition law), whilst in other areas a closer link to the humanities may be appropriate (e.g. to cultural studies for research on comparative family law).

For comparative corporate law, Corcoron (1996: 57–58) suggests that there is a 'corporate law advantage' when using the comparative method because of the following two reasons:

> The first is the historical relationships between the use of the corporate form by different legal systems. Corporations go all the way back to the Twelve Tables, the most ancient of Roman laws. Because of the strength of this historical relationship, comparative work in corporate law has a theoretical depth that does not exist in other areas of the law. The second advantage for the comparative corporate scholar is the modern relationship between corporate theory and economic theory. In the modem era corporations have provided the major vehicle for the development of capitalism and other commercial ventures. These two relationships together mean that in corporate law, the modem corporate entity has both a substantive and a structural relationship across legal systems.

This line of reasoning identifies two features of corporate law which enable comparability of legal systems, thus providing a common denominator ('*tertium comparationis*') in the terminology of comparative law (see Siems 2014: 26). However, it is the position taken in this chapter that there is more to be said about the relevance of themes of comparative law for research in comparative corporate law.

Table 1.1 summarises how comparative law can contribute to comparative corporate law. The seven categories capture the main themes of comparative law which may be applied to any area of law. In the subsequent columns these themes are then related to questions of comparative corporate law. Those will be explained in detail in the main part of this chapter. Examples will be used in order to illustrate the popularity of those approaches, their technical implementation, as well as forms of criticism.

To clarify, it seems worth noting that there may be blurred lines between the classification schemes of Table 1.1. It may often be the case that research will be concerned with more than one of the seven categories. Similarly, the divide between 'legal focus' and 'interdisciplinary perspective' has a grey area where doctrinal legal scholarship incorporates some socio-legal research into its work.

This chapter does not aim to rank the seven categories of comparative approaches to corporate law. The choice of the appropriate method cannot be assessed universally since it depends on the research topic and the countries in question, as well as the skills and the resources of the researcher (including forms of collaboration).However, it is also not suggested that 'anything goes'; rather, the following will explain the benefits and limitations of each of the seven comparative categories as applied to corporate law.

The seven categories of a comparative approach to corporate law

(1) Rule-based comparison

In both academia and legal practice, a rule-based comparison of corporate law is often a natural starting point. For example, a scholar or practitioner from a civil-law jurisdiction may want to find out whether certain incorporation requirements from her country also apply elsewhere, say, the provision of minimum share capital or the notarial authorisation requirements. If the result is then that in other countries (e.g. in some common law countries) there are no such requirements, that would already be an interesting finding for such a study (Van Hulle and Gesell 2006; see also section (4) below).

Table 1.1 Overview of relationship between comparative and corporate law

Theme of comparative law	Typical question for comparative corporate law	Examples of research:	
		with a legal focus	with an interdisciplinary perspective
(1) Rule-based comparison	*Does particular domestic rule of corporate law also exist in other countries?*	• description of differences in legal rules and principles • search for universal rules in company law	• coding of rules based on model of one country
(2) Functional comparison	*How is particular corporate problem addressed in particular countries?*	• thematically oriented country chapters • application of Common Core approach to company law	• principal-agent problems to identify similarities and differences • coding of rules based on problem case
(3) Classifications of legal systems	*How does corporate law differ at a wider level (e.g. globally)?*	• classifications according to sources of law, board models, and shareholder/stakeholder interests	• ownership structure and insider/outsider models • broad models: e.g. Anglo–Saxon, continental and Asian; legal origins
(4) Comparative law in context	*Why are insights of differences and similarities in corporate law of more general interest?*	• substitutes or complementarities of rules from different areas • role of lawyers, auditors, courts, supervisory authorities etc.	• qualitative research on specific countries • quantitative research on incorporation costs, role of culture and 'law and finance'
(5) Historical comparative perspective	*How far does history explain similarities and differences in corporate law?*	• differences in industrialisation and politics; path dependencies • historical commonalities and recent convergence	• drives for convergence, including regulatory competition • qualitative and quantitative challenges to causal effect of corporate law
(6) Transnational and comparative law	*Is a country-level perspective of corporate law still accurate?*	• beyond-state law in EU and US • OECD Principles of Corporate Governance and how they work	• Doing Business Report's index on investor protection and criticism • UN initiatives; discussion about role of limited liability in MNEs
(7) Applied comparative law	*What are possible policy implications that can follow from comparing corporate laws?*	• main beneficiaries of comparative corporate law • types of reforms from small to large-scale	• corporate law and development; empirical research • non-economic considerations

A rule-based comparison can also be of a more conceptual nature. For instance, the discussion about the applicable rules of corporate law (i.e. the private international law of corporations) typically does not start with a question about the precise legal rules but with the divide between countries that follow the 'incorporation theory' or the 'real seat theory', namely whether a country determines the applicable law only based on the place of incorporation (the 'statutory seat') or whether it also considers the place of the headquarters (the 'real seat') (Gerner-Beuerle and Schuster 2014: 310–14).

Such a more conceptual rule-based comparison can also be revealing in order to identify similarities. For instance, a controversial article by Hansmann and Kraakman (2001) suggests that across jurisdictions all modern corporate laws share the following core characteristics: full legal personality, limited liability for owners and managers, shared ownership by investors of capital, delegated management under a board structure and transferable shares. Identifying similarities of rules and concepts across countries is also important for the question of whether transnational law-makers can develop a common position that is acceptable across legal systems, for example, as far as European harmonisation is concerned (Bachner 2009, justifying a doctrinal approach for comparative corporate law) or for global benchmarks such as the OECD Principles of Corporate Governance (discussed in section (6) below).

It may seem that research with an interdisciplinary perspective would not be interested in a rule-based comparison. However, La Porta and others (1998) – an article by a group of financial economists – includes such a comparison. La Porta and others use a quantitative methodology in order to examine the differences in shareholder and creditor protection in 49 countries and its impact on financial development. For example, for shareholder protection, they use an index on 'anti-director rights' that codes (with '1' or '0') the rules on 'proxy by mail allowed', 'shares not blocked before the meeting', 'cumulative voting', 'oppressed minorities mechanism', 'share capital required to call an extraordinary shareholder meeting' and 'pre-emptive rights to new issues'.

Subsequent scholarship has identified problems with the coding of these variables (Spamann 2010), but in the present context the main problem to note is that the selection of these variables is not based on a comparative analysis of legal tools available in different legal traditions. Rather, La Porta and others usually follow the US model, thus, implicitly benchmarking how similar legal systems are to that of the US (and whether this makes a difference in terms of financial development; see also section (4) below). Such an approach is problematic because it disregards that shareholder protection – or 'anti-director rights' – may be based on other rules in other countries. Therefore, a functional comparison is often seen as preferable.

(2) Functional comparison

According to the traditional method of comparative law, the initial research question should not simply refer to the law of one legal system, but should be posed in functional terms (Zweigert and Kötz 1998: 38, 43). For example, following the approach of the Common Core project,[1] a comparatist may start with a hypothetical or real-life problem in order to examine how a problem would be solved in different legal systems. This has the advantage that preconceptions based upon the comparatist's own legal tradition will not lead to a 'false negative', with their personal bias leading them to fail to consider functional equivalents in other jurisdictions.

---

1 See www.common-core.org (last accessed 23 May 2016).

In comparative corporate law, a functional approach is very popular. The books by Fleckner and Hopt (2013) and Puchniak and others (2012) have the term 'functional' in their titles. They both deal with questions of corporate governance and derivative actions in selected jurisdictions and present those in separate country chapters. Siems and Cabrelli's (2013) *Comparative Company Law: A Case-based Approach* follows more closely the approach of the Common Core project. The main chapters of this book are based on 10 hypothetical cases, which are subsequently examined according to the laws of eight European countries, as well as the US and Japan. The project was coordinated by the two editors who appointed one or two country experts for each of the 10 jurisdictions. Each of the country experts (or the two experts from one country) also suggested one hypothetical case in order to achieve a good mix and balance of cases.

The concluding chapter of Siems and Cabrelli (2013), as well as the accompanying article by Cabrelli and Siems (2015), relate the results of the cases to differences and similarities in legal rules and sources of law. It is found that there is a strong correlation between the results of the cases (e.g. whether they favour directors or shareholders; shareholders or creditors; minority or majority shareholders) and the legal rules in question. By contrast, there is a weaker link between the relevant sources of law (case law, statute law, articles of association etc) and the results. In particular, it is not found that the case law of common law countries is a crucial determinant for higher levels of shareholder protection (a topic to be discussed further in the next section). Such a functional approach can therefore contribute to core themes of comparative corporate law.

A limitation of the approach taken in Siems and Cabrelli (2013) is that it mainly examines the legal solutions to the 10 cases. Such a 'legal focus' is in line with the books of the Common Core project. However, a functional comparative perspective by nature is not restricted to a legal approach; for example, it may be the case that the protection of shareholders provided by the law in some countries is provided by extra-legal factors in others. It is therefore no coincidence that interdisciplinary research has also used the functional approach.

One example for a functional and law-and-economics approach to comparative corporate law is Kraakman and others' (2009) book entitled *Anatomy of Corporate Law*. Following research in economics, finance and business studies (e.g. Jensen and Meckling 1976), it uses the main principal-agent problems of corporations as starting points. These, are, according to Kraakman and others (2009: 2), the potential conflicts: (i) between directors/managers and shareholders; (ii) between majority shareholders and minority shareholders; and (iii) between shareholders and non-shareholder constituencies (creditors, employees, suppliers etc). The aim of the book is therefore to 'explore the role of corporate law in minimizing agency problems', explaining that 'our analysis is "functional" in the sense that we organize discussion around the ways in which corporate laws respond to these problems' (Kraakman and others 2009: 3–4). Thus, despite the interdisciplinary perspective, here too the focus is on legal rules, even though the book does not disregard non-legal differences such as those between dispersed and concentrated ownership of public companies (see also the next section).

A further influential functional study is Djankov and others' (2008) 'Law and Economics of Self-dealing' (also noting that three of the four authors are the same as in La Porta and others 1998, discussed above). Djankov and others present a complex hypothetical case of a transaction between two companies to lawyers from 72 countries, and ask them to respond to questions such as which body of the companies has to approve the transaction in question or how the transaction's validity could be challenged. Thereafter Djankov and others code this information using various indices, and find that this new data set predicts stock market development. This generally works better than the index by La Porta and others (1998). Given this positive and significant finding, the Djankov and others (2008) index has also become part of the index on minority investor protection of the World Bank's Doing Business Report (to be discussed further in section (6) below).

The Djankov and others' study and related research is, however, not without problems. The first one is that, despite the case-based starting point, the coding is based on questions about precise legal rules; thus, this is different from the open-ended functional approach of the Common Core project. Second, the focus on 'how legal rules work' is problematic since not all laws have a predetermined function. Indeed, it is a general criticism of legal functionalism that it fails to acknowledge that function may play a small or no role in the law's creation; instead, law-makers may have responded to conflicting aims or they may simply have striven to offer a clear legal framework, being largely indifferent as to how it is used (see e.g. Michaels 2006: 354; Graziadei 2003: 118).

Third, as far as non-legal factors are concerned, quantititive work such as Djankov and others' study usually includes explanatory variables that aim to account for the influence of those factors. However, those controls do not consider how in the precise factual situation such factors may matter. Thus, in order adequately to reflect those factors, it would be necessary not only to ask lawyers from each country about the law but also to ask entrepreneurs how such problems may be resolved by extra-legal means.

The fourth and final problem is the global scope of such studies. At first sight, it seems useful that Djankov and others cover countries from all parts of the world. However, a global perspective does not sit well with functionalism. A general line of criticism of the functional method of comparative law is that it cannot be assumed that all societies face the same social problems (De Coninck 2010: 327; Husa 2003: 438). Moreover, whilst the factual situation may be identical in two countries, this does not imply that the law-makers of both societies will necessarily feel the need to promulgate legal rules on the same issue or, indeed, that the rules were created in response to the same problem. Thus, it is said to be unacceptable to impose an external measure on them, such as expecting them all to deal with a particular problem (Glenn 2007: 95; Ruskola 2002: 190). Specifically for comparative corporate law, therefore, Cabrelli and Siems (2015, footnotes omitted) justify their restriction to 10 developed countries as follows:

> It may be suggested that further countries, for example from emerging economies or the developing world, should also have been included. Yet such an inclusion may have also been contentious, since the present comparison of market economies of the developed world has the advantage that it can assess the remaining differences against a baseline of similarity in terms of the countries' histories, societies, economies, and ideologies. For example, if we had included a country such as China, a number of further considerations may have needed to be considered, such as the role of state ownership in corporate governance and the independence of the courts.

Thus, for comparative corporate law research with a global perspective other tools need to be used, as the following section will explain.

(3) Classifications of legal systems[2]

A number of classifications in comparative corporate law naturally follow from the main legal differences between countries. For example, the corporate law of common law countries is said to be less strict than that of civil law countries (see Siems 2008: 50–52). Comparatively, a strict law can be found in the German law on public companies, which states that the entire Companies Act is mandatory unless explicitly stated otherwise. In substance, French and Chinese corporate law have a similar tendency towards comprehensive regulation, leaving scarcely any room for contractual freedom. By contrast, in the US, the influential law of Delaware is an example of a 'business friendly' law that does not impose many hurdles on companies and their directors, whilst in the UK the codified corporate law is somewhat more detailed and prescriptive than in Delaware, not least owing to the influence of EU law (see also Moore 2013: 206).

Other legal taxonomies are contrastedly more closely focused on specific legal rules. In particular, comparing and classifying those rules is useful as far as they have some relevance beyond the particular problem they aim to address. For example, a frequent distinction is between countries with one and two boards of directors (Davies and others 2013). The model with just one board ('one-tier model') was the original one, and this is still the one used in common law countries. When state supervision of companies was reduced in the Germany of the nineteenth century, it was, however, decided that public companies should have two boards: a management board and a supervisory board ('two-tier model'). This German model has spread to some fellow civil law countries, whilst others, such as France, Italy and Japan allow companies to choose between different board models.

Many questions of corporate law depend on the availability and choice between those two models. This topic is also related to the role of employees in corporate law since some of the two-tier countries require employee representatives on the supervisory board. A similar question, often used for taxonomic purposes, is whether directors primarily have to consider the interests of shareholders or whether they can also consider those of other stakeholders (Gelter 2011). A typical statement is that in common law countries shareholder interests legally take primacy. The sole or at least primary object of the company is seen to be achieving a rise in the share price and the level of dividends. By contrast, in civil law countries a pluralist, stakeholder approach is often seen as prevailing since it also takes account of the social and financial interests of employees, consumers and creditors.

Moving further to interdisciplinary approaches, the corporate governance literature often makes a major distinction according to the ownership structure of large public companies: in the UK and the US, dispersed shareholder ownership is relatively common, whereas in other parts of the world ownership is more concentrated as other firms, financial institutions, families or the state hold major blocks of shares (Barca and Becht 2001). Related is the distinction between 'insider' and 'outsider' models (Aguilera and others 2012): as far as ownership of companies is concentrated, the dominant shareholders are likely to appoint board members who act on their behalf, say, in a family firm, members of that family. Thus, here, the directors are 'insiders', in contrast to firms with dispersed shareholder ownership, where newly appointed directors tend to be 'outsiders' to the company in question. The link to corporate law is that one would expect that in insider systems the main aim is

2 This section is a summary of Siems 2015.

to protect the minority against majority shareholders, whereas in outsider systems it is to protect all shareholders against possible misconduct by directors.

At a more general level, the corporate governance literature often starts with a distinction between the Anglo–Saxon and the continental European model, combining many of the individual features (e.g. shareholder primacy, stronger capital markets and more ownership dispersion in the former countries; see e.g. Goergen 2012: 68–77). Further distinctions have also been suggested, say, between Anglo–Saxon, Germanic, Latin and Japanese systems of corporate governance. Here, for example, it is said that the Latin and Japanese models are more network-oriented than the Germanic one, that stock markets are more important in the Germanic and Japanese models than in the Latin one, that the government plays a greater role in the Latin model than in the Germanic and Japanese ones, and that ownership concentration is lower in the Japanese model than in the Germanic and Latin ones (Keenan and Aggestam 2001; Weimar and Pape 1999). Research has also examined the specific problems of transition economies and emerging markets in corporate governance (Pargendler forthcoming 2017; Siems and Alvarez-Macotela 2014; Pistor and others 2000).

The studies by La Porta and Djankov and others, discussed in the previous sections, use similar categories but with a closer link to the (alleged) role of law. In both studies, the main result is that legal rules on shareholder protection have a quantifiable effect on financial development. A secondary finding of their cross-country quantifications is that the quality of legal rules varied systematically with the classification of the 'origin' of a country's legal system; that is, whether it fell into the English 'common law' or French, German or Scandinavian 'civil law' systems, which are believed to have spread to all countries of the world through conquest, colonisation and imitation (see also La Porta and others 2008). Notably, it is found that countries of English legal origin provide considerably better shareholder protection than those of the other legal origins, in particular French legal origin countries, and therefore also more developed capital markets.

The broader classifications discussed in this section have often been criticised (references in Siems 2015; see also Siems 2007 specifically on 'legal origins'). This is no surprise since classifications are bound to raise the objection that, on the one hand, they overemphasise differences between categories and, on the other hand, they underemphasise differences within these categories (i.e. in this respect they overemphasise similarities). Often, therefore, other approaches to comparative law may be preferred, notably those of comparative law in context, historical comparative research and transnationalism, which all challenge such broad classificatory schemes. Those topics will be discussed in the following three sections.

(4) Comparative law in context

A law-focused approach to comparative corporate law can be contextual, by way of examining how corporate law relates to other areas of law.

One possible focus of such research is to identify two or more areas of law that may be substitutes. For example, if the task is to compare the protection of creditors this may consider that countries may primarily use either (i) rules of corporate law that reduce the risk of default, such as minimum capital requirements, or (ii) contractual rights, including the right to take security, or (iii) aspects of insolvency law as far as they put creditors' interests at the fore (Armour and others 2009a: 605–6). Such a comparative examination of creditor protection would therefore also follow a functional approach (see section (2) above).

This method can also be used to present the role of social interests in corporate law and other areas. For example, it may be the case that countries that do not require employee co-determination on corporate boards have alternative forms of employee participation, such as works councils (cf Gospel and Pendleton 2005 for a comparison of the role of employees in corporate governance). Similarly, comparing the US with the UK, Australia and Canada, Bruner (2013: 287) suggests that, in the US, the 'weaker state-based social welfare protections have left the corporate governance system exposed to greater stakeholder-oriented political pressures'.

However, differences between legal systems may not only be of a functional nature but demonstrative of respective attitudes towards an issue. Notably, it can also be the case that one country uses multiple means to protect the same constituency, but another one uses none of them. For example, the use of extensive or few forms of creditor protection may reflect different attitudes of law-makers towards the risks that corporate creditors face owing to provision of limited liability (Foster 2007: 273–74). It is also conceivable that countries that protect social and employee interests in corporate law are also more inclined to provide such protection in other areas of law. To refer to another example: many questions of corporate law are related to corporate tax law and it may be plausible that law-makers design these laws in a way that is consistent with either encouraging or discouraging particular conduct (see e.g. Cerioni 2007 for EU corporate and tax law).

Beyond such specific examples, the literature also discusses how complementarities between different areas of law can be related to ideological differences. For instance, a well known position (Hall and Soskice 2001) distinguishes between liberal market economies such as the UK and the US on the one hand, and coordinated market economies such as Germany and Japan on the other. Comparative legal scholarship has suggested that this distinction can explain the link between country differences in corporate law and those in labour and welfare law (Ahlering and Deakin 2007; Pistor 2005; Kennedy 2012: 46–48), whilst such 'institutional complementarities' are also bound to be interconnected with other social institutions (cf Hall and Gingerich 2009; Armour and others 2009a: 596–99).

Next, a non-contextual comparison of corporate laws can be problematic as far as it disregards the role of lawyers, auditors, courts, commercial registers and supervisory authorities. In the general comparative law literature Bell (2001, 2006) urges comparatists to consider the setting of those organisations and institutions for law-in-context comparisons. For comparative corporate law the frequency of legal transplants (see section (5) below) means that the statute law may often be relatively similar for each country of a study, but through scrutiny of the operation of lawyers, courts etc it may be shown that the practical working of these rules is quite different. To provide an example, the recent introduction of derivative actions in many countries has been addressed by such contextual comparative scholarship, showing that it is not sufficient merely to compare these specific rules since only with the appropriate rules on costs and legal fees can derivative actions have the chance to become relevant in practice (Puchniak and others 2012; Siems 2012).

Interdisciplinary research considers further social, cultural and economic factors that determine how transplanted corporate law actually works. For example, the interview-based research by Deakin and others (Whittaker and Deakin 2010; Buchanan and Deakin 2008) examines whether recent reforms in Japanese corporate law have moved it in the direction of an Anglo–American or global model of corporate governance. They find that the organisational core of the Japanese firm has been retained, despite new structures aimed at providing greater flexibility in corporate decision-making. Such emphasis of context-specificity can also be found in other qualitative empirical studies of comparative company law (Jia and Tomasic (2010) for the corporate governance of resources companies in China).

More often, however, an interdisciplinary perspective of comparative corporate law in context employs quantitative methods, as the following examples illustrate.

The relevance of corporate law differences for choosing the place of incorporation has long been a topic of US corporate law and economics (see section (5) below). It is increasingly becoming so in the EU as well. Following a line of cases of the European Court of Justice starting in 1999, it is now, generally speaking, also possible that companies can choose their place of incorporation in any Member State and, by doing so, the applicable company law (Mucciarelli 2012, also for differences between the US and the EU). The study by Becht and others (2008) examines the resulting market empirically. It finds that entrepreneurs of small businesses avoid their own legal systems' minimum capital requirements and incorporate a limited company in the UK instead. In addition, Becht and others consider further set-up costs, for instance for lawyers and notaries, which are also found to have a significant effect on incorporation decisions.

For larger businesses, differences in shareholder protection have been a main topic of empirical research. For instance, research by Licht examines how far cultural factors are correlated with a tendency to protect shareholders. Licht (2001) finds that good legal shareholder protection correlates with 'individualism' and 'masculinity', seen as typical for the UK and the US, whilst the preference for 'harmony' in East Asia is correlated with weaker shareholder protection. Licht and others (2005) include rules and practices of litigation to this picture, which is then also related to the possible differences between legal families in corporate governance.

As already mentioned (see sections (2) and (3) above), La Porta and others (1998) and Djankov and others (2008) are the most prominent studies that have aimed to examine whether differences in shareholder protection matter for financial development ('law and finance'). Their positive finding is, however, not beyond doubt. From a law-in-context perspective, the most immediate response is that any such comparison of rules at the country level may be spurious if it disregards what happens at the firm level. More complete research therefore needs to consider the dynamics of corporate governance structures between the country and firm level (cf Schnyder 2015 for four countries), also considering the role of soft law, such as corporate governance codes (Kershaw forthcoming 2017) and the limits of rational behaviour in corporate governance (Marnet 2008).

One final objection is that there is unlikely to be only a one-way link between corporate law and financial development, given that law influences society in multiple ways and with various feedback mechanisms (Chong and Calderon 2000). The merely cross-sectional data sets of the La Porta/Djankov and others' studies cannot capture these dynamics. Rather, an historical perspective is needed, be it based on quantitative data with a time-dimension or more conventional historical research.

(5) Historical comparative research

Zweigert and Kötz (1998: 9) state that comparative and historical legal research are different because the former 'studies legal systems coexistent in space', whilst the latter 'studies systems consecutive in time'. But then they also suggest that both fields are closely related, for instance, because the comparatist 'has to take account of the historical circumstances in which the legal institutions and procedures under comparison evolved' (ibid). This relevance of history for comparative legal research can also be seen in comparative corporate law.

Sometimes such research uses history in order to explain the differences of today's corporate laws. For example, it has been suggested that the differences between British and continental European corporate laws can be related to Britain's early industrialisation. At that earlier time companies enjoyed great flexibility in Britain, while the later emergence of large-scale companies on the European continent happened when there was a greater willingness to regulate business (Deakin 2009). Those differences can also be related in the stronger role that social-democratic ideas played in the history of many continental European countries, consequently speaking against a narrow focus of corporate law on the interests of shareholders (Roe 1993, 2003b).

The continuation of such original differences can be supported by the notion of 'path-dependencies' which often distinguishes between weak, semi-strong and strong versions (Roe 1997). Weak path-dependence exists when different concepts lead to the same result. For instance, in comparative corporate law the extensive scope of directors' duties in common law countries may restrict certain actions that in civil law countries are pro-hibited by explicit rules (see e.g. Conac and others 2007 for self-dealing transactions). Semi-strong path-dependence means that the costs of law reform would exceed their benefits. Here, for instance, one can think of the principle of minimum capital or the separation between supervisory and management boards, since changing such rules would make it necessary to revise many areas of corporate law (Siems 2008: 295). A strong path-dependence may be assumed for the question of whether and how corporate law should consider the interests of stakeholders, such as employees, since here political considerations may hold legislators back from adopting the most economically efficient solution – whatever this may be (Bebchuck and Roe 1999: 150).

But historical arguments can also be used to show similarities. It may be said that the development of corporate law has been fairly similar across European countries, namely, at its beginnings, the establishment of colonial corporations, then the trend to make the corporate form more widely available, going hand in hand with a codification of corporate law, and subsequently its interpretation and application by courts (Siems 2008: 18–19).

Analysing recent developments, the literature discusses whether we have observed a widespread convergence of corporate laws. Gilson (2001) suggests that functional convergence is more likely than formal convergence: whilst the underlying problems are similar, there are too many obstacles in the way of formal harmonisation – where 'functional' means that a comparable result is produced, with, say, incompetent directors being removed, but along different statutory paths.

However, such line of reasoning can also be challenged by taking the historical comparative perspective. It can be shown that many rules, such as those on independent directors, audit committees and derivative actions have been popular legal transplants in recent decades (Siems 2008: 134, 195, 222), leading to convergence of formal legal rules in corporate law (also Katelouzou and Siems 2015, based on the CBR data set discussed below). But then, functionally, differences remain since the same rules often tend to operate in a diverse way across societies and cultures.

In terms of the direction of convergence, Hansmann and Kraakman (2001) suggest that the Anglo–American model of corporate law – with shareholder primacy as the main guiding principle – has won the day. Similarly, Cioffi (2010) and Barker (2010) highlight the prevalence of shareholder-oriented law reforms in/under both left and right-wing countries/governments. Thus, the argument is that – in contrast to previous work by Roe (see above) – protecting shareholders has also become an issue of concern for 'the left', for example, with the aim to appeal to new voters, to enable better monitoring of companies following financial scandals and possibly also as a result of changes to pension systems that in many countries 'turn workers into capitalists' (Gelter 2014).

By contrast, Siems (2008) finds that the corporate laws of France, Germany, the UK, the US, China and Japan have all evolved towards a mixture of three types of shareholders: in favour of the model of the 'shareholder as owner', for instance, is the fact that shareholders can in principle freely sell their shares, and are entitled to special rights. In the sense of the 'shareholder as parliamentarian', however, there are also mechanisms intended to enable the company to have an organisation with checks and balances. In view of the company's ability to attract capital, finally, the 'shareholder as investor' enters in, because finance and disclosure related provisions of corporate law are aimed primarily at them. Although legal systems may lay emphasis on one model type of shareholder, it is found that in all of the six legal systems, the overall legal situation is a hybrid one (Siems 2008: 225–6).

Adopting an interdisciplinary perspective, Siems (2008) also examines which forces may have led to this convergence, finding that the increased use of modern forms of communication, approximations in economic policy, company and shareholder structures, and the liberalisation of capital markets all account for growing legal similarities. Dignam and Galanis (2009) pursue a similar line of research and suggest that it was mainly the process of economic globalisation led by capital and product market liberalisation that has had an impact on corporate governance systems.

Another important discussion is the effect of regulatory competition on corporate laws, the main debate being whether any convergence leads to a 'race to the bottom' or 'race to the top'. This line of research started in the US (Cary 1974), given the free choice between US state corporate laws, and often uses empirical data for further analysis (Romano 1993a, 2006). Following recent developments in the EU (see section (4) above), it is now also discussed here how regulatory competition has shaped corporate law reforms in the EU Member States (Ringe 2013).

As already suggested (see section (4) above), historical comparative research may help answer the question of whether differences in corporate law 'matter'. Qualitative historical work often doubts such a claim. According to Cheffins (2001) and Coffee (2001), the experience of the UK and the US shows that only after the number of investors and the importance of the capital market increased was shareholder protection strengthened. In particular, it can be shown that in the UK some ownership dispersion had already emerged without high quality shareholder protection (Cheffins 2008). A similar scepticism of broad causal claims is apparent from books dealing more generally with the history of corporations and corporate governance of various countries (Colli and others 2012; Morck 2007).

Recent quantitative historical comparative work has also challenged the 'law matters' claim. Two studies specifically examined the situation in the UK and the US (Franks and others 2009; Cheffins and others 2013). Moreover, a project on Law, Finance and Development at the Centre for Business Research (CBR) of the University of Cambridge collected time-series information on shareholder protection law of up to 30 countries and 36 years.[3] The legal data sets of this project have been called 'more sophisticated' (Pacces 2011: 304) than the La Porta/Djankov and others ones (see previous sections). The time dimension of this data set also provides the potential to identify whether corporate law really affects financial development. However, such a causal relationship could not be confirmed in most of the specifications (Armour and others 2009b; see also Siems and Deakin 2010).

---

3 See http://www.cbr.cam.ac.uk/research/research-projects/completed-projects/law-finance-development/ (two shareholder protection indices, each coding a different number of years and countries) (last accessed 23 May 2016).

(6) Transnational and comparative law

In sections (1) to (5) the main focus has been on laws at the country level. This is in line with traditional comparative law (cf Siems 2014: 15).However, nowadays in most, if not all, areas of law there is also the need to consider the area of 'transnational law', referring to any law that transcends nation states (Senn 2011: 197–8).

In the EU, some directives have harmonised aspects of company law. But the scope of harmonisation has been called 'trivial' (Enriques 2006), with a growing preference for regulatory competition as a means of 'negative integration' (Johnston 2009; see also section (5) above). This can be contrasted with the deeper European harmonisation in securities law (see e.g. Moloney 2014), which also addresses some aspects that overlap with topics of company law (e.g. remedies for wrongful disclosure). Beyond formal rules, there is an initiative for a European Model Company Act,[4] apparently influenced by the Model Business Corporation Act (MBCA) of the US, where it has led to significant convergence of state corporate laws (Carney 1998). Another parallel is that in the US too securities law is unified to a larger extent, also extending to some themes that could also be addressed by state corporate law (see e.g. Roe 2003a).

More frequently the literature about transnational law is, however, concerned with laws that are not only relevant to a particular territory, such as the EU (or the US). For transnational laws related to companies, there are detailed non-binding rules in accounting and securities law – the International Financial Reporting Standards and various principles by the International Organization of Securities Commissions (IOSCO).

With respect to corporate law, the main general transnational set of norms are the OECD Principles of Corporate Governance (see Siems and Alvarez-Macotela 2014). The initial version of the OECD Principles was adopted in 1999; it was revised in 2004 and 2015 (and then renamed as G20/OECD Principles).. In substance, they reflect the common principles of the corporate laws of the 34 OECD member states. There are also some examples where choices have been made. For instance, the statement that there should be a 'sufficient number of non-executive board members capable of exercising independent judgement [sic]' (section VI.E1 of the Principles) is based on the use of independent board members in Anglo–Saxon countries. By contrast, the relevance of stakeholder interests in corporate governance (section IV, VI.C of the Principles) is likely to be the result of continental European models.

OECD accession requires a country's 'positioning' to the existing OECD instruments, including the Corporate Governance Principles. For existing members the Principles are not legally binding and compliance is only assessed selectively through thematic peer review. Rather, it is the case that the Principles are primarily aimed at law-makers in emerging markets and developing economies, those not being members of the OECD. For those countries the voluntarity of the Principles may be reduced in practice. The Financial Stability Board (FSB), the World Bank and the IMF regard the OECD Principles as one of the international standards countries are urged to adopt, notably as part of the World Bank Reports on the Observance of Standards and Codes (ROSCs).

The use of the OECD Principles can also be the result of market pressure as far as countries want to stimulate foreign investment. At the level of companies it may simply be the case that they have to apply laws based on the OECD Principles. In addition, as far as

---

4 http://law.au.dk/en/research/projects/european-model-company-act-emca/ (last accessed 10 June 2016).

corporate laws leave options for companies, the OECD Principles function as guidance for good practice. Here too, then, it may matter that companies may be interested in implementing the Principles in order to attract investments. This is also fostered by the fact that some rating agencies use the OECD Principles in order to rank the quality of firm level corporate governance.

In the recent ROSCs, reference is also made to another set of transnational indicators: the index on minority investor protection of the World Bank's Doing Business Report (DBR).[5] This dual approach is interesting since this latter index is drafted in a different style, being more concerned with legal details than the high-level standards of the OECD Principles. In particular, it is worth noting that the minority investors' protection index is partly based on the study by Djankov and others (2008), and that other parts of the DBR also incorporate further studies by La Porta/Djankov and others.

Moreover, the DBR has a narrower substantive orientation, which has been a major point of concern for researchers critical of a pure market approach to corporate and commercial law. For example, the DBR is said to promote 'a narrow neo-liberal conception of law as a platform for private business and entrepreneurial activity' (Krever 2013), with an emphasis on investor interests 'at the expense of non-economic values and interests' (Perry-Kessaris 2011). The relevance of such orientation is also relevant in practice since the DBR is more influential than the OECD Principles: countries that rely on World Bank funding have little choice than to comply with these standards, and some have engaged in an explicit strategy to perform well in the annual DBR rankings (Schueth 2011, explaining the 'investment-promotion campaign' of the Republic of Georgia).

There are also transnational initiatives that support social aspects of corporations, in particular considering the growing importance of multinational enterprises and corporate social responsibility (Zerk 2006; Dine 2005). The main ones are the OECD Guidelines for Multilateral Enterprises, the UN Global Compact and the UN Framework on Human Rights and Business. Those are also of a non-binding nature. Their effectiveness therefore depends on how such rules may have an appeal across countries, industries and firms (see e.g. Perkins and Neumayer 2010 for the Global Compact; Muchlinski 2012 for the UN HR Framework).

A similar interdisciplinary debate about the social dimension of multinational corporations recently re-emerged about the limited liability in corporate groups. For example, it is suggested that global firms are able to avoid risks of liability owing to their complex network of subsidiaries. A legal response may be that a law of groups of companies is needed (see Hopt forthcoming 2017). In other disciplines, debates address broader issues. For example, research that deals with subsidiaries located in developing countries incorporates aspects of international relations,[6] and research that analyses how big companies and wealthy individuals use corporate forms in order to escape accountability discusses problems of power and exploitation (CJE 2010).

---

5 www.doingbusiness.org/data/exploretopics/protecting-minority-investors (last accessed 23 May 2016).
6 See the project at the Centre for International Studies and Diplomacy (SOAS, University of London) at www.cisd.soas.ac.uk/research/corporate-accountability-and-limited-liability,45734805 (last accessed 24 May 2016).

(7) Applied comparative law

It is sometimes doubted whether comparative law should be used for normative purposes. For example, the mere fact that a majority of jurisdictions follows a particular legal model does not mean that this model is better than that of the minority. It has also been said that 'the comparatist is not seeking to be judgmental about legal systems in the sense of whether he believes them to be "better" or "worse" than any other given system' (De Cruz 2007: 224). However, the majority of comparatists support the idea of 'applied comparative law'. For example, Zweigert and Kötz (1998: 47) state that 'the comparatist is in the best position to follow his comparative researches with a critical evaluation', and add that 'if he does not, no one else will do it'.

In comparative corporate law, an applied approach is possible at various levels. At the transnational level, organisations such as the EU and the OECD that are involved in drafting common rules use the experience from domestic corporate laws as comparative guidance (e.g. Ventoruzzo 2014, comparing the EU and the US). Frequently, comparisons of corporate laws are also conducted at the domestic level – by law-makers, for example prior to the UK reform leading to the Companies Act (CA) 2006 (see Jordan 1998) and occasionally also by courts (see Gelter and Siems 2014: 62–3 on corporate law decisions by the Austrian Supreme Court citing German case law). As far as there is flexibility, foreign models (or transnational models such as the OECD Principles) can also be helpful for the drafting of articles of association.

More specifically, consulting foreign company legislation for domestic law-making may be useful where the concept in question is relatively undisputed but the foreign legal system has already tried to put it into words. For example, a law-maker that wants to codify directors' duties may consider sections 170–81 of the UK CA 2006 (consolidating prior case law), as well as section 93 of the German AktG (codifying the business judgment rule). More fundamental changes may also be inspired by foreign models. However, using those may be more contentious, for example, considering the question of whether US corporate law should take inspiration from Germany and Japan in embracing stakeholder interests (see Romano 1993b, rejecting such a suggestion).

Another response to the diversity of models can be the introduction of additional forms of business entities, thus leaving it to the market to decide which one will win the day. Following the introduction of limited liability partnership (LLP) and limited liability company (LLC) laws in US states, this has indeed happened in a number of countries (McCahery and others 2010, e.g. referring to Japan and Singapore). At the level of EU law, a related development also took place: given the limited success of company law harmonisation, the EU enacted a European form of public company (called *Societas Europaea* or 'SE') in 2004, and the introduction of a European one-person private company (called *Societas Unius Personae* or 'SUP') is currently under discussion.

The transition of the former communist countries of central and eastern Europe to market economies also shows the relevance of applied comparative corporate law. The drafting of new laws was often co-authored by foreign legal scholars who took existing models into account. For instance, the Russian Law on Joint-Stock Companies of 1999 was partly influenced by US law. In addition, however, the two US professors who drafted the text aimed to consider the Russian context by way of implementing a 'self-enforcing' approach to corporate law, meaning that it should require minimal resort to courts (Black and Kraakman 1996). Another example is the 'Model Company Law for Transition Economies' by Dine and others (2007): the text of this law is a hybrid but the explanatory notes also mention that the former Yugoslavian law was used as a starting point in order to make use of a corporate law that includes consideration of stakeholder interests.

Law reforms for development are also a theme of development politics and economics. Whilst the 'law and development' initiatives of the 1960s and 70s were mainly concerned with the modernisation of legal education and the legal profession, in the 1980s a market-oriented approach to development, called the 'Washington Consensus' (Williamson 1989) became the dominant one. Among its typical recommendations were the reduction of public spending, the liberalisation of trade and investment, privatisation, deregulation and strong protection of property rights. Those precepts have then also been applied to corporate law, for example, with Dam (2006) and Cooter and Schäfer (2011) referring to the need for secure property rights, rules of investor protection and an effective judicial system, and with the World Bank including an index on minority investor protection in its Doing Business Report (see section (6) above).

The question, however, is whether, with respect to corporate law, this approach has a sound empirical basis. To summarise the research discussed earlier: on the one hand, the cross-sectional studies by La Porta and others (1998) and Djankov and others (2008) indeed found that shareholder protection is a determinant for financial development (see sections (1), (2) and (4) above). On the other hand, quantitative research with a time dimension did not confirm such a causal relationship (Armour and others 2009b), and qualitative research found the reverse causality, namely that it is financial development that stimulates law reforms (see section (5) above).

A further reason for scepticism is that today many support a more comprehensive view of development. For example, Amartya Sen suggests the notion of 'development as freedom', meaning that the main aim should be to enable everyone 'to be able to do and be'. This requires elementary 'capabilities', not simply income and wealth but, for example, education, social security, personal liberties, equal opportunities and fairness. Law and justice are therefore also not merely seen as a means to another end (say, for economic development); rather, they are an important part of the development process on their own (Sen 1999, 2009). For corporate law it may therefore also be followed that its normativity should not be restricted to the need to fix economic agency problems.

Conclusion: overcoming separations

It was the aim of this chapter to show how seven core approaches of comparative law can support research on comparative corporate law. Establishing such links was not an easy endeavour since previous literature on comparative corporate law has largely disregarded modern discussions in comparative law, whilst mainstream comparative law has typically not been interested in corporate law but has focused on contract law, tort law and civil procedure. Thus, as a first recommendation, this conclusion suggests overcoming the separation between comparative and corporate law research.

In this chapter the division into seven categories was used for didactic purposes. In practice, it is likely that any substantial research will be based on at least two or three of these approaches. Moreover, it is important to be familiar with all of those seven categories in order to justify one's choices and in order to be aware of the limitations of one's chosen method. For a thorough treatment of a particular topic of comparative corporate law, it may even be unavoidable to use all of those approaches. As far as appropriate, secondly, it is therefore suggested to overcome any superficial separation between the seven categories.

Throughout the chapter, the discussion about the methods of comparative corporate law distinguished between comparative corporate law research with a legal focus and with an interdisciplinary perspective. This was done in order to reflect, on the one hand, the preference of some corporate law scholars for relatively narrow legal approaches and, on the other hand, the widespread interest of researchers from other disciplines (management, economics, politics etc) in topics that have a corporate law dimension. This is not ideal. Therefore, thirdly, corporate legal scholars should try to overcome the separation between legal and interdisciplinary perspectives of comparative corporate law.

Bibliography

Aguilera, Ruth V., Kurt A. Desender and Luiz Ricardo Kabbach de Castro (2012) 'A Bundle Perspective to Comparative Corporate Governance' in Thomas Clarke (ed) *The Sage Handbook of Corporate Governance*, London: Sage, pp. 380–405.

Ahlering, Beth and Simon Deakin (2007) 'Labour Regulation, Corporate Governance and Legal Origin: A Case of Institutional Complementarity?', *Law & Society Review*, 41: 865–98.

Andenas, Mads and Frank Wooldridge (2009) *European Comparative Company Law*, Cambridge: Cambridge University Press.

Armour, John, Simon Deakin, Priya Lele and Mathias Siems (2009a) 'How Do Legal Rules Evolve? Evidence From a Cross-Country Comparison of Shareholder, Creditor and Worker Protection', *American Journal of Comparative Law*, 57: 579–629.

Armour, John, Simon Deakin, Prabirjit Sarkar, Mathias Siems, and Ajit Singh (2009b) 'Shareholder Protection and Stock Market Development: A Test of the Legal Origins Hypothesis', *Journal of Empirical Legal Studies*, 6: 343–80.

Bachner, Thomas (2009) *Creditor Protection in Private Companies: Anglo-German Perspectives for a European Legal Discourse*, Cambridge: Cambridge University Press.

Barca, Fabrizio and Marco Becht (eds) (2001) *The Control of Corporate Europe*, Oxford: Oxford University Press.

Barker, Roger M. (2010) *Corporate Governance, Competition, and Political Parties: Explaining Corporate Governance Change in Europe*, Oxford: Oxford University Press.

Bebchuk, Lucian Arye and Mark J. Roe (1999) 'A Theory of Path Dependence in Corporate Ownership and Governance', *Stanford Law Review*, 52: 127–70.

Becht, Marco, Colin Mayer and Hannes F. Wagner (2008) 'Where Do Firms Incorporate? Deregulation and the Cost of Entry', *Journal of Corporate Finance*, 14: 241–56.

Bell, John (2001) *French Legal Cultures*, London: Butterworths.

Bell, John (2006) *Judiciaries within Europe: A Comparative Review*, Cambridge: Cambridge University Press.

Black, Bernard and Reinier Kraakman (1996) 'A Self-Enforcing Model of Corporate Law', *Harvard Law Review*, 109: 1911–82.

Bruner, Christopher M. (2013) *Corporate Governance in the Common-Law World: The Political Foundations of Shareholder Power*, New York: Cambridge University Press.

Buchanan, John and Simon Deakin (2008) 'Japan's Paradoxical Response to the New "Global Standard" in Corporate Governance', *Zeitschrift für Japanisches Recht*, 13: 59–84.

Cabrelli, David and Mathias Siems (2015) 'Convergence, Legal Origins and Transplants in Comparative Corporate Law: A Case-Based and Quantitative Analysis', *American Journal of Comparative Law*, 63: 109–53.

Cahn, Andreas and David C. Donald (2010) *Comparative Company Law*, Cambridge: Cambridge University Press.

Carney, William J. (1998) 'The Production of Corporate Law', *Southern California Law Review*, 71: 715–80.

Cary, William L. (1974) 'Federalism and Corporate Law: Reflections Upon Delaware', *Yale Law Journal* 83: 663–707.

Cerioni, Luca (2007) *EU Corporate Law and EU Company Tax Law*, Cheltenham: Edward Elgar.

Cheffins, Brian R. (2001) 'Does Law Matter? The Separation of Ownership and Control in the United Kingdom', *Journal of Legal Studies*, 30: 459–84.

Cheffins, Brian R. (2008) *Corporate Ownership and Control: British Business Transformed*, Oxford: Oxford University Press.

Cheffins, Brian R., Steven A. Bank and Harwell Wells (2013) 'Questioning "Law and Finance": US Stock Market Development, 1930–70', *Business History*, 55: 601–19.

Chong, Alberto and Cesar Calderon (2000) 'Causality and Feedback Between Institutional Measures and Economic Growth', *Economics and Politics*, 12: 69–81.

Cioffi, John W. (2010) *Public Law and Private Power: Corporate Governance Reform in the Age of Finance Capitalism*, Ithaca NY: Cornell University Press.

CJE (2010) 'Corporate Accountability and Legal Liability: On the Future of Corporate Capitalism', special issue in *Cambridge Journal of Economics* (CJE), volume 34, issue 5.

Coffee, John C. (2001) 'The Rise of Dispersed Ownership: The Roles of Law and the State in the Separation of Ownership and Control', *Yale Law Journal* 111: 1–81.

Colli, Andrea, Abe Jong and Martin Jes Iversen (eds) (2012) *Mapping European Corporations; Strategy, Structure, Ownership and Performance*, London: Routledge (also published in *Business History*, 53, issue 1).

Conac, Pierre-Henri, Luca Enriques and Martin Gelter (2007) 'Constraining Dominant Shareholders' Self-dealing: The Legal Framework in France, Germany, and Italy', *European Company and Financial Law Review*, 491–528.

Cooter, Robert D. and Hans-Bernd Schäfer (2011) *Solomon's Knot: How Law Can End the Poverty of Nations*, Princeton: Princeton University Press.

Corcoron, Suzanne (1996) 'Comparative Corporate Law Research Methodology', *Canberra Law Review*, 3: 54–61.

Dam, Kenneth W. (2006) *The Law–Growth Nexus: The Rule of Law and Economic Development*, Washington DC, Brookings Institution Press.

Davies, Paul, Klaus Hopt, Richard Nowak and Gerard van Solinge (eds) (2013) *Corporate Boards in Law and Practice: A Comparative Analysis in Europe*, Oxford: Oxford University Press.

De Coninck, Julie (2010) 'The Functional Method of Comparative Law: Quo Vadis?', *Rabels Zeitschrift für ausländisches und internationales Privatrecht*, 74: 318–50.

De Cruz, Peter (2007) *Comparative Law in a Changing World*, 3rd edn, London: Routledge Cavendish.

Deakin, Simon (2009) 'Legal Origin, Juridical Form and Industrialisation in Historical Perspective: the Case of the Employment Contract and the Joint-stock Company', *Socio-Economic Review*, 6: 35–65.

Dignam, Alan and Michael Galanis (2009) *The Globalization of Corporate Governance*, Farnham: Ashgate.

Dine, Janet (2005) *Companies, International Trade and Human Rights*, Cambridge: Cambridge University Press.

Dine, Janet, Marios Koutsias and Michael Blecher (2007) *Company Law in the New Europe: The EU Acquis, Comparative Methodology and Model Law*, Cheltenham: Edward Elgar.

Djankov, Simeon and Rafael La Porta, Florencio Lopez-de-Silanes and Andrei Shleifer (2008) 'The Law and Economics of Self-Dealing', *Journal of Financial Economics*, 88: 430–65.

Doing Business Reports (various years), World Bank, http://www.doingbusiness.org/reports (last accessed 10 June 2016).

Enriques, Luca (2006) 'EC Company Law Directives and Regulations: How Trivial Are They?', *University of Pennsylvania Journal of International Economic Law*, 28: 1–78.

Fleckner, Andreas M. and Klaus J. Hopt (eds) (2013) *Comparative Corporate Governance: A Functional and International Analysis*, Cambridge: Cambridge University Press.

Foster, Nicholas H.D. (2007) 'Comparative Commercial Law: Rules or Context?' in Esin Örücü and David Nelken (eds) *Comparative Law: A Handbook*, Oxford: Hart, pp. 263–85.

Franks, Julian, Colin Mayer and Stefano Rossi (2009) 'Ownership: Evolution and Regulation', *Review of Financial Studies*, 22: 4009–56.

Gelter, Martin (2011) 'Taming or Protecting the Modern Corporation? Shareholder-Stakeholder Debates in a Comparative Light', *NYU Review of Law and Business*, 7: 641–730.

Gelter, Martin (2014) 'From Institutional Theories to Private Pensions', Fordham Law Legal Studies Research Paper No 2463275, forthcoming in *Company Law and CSR: New Legal and Economic Challenges* (Ivan Tchotourian ed), Bruylant).

Gelter, Martin and Mathias Siems (2014) 'Citations to Foreign Courts – Illegitimate and Superfluous, or Unavoidable? Evidence from Europe', *American Journal of Comparative Law*, 62: 35–85.

Gerner-Beuerle, Carsten and Edmund Schuster (2014) 'The Costs of Separation: Friction between Company and Insolvency Law in the Single Market', *Journal of Corporate Law Studies*, 14: 301–46.

Gilson, Ronald J. (2001) 'Globalizing Corporate Governance: Convergence of Form or Function', *America Journal of Comparative Law*, 49: 329–57.

Glenn, H. Patrick (2007) 'Com-paring' in Esin Örücü and David Nelken (eds) *Comparative Law: A Handbook*, Oxford: Hart, pp. 91–108.

Goergen, Marc (2012) *International Corporate Governance*, Harlow: Pearson.

Gospel, Howard and Andrew Pendleton (eds) (2005) *Corporate Governance and Labour Management: An International Comparison*, Oxford: Oxford University Press.

Graziadei, Michele (2003) 'The functionalist heritage', in Pierre Legrand and Roderick Munday (eds.) *Comparative Legal Studies: Traditions and Transitions*, Cambridge: Cambridge University Press, pp. 100–27.

Hall, Peter A. and Daniel W. Gingerich (2009) 'Varieties of Capitalism and Institutional Complementarities in the Political Economy: An Empirical Analysis', *British Journal of Political Science*, 39: 449–82.

Hall, Peter A. and David Soskice (2001) 'An Introduction to Varieties of Capitalism', in Peter A. Hall and David Soskice (eds) *Varieties of Capitalism: The Institutional Foundations of Comparative Advantage*, Oxford: Oxford University Press, pp. 1–68.

Hansmann, Henry and Reinier Kraakman (2001) 'The End of History for Corporate Law', *Georgetown Law Journal*, 88: 439–68.

Hopt, Klaus J. (forthcoming 2017) 'Groups of Companies' in Jeffrey Gordon and Georg Ringe (eds) *The Oxford Handbook of Corporate Law and Governance*, Oxford: Oxford University Press.

Husa, Jaakko (2003) 'Farewell to Functionalism or Methodological Tolerance?', *Rabels Zeitschrift für ausländisches und internationales Privatrecht*, 67: 419–47.

Husa, Jaakko (2015) *A New Introduction to Comparative Law*, Oxford: Hart Publishing.

Jensen, Michael C. and William H. Meckling (1976) 'Theory of the Firm: Managerial Behavior, Agency Costs and Ownership Structure', *Journal of Financial Economics* 3: 305–60.

Jia, Xinting and Roman Tomasic (2010) *Corporate Governance and Resource Security in China – The Transformation of China's Global Resources Companies*, New York: Routledge.

Johnston, Andrew (2009) *EC Regulation of Corporate Governance*, Cambridge: Cambridge University Press.

Jordan, Cally (1998) *An International Survey of Companies Law in the Commonwealth, North America, Asia and Europe*, London: DTI http://ssrn.com/abstract=1141874 (last accessed 24 May 2016).

Katelouzou, Dionysia and Mathias Siems (2015) 'Disappearing Paradigms in Shareholder Protection: Leximetric Evidence for 30 Countries, 1990–2013', *Journal of Corporate Law Studies*, 15: 127–60.

Keenan, James and Maria Aggestam (2001) 'Corporate Governance and Intellectual Capital: Some Conceptualisations', *Corporate Governance: An International Review*, 9: 259–75.

Kennedy, Duncan (2012) 'Political ideology and comparative law' in Mauro Bussani and Ugo Mattei (eds) *Cambridge Companion to Comparative Law*, Cambridge: Cambridge University Press, pp. 35–56.

Kershaw, David (forthcoming 2017) 'Corporate Law and Self-regulation' in Jeffrey Gordon and Wolf-Georg Ringe (eds) *The Oxford Handbook of Corporate Law and Governance*, Oxford: Oxford University Press.

Kraakman, Reinier and others (2009) *The Anatomy of Corporate Law: A Comparative and Functional Approach*, 2nd edn, Oxford: Oxford University Press.

Krever, Tor (2013) 'Quantifying Law: Legal Indicator Projects and the Reproduction of Neoliberal Common Sense', *Third World Quarterly*, 34: 131–50.

La Porta, Rafael, Florencio Lopez-de-Silanes, Andrei Shleifer and Robert W. Vishny (1998) 'Law and Finance', *Journal of Political Economy*, 106: 1113–55.

La Porta, Rafael, Florencio Lopez-de-Silanes and Andrei Shleifer (2008) 'The Economic Consequences of Legal Origins', *Journal of Economic Literature*, 46: 285–332.

Licht, Amir N. (2001) 'The Mother of All Path Dependencies: Towards a Cross-Cultural Theory of Corporate Governance-Systems', *Delaware Journal of Corporate Law*, 26: 147–205.

Licht, Amir N., Chanan Goldschmidt and Shalom H. Schwartz (2005) 'Culture, Law, and Corporate Governance', *International Review of Law and Economics*, 25: 229–55.

Marnet, Oliver (2008) *Behaviour and Rationality in Corporate Governance*, Abingdon: Routledge.

McCahery, Joseph A., Erik P.M. Vermeulen, Masato Hisatake and Jun Saito (2010) 'The New Company Law: What Matters in an Innovative Economy' in Joseph A. McCahery, Levinus Timmerman and Erik P.M. Vermeulen (eds) *Private Company Law Reform: International and European Perspectives*, The Hague: T.M.C. Asser Press, pp. 71–118.

Merryman, John Henry (1999) *The Loneliness of the Comparative Lawyer – And Other Essays in Foreign and Comparative Law*, The Hague: Kluwer.

Michaels, Ralf (2006) 'The Functional Method of Comparative Law' in Mathias Reimann and Reinhard Zimmermann (eds) *The Oxford Handbook of Comparative Law*, Oxford: Oxford University Press, pp. 339–82.

Moloney, Niamh (2014) *EU Securities and Financial Markets Regulation*, Oxford: Oxford University Press.

Moore, Marc T. (2013) *Corporate Governance in the Shadow of the State*, Oxford: Hart Publishing.

Morck, Randall K. (ed.) (2007) *A History of Corporate Governance Around the World: Family Business Groups to Professional Managers*, Chicago: University of Chicago Press.

Mucciarelli, Federico (2012) 'The Function of Corporate Law and the Effects of Reincorporations in the U.S. and the E.U.', *Tulane Journal of International and Comparative Law*, 20: 421–68.

Muchlinski, Peter (2012) 'Implementing the New UN Corporate Human Rights Framework: Implications for Corporate Law, Governance and Regulation', *Business Ethics Quarterly*, 22: 145–77.

Pacces, Alessio M. (2011) 'How Does Corporate Law Matter? "Law and Finance" and Beyond', in Michael Faure and Jan Smits (eds) *Does Law Matter? On Law and Economic Growth*, Antwerp: Intersentia, pp. 297–329.

Pargendler, Mariana (forthcoming 2017) 'Corporate Governance in Emerging Markets' in Jeffrey Gordon and Wolf-Georg Ringe (eds) *The Oxford Handbook of Corporate Law and Governance*, Oxford: Oxford University Press.

Perkins, Richard and Eric Neumayer (2010) 'Geographic Variations in the Early Diffusion of Corporate Voluntary Standards: Comparing ISO 14001 and the Global Compact', *Environment and Planning*, 42: 347–65.

Perry-Kessaris, Amanda (2011) 'Prepare Your Indicators: Economics Imperialism on the Shores of Law and Development', *International Journal of Law in Context*, 7: 401–21.

Pistor, Katharina (2005) 'Legal Ground Rules in Coordinated and Liberal Market Economies' in Klaus Hopt and others (eds) *Corporate Governance in Context: Corporations, States and Markets in Europe, Japan and the U.S.*, Oxford: Oxford University Press, pp. 249–80.

Pistor, Katharina, Martin Raiser and Stanislaw Gelfer (2000) 'Law and Finance in Transition Economies', *Economics of Transition*, 8: 325–68.

Puchniak, Dan W., Harald Baum and Michael Ewing-Chow (eds) (2012) *The Derivative Action in Asia: A Comparative and Functional Approach*, Cambridge: Cambridge University Press.

Ringe, Wolf-Georg (2013) 'Corporate Mobility in the European Union – a Flash in the Pan? An Empirical Study on the Success of Law-making and Regulatory Competition', *European Company and Financial Law Review*, 10: 230–67.

Roe, Mark J. (1993) 'Some Differences in Corporate Structure in Germany, Japan, and the United States', *Yale Law Journal*, 102: 1927–2003.

Roe, Mark J. (1997) 'Path Dependence, Political Options, and Governance Systems', in Klaus J. Hopt and Eddy Wymeersch (eds) *Comparative Corporate Governance – Essays and Materials*, Berlin: de Gruyter, pp. 165–84.

Roe Mark J. (2003a) 'Delaware's Competition', *Harvard Law Review*, 117: 588–646.

Roe, Mark J. (2003b) *Political Determinants of Corporate Governance*, Oxford: Oxford University Press.

Romano, Roberta (1993a) *The Genius of American Corporate Law*, Washington: AEI Press.

Romano, Roberta (1993b) 'A Cautionary Note on Drawing Lessons from Comparative Corporate Law', *Yale Law Journal*, 102: 2021–36.

Romano, Roberta (2006) 'The State as a Laboratory: Legal Innovation and State Competition for Corporate Charters', *Yale Journal of Regulation*, 23: 209–349.

Roth, Günter H. and Peter Kindler (2014) *The Spirit of Corporate Law*, Oxford: Hart Publishing.

Ruskola, Teemu (2002) 'Legal Orientalism', *Michigan Law Review*, 101: 179–234.

Samuel, Geoffrey (2014) *An Introduction to Comparative Law Theory and Method*, Oxford: Hart Publishing.

Schnyder, Gerhard (2015) 'The Drivers of Change in National Corporate Governance Systems: Longitudinal Firm-level Evidence From Four European Countries', Working Paper.

Schueth, Sam (2011) 'Assembling International Competitiveness: The Republic of Georgia, USAID, and the Doing Business Project', *Economic Geography*, 87: 51–77.

Sen, Amartya (1999) *Development as Freedom*, New York: Knopf.

Sen, Amartya (2009) *The Idea of Justice*, London: Allen Lane.

Senn, Myriam (2011) *Non-State Regulatory Regimes: Understanding Institutional Transformation*, Heidelberg: Springer.

Siems, Mathias (2007) 'Legal Origins: Reconciling Law & Finance and Comparative Law', *McGill Law Journal*, 52: 55–81.

Siems, Mathias (2008) *Convergence in Shareholder Law*, Cambridge: Cambridge University Press.

Siems, Mathias (2012) 'Private Enforcement of Directors' Duties: Derivative Actions as a Global Phenomenon' in Stefan Wrbka, Steven Van Uytsel and Mathias Siems (eds) *Collective Actions: Enhancing Access to Justice and Reconciling Multilayer Interests?*, Cambridge: Cambridge University Press, pp. 93–116.

Siems, Mathias (2014) *Comparative Law*, Cambridge: Cambridge University Press.

Siems, Mathias (forthcoming 2017) 'Taxonomies and Leximetrics' in Jeffrey Gordon and Wolf-Georg Ringe (eds) *The Oxford Handbook of Corporate Law and Governance*, Oxford: Oxford University Press.

Siems, Mathias and Oscar Alvarez-Macotela (2014) 'The OECD Principles of Corporate Governance in Emerging Markets: A Successful Example of Networked Governance?' in Mark Fenwick, Steven Van Uytsel and Stefan Wrbka (eds), *Networked Governance, Transnational Business and the Law*, Berlin: Springer, pp. 257–84.

Siems, Mathias and David Cabrelli (eds) (2013) *Comparative Company Law: A Case-Based Approach*, Oxford: Hart Publishing.

Siems, Mathias and Simon Deakin (2010) 'Comparative Law and Finance: Past, Present and Future Research', *Journal of Institutional and Theoretical Economics*, 166: 120–40.

Spamann, Holger (2010) 'The "Antidirector Rights Index" Revisited', *Review of Financial Studies*, 23: 468–83.

Van Hulle, Karel and Harald Gesell (eds) (2006) *European Corporate Law*, Baden Baden: Nomos.

Ventoruzzo, Marco (2014) 'The Role of Comparative Law in Shaping Corporate Statutory Reforms', *Duquesne Law Review* 52: 151–72.

Ventoruzzo, Marco, Pierre-Henri Conac, Gen Goto, Sebastian Mock, Mario Notari and Arad Reisberg (2015) *Comparative Corporate Law*, St. Paul, MN: West Academic.

Weimar, Jeroen and Joost Pape (1999) 'A Taxonomy of Systems of Corporate Governance', *Corporate Governance: An International Review*, 7: 152–66.

Whittaker, D. Hugh and Simon Deakin (eds) (2010) *Corporate Governance and Managerial Reform in Japan*, Oxford: Oxford University Press.

Williamson, John (1989) 'What Washington Means by Policy Reform' in John Williamson (ed) *Latin American Readjustment: How Much has Happened*, Washington: Institute for International Economics.

Zerk, Jennifer A. (2006) *Multinationals and Corporate Social Responsibility*, Cambridge: Cambridge University Press.

Zweigert, Konrad and Hein Kötz (1998) *An Introduction to Comparative Law*, 3rd edn, Oxford: Clarendon Press.

2

The de-privatisation of Anglo–American corporate law?

Marc T Moore

Introduction

The way in which scholars and students characterise a phenomenon academically is of enormous – and often underappreciated – significance, especially when it comes to aspects of the law. How we characterise an area of law – or, in other words, what the dominant academic *paradigm* of that subject is – affects how we customarily think about it, write about it and teach it. Crucially, it also affects our *normative* perspective on that subject. That is to say, it determines what we regard to be its strengths and weaknesses, its 'rights' and 'wrongs', and the appropriate course of its future development. The opinions and attitudes that are shaped in legal monographs, law review articles and law school classrooms do not just echo around the proverbial ivory towers of elite academic institutions. Ultimately – albeit often very gradually – they trickle down into the so-called 'real world', either when former students of the law later become influential practitioners of it or when leading academic texts are used by judicial or policy-making figures to help shape their critical understanding of challenging legal issues.

Within the Anglo–American environment, the dominant academic characterisation of corporate law is as an aspect of 'private' or facilitative law. As such, corporate (or – to use English parlance – 'company') law is conventionally bracketed alongside other traditional private law subjects such as contract, property, equity, agency and trusts law. Accordingly, the efficacy of corporate law in the US and UK is ordinarily judged by reference to how responsive those rules are to the supposed private preferences of key corporate participants or 'contractors'. For the most part, this category is normally restricted to include the common or ordinary shareholders who supply the corporation's equity or risk capital, and the managerial officers (including directors) who are appointed to make executive policy decisions on shareholders' collective behalf.

It follows from this premise that the core and motivating purpose of corporate law should be to reflect or 'mimic' the notional 'terms' that shareholders and managers would be inclined to agree upon with one another privately, in the hypothetical situation where no antecedent laws exist and therefore all norms stand to be determined by private negotiation alone. This is what is commonly known as the 'contractarian' or 'nexus of contracts' paradigm of corporate law (see, e.g. Black 1990; Easterbrook and Fischel 1991; Hansmann and Kraakman 2000).

Correspondingly, corporate law is ordinarily *not* characterised as an aspect of 'public' or regulatory law, in the way that subjects such as tort, criminal, environmental, antitrust (or competition) and securities law are. That is to say, unlike the above areas of law, corporate law is typically not perceived as being designed to coerce social-behavioural change, or to bring about direct distributional outcomes within society whether in terms of risk, power or wealth. Therefore, academic characterisations of corporate law normally do not seek to portray the laws and norms in this field as exhibiting such characteristics, which would run counter to their purportedly facilitative – and thus fundamentally *non*-socially-determinative – nature (on the private/public divide in corporate law generally, see Bottomley in this volume; Hadfield and Talley 2006).

Just as the purpose of an artistic caricature is to accentuate the most distinctive or noteworthy features of a person rather than portray her every literal detail, the objective of an academic characterisation is to emphasise and draw on the key distinguishing features of a subject rather than to document that phenomenon in all of its complexity. Inevitably, therefore, the process of academic characterisation – in law as elsewhere – involves some marginal degree of papering over the empirical cracks. That is to say, the occasional outlying or idiosyncratic feature is conveniently (and quite acceptably) elided so as not to detract from the essential qualities of the subject that the writer is seeking to accentuate.

Therefore an academic characterisation of an area of law, like an artistic caricature, need not be 100 per cent comprehensive in documenting a subject, nor sensitive to its every empirical nuance. As a minimum requirement, however, the characterisation must be capable of incorporating *all materially significant* features of its subject matter, or else the ensuing model will lose its essential representational quality.

Moreover, the process of academically characterising a subject – and especially an area of law – involves not just an empirical but also a normative dimension. These two elements necessarily overlap and reinforce one other. Inevitably, the answer to the empirical question – that is, what essentially *is* a given phenomenon – affects our answer to the ensuing normative question – that is, what essential form or qualities *should* that phenomenon embody? Thus, in any field of social science, constructive academic debate involves scholars providing competing characterisations of the essential (empirical) nature of a thing on a definitional level, in order to establish (or change) the points of references in accordance with which the efficacy or desirability of that phenomenon can subsequently be judged from a more critical perspective.

In short – in law, as elsewhere – *ought* judgments are ultimately dependent to a large extent on *is* judgments because, in order to be able critically to evaluate a subject, we must first of all understand its key attributes and qualities.[1] It follows that, where a particular characterisation of an area of law lacks adequate empirical foundations (in the sense of failing to represent any materially significant features of the relevant subject matter), any normative conclusions that are drawn on that basis are either void – or, at the very least – become subject to further questioning as a precondition to their continuing acceptance by others.

---

1 On the 'is–ought' distinction in legal discourse generally, see MacCormick 2007: chs 1–2; MacCormick 1999: ch 1.

In the field of corporate law, the main 'is' dispute concerns the alleged 'private' versus 'public' nature of the laws in this field – that is, to what extent can corporate law properly be regarded as the outcome of decentralised market or civil society bargaining, in contrast to centralised regulatory state imposition? Or, to put the issue another way: is corporate law at its core an organic ('bottom-up') or synthetic ('top-down') creation? Where one adopts the former view as regards the fundamental nature of corporate law, they are ordinarily led to the ensuing normative position that the relevant laws in future *should* rightfully be developed along the same basic path: that is, law-making in this field should be *responsive* to private preferences, rather than determinative of them.

Vice versa, proponents of the latter (synthetic) view of corporate law tend consequently to arrive at the contrary normative position. That is, that the laws in this field should be coercive and socially-determinative, aimed at eliciting direct change in the behavioural patterns and relative resources of key corporate participants in line with general democratic opinion in society; and irrespective of whether or not such regulatory outcomes are consistent with the affected participants' (especially shareholders') private preferences.

Against the above background, this chapter accordingly examines and challenges the dominant academic portrayal of Anglo–American corporate law as an aspect of private law, and argues for a recharacterisation of the subject that reflects the centrality of public regulation to its core dynamics. It first explores the purported 'privity' (or privateness) of corporate law as it is most commonly understood and taught within the Anglo–American environment. In doing so, it makes reference to some of the most notable quasi-contractual aspects of US and UK corporate law, which would appear to provide empirical support for the dominant contractarian paradigm of the subject. The chapter then highlights an apparent 'de-privatisation' trend in Anglo–American corporate law over recent years, including the impact of increasing federalisation of corporate law in the United States under the Sarbanes–Oxley and Dodd–Frank reforms, and also the effect of increasing juridification of corporate law in the United Kingdom at both domestic and EU level.

The chapter subsequently examines the normative implications of this de-privatisation trend. It demonstrates that the developments in question – on closer inspection – are in fact considerably less material than might first appear to the overall character of Anglo–American corporate law, which has for a long time exhibited significant public-regulatory features. However, insofar as these more publicly oriented aspects of corporate law have tended to be rationalised under the separate head of *securities* (or capital markets) law reforms, their existence has generally not been seen as threatening the continuing private dynamic of 'corporate' law as a distinct system in itself. As against this, however, the chapter argues that once the inherent artificiality of the conventional corporate/securities law divide is recognised, the prevailing academic characterisation of Anglo–American corporate law as an inherently private phenomenon is rendered unsustainable, both descriptively and normatively.

The purported 'privity' of Anglo–American corporate law

For much of the past century, corporate law scholars in the United States and United Kingdom have sought to develop the academic contours of their subject as an essentially private, functional and politically colourless field of enquiry. The precise jurisprudential trajectories along which these developments have occurred on each side of the Atlantic bear their own unique characteristics. Nonetheless, a common and fundamental feature of the so-called 'Anglo–American' corporate law systems is the dominant scholarly perception of the subject as a dynamic and self-determinative aspect of *private* law lying beyond the meddling reach of the 'public' or interventionist regulatory state. As such, corporate law arguably is – and, moreover, *should be* – focused more or less exclusively on giving legal effect to the terms and essential substance of arrangements constituted by decentralised persons acting on their own behalf, whether in an individual or private–organisational capacity.

The perceived 'privity' (or privateness) of Anglo–American corporate law is attributable in large part to the pervasive influence of what has variously been termed the 'contractarian', 'nexus of contracts' or 'private ordering' theory of the firm. Originally an invention of US-based financial economists in the 1970s, contractarianism has expanded in depth and influence over recent decades to become the dominant conceptual and normative lens through which the corporation and its constituent laws are conventionally studied across the English-speaking world.

On a jurisprudential level, contractarianism in effect instils the logic of private law into the internal structure and functioning of modern business corporations, by asserting that 'public' or widely held corporate entities – in spite of their typically enormous organisational scale, extensive social impact and peculiar ownership/control dynamic (including the lack of any distinct proprietary or entrepreneurial presence) – should nonetheless be regarded as essentially private and quasi-contractual institutions, which are subject to qualitatively similar market dynamics and pressures to those affecting orthodox (i.e. closely held) business entities (Ireland 2003). In particular, contractarian scholars emphatically refuse to afford any conceptual significance to the corporation's formal legal autonomy or 'personhood', instead regarding the incorporated firm as a mere structural convenience that serves the collective, contractually communicated interests of its various human participants at any given point in time (see e.g. Cheffins 1997: 31–41; Easterbrook and Fischel 1985). It is therefore un-surprising that the contractarian theory of the firm has tended in general to exhibit a strong anti-regulatory hue.

To a significant extent the contractarian characterisation is empirically validated – albeit in different ways – by the actual form and substance of corporate law as it exists in both the United States and the United Kingdom. In the United States, the pervasive influence of the contractarian paradigm inheres at least as much in the peculiar *form* that many core corporate law rules take, as in the inherent substance of those doctrines themselves. Consistent with the general ideological impetus of the contractarian position, corporate law scholars in the United States tend in general to show a preference for legal rules that are flexible and adaptable in their application.

From the contractarian assertion that there is no universally determinable 'right' way to structure a corporation's internal governance arrangements, there derives a commonly held view in the United States that corporate law rules should be designed so as to allow ample space for deviation and diversity by contractors from the regulatory norm. Therefore, in con-trast to the orthodox 'command' conception of laws as a coercive means of engendering conformity by citizens with universally applicable sovereign decrees, US business entities law by contrast is commonly depicted in terms of an essentially *facilitative*, transaction-cost saving device or 'tool' that contracting parties are free to adopt or reject at their personal whim (see e.g. Easterbrook and Fischel 1989).

Furthermore, since in the absence of state-promulgated corporate laws, shareholders and managers would be inclined to work out their own ad hoc contractual solutions to corporate governance problems in any event, the law in this context should – it is argued – rightfully be viewed as having no socially determinative value in its own right. Rather, the purpose of corporate law within the contractarian paradigm is simply to 'mimic' ex ante those contractual outcomes that hypothetical corporate participants would in general be inclined to favour if given the opportunity to bargain free of charge over the internal division of power, rights and entitlements in respect of their mutual venture (Black 1990: 552–5).

From this understanding of law there derives a legislative preference (at least at state level) for providing generally – but not universally – accepted 'default' legal rules that are freely 'reversible' at the behest of key corporate participants (Bainbridge 2008: 35–7). Such reversibility is achieved by granting directors and/or shareholders an ad hoc licence to 'opt out' of any rule or doctrine that appears ill-suited to their firm's peculiar characteristics or environment, by including a provision to this effect within a corporation's internal constitutional documents (Bebchuk 1989: 1396–7).

The long-standing trailblazer of the opting-out (and, vice versa, opting-in) tradition in US corporate law is the State of Delaware, which has over the past century developed a highly flexible corporate law statute permitting individual firms significant leeway in their application of core governance norms (Bowman 1996: 60). This includes the freedom to limit or negate in respect of any one firm the effect of important statutory and common law rules concerning the balance of power, influence and accountability between shareholders and directors. Largely for this reason, Delaware has become the state domicile of choice for a majority of publicly listed corporations in the United States.

Moreover, the tradition of adaptability and opting-out in US corporate law is reinforced by the country's unique competitive-federalist law-making system. Ingrained into the jurisprudential fabric of US corporate law is the long-standing 'internal affairs' doctrine, which dictates that the state of incorporation – as the formal source of a corporation's legal existence – has exclusively regulatory prerogative over intra-firm affairs involving the rights and powers of shareholders, directors and managers (DeMott 1985; Tung 2006).

Thus incorporators – both 'start-up' first-time incorporators and 'midstream' reincorporating firms – enjoy a legally uninhibited choice of 51 intra-national jurisdictions[2] as the formal legal domicile for their company. Moreover, applicable rules of US corporate law – in contrast to other aspects of civil or criminal law – are determined purely by a corporation's state of registration, irrespective of whereabouts in the country (or world) its physical activities and transactions are subsequently carried out (Romano 1993: 1). This means that, with respect to corporate law at least, the choice of state of incorporation in effect amounts to a choice *of law*, thereby creating a quasi-consumerist tendency to view each individual state's corporate law system as an effective 'menu' of choices that can be weighed up against those competing regulatory 'products' offered by other states (Easterbrook and Fischel 1991: 5).

Accordingly, just as corporations compete with each other to offer the securities and governance systems that appeal to investors, at a higher level states can also be seen as competing with one another to offer the legal 'terms' that corporations themselves are likely to find attractive (Bainbridge 2006: 1742). Whereas the imputed motivating force for a corporation in offering attractive terms to investors is reduction of its cost of capital and, ultimately, profit maximisation, for states, the corresponding imperative is perceived to be maximisation of incorporation revenues and attendant benefits (Bebchuk 1992: 1451). In this way, the orthodox chain of regulatory cause and effect is reversed in the sense that regulatees, as notional 'consumers' of legal rules, dictate the decisions of regulators as notional 'producers' on the corporate law marketplace.

---

2 This figure includes all 50 US states plus the District of Columbia, which operates its own incorporations regime.

Such a portrayal of the rule-making process, moreover, aligns logically with the above-mentioned 'opting out' tradition in corporate law. On a private ordering analysis it could thus be said that an incorporator, having chosen to 'purchase' a particular set of rules by incorporating her firm within a chosen jurisdiction, should thereafter be free as the notional 'owner' of those rules to adapt them to her personal preference, just as one might wish to make perceived improvements to a house or car following its purchase.

In contrast to the US model of corporate law-making outlined above, the corresponding British system is for most practical intents and purposes *unitary* in nature.[3] Furthermore, in respect of the majority of significant corporate governance matters the UK's principal corporate law statute, the Companies Act 2006, operates on a mandatory and thus irreversible basis. More generally, the use of mandatory and irreversible statutory rules to afford protection to shareholders of UK corporations has been widely accepted and thus seldom questioned, either academically or judicially.

Notwithstanding, the dual contractual qualities of flexibility and reversibility of laws are maintained within the British company law framework in other important respects. Insofar as publicly listed companies are concerned, a particularly distinctive dimension of UK corporate law's rich private ordering heritage is its extensive resort to non-statist 'soft law' techniques that lie *beyond* the orthodox realm of statutory and common law, and which (theoretically at least) provide scope for flexibility, diversity or opt-out at the point of firm-specific norm application. This comparatively peculiar aspect of UK corporate law can be attributed to the cultural path dependencies underlying the so-called 'London approach' to financial market regulation (FRC 2006), a central characteristic of which is the implicit devolution – by government – of far-reaching regulatory responsibilities to individuals or groups directly affected by the ensuing rules (Cheffins 1997: 366).

In the field of corporate governance, meanwhile, the so-called 'soft law' phenomenon has manifested itself in two main forms. The first of these is the system for regulation of listed company board structures and risk oversight practices under the UK Corporate Governance Code: an informal body of norms promulgated by the non-governmental Financial Reporting Council (FRC), and whose enforcement is characterised by the dynamic and (theoretically) investor-driven practice of 'comply or explain' (FRC 2014: 4; Moore 2009: 104–7). The second of such forms is the UK's so-called 'privatised' system of corporate takeover regulation under the remit of the Panel on Takeovers and Mergers: a non-statist rule-making and executive body comprised mainly of appointees from financial institutions that are broadly representative of the City of London's institutional shareholder (and associated professional) community. The Panel administers and adjudicates on the application of its influential Takeover Code,[4] and also publishes regular updates to the Code in response to developing market practices.

Successive UK governments from both sides of the political spectrum have consistently resisted the populist temptation to displace the perceived prerogatives of the FRC and Takeover Panel in determining the substantive content of the codes, or to transplant any core code provisions onto a legally binding statutory basis. An important political consequence of this is that the codes' respective rule frameworks – in spite of bringing about significant

---

3 This is notwithstanding the effects of (internal) devolution and legal pluralism, and (external) European Union membership, on the UK's national law-making dynamics. On the latter of these factors, see below.

4 See Panel on Takeovers and Mergers, *The Takeover Code* (May 2013) http://www.thetakeoverpanel. org.uk/the-code (last accessed 24 May 2016).

and far-reaching innovations to UK corporate governance practices over recent decades – have nevertheless slipped under the proverbial public policy radar by largely eliding formal democratic scrutiny. As such, the codes have tended to derive their general social acceptability from two alternative – albeit overlapping – normative sources.

The first of these is the codes' reputed quasi-contractual status as relatively flexible and investor-determinable norms, which purport only to consolidate pre-existing 'best practice' rather than having any socially determinative effect in their own right (Cheffins 1997: 370; Amour and Skeel 2007: 1729). Second, there is the apparently neutral-technocratic system by which the respective codes are formulated, whereby leading financial and legal intermediaries devise rules in an apparently practical and politically colourless forum, guided by a prevailing professional sense of what regulatory outcomes are functionally 'correct' – in the sense of optimally efficient – from the perspective of industry and financial market participants generally. According to this view, the purported 'neutrality' – and, by implication, public defensibility – of the codes inheres in the fact that the members of the relevant rule-making bodies (that is, the FRC and Takeover Panel) are elected exclusively on the basis of their perceived practical expertise in the relevant fields, and correspondingly *not* on account of any particular political or ideological predisposition that they seek to bring to bear on their respective regulatory and supervisory tasks.[5]

Therefore, the continuing normative acceptability of the codes is based principally on private (prudential and professional) rather than public (democratic or policy-based) criteria. Substantively, this important institutional characteristic of the codes is exemplified in their common investor-protectionist ethos, and corresponding general disregard for public policy concerns extraneous to considerations of shareholder welfare.[6]

The recent 'de-privatisation' trend in Anglo–American corporate law

Developments in the United States

Academic concern about a perceived 'de-privatisation' trend in Anglo–American corporate law has been expressed most vehemently in the United States, which over recent years has witnessed increasing federal government involvement in the traditionally state-dominated realm of internal corporate governance affairs. Regulatory limitations on the permissible scope for private ordering in US corporate law have tended to derive from the expanding involvement of federal government in corporate governance, a process that has been described (in somewhat pejorative terms) as one of federal regulatory 'creep' (Bainbridge 2009: 44).

A major consequence of the long-standing internal affairs doctrine in US corporate law – which regards the regulation of intra-firm decision-making processes as being the exclusive preserve of individual states – is that federal interventions in this area have historically tended to take the form of securities market measures aimed principally at enhancing the public transparency of corporate performance and dealings.[7] With limited exceptions (such as the

---

5 On technocratic approaches to establishing economic-regulatory legitimacy generally, see Prosser (1999).

6 In this regard see in particular the pivotal 'no-frustration/board neutrality' doctrine established by General Principle 3 and Rule 21 of the Takeover Code.

7 The dual legislative basis of the federal government's securities law-making function in the US is the Securities Act of 1933 and the Securities Exchange Act of 1934, together with regulations promulgated

federally prescribed system of proxy solicitation under SEC Rule 14), these interventions have tended to affect US corporate governance practices only in an *indirect* and largely uncontroversial way, insofar as informationally efficient securities markets are widely regarded as an institutional prerequisite of effective managerial monitoring and discipline within widely held corporations (Moore and Reberioux 2011: 88–90).

In a notable break from this trend, however, the corporate governance components of the 2002 Sarbanes-Oxley and 2010 Dodd-Frank Acts sought – respectively – to increase directly the formal accountability of listed company boards to shareholders, and to empower shareholders to influence matters formerly subject to the exclusive prerogative of the board under state law. Both Acts take the form of wide-reaching legislative or regulatory measures that, whilst formally billed as *extra*-corporate financial reforms, have nevertheless had a considerable 'overspill' impact on *intra*-corporate governance norms and practices. From an orthodox contractarian point of view, these developments are doubly controversial insofar as they represent a limited erosion of the traditional division of law-making functions between federal and state level, and also a regulatory concretisation of formerly flexible corporate governance practices (Bainbridge 2012; Barden 2005).

The first such prima facie financial reform measure with a corporate law 'sting in the tail' was the Sarbanes-Oxley (or 'SOX') Act of 2002, which was enacted in the immediate wake of the Enron and WorldCom scandals at the turn of the century. SOX was presented as a comprehensive regulatory response to the extensive accounting fraud and financial audit failures exposed in the aftermath of these and other high-profile corporate collapses of the time.

From a private ordering perspective, arguably the most controversial implication of SOX for US corporate law was its 'top-down' implementation of compulsory intra-firm accountability processes that, in terms of procedural rigour, went significantly above and beyond previously accepted norms of self-regulatory best practice. Most notable in this regard are the oft-criticised internal control requirements laid down by sections 302 and 404 of SOX. Taken together, these provisions have the effect of vesting a corporation's senior managerial officers – and, in particular the chief executive officer (CEO) and chief finance officer (CFO) – with responsibility to act as ultimate guardians of the firm's internal system of financial information flows by formally certifying the reliability and integrity thereof.

Prior to 2002, the offices of CEO and especially CFO had been regarded as contractually contingent organisational functions. Accordingly, the existence and contours of these offices were determinable privately by boards in exercise of their inherent right to delegate and sub-divide executive powers on a flexible and discretionary basis, and to structure a firm's managerial hierarchy accordingly. However, a largely unwelcome by-product of SOX has been its effect in affording express statutory recognition to the formerly endogenous CEO and CFO positions, thereby establishing these phenomena as formal legal role definitions.

Other post-Enron regulatory measures in the United States took the (comparably less controversial) approach of concretising previously informal and self-regulatory norms of best practice on a mandatory and legally prescribed basis. The most notable such reforms were the introduction in US stock exchange listing rules of express requirements for majority-independent boards and fully independent sub-board nominating and compensation committees, together with a detailed supporting definition of directorial 'independence' for these

---

thereunder by the US securities market regulator (itself established under the latter Act), the Securities and Exchange Commission (SEC).

purposes.[8] Also noteworthy in this regard was the more demanding definition of independence established under section 301 of SOX for application to audit committees. Whilst these latter types of reform – unlike the former – did not in general seek to elicit fundamental change in established practices, they were nevertheless problematic from a contractarian perspective in that they both universalised and formalised certain corporate governance norms that had previously been susceptible to inter-firm variation or occasional exception.

More recently, the Obama administration's principal legislative response to the financial crisis of 2007 and 2008, namely the Dodd-Frank Wall Street Reform and Consumer Protection Act of 2010, continued in the trend of SOX by introducing significant federal amendments to US corporate governance under the apparent head of financial regulatory reform. However, in contrast to SOX's focus on reforming the internal monitoring function of corporate boards, the corporate governance aspect of Dodd-Frank was concerned primarily with increasing the direct external influence of shareholders within the corporate decision-making process.

In particular, Dodd-Frank sought (inter alia) to recalibrate the traditional state law division of power between boards and shareholders in the latter group's favour with a view to ensuring greater managerial accountability and improved standards of shareholder risk oversight. The two principal regulatory innovations that Dodd-Frank sought to introduce in purported fulfilment of this objective were: (i) shareholder access to the corporate election ballot, and (ii) the introduction of precatory 'say on pay' procedures within US-listed firms, including (inter alia) on corporate disclosures relating to the highly controversial issue of CEO–worker pay ratios.

Under the first of these reforms, the Securities and Exchange Commission was vested with delegated statutory authority (under § 971 of Dodd-Frank) to formulate rules permitting shareholders of US-listed corporations to nominate their own candidates for election to the board of directors. This so-called 'proxy access' provision was designed so as to permit significant change to be made to the long-established traditional process for electing directors in US corporations, whereby the board of directors (and, indirectly, management) itself is vested with the exclusive right to determine the particular 'slate' of candidates that will be proposed to shareholders for election or re-election to the board each year (Bebchuk 2003).

In exercise of its rule-making authority in this regard, the SEC in 2010 promulgated the highly controversial Exchange Act Rule 14a-11 (see SEC 2010). Proposed SEC Rule 14a-11 purported to allow any 'significant, long-term' shareholder satisfying certain minimum ownership and holding requirements[9] to have his or her directorial nominee or nominees[10] included in the proxy voting card that is circulated by the corporation in advance of its annual shareholders' meeting, alongside and in opposition to those candidates nominated by the board.

By virtue of the second of the above reforms, shareholders of US listed corporations were statutorily vested (under § 951 of Dodd-Frank) with the collective right to pass a periodic precatory (i.e. advisory) vote on the compensation arrangements for executive officers. This

---

8 See § 303A.02.

9 Specifically, the rule would have required a shareholder to have held at least three per cent of the company's voting equity capital on a continuous basis for at least three years, before being entitled to invoke the directorial nomination procedure.

10 Under the proposed rule, a qualifying shareholder would have been entitled to nominate one director, or a number of directors together constituting no more than 25 per cent of the seats on the company's board of directors (whichever is the greater).

is an amended version of the so-called 'say on pay' procedures that have been a fixture of UK public company annual general meetings since 2002 (Gordon 2009). In a clear rejection of the contractarian paradigm, the SEC resolutely adopted the position that the proposed 14a-11 proxy access requirement should supersede any conflicting rules of state law, and also that its effect should be incapable of reversal or reduction by means of any corporate constitutional 'opt-out' provision (SEC 2010: 17–19).

Likewise, whilst the legislation granted a degree of leeway to firms in respect of the frequency of 'say on pay' resolutions,[11] its basic position was nevertheless that such votes *must* be held at least once every three years, regardless of whether there is material investor demand to this effect (Gordon 2009). Moreover, in addition to mandating disclosure on orthodox compensation-related concerns relating to the correlation between executive pay and firm performance, Dodd-Frank (specifically, § 953(b) thereof) imposed a further requirement on US-listed corporations to disclose annually the ratio between: (i) the total amount of pay received by the firm's CEO over the most recent year, and (ii) the median level of pay received by the rest of the firm's employees (the so-called 'pay ratio disclosure').

In spite of the considerable procedural and substantive limitations on the above regulatory provisions, both the proxy access and 'say on pay' (including pay ratio disclosure) reforms attracted widespread criticism within the business and academic communities for a number of reasons (see e.g. Bainbridge 2012; Fisch 2012; Sharfman 2012; Kahan and Rock 2011; Bratton and Wachter 2010; Gordon 2009). A prominent cause of concern was the common perception of these rules as a further sharp lurch in the direction of widespread federalisation of 'core' US corporate law, and the concomitant threat that this posed to corporate law's traditional private ordering dynamic (Bainbridge 2012).

A further source of unease was the fact that, since the relevant rules' mandatory status renders them unsusceptible to bargaining and market 'pricing' by those persons whose interests are directly affected by them (i.e. investors and managers), they would be more likely to exhibit inefficiencies and, consequently, to have an overall wealth-*reducing* effect on the US corporate sector as a whole (Sharfman 2012). As regards the CEO–worker pay ratio disclosure requirement in particular, there was widespread unease amongst the managerial and professional-advisory communities as to the arguably doubtful practical worth of such information to investors, which seemed to bear little obvious relevance to orthodox corporate financial-performance criteria (SEC 2013: 96; although for a counter-perspective on this, see Moore 2015).

In respect of the proxy access issue, the above debate was rendered largely academic (in the pejorative sense) by the July 2011 decision of the DC Circuit Court of Appeals in *Business Roundtable v SEC*,[12] which struck down proposed SEC Rule 14a-11 on Administrative Procedure Act grounds (see Fisch 2013; Brown 2011). Notwithstanding the invalidation of Rule 14a-11, the SEC nevertheless proceeded with the introduction of proxy access on a non-mandatory 'opt-in' basis by removing the former restriction in Rule 14a-8 on the tabling of shareholder resolutions relating to the reform of directorial election procedures. The effect was to slant the private ordering process considerably more in shareholders' favour, whilst leaving companies ultimately free to determine their own procedures for

---

11 Specifically, Dodd-Frank prescribes that 'say on pay' votes take place either on a yearly, two-yearly or three-yearly basis, as determined by shareholders via a separate resolution on 'say on pay' vote frequency, itself to be held at least once every six years. See Dodd-Frank § 951(b).
12 647 F.3d 1144 (DC Cir 2011).

nomination of directors, as opposed to supplanting private ordering altogether with a regulatorily determined election procedure.

In contrast, the equally controversial 'say on pay' requirement *was* successfully brought into effect in its entirety in 2011. However, the SEC's additional rules including CEO–worker pay ratio disclosure as part of the mandatory 'say on pay' process were (following significant public and political challenge) not implemented until August 2015. Moreover, even though the proxy access issue is now apparently off the public policy agenda (at least for the foreseeable future) – the Rule 14a-11 experience as a whole at least evidences the federal government's occasional political resolve to attempt to override US (state) corporate law's traditional private ordering dynamic where political circumstances would seem to necessitate a more interventionist regulatory stance (on this tendency generally, see Coffee 2012).

Developments in the United Kingdom

In the markedly different legal culture and political climate of the United Kingdom, there are signs of a corresponding de-privatisation trend within corporate law over recent years. Just as the US reforms discussed above have proved controversial within that country's peculiar federalist and market-liberal law-making environment, some recent developments in the UK have created challenges that are in large part specific to Britain's own path-dependent corporate governance system.

In respect of internal matters of board structure and function, the UK regulatory response to Enron and other corporate failures at the turn of the century was similarly extensive compared to the above-mentioned US reforms in terms of its impact on established national corporate governance practices. Ensuing British reforms came in the form of the Financial Reporting Council's significant revisions to the UK's (then-called) Combined Code on Corporate Governance in 2003, following the influential recommendations in 2002 of the Higgs and Smith Committees. These changes included the introduction of a requirement for US-style majority-independent boards within UK FTSE 350 companies, which represented a significant change to the executive-dominated, 'majority-insider' board model that had previously been customary within the British listed company sector. Also affirmatively required for the first time by the 2003 version of the code were fully independent and financially skilled audit committees, independent non-executive chairmen and senior independent directors. These requirements were reinforced, moreover, by a rigorous regulatory definition of directorial independence that established an effective presumption against long periods of office holding.

The 2003 Code reforms were by no means free from controversy in the UK (see e.g. Alcock 2003). Nevertheless, they largely escaped many of the criticisms levelled against the contemporaneous regulatory reforms in the US on account of the code's officially 'soft' presumptive status as a set of non-statutory 'best practice' norms, underpinned by the market-invoking principle of 'comply or explain', rather than the binding and absolute force of state sanction. This feature of the code makes it difficult for critics of corporate governance reforms in the UK to raise SOX-esque concerns of 'ill-fit' with pre-existing norms, given the continuing flexibility afforded to British boards (formally if not always practically) to opt for reasoned non-compliance in cases where maladaptation concerns apparently render full code compliance cost-ineffective at the individual firm level.

The UK Corporate Governance Code (as it is called today) has thus been able to maintain its self-claimed status as a fundamentally facilitative and non-coercive institution, in spite of the typically limited degree of deviation from its core norms that tends to occur in practice (on this, see Moore 2009: 117–29). The code's perceived quasi-contractual 'neutrality' in the above regard has been crucial for maintaining its continuing legitimacy as a private ordering mechanism, and also the legitimacy of its promulgator – the Financial Reporting Council – as a non-statist rule-making body. This is in spite of the deep and sweeping reforms to British boardroom norms and practices that the code is widely acknowledged to have brought about over the past two decades, within a national political climate generally favourable to the increased regulation of corporate activities in the public interest.

Notwithstanding the general resilience of UK corporate law's underpinning normative fabric to the regulatory developments described above, the characteristic privity of the UK corporate governance system has by no means been immune from challenge over recent years. Most notably in this regard, the UK has witnessed a growing trend of statutory 'spread' in corporate law, which would appear to evoke fundamentally similar concerns to those that have arisen with respect to the above-mentioned US regulatory reforms.

Domestically, the principal factor in this trend was the Blair/Brown Governments' promulgation and implementation of the Companies Act 2006 which, at over 1300 sections long, constitutes the longest piece of legislation in British legal history. The most controversial aspect of the new Act has been its perceived 'juridifying' effect. Accordingly, an increased number of core corporate governance concerns in the UK, the most notable of which being the formulation and content of directors' general duties, were displaced from their traditional common law or equitable realm into the arguably more rigid and politically reactive territory of statute law.

Additional to this has been the significant influence of EU harmonisation measures as an extraneous juridifying constraint on the operation and development of UK corporate law. Indeed, the notion of inter-jurisdictional harmonisation in the European sense is arguably antithetical to the rationality of private ordering. Whereas US-style competitive federalism operates on an endogenous 'bottom-up' basis, with any inter-state 'harmonising' initiatives (e.g. the American Bar Association's influential Model Business Corporation Act) merely reflective of pre-established regulatory best practice; EU-style harmonisation by contrast works in an exogenous 'top-down' manner, and for the express purpose of driving substantive convergence between different legal systems where it would not otherwise be inclined to exist.

Therefore, in spite of what may be connoted by the notion of 'harmony', harmonisation of laws is in reality a process that entails varying degrees of mandated regulatory conformity at the individual state level, at least insofar as the subject state wishes to remain part of the relevant inter-state order. These characteristics contradict the basic tenets of voluntariness and unanimity that underpin the contractarian concept of the 'prudential state' as an individually rational rule-selector. Furthermore, harmonisation measures require formal implementation within a member state's legal system in order for the relevant state to be deemed compliant with its treaty obligations. The effect is that statutory entrenchment of practices and institutions becomes the regulatory norm, in some cases at the expense of institutional flexibility or diversity.

In UK corporate law, the most conspicuous and controversial example of EU-compelled juridification has occurred in the area of takeover regulation. As explained above, the regulation of public company takeovers in the UK is administered on a relatively informal basis by the non-governmental Panel on Takeovers and Mergers, which promulgates and enforces the non-statutory UK Takeover Code. In light of the Panel and Code's widely acknowledged success in this regard, the EU Takeover Directive – which came into force in 2004 – was designed with a view to extending long-established features of the UK's flexible and market-liberal system of takeover regulation (including, inter alia, the mandatory bid requirement and 'no-frustration' doctrine) across EU Member States as a whole. The ultimate policy objective was to afford heightened protection to cross-border investors in respect of control-related issues and, in turn, facilitate the free movement of corporate capital on a Community-wide basis.[13]

However, whilst the content of the directive has been heavily influenced by pre-existing UK takeover norms, the subsequent trans-European harmonisation of these rules has necessarily entailed that the UK *itself* formally implement the provisions of the directive, thereby reducing to an extent the previous informality of the relevant norms at domestic level. Thus, a curious side-effect of the directive has been to require the UK to give statutory authorisation to the Takeover Panel in formal support of its rule-making, executive and adjudicative functions, notwithstanding the fact that the Panel has been carrying out these functions for the past four decades. More fundamentally, Part 28 of the UK Companies Act 2006 – in addition to formally establishing the Panel's powers and its new right of judicial recourse for enforcement of sanctions – also gives express statutory recognition to the Panel for the first time in its history. As a result, the Panel has – somewhat inadvertently – become entrenched as an indirect part of the British Government apparatus, thereby transforming it from a private sector institution into a quasi-public regulatory agency.

Normative implications of the de-privatisation trend in Anglo–American corporate law

The analysis above does not purport to provide a remotely comprehensive survey of the US and UK corporate governance systems by any means. Rather, the purpose of the foregoing discussion is simply to highlight an arguable trend towards greater mandatory regulatory intervention in core aspects of Anglo–American corporate governance, as manifested in some conspicuous key respects. From a contractarian perspective, it could be said that this trend – if it continues – potentially threatens the characteristic privity of Anglo–American corporate law, by undermining its traditionally perceived nature as a facilitative body of rules reflective of prudential contractual choices. However, on closer examination, these regulatory reforms and initiatives are not particularly unusual within the wider institutional framework of Anglo–American corporate law as a whole. In fact, both US and UK corporate law (understood in a broad and inclusive sense) have for a long time exhibited significant mandatory components that, prima facie at least, take the form of public-interventionist regulation rather than quasi-contractual norms.

In particular, it is largely beyond question today (even amongst adherents to the contractarian paradigm of corporate law) that the mandatory regulation of corporate securities markets – specifically, the regulatory compulsion of corporate information disclosure to the investing public – is a structurally necessary component of any effective corporate financing and governance system. Indeed, it is commonly accepted that in any market environment (but especially in complex financial securities markets) information has the special status of a 'public good': that is to say, it is both *non-excludable* and *non-divisible*. The former quality denotes that those who expend the costs involved in producing and verifying information

---

13 See Directive 2004/25/EC (preamble).

cannot exclude those who have not paid for it from benefiting from it, insofar as information is by its very nature capable of (and also prone to) being circulated beyond its immediate recipients. The latter quality indicates that information – unlike most other commodities – is not exhausted or diminished in utility by being used, with the effect that those who pay to receive information will continue to derive significant use value from it even in the presence of a number of 'free-riders' who also stand to benefit from it indirectly (Easterbrook and Fischel 1984: 681).

Against this background, where information is generated and verified by private actors alone, those paying for the information will – owing to the inevitability of free-riders – be incapable of appropriating all of the benefits of their search efforts (Coffee 1984: 726–7). As a result, such persons will be disinclined to invest in acquiring information to the optimal extent that they would if they could exclusively exploit the full economic benefits thereof. It follows that corporate information will be systematically under-produced; or, more likely, over-produced in certain isolated respects (that paying investors value most), whilst under-produced in others (Easterbrook and Fischel 1984: 681–2).

This is one of the classic economic situations where the pursuit (by investors) of individual rationality *en masse* leads not to overall allocative efficiency, but rather to the 'collective folly' of a socially sub-optimal outcome (specifically, informational incompleteness and imbalance in corporate securities markets). Accordingly, since private actors (i.e. investors) will not be inclined to generate individually the quantity and quality of company data that they would ideally wish for as a general group, a mandated universal system of disclosure is arguably necessary in order to 'correct' this innate disparity between individual and collective rationality, so as to produce an optimal level of information from the perspective of investors (and, in turn, society) as a whole.

On a normative level, the accommodation of mandatory disclosure regulation within an institutional paradigm otherwise hostile to regulatory interference in private ordering is achieved by drawing a (frequently grey) conceptual 'dividing line' between the purportedly distinct spheres of: (i) *corporate/company* law, and (ii) *securities/capital markets* law. The former is presented as an aspect of facilitative private law, and the latter – contrarily – as a subset of public-regulatory law. Accordingly, securities law is purportedly dedicated to the mandatory and pre-contractual 'correction' of structural market failures that would otherwise inhibit the efficient operation of private ordering processes within corporate law. On this basis, federal legislative and administrative control over corporate disclosure regulation has been widely accepted in the United States as both functionally necessary and politically legitimate, in spite of the internal affairs doctrine's formal hostility to supra-state intervention in other areas of corporate governance.

Given the irrelevance of such intra-national federalist concerns to UK corporate governance, the importance of ensuring a distinct division between company and capital markets law has been of lesser normative importance within the British regulatory environment. Here the principal legal rules pertaining to the disclosure and verification of information in respect of UK-listed companies are situated in a somewhat disorderly and seemingly illogical domain, spanning parts of orthodox corporate law and financial markets legislation, as well as the listing requirements of the London Stock Exchange.

Irrespective of the specific national institutional environment, however, understanding corporate disclosure regulation as a *non*-corporate law field is – for a variety of reasons – highly convenient both doctrinally and politically. On a policy level, it legitimises federal interventions in the US (such as the SOX and Dodd-Frank reforms discussed above) that, whilst formerly billed as aspects of securities law, nevertheless carry a significant internal corporate governance 'sting in the tail'. In the UK and wider European context, meanwhile, the normative effect of branding a particular EU regulatory innovation in corporate governance (e.g. the Takeover Directive or Shareholder Rights Directive[14]) as an aspect of capital markets rather than company law is to legitimise it on common market grounds as a facilitator of cross-border free movement of financial capital. In such instance, the political impediments to successful trans-national importation of the provision in question are likely to be less severe (although by no means absent) than if the relevant innovation purported to be concerned exclusively with the so-called 'social dimension' of European integration as it applies to intra-company governance relations and the distribution of power and wealth between corporate participants.

Moreover, regarding corporate and securities law in distinction from one another matters a great deal on a conceptual level, insofar as it enables the validity of the contractarian paradigm in corporate law to be continually asserted notwithstanding the arguable incongruity between the theoretical ideal and empirical reality. This is because aspects of corporate governance – such as mandatory disclosure regulation – that fail to fit the facilitative, private ordering blueprint can effectively be 'carved out' of the conceptual picture, leaving only those features of the law that support the prevailing theoretical characterisation of the subject-matter.

An outstanding definitional difficulty with this distinction, however, is that some commonly accepted elements of so-called securities or capital markets law – including proxy rules, anti-fraud legislation and significant/extraordinary transaction approval requirements – affect corporate governance in ways beyond merely mandating ongoing corporate transparency. However, even in 'standard' situations where compulsory corporate disclosure regulation does little more than render corporate affairs and performance more conspicuous to the investor community, it cannot be said that this outcome is either extraneous to, or formally separable from, so-called 'core' corporate governance processes and norms (as the US internal affairs doctrine would seem to imply). Mandated corporate transparency, even in the most basic form of requiring periodic disclosures on ongoing financial performance, entails the regulatory state going considerably above and beyond its limited neo-liberal remit of enforcing contracts, property rights and surrounding 'rules-of-the-game' (on this notion, see Friedman 1962: 27).

Rather, a publicly mandated disclosure regime for the benefit of investors constitutes direct governmental action aimed at mitigating the informational disparity between managers and shareholders, so as to recalibrate – by means of interventionist regulation – the prevailing balance of governance power in the latter constituency's favour. This is arguably at least as much an aspect of direct investor protectionism inspired by political-distributional considerations, as it is a technical means of correcting failures in securities market pricing mechanisms.

Consequently, mandatory securities laws are not as readily susceptible to conceptual expulsion from the realm of 'internal' corporate to 'external' regulatory law as contractarian theorists have sought to infer. This important finding has the normative effect of blurring the conventionally perceived boundaries of corporate law as a subject and, in turn, undermining the purported privity of Anglo–American corporate law as asserted within the dominant contractarian frame of reference.

---

14 Directive 2007/36/EC.

Conclusion

The long-standing presence of mandatory and irreversible corporate law rules, in whatever rhetorical guise, poses a difficult descriptive challenge for those who seek to present corporate law as a principally private-contractual, rather than public-regulatory, phenomenon. Moreover, once the inherent artificiality of the corporate/securities law divide is recognised, it becomes impossible to rationalise these features by reference to the orthodox conceptual reference points of private ordering and market failure analysis.

The unavoidable conclusion is that Anglo–American corporate law is an undeniably public phenomenon, whose innate regulatory dimensions cannot readily be explained away by recourse to contractarian logic. Only when scholars and students of the subject on both sides of the Atlantic are willing to accept this fundamental descriptive premise will it become possible to develop a new normative theory of corporate law that might displace the incumbent contractarian paradigm.

Bibliography

Alcock, A, 'Higgs – The Wrong Answer' (2003) 24 Company Lawyer 161.

Armour, J and Skeel, DA, 'Who Writes the Rules for Hostile Takeovers, and Why? – The Peculiar Divergence of US and UK Takeover Regulation' (2007) 95 *Georgetown Law Journal* 1727.

Bainbridge, SM, 'Director Primacy and Shareholder Disempowerment' (2006) 119 *Harvard Law Review* 1735.

Bainbridge, SM, *The New Corporate Governance in Theory and Practice* (New York, Oxford University Press, 2008).

Bainbridge, SM, 'Is "Say on Pay" Justified', *Regulation* (Spring 2009) 42.

Bainbridge, SM, *Corporate Governance after the Financial Crisis* (New York, Oxford University Press, 2012).

Barden, A, 'US Corporate Law Reform Post-Enron: A Significant Imposition on Private Ordering of Corporate Governance?' (2005) 5 *Journal of Corporate Law Studies* 167.

Bebchuk, LA, 'The Debate on Contractual Freedom in Corporate Law' (1989) 89 *Columbia Law Review* 1395.

Bebchuk, LA, 'Federalism and the Corporation: The Desirable Limits on State Competition in Corporate Law' (1992) 105 *Harvard Law Review* 1435.

Bebchuk, LA, 'The Case for Shareholder Access to the Ballot' (2003) 59 *The Business Lawyer* 43.

Black, B, 'Is Corporate Law Trivial? A Political and Economic Analysis' (1990) 84 *Northwestern University Law Review* 542.

Bowman, SR, *The Modern Corporation and American Political Thought: Law, Power and Ideology* (PA, Penn State University Press, 1996).

Bratton, WW and Wachter, ML, 'The Case against Shareholder Empowerment' (2010) 158 *University of Pennsylvania Law Review* 653.

Brown, JR, 'Shareholder Access and Uneconomic Economic Analysis: Business Roundtable v SEC' (2011) 88 *Denver University Law Review Online*.

Cheffins, BR, *Company Law: Theory, Structure and Operation* (Oxford, Oxford University Press, 1997).

Coffee, JC, 'Market Failure and the Economic Case for a Mandatory Disclosure System' (1984) 70 *Virginia Law Review* 717.

Coffee, JC 'The Political Economy of Dodd-Frank: Why Financial Reform Tends to be Frustrated and Systemic Risk Perpetuated' (2012) 97 *Cornell Law Review* 101.

De Mott, D, 'Perspectives on Choice of Law for Corporate Internal Affairs' (1985) 48 *Law & Contemporary Problems* 161.

Easterbrook, FH and Fischel, DR, 'Mandatory Disclosure and Protection of Investors' (1984) 79 *Vanderbilt Law Review* 669.

Easterbrook, FH and Fischel, DR, 'Limited Liability and the Corporation' (1985) 52 *University of Chicago Law Review* 89.

Easterbrook, FH and Fischel, DR, 'The Corporate Contract' (1989) 89 *Columbia Law Review* 1416.

Easterbrook, FH and Fischel, DR, *The Economic Structure of Corporate Law* (Cambridge, MA, Harvard University Press, 1991).

Financial Reporting Council (FRC), *The UK Approach to Corporate Governance* (November 2006).

Financial Reporting Council (FRC), *The UK Corporate Governance Code* (September 2014).

Fisch, JE, 'The Destructive Ambiguity of Federal Proxy Access' (2012) 61 *Emory Law Journal* 435.

Fisch, JE, 'The Long Road Back: Business Roundtable and the Implications for Future SEC Rule-Making' (2013) 36 *Seattle University Law Review* 695.

Friedman, M, *Capitalism and Freedom* (Chicago, The University of Chicago Press, 1962).

Gordon, JN, '"Say on Pay": Cautionary Notes on the UK Experience and the Case for Shareholder Opt-In' (2009) 46 *Harvard Journal on Legislation* 323.

Hadfield, G and Talley, E, 'On Public versus Private Provision of Corporate Law' (2006) 22 *The Journal of Law, Economics, & Organization* 414.

Hansmann, H and Kraakman, R, 'The Essential Role of Organizational Law' (2000) 110 *Yale Law Journal* 387.

Ireland, P, 'Property and Contract in Contemporary Corporate Theory' (2003) 23 *Legal Studies* 453.

Kahan, M and Rock, E, 'The Insignificance of Proxy Access' (2011) 97 *Virginia Law Review* 1347.

MacCormick, N, *Questioning Sovereignty: Law, State, and Nation in the European Commonwealth* (Oxford, Oxford University Press, 1999).

MacCormick, N, *Institutions of Law: An Essay in Legal Theory* (Oxford, Oxford University Press, 2007).

Moore, MT, '"Whispering Sweet Nothings": The Limitations of Informal Conformance in UK Corporate Governance' (2009) 9 *Journal of Corporate Law Studies* 95.

Moore, MT, 'Corporate Governance, Pay Equity, and the Limitations of Agency Theory' (2015) 68 *Current Legal Problems* 431.

Moore, MT and Reberioux, A, 'Revitalizing the Institutional Roots of Anglo–American Corporate Governance' (2011) 40 *Economy and Society* 84.

Prosser, T, 'Theorising Utility Regulation' (1999) 62 *Modern Law Review* 196.

Romano, R, *The Genius of American Corporate Law* (Washington, DC, AEI Press, 1993).

Securities and Exchange Commission (SEC), 'Facilitating Shareholder Director Nominations (Final Rule)' (15 November 2010).

Securities and Exchange Commission (SEC), 'Pay Ratio Disclosure: Proposed Rule' (18 September 2013).

Sharfman, BS, 'Why Proxy Access is Harmful to Corporate Governance' (2012) 37 *Journal of Corporation Law* 387.

Tung, F, 'Before Competition: Origins of the Internal Affairs Doctrine' (2006) 32 *Journal of Corporation Law* 33.

3

What is corporate law?

An Australian perspective

Stephen Bottomley

Introduction

What is corporate law? What is it that corporate lawyers in the early decades of the twenty-first century are practising, enforcing, researching and teaching? Is corporate law a doctrinally coherent and cohesive branch of law with its own unique place in the legal landscape, or is it largely a collection of concepts and rules borrowed and adapted from other areas of law, bundled together simply because they have some bearing on corporate activity? Is corporate law an essentially pragmatic and reactive discipline that develops sporadically in response to the crisis of the day, or is it principled and proactive, embodying social norms and anticipating and shaping the course of corporate behaviour (Eisenberg 1999)?

Surprisingly, little attention has been given to this line of questions. For some, perhaps, this may not be a surprise; after all, in the widely cited claim of US corporate law scholars Henry Hansmann and Reinier Kraakman, we reached 'the end of history for corporate law' sometime around the end of the twentieth century, when corporate law systems around the globe allegedly converged on the shareholder primacy model of corporate governance (Hansmann and Kraakman 2001).[1]

For others, the immediate response to the question may be: 'why does it matter?' Perhaps, it might be said, we have a sufficiently understood and practically robust idea of what corporate law is (and what it is not) that is enough to allow us to get on with the everyday tasks of doctrinal application and dissection, and legislative critique and reform. This chapter proceeds, nevertheless, on the assumption that there is still much to ask and to be learned about the nature and role of corporate law in the post-twentieth-century world. If for no other reason, this is because, as Kent Greenfield observes, 'corporate law determines the rules governing the organization, purposes, and limitations of some of the largest and most powerful institutions in the world' (Greenfield 2006: 4). More fundamentally, corporate law determines and constitutes the key roles, relations and interests that drive those institutions (see Cioffi 2010: 4–5).

---

1 Those authors have since acknowledged the hyperbolic tone of the paper's title, whilst reaffirming its central thesis (Hansmann and Kraakman 2012).

Nor is the importance of corporate law limited to its impact on 'the big end of town'. Increasingly more is asked of corporate law. The rules and doctrines that are grouped under that label are now applied to a diversity of corporate forms, spanning the private and government sectors, commercial and not-for-profit purposes, and local and global operations. As the corporate form is put to wider and more diverse uses, so too those rules and doctrines take on more expanded roles and greater significance.

Even in the practical application and formulation of corporate law rules the question is important. For one thing, the distribution of corporate law enforcement responsibilities between the courts, government agencies and the private sector presumes some conception of what corporate law is and what its purposes are.

Another reason for reflecting on the nature of corporate law as a discipline is that it assists in responding to conceptual and policy challenges posed by other disciplines and areas of inquiry. In Australia, as in the United States and the United Kingdom, corporate law doctrine and theory has confronted questions posed by the discipline of economics (or, more particularly, by 'law and economics' (Miller 2011) and by the social sciences more generally (see, for example, Whincop 2001; Canberra Law Review 1996). For example, is the purpose of corporate law to be determined by reference to ideas such as efficiency, human rights and social responsibilities (e.g. Addo 1999) or accountability and deliberation (Bottomley 2007)?

Nor do we need to look to other disciplines for conceptual challenges. Corporate lawyers have their own boundary disputes, taking different positions on whether insolvency law, financial services regulation, or the regulation of investment funds are part of, or separate from, 'real' corporate law. Corporate law jurisprudence also harbours a number of tensions and dichotomies that shape an understanding of the nature of the corporate law discipline. For example, the history of corporate law in Australia reveals continuing tensions and shifts between common law and statutory sources of law, and between legal principle and political process (especially constitutional politics). This, in turn, raises increasingly important questions about whether corporate law is essentially private or public (or, perhaps, hybrid) in nature, and long-established questions about whether its primary purpose is facilitative and enabling or, instead, directive and mandatory (Coffee 1989).

The purpose of this chapter, then, is to examine some of the ways in which the question: 'what is corporate law?' has been, and might be, answered, and to suggest what I think are some important considerations in formulating an answer.

One preliminary point should be emphasised at the outset: there can be no single answer to the question. Importantly, the answers will differ depending on the context and jurisdiction in which the question is posed. This goes beyond the obvious differences between common law and civil law jurisdictions. Even between common law systems, and despite superficial similarities, there are considerable variations. As Bruner demonstrates, a comprehensive or holistic global theory of corporate governance is not possible (Bruner 2013). Differences in political structure, constitutional allocations of legislative power, the role and structure of regulators, legal and business cultures, amongst other factors, will shape the answers. Necessarily then, this chapter must take a broad approach. However, in doing so it draws primarily on the Australian corporate law experience. That experience has been heavily influenced by corporate law thinking in the United Kingdom and the United States, and so (as is already apparent) the chapter also draws on that material, with the general framework being common law systems.

Some definitions

As already noted, there have been surprisingly few attempts in the corporate law literature to investigate the question: 'what is corporate law?' One brief example is found in Bernard Black's definition of corporate law as including 'laws – whether made by legislators, judges or regulators – that primarily govern the relationship between a company's managers and investors'. He goes on to exclude, without saying why, 'laws that regulate corporate action primarily to benefit others, such as employees, neighbours, and local communities' (Black 1990: 547). Black's top-down definition is thus referenced to laws that relate to matters of internal corporate structure and governance, rather than to corporate finance and so, presumably, would exclude the law that regulates financial services markets and the law that regulates public capital raising, both of which feature in the primary corporate law statute in Australia (Corporations Act 2001 (Cth)), but not in the UK Companies Act 2006. It is a definition that also excludes laws that bear on corporate social responsibility insofar as they require or encourage company managers to consider the interests of non-investor stakeholders, such as section 172 of the Companies Act 2006 (UK).

Armour, Hansmann and Kraakman provide a more extended answer to the question in the opening chapter to the collection of essays in *The Anatomy of Corporate Law* (Kraakman and others 2009). They begin with the proposition that corporate law (or as they emphasise, 'corporate law everywhere') derives its essential identity from five basic characteristics of the business corporation: legal personality, limited liability, transferable shares, a board structure with delegated management and investor ownership (Armour, Hansmann and Kraakman 2009: 1). It follows, they argue, that: 'a principal function of corporate law is to provide business enterprises with a legal form that possesses these five core attributes' (Ibid: 2).

Two points can be noted about this way of defining corporate law. First, Armour, Hansmann and Kraakman focus their analysis primarily on 'the business corporation'.[2] Thus the boundaries of corporate law – what is 'in' and what is 'out' – are determined exclusively by what the authors consider to be the unique and core characteristics of the corporate firm, which, in turn, is defined primarily by reference to the needs of business corporations operating under the shareholder–primacy model. Interestingly, whereas in an earlier edition of their chapter certain topics, such as insolvency law, were excluded from the ambit of corporate law (Hansmann and Kraakman 2004: 17), these authors have later included areas such as insolvency law, tax law and labour law within their definition, to the extent that those laws are 'specifically tailored for the corporate form in ways that have important effects on corporate structure and conduct' (Armour, Hansmann and Kraakman 2009: 19).

Second, the Armour, Hansmann and Kraakman approach to defining corporate law is facilitative and functional. Corporate law must respond to 'the economic exigencies of the large business enterprise' (Ibid: 1). In particular, it is the task of corporate law, they say, to respond to three value-reducing forms of conflict within the corporation: conflicts between managers and shareholders, between shareholders themselves, and between shareholders and other constituencies such as creditors and employees (Ibid: 2).

---

2 Later they acknowledge the existence of 'secondary or partial corporate law statutes' that address special classes of corporation such as government-owned enterprises and close corporations (Armour, Hansmann and Kraakman 2009: 17).

We may debate the particular features of this definition of corporate law, including the claim that it has global application (because, they argue, 'corporate law everywhere' is converging on the shareholder primacy model). But one virtue of their approach to answering the question is that it is based on an articulation (contestable though it may be) of the purpose of the corporate form and corporate activity. Theirs is a normative, not simply a positive, definition.

As noted above, however, there are relatively few instances in the corporate law literature where the question of 'what is corporate law' has been examined directly. For the most part the shape and content of corporate law is either simply assumed, or is left to be inferred from the way in which the topic is discussed. As Greenfield points out: '[t]he present-day guardians of these assumptions are the hundreds of legal scholars who teach and write about corporate law and the scores of judges who put the assumptions into practice' (Greenfield 2006: 125).

The influence of legal educators

In Australia one illustration of the joint role played by corporate law teachers, judges and the profession in shaping the boundaries of corporate law is found in the way in which the university corporate law curriculum is defined. This is not left to the sole discretion of the corporate law teacher. Minimum course content requirements for law degrees in general are prescribed by a committee representing law admissions authorities, law deans, practical legal training authorities and the peak body of the Australian legal profession. This committee (the Law Admissions Consultative Committee) is generally responsible to the Australian and New Zealand Council of Chief Justices.

The course requirements are specified in 11 'Prescribed Areas of Knowledge', one of which is 'company law'. The prescribed areas of knowledge for 'company law' are: corporate personality, the incorporation process, the corporate constitution, company contracts, administration and management of the business of companies, duties and liabilities of directors and officers, share capital and membership, members' remedies, company credit and security arrangements, winding up of companies (Law Admissions Consultative Committee 2015). These prescriptions have remained unchanged from the time they were first determined in 1992. In what is now a much more diverse and globalised corporate climate, we might question their currency and sufficiency. Such a debate would, presumably, entail some forming a view about what contemporary corporate law is.

The prescriptions listed in the previous paragraph have a familiar look to anyone who is acquainted with the standard corporate law texts that have populated Anglo–Australian corporate law scholarship since the 1960s. Indeed, closely related to curriculum and teaching, another important way in which legal scholarship has shaped our understanding of the corporate law discipline is through the role and impact of the seminal corporate law texts.

Corporate law in the textbooks

To a considerable extent, our understanding of the content and dimensions of corporate law is mediated and shaped by corporate law textbooks, even if few of those texts directly address the question posed by this chapter (but see Wishart 1994). The impact of the textbook in shaping our understanding of corporate law is significant. This is true not just for the content of the law, but also for how we conceive of its overall structure and ordering.

Historically, one of the primary tasks of law textbooks in Anglo–Australian jurisprudence has been to impose a sense of order and coherence onto what otherwise appears as a body of rules and doctrine that is 'irrational, chaotic and particularistic' (Sugarman 1986: 26). As David Sugarman has pointed out: '[t]he exposition and systematization of . . . general principles, and the techniques required to find and apply them and the rules that they underpin, are largely what legal education and scholarship are all about' (Sugarman 1986: 26).

In Australia, as elsewhere, there is now a daunting array of corporate law textbooks on the market, but to explore this point further it is convenient to use, as a case study, the book that would now generally be acknowledged as the standard reference, Professor Harold Ford's *Principles of Company Law*, first published in 1974 (Ford 1974). To be clear, this was not the first text to deal with Australian company law. For example, by 1968 Sir Keith Yorston had co-authored three editions of his book *Company Law* (Yorston and Brown 1968). There were also extensive volumes of annotated legislation, and texts that dealt with specific aspects of company operations, such as meetings and annual reports (for example, Wallace and Young 1965; Paterson and Ednie 1962; Joske 1963; Chambers 1955). Professor Gower's earlier seminal text, *The Principles of Modern Company Law* published in the United Kingdom in 1954 (Gower 1954), was also widely used in Australia, with local supplements being published to bridge the growing difference between UK and Australian corporate law developments, particularly as a consequence of statutory developments in Australia (see, for example, Baxt 1974).

However, just as Gower had done in the United Kingdom, it was Ford's book which cemented the modern corporate law textbook tradition in Australia. The book was intended to be more than a simple description of company law rules and doctrines. In the Preface to the first edition, Ford emphasised the importance of understanding the way in which case law principles 'have been fashioned'. One purpose of writing the book, he said, was 'to provide, in a treatment of reasonable length, a rounded view of the legislation in relation to the judge-declared law', and 'to explain the causes which prompted the enactment' of legislative amendments (Ford 1974: v).

In 2013, the 15th edition of what had become Robert Austin and Ian Ramsay's *Ford's Principles of Corporations Law* carried a tribute to the late Professor Ford, who died in 2012, which reflected on Professor Ford's lasting impact on the corporate law discipline in Australia, pointing to the way his 'fundamental conceptual contribution . . . gave us the shape of our modern subject'. It is the impact of this text on how we conceive the 'shape' of corporate law that I want to emphasise. Bearing out Sugarman's point, Austin and Ramsay emphasised that it is Ford's text that gave Australian corporate lawyers 'the coherency of the subject [of corporate law] as an academic discipline' (Austin and Ramsay 2013: xi–xii).

That sense of coherence is evident in the gradual evolution of the book's content in the 40 years between the first and 16th editions. In 1974 the first edition of what became known simply as *Ford* contained 21 chapters, and ran to 493 pages of text. The chapters were grouped into five parts: an Introduction (dealing with corporate personality, the history of corporate law and the corporate constitution); the company as a corporate entity; company finance; management and control; and company reorganisation, takeovers and liquidation. Today there is a familiarity to this selection and sequence of topics, and it continues to be reflected, with some modifications, in contemporary editions of the text (and, indeed, many other Australian corporate law text books).

Indicative of the growing complexity of the corporate world, the 16th edition (current at the time of writing this chapter) has 1787 pages of text and 28 chapters divided into seven parts: companies and company law (covering similar territory to the original Introduction but, significantly, adding a discussion about the regulation of companies); the company as a corporate entity; the law of corporate governance; corporate liability; corporate finance; corporate control and restructuring; and external administration. Of course, whilst the overall structure of the book has endured, the content has changed. Some of those changes point to significant ways in which the shape of corporate law doctrine has changed, but they also reflect the growing dominance of the statute over the common law of corporations.

Corporate law textbooks have a significant role in defining, if only by implication, what is 'in' and what is 'out' when it comes to understanding the dimensions and content of corporate law. But it is not an exclusive role. For the most part, the treatment of corporate law in *Ford* (and other texts) has derived its understanding of the content and shape of corporate law by reference to the formal statutory and judicial sources of that law. Whilst it is the textbook writer's aim to impose some analytical order onto that material, it is that material which had tended to provide the definitional parameters for that analysis. In short, the answer to the question: 'what is corporate law?' that one derives from most corporate law textbooks is that it is the law that is found in the primary statute (in Australia, the Corporations Act 2001) and the associated case law. It is necessary, then, to turn to those sources,

Statute and common law

In a recent essay on the development of the common law, Justice Mark Leeming urged that lawyers should not forget the role of statutes when considering the Australian legal system: 'statutes', he observes, 'are an under-appreciated component in the academic literature on the Australian legal system'. To the Australian corporate lawyer this reminder is hardly necessary. Whilst corporate lawyers in the Anglo–Australian tradition typically think of corporate law as a mixture of common law – or general law – principles and statute law, the emphasis is now firmly on the latter. Contemporary corporate law is dominated by legislation. Indeed, corporate law has become a paradigmatic example of the shift to 'the age of statutes' (Ramsay 1992). To the lay observer it is Parliament more than the courts that is responsible for defining the parameters and content of contemporary corporate law.

Indeed, whilst it is clear that corporate law is now dominated by statute, the risk for corporate lawyers runs in the opposite direction to the concerns raised by Justice Leeming: a preoccupation with the primary statute can deflect attention away from other important dimensions of, and influences on, corporate law.

In what follows I begin by considering the impact of legislation in shaping our understanding of corporate law. I then look outside the statute, particularly at the common law but also to non-legal (or extra-legal) factors.

The statute

'All jurisdictions with well-developed market economies have at least one core statute that establishes a basic corporate form' (Armour, Hansmann and Kraakman 2009: 16). However, if we were to point to that core statute as the text that definitively answers the question: 'what is corporate law?', we may risk an answer that is both over-inclusive and under-inclusive.

Using the Australian Corporations Act 2001 as an example, the answer would be over-inclusive because, in its current form, the Act covers subject matter that ranges from what might be regarded as 'core' corporate law topics – rules dealing with the creation, constitution and governance of corporations – through to what might be described as 'consequential' or 'applied' matters, for example managed investment schemes and financial markets regulation.

There is no articulated rationale for the inclusion of some of these topics in the Act. Certainly, the inclusion of rules governing financial services within the general corporate law statute is at odds with the legislative regimes in other comparable jurisdictions such as the United Kingdom,[3] the United States,[4] Canada[5] and New Zealand.[6] In Australia, the inclusion under one legislative umbrella of this wide range of laws covering corporations and securities dealings appears to be a by-product of political manoeuvring between federal and state governments, rather than focused legal or policy considerations. The Corporations Act is a federal statute. Before it came into force, corporate legislation was the responsibility of the various state parliaments. From 1981 to mid-1989, the state legislation which formed the national cooperative scheme for corporate law provided separately for the Companies Code, the Acquisition of Shares Code, the Securities Industry Code and the Futures Industry Code.

The first attempt at federal legislation in 1989 brought this all together under the Corporations Act 1989, although separate legislation for close corporations was proposed, but later rejected. There appears to have been no specific reason given for amalgamating the subject matter of the prior statutes into one piece of legislation. Indeed, the wide-ranging discussion at the time concerning the proposed federal takeover of corporate law responsibility seems to have conflated the idea of having uniform legislation to apply Australia-wide with the idea of having a single piece of corporate legislation. In Parliament the then federal Attorney-General, Lionel Bowen stated simply that:

> We need one piece of legislation on a national basis. . . . We have to bear in mind that there is one share market, there is one dollar and there is virtually one stock exchange, if we want to put it that way, and it is about time we adopted the concept of having uniform legislation which is effective.
>
> *(Commonwealth of Australia 1987)*

The later Corporations Law Simplification Program also did not contemplate the possibility of 'dis-amalgamating' the increasingly voluminous Corporations Law (as it was then known), with its June 1995 paper 'Organising the Law' focused exclusively on an internal reorganisation of the Act (Simplification Task Force 1995).

A further reason why the Corporations Act is an insufficient source for defining the scope of corporate law is that it represents only the tip of the legislative iceberg. It presents an under-inclusive image of the scope of corporate law legislation and rules. As I have noted elsewhere (Bottomley 2005), the Corporations Act is not the only body of corporate law rules that guides our understanding of corporate law nor, in everyday practice, is it always the most important body of such rules, Beneath, or alongside, the Act there is a plethora of delegated and non-legislative rules and standards, including the Corporations Regulations 2001 (which rival the Act in length and complexity), orders and other regulatory guides issued by the corporate regulator, the Australian Securities and Investments Commission,

3 Companies Act 1986 (UK) c 46; Financial Services and Markets Act 2000 (UK) c 8.
4 Securities Act of 1933; e.g. in Delaware, Delaware General Corporation Law.
5 Canadian Business Corporations Act, RSC 1985, c C-44; e.g. in Ontario, Securities Act, RSO 1990 c S.5.
6 Companies Act 1993 (NZ); Securities Act 1978 (NZ).

securities exchange listing and operating rules, accounting and auditing standards and corporate governance codes of best practice.

With regard to the Corporations Regulations, it is important to note an emerging practice in Australian legislative drafting (at least at the federal level) in which more detailed regulation is now deliberately left to delegated or subordinate legislation, leaving the primary statute to set the broad framework and principles. According to the Office of Parliamentary Counsel (OPC), when legislation deals with matters of great detail, this practice has the virtue of 'leaving the Act uncluttered to deal with the core policy, but it does result in shifting the detail to another document' (Office of Parliamentary Counsel 2014: 14). Greater reliance on subordinate legislation is also appropriate, according to the OPC, when legislative drafters are faced with tight timelines on a legislative project.

Recent amendments to the Corporations Act 2001 show ample evidence of this practice. Taking two examples, the Explanatory Memorandum to the Corporations Amendment (Future of Financial Advice) Act 2012 noted, with regard to several sections that provide for subordinate rule making power, that:

> [the] regulation-making power therefore serves several functions, including keeping the legislation up to date, providing commercial certainty quickly and efficiently to industry participants, and to provide efficacy to the legislation.
>
> *(Commonwealth of Australia 2011: 1.17, 1.22)*

Similarly, when the Corporations Amendment (Short Selling) Act 2008 (Cth) inserted various regulation-making powers into the Corporations Act 2001, covering disclosure in relation to short sales in certain instances, the Explanatory Memorandum explained that this flexibility was needed 'to allow the law to respond to an environment of rapid change, including technological innovation and ongoing developments in the conduct and structures of financial markets' (Commonwealth of Australia 2008: 4.48).

As Mark Aronson has pointed out, the risk with such a practice is: 'the transfer of substantively important legislative power from the parliament to the executive, and the diminution in the transparency of a legislative process increasingly conducted without parliamentary debate' (Aronson 2011: 5). For the purposes of this chapter, this points to an approach to defining corporate law that, at the very least, must take into account the ideas and influence of the executive arm of government. In this regard it is worth noting that in Australia, since 2001, executive responsibility for the Corporations Act has resided in the Treasury Department rather than the Attorney-General's Department (as was previously the case), underlining an executive perception of corporate law as a species of economic and market regulation, rather than having wider social or political application.

The role of common law

'[E]ven if you know the statute . . . backwards and inside out, you will still not know the law that governs corporations: the only way of understanding corporations law properly is as part of an interrelated, intermeshed, entire system of law' (Campbell 2015: 238). As noted already, the balance between statute and common law in shaping Australian corporate law has shifted considerably over its history. This is evident from a simple comparison between the Uniform Companies Act 1961, when many aspects of corporate law (e.g. pre-incorporation contracts, shareholder rights of action, the determination of dividends) were predominantly, if not exclusively, determined by common law, and the present-day

Corporations Act 2001, which has increasingly brought these and many other areas under the statutory umbrella whilst, at the same time, adding whole new areas to the statutory menu (e.g. voluntary administration, managed investments).

However, notwithstanding its more comprehensive form, the Corporations Act retains a complex relationship with common law (using that term in its broad sense to include all judge-made law). Understanding that complexity is one of the first challenges in understanding the structure of corporate law in Australia, noting that in some places the Act purports to cover the field (e.g. shareholder derivative actions), in others it attempts to supplement or build upon common law principles (e.g. contracting with a company), whilst elsewhere it sits alongside and purportedly restates the common law (e.g. directors' duties).

The Australian case law on the statutory duty of care and diligence and on directors' powers of delegation and reliance provides an illustration of this complexity. The courts have depicted the relationship between common law and statute in this area in a number of ways. In *ASIC v Adler (No 3)*, Santow J described the Act as 'codifying' the general law on director's responsibilities for the actions of delegates.[7] In *Vines v ASIC*, Spigelman CJ stated that the statutory duty of care 'operates in parallel' with the common law duty, adding later that the language in the statute was 'plainly derived from the civil case law'.[8]

Perhaps unintentionally, the descriptor 'parallel' carries the implication that, like parallel lines, the two sources of law follow the same direction without ever coming into contact with each other. In *ASIC v Macdonald (No 11)*, Gzell J adopted the view of Brereton J in *ASIC v Maxwell* that the statutory duty of care 'reflects, and to some extent refines' the duty at general law.[9] In his detailed analysis of the duty of care in *ASIC v Rich*, Austin J noted that 'the content of the statutory standard of care and diligence is . . . informed by, and generally the same as, the general law standard'.[10]

The general consensus in all this is that the common law can be called on as a reference point to guide the interpretation and application of the statute. For example, in *Daniels v Andersen*, Clarke and Sheller JJA used the common law of negligence to interpret and explain the objective standard of care which they saw was required by section 232(4) of the Corporations Law.[11] The impression, then, is that at least with regard to directors' duties it is the statute that dominates. This impression is reinforced by the fact that the case law is itself largely the product of actions brought by ASIC under the civil penalty provisions in the Corporations Act. The application and enforcement of directors' duties has, in practice, become a matter of public regulation, and therefore subject to the strategic regulatory preferences of the corporate regulator (Welsh 2014). Whether for reasons of complexity or cost, there are few if any private actions brought against directors under general law.

This 'statutorification' of corporate law (Kingsford-Smith 1999: 161) has led to a stronger argument about the relationship between these two sources of law. Where principles of common law, particularly equity, continue to operate in relation to corporate law, there is an argument that those principles should be developed and applied in a way that is consistent with the prevailing statutory scheme. For example, where the Corporations Act provides for accessorial liability in relation to breach of the good faith, use of position and use of information duties in sections 181–183, but not for the care and diligence duty in section

---

7 [2002] NSWSC 171 [372].
8 [2007] NSWCA 75 [100].
9 [2009] NSWSC 287 [236], citing [2006] NSWSC 1052 [99].
10 [2009] NSWSC 1229 [7192].
11 (1995) 13 ACLC 614, 665.

180, should equity fill that gap? Gummow, previously a judge of the High Court of Australia, suggests not. Referring to the principle of coherence, he argues that: 'the better view is that it would be a misstep for equity to fix criteria more severe for the third party than those (if any) for which the statute provides. Where the statute provides for no accessorial liability . . . equity should not do so' (Gummow 2013: 758).

Corporate law and the public/private debate

The debate about the relative roles of common law and statute can also be mapped onto equally long-standing arguments about the status of post-20th century corporate law as being either essentially private, with a concern to enable and facilitate or public, with a focus on regulating and controlling corporate conduct. The former view is expressed with most force in the well known arguments of law and economics scholars. Armour, Hansmann and Kraakman, for example, argue that: '[a] significant part of corporate law – more in some jurisdictions, less in others – consists of default provisions [which offer] a standard form contract that parties can adopt, at their option, in whole or in part' (2009: 20). On this view, the purpose of corporate law is to simplify the otherwise costly exercise of entering into often complex and presumptively voluntary intra-corporate agreements. Corporate law thus supplements the private law of contract. Even the presence of mandatory rules is said to support this view: mandatory rules are a response to 'contracting failure' and 'serve a useful standardizing function' (2009: 22).

Against this is the argument that corporate law is (or has become) public in nature. There are two slightly different versions of this argument. One is that corporate law rules and doctrines have strong similarities to those in other branches of public law. This is not a new claim. In 1984, for example, Gerald Frug presented a powerful analysis of the similarities between corporate and administrative law, arguing that 'these two fields have relied on the same basic ideas in their attempt to assuage the longstanding fear that bureaucracy is a form of human domination' (Frug 1984: 1277–78). More recently, analyses of Australian corporate law have argued that it increasingly assumes 'emblems and norms that resemble those of public law' such that it makes sense to talk of the 'publicisation' of corporate law (Whincop and Keyes 1997: 54; Welsh 2014).

The second version of the 'corporate law is public' argument builds on the first to argue that it is indeed preferable to view corporate law – and corporate activity – through a public lens. Kent Greenfield has urged that: 'the laws controlling corporations should . . . be evaluated more as a branch of *public* law, the kind of law that concerns societies more generally' (Greenfield 2006: 2, emphasis supplied). What lies behind this argument is a different view about the role of corporations in modern society. Instead of corporations as private actors, this view emphasises corporations as political entities – not in the obvious sense that they exert political and economic power, but because corporations are governance systems. They are:

> arenas in which power and authority, rights and obligations, duties and expectations, benefits and disadvantages, are allocated and exercised, either actively or passively, collectively or individually, in relationships that can be characterised by conflict, control, competition, or co-operation.
>
> *(Bottomley 2007: 37)*

The better view, I suggest, is that corporate law is not classifiable as *either* private *or* public. Neither is it useful to reduce corporate law rules to a simple mandatory or enabling dichotomy. Again, this is not a new or recent observation. Back in 1982, even while he emphasised the importance of the distinction – 'a good society needs a commitment that public/private matters' – Christopher Stone noted 'how seamless and forbidding the public/private distinction can become' (Stone 1982: 1443). Similarly, John Coffee's challenge to the mandatory/enabling distinction holds as true today as it did in 1989 (Coffee 1989; also Ramsay 1998).

Corporate law presents a complex, hybridised mixture of private law notions, derived largely from contract law and equity, such as trust, obligation and individual autonomy, and of public law values such as accountability, procedural propriety and rational decision-making. Importantly, this hybridisation goes beyond the formal rules and structures that are familiar to corporate lawyers, be they legislative or common law, parliamentary, executive or judicial. On this view:

> There are many different rules and sets of rules that interact with each other and with other formal and informal forms of conduct to produce outcomes. For example, there are many different regulatory schemes which affect the conduct of directors and the systems of corporate governance adopted by corporations.
>
> *(Corbett and Bottomley 2004: 64–65)*

The suggestion is that instead of 'corporate law' it would make more sense – that is, it would be more practically relevant – to consider a broader category of regulatory practices, processes and structures that can be grouped under the heading 'corporate governance'. This is a regulatory field that exhibits features that are both public and private, legislative and common law, formal and informal, global and local. I now turn to the last of these dichotomies.

Is corporate law global or local?

The argument that corporate law can be assessed at the global scale has been strongly influenced by the idea that corporate law systems around the world are converging on a single model. As Hansmann and Kraakman describe it:

> Powerful new pressures are pushing corporate law into another phase of convergence. Chief amongst these pressures is a widespread acceptance of a shareholder-centered ideology of corporate law among international business government and legal elites. . . . This emergent consensus has already profoundly affected corporate governance practices throughout the world; its influence increasingly conditions the reform of corporate law as well.
>
> *(Hansmann and Kraakman 2002: 56)*

In effect, this argument conflates the global with the local, at least if 'the local' is understood in terms of the particular model of corporate governance that operates in the United States. The convergence thesis posits that that corporate governance rules around the world will inevitably converge because, as Jennifer Hill summarises it, 'jurisdictions with substandard legal rules would succumb to the siren song of economic efficiency, by adopting superior legal rules', and those superior legal rules are built on the shareholder primacy model of corporate governance (Hill 2005: 744).

The convergence thesis has received considerable criticism. In part this is because it does not match observed global patterns (Bruner 2013: 116–18). Moreover, the idea of convergence entails a significant disregard for the local legal, regulatory, political, economic and social conditions that shape corporate practice. One counter to convergence theory is the idea that 'there are significant sources of path dependence in a country's patterns of corporate ownership structure', which play a significant role maintaining differences in corporate structures (Bebchuk and Roe 2004). The convergence argument shares similar territory with the so-called 'law matters' thesis proffered by La Porta and colleagues (La Porta and others 1999), which emphasises the fundamental role of legal systems and legal rules in the development of strong financial systems and asserts the superior nature of common law systems over civil law systems in fostering 'vibrant equity markets' (Jordan 2005: 988).[12]

This argument attracts similar criticism. Whilst it is certainly arguable that law matters, so too do history, politics, custom and tradition. Like the convergence argument, the 'law matters' thesis overlooks the important role of localised non-law influences. It also overlooks what has long become commonplace in the sociological analysis of law – the importance of moving beyond the 'law in the books' to consider 'the law in action'. Importantly, the 'law matters' thesis also confuses – or, at least, it makes an overly simplified assumption about – cause and effect. As John Coffee has pointed out, there is good historical evidence to suggest that legal change has 'tended to follow, rather than precede, economic change' (Coffee 2001: 7).

As Jennifer Hill has emphasised, notwithstanding (and without disregarding) global influences, many recent corporate law reforms have responded specifically to local issues (Hill 2007: 118). Issues such as shareholder activism, management remuneration, auditor independence or financial advice regulation play out differently in different local settings. For example, as John Braithwaite observes:

> The ... corporate law reform debate that began in 2002 in Australia addressed many of the same issues as the US Sarbanes-Oxley Act of 2002, though in different and in some respects less interventionist ways.
>
> *(Braithwaite 2008: 35)*

Put another way, there are significant global trends and influences that shape an understanding of corporate law and, whilst corporate law scholars from around the globe can discuss these trends using a common corporate law language, they do so with different local corporate governance dialects. Those dialects signify local history, customs and practices that should not be ignored.

Conclusion

The purpose of this chapter has been to explore some of the ideas and issues that are raised when one attempts to answer the question: 'what is corporate law?' As I signalled in the Introduction, the chapter offers no conclusive answer to the question – indeed, to use an overworked aphorism, it is the journey more than the destination that matters. In that light, I offer some brief suggestions as to how I would construct my answer to the question.

Corporate law is a hybrid area of knowledge and practice. It is comprised of legal concepts and doctrines that are sui generis (the prime example being the idea of corporate legal personality), others that are adapted to suit the changing demands of corporate practice and

---

12 For a review and critique of the law matters thesis see Cheffins (2003).

varied usage of the corporate form, and yet others that are adopted with little modification. It is not confined to the pages of the statute or the case reports. It is neither exclusively private nor public in orientation and application. It is shaped by, and it shapes, domestic and global conditions.

In many ways, corporate law has become a disciplinary chameleon. It can blend into the varied discourses of legal theory, economic theory, regulatory theory, or managerial theory (to take just four examples). More specifically, it is able to house the specialist expertise of the corporate governance lawyer, the insolvency lawyer, the mergers and acquisitions lawyer, the private equity lawyer, the capital raisings lawyer and the financial markets lawyer.[13] This suggests that corporate law is not so much a disciplinary specialisation as a conceptual umbrella.

Perhaps this is the reason why it lends itself so well to contextual and inter-disciplinary study. But, equally, perhaps its hybrid qualities point to the possibility of fragmentation and sub-disciplinary secession. It may be that corporate law does not have a future as a single unifying disciplinary framework.

Bibliography

Addo, M.K. (ed) (1999) *Human Rights Standards and the Responsibility of Transnational Corporations*, The Hague: Kluwer Law International.

Armour, J., Hansmann, H. and Kraakman, R. (2009) 'What is Corporate Law?' in R. Kraakman and others (eds) *The Anatomy of Corporate Law: A Comparative and Functional Approach*, New York: Oxford University Press.

Aronson, M. (2011) 'Subordinate Legislation: Lively Scrutiny or Politics in Seclusion', *Australasian Parliamentary Review*, 26(2), 4–19.

Austin, R.P. and Ramsay I.M. (2013) *Ford's Principles of Corporations Law*, 15th edn, Sydney: LexisNexis.

Australian Law Reform Commission (1998) *General Insolvency Inquiry*, Report No 1, Volume 1, Canberra: Australian Government Printing Service.

Baxt, R. (1974) *Second Australian Supplement to the Third Edition of Gower's Modern Company Law*, Sydney: Law Book Company.

Bebchuk, L.A. and Mark J Roe, M.A. (2004) 'A Theory of Path Dependence in Corporate Ownership and Governance', in J.N. Gordon and M.J. Roe (eds), *Convergence and Persistence in Corporate Governance*, Cambridge: Cambridge University Press.

Black, B. (1990) 'Is Corporate Law Trivial? A Political and Economic Analysis', *Northwestern University Law Review*, 84: 542–93.

Bottomley, S. (2005) 'A Framework for Understanding the Interpretation of Corporate Law in Australia' in S. Corcoran and S. Bottomley (eds) *Interpreting Statutes*, Sydney: The Federation Press.

Bottomley, S. (2007) *The Constitutional Corporation: Rethinking Corporate Governance*, Aldershot: Ashgate Publishing.

Braithwaite, J. (2008) *Regulatory Capitalism: How it Works, Ideas for Making it Better*, Cheltenham: Edward Elgar.

Bruner, C. (2013) *Corporate Governance in the Common-Law World – The Political Foundations of Shareholder Power*, New York: Cambridge University Press.

Campbell J.C. (2015) 'Corporate Law, the Courts and Corporate Personality', *Company and Securities Law Journal*, 33: 227–38.

Canberra Law Review (1996) 'Special Issue on Corporate Law Research Methods and Theory', *Canberra Law Review*, 3: 1–115.

---

13 A review of the websites of six of the larger law firms operating in Australia reveals some diversity in what specialisations are included under the heading 'corporate practice'. Whilst commercial contracts, capital raisings, private equity and mergers and acquisitions are common, some firms add insurance, outsourcing, privatisation and climate change to the list.

Chambers, R.J. (1955) *Company Annual Reports*, Sydney: Law Book Co.

Cheffins, B. (2003) 'Law as Bedrock: The Foundations of an Economy Dominated by Widely Held Companies', *Oxford Journal of Legal Studies*, 23: 1–23.

Cioffi, J. (2010) *Public Law and Private Power: Corporate Governance Reform in the Age of Finance Capitalism*, Ithaca: Cornell University Press.

Coffee, J. (1989) 'The Mandatory/Enabling Balance in Corporate Law: An Essay on the Judicial Role', *Columbia Law Review*, 89: 1618–91.

Coffee, J. (2001) 'The Rise of Dispersed Ownership: The Roles of Law and State in the Separation of Ownership and Control', *Yale Law Journal*, 111: 1–82.

Commonwealth of Australia (1987), *Parliamentary Debates*, House of Representatives, 18 February 1987, 220 (Lionel Bowen).

Commonwealth of Australia (2011) *Explanatory Memorandum to the Corporations Amendment (Future of Financial Advice) Bill 2011*, https://www.comlaw.gov.au/Details/C2011B00208/Explanatory%20 Memorandum/Text (last accessed 9 June 2016).

Commonwealth of Australia (2008) *Explanatory Memorandum to the Corporations Amendment (Short Selling) Bill 2008* https://www.comlaw.gov.au/Details/C2008B00261/Explanatory%20 Memorandum/Text (last accessed 9 June 2016).

Corbett, A. and Bottomley, S. (2004) 'Regulating Corporate Governance' in C. Parker, C. Scott, N. Lacey and J. Braithwaite (eds) *Regulating Law*, Oxford: Oxford University Press.

Eisenberg, M. (1999) 'Corporate Law and Social Norms', *Columbia Law Review*, 99: 1253–92.

Ford, H.A.J. (1974) *Principles of Company Law*, Sydney: Butterworths.

Frug, G. (1984) 'The Ideology of Bureaucracy in American Law', *Harvard Law Review*, 97: 1276–388.

Greenfield, K. (2006) *The Failure of Corporate Law: Fundamental Flaws and Progressive Possibilities*, Chicago: University of Chicago Press.

Gower, L.C.B. (1954) *The Principles of Modern Company Law*, London: Stevens and Sons.

Gummow, W. (2013) 'The Equitable Duties of Company Directors', *Australian Law Journal*, 87: 753–60.

Hansmann, H. and Kraakman, R. (2001) 'The End of History for Corporate Law', *Georgetown Law Journal*, 89: 439–68.

Hansmann, H. and Kraakman, R. (2002) 'Toward a Single Model of Corporate Law?' in J. McCahery, P. Moerland, T. Raaijmakers and L. Renneboog (eds) *Corporate Governance Regimes: Convergence and Diversity*, Oxford and New York: Oxford University Press.

Hansmann, H. and Kraakman, R. (2004) 'What is Corporate Law?' in R. Kraakman and others (eds) *The Anatomy of Corporate Law: A Comparative and Functional Approach*, New York: Oxford University Press.

Hansmann, H. and Kraakman, R. (2012) 'Reflections on the End of History for Corporate Law' in A. Rasheed and T. Yoshikawa (eds) *The Convergence of Corporate Governance: Promises and Prospects*, Basingstoke: Palgrave-Macmillan.

Hill, J. (2005) 'The Persistent Debate about Convergence in Comparative Corporate Governance', *Sydney Law Review*, 27: 743–52.

Hill, J. (2007) 'Evolving "Rules of the Game" in Corporate Governance Reform' 1(2) *GovNet eJournal*, 1: 112–39 http://www.austlii.edu.au/au/journals/GovNeteJl/2007/4.pdf (last accessed 10 June 2016).

Jordan, C. (2005) 'The Conundrum of Corporate Governance', *Brooklyn Journal of International Law*, 30: 983–1028.

Joske, P.E. (1963) *The Law and Procedure of Meetings*, 4th edn, Sydney: Law Book Co.

Kingsford-Smith, D. (1999) 'Interpreting the Corporations Law – Purpose, Practical Reasoning and the Public Interest', *Sydney Law Review*, 21: 161–201.

Kraakman, R.H. and others (eds) (2009) *The Anatomy of Corporate Law: A Comparative and Functional Approach*, 2nd edn, New York: Oxford University Press.

La Porta, R., Lopez-De-Silanes, F. and Shleifer, A. (1999) 'Corporate Ownership around the World', *Journal of Finance*, 54: 471–517.

Law Admissions Consultative Committee (2015) Model Admission Rules 2015, http://www. lawcouncil.asn.au/LACC/images/LACC_Uniform_Admission_Rules_2014.pdf (last accessed 9 June 2016).

Miller, G.P. (2011) 'Law and Economics versus Economic Analysis of Law', *American Bankruptcy Institute Law Review*, 19: 459–70.

Office of Parliamentary Counsel (2014) *Guide to Reducing Complexity in Legislation* http://www.opc. gov.au/about/documents.htm (last accessed 9 June 2016).

Paterson, W.E. and Ednie, H.H. (1962) *Australian Company Law*, Melbourne: Butterworths.

Ramsay, I. (1992) 'Corporate Law in the Age of Statutes', *Sydney Law Review*, 14: 474–94.

Ramsay, I. (1998) 'Models of Corporate Regulation: The Mandatory/Enabling Debate' in R. Grantham and C Rickett (eds), *Corporate Personality in the 20th Century*, Oxford: Hart Publishing.

Simplification Task Force (1995), Corporations Law Simplification Program – Drafting Issues: Organising the Law, Canberra: Commonwealth Attorney-General's Department.

Stone, C.D. (1982) 'Corporate Vices and Corporate Virtues: Do Public/Private Distinctions Matter?', *University of Pennsylvania Law Review*, 130: 1441–509.

Sugarman, D. (1986) 'Legal Theory, the Common Law Mind and the Making of the Textbook Tradition' in W. Twining (ed) *Legal Theory and Common Law*, Oxford: Basil Blackwell, Oxford.

Wallace, G. and Young, J. (1965) *Australian Company Law and Practice*, Sydney: Law Book Company.

Welsh, M. (2014) 'Realising the Public Potential of Corporate Law: Twenty Years of Civil Penalty Enforcement in Australia', *Federal Law Review*, 42: 217–40.

Whincop, M. and Keyes, M. (1997) 'Corporation, Contract, Community: An Analysis of Governance in the Privatization of Public Enterprise and the Publicisation of Private Corporate Law', *Federal Law Review*, 25: 51–96.

Whincop, M. (2001) *An Economic and Jurisprudential Genealogy of Corporate Law*, Aldershot: Ashgate.

Wishart, D. (1994) *Company Law in Context*, Auckland: Oxford University Press.

Yorston, R.K. and Brown, S.R. (1968) *Company Law: A concise manual of the principles and practice of company law incorporating the legislation of New South Wales, Victoria and Queensland*, 3rd edn, Sydney: Law Book Company.

4

How corporate law matters

The debate as to the inter-relationship between legal origin and economic performance

Rob McQueen

1 Introduction: the La Porta thesis and its critics

Lack of time, combined with the jurisdictionally focused demands of most law programs generally dictates that larger questions regarding the history and/or jurisdictional specificity of particular corporate law regimes are rarely explored in any detail in courses devoted to the law of corporations. However, in our current age of borderless transactions, international-isation of share trading and the almost immediate exposure of jurisdictionally located stock exchanges to international developments, this jurisdictional myopia seems somewhat anachronistic.

However, one area in which such issues have recently been ventilated in the academic literature is in respect of the perceived 'efficiency' of structural aspects of the legal architecture of corporate and investment regimes in specific jurisdictions. Particular attention has been paid to the relative 'efficiency' of common law and civil law regimes in their respective diasporas, as former colonies became independent states.

Such studies, examining the comparative efficacy of differing legal regimes, have become an increasingly important and growing area of analysis in recent decades, often driven by donor countries and international agencies concerned to ensure that aid and other funding provided to recipient countries is efficiently deployed. One particularly influential group of such studies, regarding the relative 'efficiencies' of common law and civil law systems of law when introduced into former colonial economies, have been those undertaken by Rafael La Porta and his collaborators. In this body of work it is posited that the 'legal origin' of the corporate laws of a formerly colonised state is a strong determinant of the relative 'efficiency' of its corporate sector into the present.

One group of scholars has noted the following regarding the postulated relative efficiency of these two differing legal systems (civil and common law) as established through these studies, and the possible reasons for an apparent superior effectiveness of one system of law over the other:

> The legal origin hypothesis states that the performance of firms is related to the legal origin of their country of origin. It links the corporate governance structure of a country as defined by its legal system to a firms' performance. For this reason it is maintained that the legal origin of a country affects the extent of agency problems.
>
> *(Andersson and others 2014: 5)*

La Porta and his colleagues (1998) have maintained that the legal origin of a country affects the extent of agency problems. The efficiency of corporate governance rules will accordingly differ between legal traditions. La Porta and his colleagues have shown that common law countries (English legal origin) have stronger legal protection of investor rights than civil law countries (French, German and Scandinavian legal origin). Because of this, agency problems are expected to be stronger in civil law countries compared with common law countries. Empirical research has shown that the Anglo–Saxon system turns out to be most efficient in protecting the rights of shareholders against management and majority owners, followed in order by the Scandinavian and the German systems of law.

La Porta and his colleagues (2002) and Gugler and his (2003, 2004) do indeed show that firms originating from countries with British origin on average perform better than firms from countries with Scandinavian, German or French origin. Moreover, the French legal system seems to be 'worst', whereas Scandinavian and German are in between the French and English-origin average (Andersson and others 2014: 5).

Nonetheless, despite the influence that this body of work initiated by La Porta and his colleagues has exerted on the decisions of international aid and other agencies, it has not been without its critics. A recent study by Mathias Siems has noted that, whilst law and finance scholars have, in recent years, increasingly relied upon comparative law, particularly with regard to determining the 'relative efficiencies' of the two major colonial systems of law transplanted into these now former colonies, civil and common law, it is nonetheless the case that many, if not all, such studies appear to have 'routinely adopted the traditional distinction between civil law and common law countries'. Siems continues by stating his and a number of other scholars' scepticism in regard to this methodology and, furthermore, notes that it is a 'matter of considerable debate' whether such a revival of 'legal families' (or 'legal origins') as a conceptual tool in this arena is a 'useful way forward' (Siems 2007: 55).

La Porta, along with his collaborators Florencio de Silanes and Andrei Shleifer, in a short article published in 2008, responded to the above critics and, after reiterating the central propositions of their thesis, noted that:

> When common and civil law were transplanted into much of the world through conquest and colonization, not only the rules, but also human capital and legal ideologies, were transplanted as well ... Despite much local legal evolution, the fundamental strategies and assumptions of each legal system survived, and have continued to exert substantial influence on economic outcomes ... In our conception, legal origins are central to understanding the varieties of capitalism.
>
> *(La Porta and others 2008: 285)*

Beck and Levine, who are themselves former collaborators with La Porta, have observed in respect of these critiques that, whilst the different legal traditions of the common law and civil law countries which were spread across the globe through conquest, colonisation and imitation might provide an explanation for cross-country differences in investor protection, the contracting environment, and financial development today, these two major legal traditions also, in particular, differ significantly in their formalism and therefore their capacity to evolve with changing conditions. Beck and Levine continue by postulating that the more formal civil law system is 'less efficient' than common law owing to the larger 'gap' it maintains between the 'contracting needs of the economy' and the legal systems capabilities to fulfil the needs of those who drive the economy (Beck and Levine 2008: 251).

In Beck and Levine's view, civil law is a less flexible, and thereby, a less efficient system of law. They also note, however, that not all in this field of research subscribe to such a view and, even then a number of researchers who do subscribe to the notion that civil law is less flexible, and thus 'less efficient' than common law, nonetheless disagree with a number of the key conclusions reached by Beck and Levine as to what are the actual, rather than the postulated, effects of such differing levels of 'efficiency' as between these two major legal systems:

> Countervailing theories and evidence challenge both parts of the law and finance theory ... Many researchers accept that effective investor protection facilitates efficient corporate financing and growth-enhancing financial development, but reject the law and finance's view that legal origin is a central determinant of investor protection laws and financial development.
>
> *(Beck and Levine 2008: 251)*

Accordingly, whilst Beck and Levine do not go as far as denying that there is an apparent correlation between colonial antecedents and later economic performance, they nonetheless do acknowledge that the underlying key factors in such correlations have been and continue to be hotly contested in the academic literature. In this regard a number of researchers in the field have noted that there is indeed a complex array of plausible factors, which might explain the differing economic performance between various colonised states, of which the respective implantation of either a common or civil law system is but *one* amongst a wide range of other factors, many of which may also strongly correlate with later economic performance:

> The reason almost all legal systems of the world belong to either the common or the civil law family is that the European powers imposed their legal system on their colonies. Consequently, *'legal origin'* is almost perfectly congruent with 'colonial history' understood as the identity of the dominant colonizing power. Nevertheless, the legal regime was just one of many differences between the various colonial powers. Colonizing powers differed in their policies relating to education, public health, infrastructure, European immigration, and local governance. In addition, colonizing powers did not choose their colonies randomly, so colonies may differ in characteristics such as climate and natural resources. Disentangling these factors is not merely of historic interest. To the extent that policy lessons can be learned from the *legal origin* literature, they depend critically on identifying the causes of the observed effects. (emphases added)
>
> *(Beck and Levine 2008: 252)*

With regard to the variety and complexity of factors that might explain differences in post-colonial economic performance, Klerman and his collaborators, using a sample of 49 former colonies around the world for the period 1960–2003, found that differences in educational policies, not legal origin, were, in fact, the main reason why former British colonies' economies had grown faster than former French colonies (Klerman and others 2011: 380).

In addition, Klerman and others specifically noted the following regarding La Porta and his colleagues' research:

> La Porta et al. 'adopt a broad conception of legal origin as a style of social control of economic life.' Under this view, legal origin is not just whether a country has a legal system based on the Code Napoléon or on the precedents of the English common law. Nor is legal origin simply about whether the judiciary is a bureaucracy tasked with textual interpretation rather than a high-status independent group with de facto lawmaking powers.
>
> Rather, legal origin stands for 'strategies of social control' that either 'support private market outcomes' or implement specific state policies. . .This broad conception of legal origin might be better measured by the identity of the dominant colonial power than by comparative lawyers' classification of legal systems. Strategies of social control might be more influenced by educational systems and governmental structure than by whether code or precedent was the dominant source of law, or whether judges or juries were the principle fact finders (ibid: 393).

2 The 'initial endowments thesis' of post-colonial economic success

As stated above, proxies for broader colonial policy – but not proxies for legal origin – can explain much of the growth differential between the civil law and common law colonial groupings (ibid: 409). These findings thereby lend considerable support to the alternative 'initial endowments' hypothesis as being the best explanation for the superior performance of one group of colonised states over all others, rather than this performance differential being explicable by means of the identity of any particular colonising power, or by means of the respective legal systems that European powers implanted into their colonies. It seems that differences in the pre-colonisation 'initial conditions' of these states, rather than any possible differences in colonial policy (legal, educational, or other), constitute the best explanation for the differing growth rates amongst former colonies (Beck and others 2002: 2).

Klerman and his collaborators have further observed that if the above is true then the premise behind La Porta's work seriously falls into question (Klerman and others 2011: 382). This would perhaps not matter so much if La Porta's initial study had, after its publication, remained simply an interesting, but yet unproven, thesis to be debated amongst academics. However, quite the contrary has occurred as, rather than remaining one potentially interesting thesis amongst many others, La Porta's work has, instead, exercised significant influence on major international bodies with regard to their funding allocations to 'developing' nations over the past decade or more (Garoupa and Ligüerre 2011).

Thus, the 'legal system' thesis championed by La Porta and his colleagues for the past few decades may not only be wrong; it may also have done irreparable damage to the future prospects of a number of emerging nations. Those most likely to be particularly affected would be those nations that, as a result of La Porta's thesis, have consistently failed to gain significant international funding or support for development projects in their respective nations.

As a consequence of these mounting concerns regarding past funding allocations, a major reexamination of the initial propositions upon which La Porta and his colleagues' analyses were based has recently been undertaken. A number of such studies have been conducted by researchers previously supportive of La Porta's thesis. These revisionary initiatives have largely been directed at the generally uncritical acceptance of La Porta's thesis by many major international funding bodies over the past decade or more as a major basis for their funding decisions, even in the face of the ever-mounting number of critiques of La Porta's thesis by independent scholars during this period.

A number of such critiques of La Porta's research have also recently noted the transformed nature of the legal systems in a number of those states that had previously been deemed 'inefficient' by La Porta in his earlier studies. Despite such significant changes in these states since the earlier studies of La Porta and, in a number of instances, consequent major re-organisations of their economies, these states were nonetheless still categorised in later reports by La Porta and his colleagues as inefficient 'civil law' states, based on research they had conducted some decades ago, without reference to the growing body of new studies by other researchers suggesting this that such assumed 'inefficiency' was no longer the case.

3 La Porta's response to his critics

La Porta and his collaborators have, not surprisingly, responded to this growing body of criticism in regard to their original thesis, specifically commenting on the challenges presented to their theory by the transformation of the legal 'landscape' which they had described in their original research:

> There are many arguments for convergence. Globalization leads to a much faster exchange of ideas, including ideas about laws and regulations, and therefore encourages the transfer of legal knowledge. Globalization also encourages competition among countries for foreign direct investment, for capital, and for business in general, which must as well put some pressure toward the adoption of good legal rules and regulations. The convergence is [a result of] civil law countries increasingly accepting common law solutions, and vice versa.
>
> *(La Porta and others 2008: 332)*

Nevertheless, in the conclusions to this 2008 article La Porta and his colleagues, after acknowledging the possibility of some degree of convergence as between the two major legal systems occurring, stated that even if one were to accept the possibility of a true convergence of legal systems over time, this would still leave open the question as to what legal rules and regulations these countries would most likely move towards in such a situation.

La Porta and his colleagues then concluded this response to their critics in the following manner:

> The world economy in the last quarter century has been surprisingly calm, and has moved sharply toward capitalism and markets. In that environment, our framework suggests, the common law approach to social control of economic life performs better than the civil law approach. When markets do or can work well, it is better to support than to replace them. As long as the world economy remains free of war, major financial crises, or other extraordinary disturbances, the competitive pressures for market-supporting regulation will remain strong, and we are likely to see continued liberalization. Of course, underlying this prediction is a hopeful assumption that nothing like World War II or the Great Depression will repeat itself. If it does, countries are likely to embrace civil law solutions, just as they did back then.
>
> *(La Porta and others 2008: 332)*

In many ways this *caveat* to La Porta and others' predictions in respect of the continuing health of the world economy, which they note would be contingent on its continuing prosperity and avoiding any major financial crises, seems somewhat ominous in a commentary published in 2008. The off-the-cuff pronouncements in the paper as to the possible global consequences in the 'unlikely eventuality' of such a crisis actually occurring, are unfortunate, given the then imminence of the GFC, which has been referred to by many economists as the worst financial crisis since the Great Depression of the 1930s.[1]

4 The critics' response

Another major figure in corporate law theory, John Coffee, the Adolf A. Berle Professor of Law at Columbia University Law School, has stated in respect of the form of legal convergence needed to remove the apparent differences in 'efficiency' of common law and civil law systems, that this may not, in fact, entail wholesale changes to existing civil law systems. Indeed, it might not entail much change in formal structures at all, as 'formal legal convergence may be less important than functional convergence' (Coffee 1999: 15).

Coffee's approach to this important issue as to the possible nature and consequences of a prospective future convergence of legal systems is, in fact, congruent with the views expressed in another significant study by Nuno Garoupa and Carlos Gomez Ligüerre. Their study centred on the consequences or lack thereof of the alleged differences in 'efficiency' of common and civil law systems and thereby their respective capacity to foster or fail in ensuring economic success in these former colonies after colonisation has ended. In describing the *purpose* of their research, they state their aims as follows:

> Our thesis is that without a detailed analysis of common law and French law institutions, it is not possible to theorize the legal origins literature. However, when such detailed analysis is performed, it is not obvious which legal system has more pro-market or pro-economic growth legal institutions. The persistence of the alleged superiority of the common law requires a proper theorization that will be complex and intrinsically difficult.
>
> *(Garoupa and Ligüerre 2011: 293–4)*

---

1 For instance, Russell Cooper, Professor of Economics at the European University Institute in Florence, Italy and Andrew John, Associate Professor of Economics at the Melbourne Business School, in the introduction to Chapter 15 of their widely read text, *Theory and Applications of Macroeconomics* http://2012books.lardbucket.org/books/theory-and-applications-of-macroeconomics/s19-00-the-global-financial-crisis.html (last accessed 26 May 2016), note the following:

> As we wrote this chapter in 2011, the world economy was slowly emerging from the worst financial crisis since the Great Depression. Economists and others formerly thought that the Great Depression was an interesting piece of economic history and nothing more. After all, they thought, we now understand the economy much better than did the policymakers at that time, so we could never have another Great Depression. But this belief that monetary and fiscal policymakers around the world knew how to ensure economic stability was shattered by financial turmoil that began in 2007, blossomed into a full-fledged global crisis in the fall of 2008, and led to sustained downturns in many economies in the years that followed.
>
> That was the background to the November 2008 meeting of the G-20 countries. The world leaders attending that meeting were attempting to cope with economic problems that they had never even contemplated. The events that led to this meeting were unprecedented since the Great Depression, in part because of the magnitude and worldwide nature of the crisis.

This research clearly flies in the face of the orthodoxy established by La Porta and his associates, and therefore demands serious attention. This is particularly so because, as we have noted earlier, the funding decisions of many international bodies with respect to economic assistance and other forms of aid funding to emergent nations have, over the past decade or more, been significantly influenced by La Porta's studies.

Unlike speculative theses in other areas of law, which are often no more than mere debating points between different schools of academic thought, La Porta and his associates' research has, however, exerted significant influence on 'real world' funding decisions for the past few decades. New data, such as that recently provided by Garoupa and Ligüerre is therefore an important contribution, and particularly prescient given that, despite La Porta and his colleagues' oft-repeated assurances that their research is 'evidence based', it is their interpretation of that evidence, rather than the underlying data itself, which has recently been brought into question.

In addition, the core assertion of La Porta's thesis respecting the relative 'efficiencies' of civil versus common law has been contested by other researchers in the field for some time, and continues to be so contested. Whilst up to now La Porta's research has remained influential in respect to the funding decisions of international agencies, this prior unquestioning acceptance of La Porta's research as a basis for aid and other financial allocations now appears to be coming to an end.

In the past, it was, presumably, the simplicity that La Porta and his colleagues' research offered to international funding bodies in respect to their decision-making that was its allure. It permitted a rational, apparently scientific basis for differentiating between various post-colonial states in respect to the allocation of aid and financial development funding on the basis of measured levels of economic 'efficiency' and/or 'inefficiency' between these formerly colonised states. The ability of La Porta's research to provide such a 'league table' of the prospects of differing states' claims for aid and other funding led those bodies to accept this particular body of research as the basis for their funding decisions. To them it would have seemed both defensible as a basis for decision-making and also had the benefit of appearing to be both 'scientifically based' and fair.

With the benefit of hindsight, this seems to have been somewhat foolish, particularly when there was a competing body of research which suggested the main difference between 'successful' and 'unsuccessful' decolonising states was their 'initial endowments', whether that be mineral wealth, prime agricultural land, good fisheries etc, rather than that post-colonial success or failure being principally contingent on their inherited legal systems, or the efficiency or otherwise of such legal systems.

This is, however, not the only the significant problem with La Porta's research results. Another important issue is the inability of research to demonstrate that the same or similar post-colonial 'performance inefficiencies' evident in former French civil law colonies was also extant in a range of other now post-colonial states that inherited civil law systems, either from German or Scandinavian colonial pasts (Nunn 2009: 67).

Consequently, despite the significant influence that the body of work initiated by La Porta and his colleagues has exerted on the decisions of international aid and other agencies for at least the past few decades, it has also been the case that, during this period, their research has attracted a growing assembly of critics.

These commentators have been particularly sceptical of La Porta's measures of 'efficiency' in a context in which one is never comparing like with like, given the disparate array of 'other factors' which might be impacting on performance in what was a wide variety of colonial settings in terms of geography, soil fertility, natural resources, workforce skills etc.

This exercise is thus not one in which the observer is comparing 'like with like', as the colonies being compared did not start out with the same natural endowments and therefore neither had the same opportunities for future development at the time of their colonisation, nor do so in the present.

La Porta, along with his collaborators Florencio de Silanes and Andrei Shleifer, have nonetheless steadfastly responded to this growing array of critics by continuing to reiterate the central propositions of their original thesis as follows:

> Legal Origin Theory traces the different strategies of common and civil law to different ideas about law and its purpose that England and France developed centuries ago. These broad ideas and strategies were incorporated into specific legal rules, but also into the organization of the legal system, as well as the human capital and beliefs of its participants. When common and civil law were transplanted into much of the world through conquest and colonization, the rules, but also human capital and legal ideologies, were transplanted as well . . . we show how these styles of different legal systems have developed, survived over the years, and continued to have substantial economic consequences. In our conception, legal origins are central to understanding the varieties of capitalism.
>
> *(La Porta and others 2008: 285)*

Sometime collaborators with La Porta, Thorston Beck and Ross Levine have, however, observed the following regarding the nature of the different schools of thought on *how to interpret* the findings as to apparent differences in relative 'efficiency' as between these two colonising legal regimes:

> Law and finance theory emphasizes that the different legal traditions that emerged in Europe over previous centuries and were spread internationally through conquest, colonization, and imitation help explain cross-country differences in investor protection, the contracting environment, and financial development today . . . Countervailing theories and evidence challenge both parts of the law and finance theory . . . Many researchers accept that effective investor protection facilitates efficient corporate financing and growth-enhancing financial development, but reject the law and finance's view that *legal origin* is a central determinant of investor protection laws and financial development (emphasis added)
>
> *(Beck and Levine 2005: 252)*

Hence, whilst different schools of thought may actually agree on the apparent correlation between colonial antecedents and later economic performance, the underlying reasons for such correlations nonetheless continue to be *hotly contested* in the academic literature by these different schools of thought. In this regard, a number of researchers in the field have noted that it is not any single factor, but rather the synergies existing between a complex array of factors, which might best explain the differing economic performance between various colonised states. Of these, the respective implantation of either a common or a civil legal system is but *one* in a diverse range of diverse factors that may correlate with this later economic performance or lack thereof:

> 'Legal origin' is almost perfectly congruent with 'colonial history' understood as the identity of the dominant colonizing power. Nevertheless, the legal regime was just one

of many differences between the various colonial powers. Colonizing powers differed in their policies relating to education, public health, infrastructure, European immigration, and local governance. In addition, colonizing powers did not choose their colonies randomly, so colonies may differ in characteristics such as climate and natural resources. Disentangling these factors is not merely of historic interest. To the extent that policy lessons can be learned from the legal origin literature, they depend critically on identifying *the causes* of the observed effects. (emphasis added)

(Beck, Demirgüç-Kunt and Levine 2003: 654)

With regard to the variety and complexity of factors that might explain these differences in post-colonial economic performance, Beck and his collaborators, as previously noted, demonstrated that *colonial origin* did not matter after geographical factors were controlled (ibid: 674, emphasis added). This finding lends significant support to the alternative 'initial endowments' hypothesis, and accounts for the results in those studies which have indicated that performance differences between common and civil law systems were most pronounced in former French colonies, something which might be best explained by one specific artefact of French colonisation, the particular geographical characteristics of their colonial possessions.

Other scholars who have agreed with La Porta and his associates as to some form of differentiation existing between the post-colonial economic performance of formerly 'common law colonies' compared with 'civil law colonies' have, nonetheless, challenged the notion that this necessarily means there is some form of *direct relationship* between the nature of the inherited legal system of a former colony and its later, post-colonial, economic performance.

Thus, whilst Klerman and his associates (2011) do not deny that there is a definite correlation between legal origins, modern regulation, and economic outcomes, they nonetheless persuasively argue that these correlations are not principally the result of the specific form of legal system introduced into these states, whether common law or civil law in origin. They, in fact conclude their study by suggesting that such correlations, at least with regard to their potential as a predictive factor of later economic performance, are not reliable. They further note that such correlations have been demonstrated, in a range of independent research in the area, to instead be predominantly attributable to the broader policy frameworks in which colonisation occurred, rather than being a result of whether a newly post-colonial state inherited a common or a civil system of law at the time of independence (ibid: 386).

Klerman and his associates also observe that:

> Where legal origin is exogenous, however, it is almost perfectly correlated with another set of potentially relevant background variables: the colonial policies of the European powers that spread the 'origin' legal systems through the world. We find strong evidence in favor of non-legal colonial explanations for economic growth (ibid: 379).

Thus, a single factor explanation, such as one positing that the nature of the adopted legal system in any particular colonised state is able to explain subsequent differing levels of economic performance appears not to be sustainable. Rather, it appears that a range of diverse factors brought to bear on specific colonial possessions by particular colonial powers, would significantly influence the later, post-colonial economic prospects of particular states. These factors might include characteristics of the particular bureaucratic apparatus of such states, alongside the often significant differences in governance styles adopted in those colonies by the colonising power. These and other related factors have proved to be crucially important factors in later economic development, or the lack thereof.

In explaining variations between specific colonies Klerman and his associates have observed, respecting their own research method, that they 'exploit the imperfect overlap of colonizer and legal origin' by looking at possible channels. These could include a variety of possibilities, such as the differing bureaucratic structures and other arrangements pertaining to the legal systems in force across a range of colonial states, rather than their common or civil law origins, as being the main determinants of which factors influence contemporary economic outcomes (Klerman and others 2011: 379).

This body of research thereby suggests that there are a group of exogenous, non-legal factors associated with later economic performance, which are both variable and synergistic in nature and, whilst ever-present, are, individually, somewhat unpredictable determinants of post-colonial economic performance.

It appears to have been the case, therefore, that such a bundle of varying factors exogenous to the inherited legal system of these formerly colonised states were, through their interaction, the principal drivers of later economic success, or its obverse, in the post-colonial period, rather than such success or failure being attributable to any single specific factor.

5 A better understanding of the causes of post-colonial success or failure?

It is thus, according to the above viewpoint, the synergy between an array of factors, or the lack thereof, which constitutes the principal determinant of whether a former colonised state would enjoy later economic success, or alternatively, economic failure. Single factor explanations, such as the civil or common law origin of the legal systems inherited by specific former colonial possessions are now dismissed by most researchers in the field as being far too simplistic to be able properly to describe the complex processes at the heart of the post-colonial development in such states or, in some cases, the lack thereof. In this regard, Klerman and his collaborators have noted that:

> 'legal origin' is almost perfectly congruent with 'colonial history' understood as the identity of the dominant colonizing power. Nevertheless, the legal regime was just one of many differences between the various colonial powers. Colonizing powers differed in their policies relating to education, public health, infrastructure, European immigration, and local governance. In addition, colonizing powers did not choose their colonies randomly, so colonies may differ in characteristics such as climate and natural resources. Disentangling these factors is not merely of historic interest. To the extent that policy lessons can be learned from the legal origin literature, they depend critically on identifying the causes of the observed effects.
>
> *(Klerman and others 2011: 381)*

Similar comments regarding the synergy existing between a wide range of factors as being crucial in determining the 'performance' or otherwise of particular states economies in the post-colonial period have been made by a number of other scholars in recent studies. For instance, Mahy and Ramsay, in their examination of the effects of transplanted British company laws in Malaya, have noted:

> Pistor and others have found that company law in common law 'origin' countries has tended to be more adaptable than in civil law 'origin' jurisdictions. However, they also

found that in 'transplant' countries the law developed very differently to that of its relevant parent legal family. Pistor and others demonstrated that transplanted law is unlikely to correspond to local demand and thus often displays patterns of erratic change or long periods of stagnation rather than incremental co-evolution with economic and social developments. Overall, that study, together with other related work, argues that this 'transplant effect', and the way that law was received, is much more important than the legal family in determining outcomes of the law in 'transplant' countries.

(Mahy and Ramsay 2014: 124–25)

A further group of scholars has also, from a somewhat different angle, recently questioned the potentially erroneous and oversimplified nature of the supposed correlation between the nature and form of the legal system introduced by a colonising nation and any specific colonies' subsequent economic performance, both before and after decolonisation:

While contemporary scholars no longer see colonialism as unambiguously positive, they do agree on its importance. A series of quantitative studies, both within and across nations, have linked colonial-era policies and institutions to post-independence variation in economic growth, public goods provision, democracy, and corruption. One strand of this literature suggests that colonization by the British led to better outcomes than colonization by the French or by the smaller colonial powers, because of either the adaptability of British legal institutions to the market economy or the higher levels of personal freedom provided by British culture . . .

One major shortcoming of such studies is, however, that they conceal a large amount of unobserved heterogeneity in 1) the preexisting conditions of the areas colonized, 2) the institutions imposed by the colonizer, and 3) the post-independence political histories of these countries. As such, any estimation of 'colonizer effects' may be *biased*, and this bias could be particularly strong with respect to the British Empire . . .

(Schultz 2012: 401, emphasis added)

On the basis of such evidence, it would seem the influence on subsequent development of the legal system in force in any particular former colonial state is generally overshadowed by other aspects of colonial policy in a wide range of areas – education, involvement of indigenes in the civil service and the relative economic status of the colonisers and the elites of the colonised. It also appears from the above research data, along with that of a number of other researchers in the field, that the 'initial endowments' of any specific colony are often a crucial factor in later development or lack thereof; more so, for instance, than the nature of the implanted legal system.

It is also important to consider factors such as a colonised population's 'understanding' of the specific measures introduced by a colonial power, and the manner and degree to which the subjugation of indigenous populations within a colonised state may have influenced later developments, particularly where such subjugations have significantly disrupted prevailing cosmologies, economic organisation and many other aspects of pre-colonial life in the now colonised state:

There is no question that bringing legal history into the economic debate was an important and welcome innovation. . . . Yet, the main difficulty with the argument derives from the econometric and analytical interpretation of this very notion: 'legal origin' is used as a country-specific, time-invariant parameter, which is expected to have permanent effects on institutions and on economic performances. This assumption is actually required, if the endogeneity problem is to be solved neatly.

Hence, the underlying paradox: whereas the overall approach comes with a strong smell of Northian historiography, the actual use of history, or duration, is profoundly a-historical. It does not and cannot account for phases or cycles in economic or political development . . . 'legal origins' are supposed to have emerged in a given historical context and to have then crystallized: they are interpreted as some essential hard-core identity, which would lie beyond the reach of either economic or political competition. This obviously raises concerns. To start with, no empirical evidence has been presented which would support this proposition.

(Sgard 2006: 11, emphasis added)

Ian Ramsay and Petra Mahy, in a similar vein, have recently observed the following regarding the apparent 'abnormal' nature of the gestation of corporate law in a specific colonial setting, and the subsequent need and capacity for such formerly colonised states, in this case, Malaya, to develop and adapt such laws to their own needs after colonisation ceases:

[One] line of debate in respect to the implantation of colonizing states corporate law systems into colonial 'possessions' is as to whether the introduction and effects of company law in the colonial context is best understood as 'imperialism'. This debate, too, is concerned with innovation and the adaptability of the law to local conditions.

(Mahy and Ramsay 2014: 125)

In an earlier paper I myself have argued that these past interventions might indeed be best characterised as constituting company law as an instrument of imperialism, and that local populations indeed had little agency in preventing this, despite an awareness of the unsuitability of British (or United States or European) company law statutes to local conditions. Local entrepreneurs were often acutely aware that the corporate laws introduced by the colonisers, in looking towards home country based commercial interests, often served to impede local commercial endeavor and local economic development rather than assist it (McQueen 1995: 187).

This reinforces the notion that local interests in the colonies did not see 'history' as implacably headed in the direction it had been set upon by the colonising power; rather, they saw history as prospective rather than retrospective, and it was now very much in their control, rather than in the hands of the coloniser. To them history mattered, but in this case it was the historical evolution of their future as an independent nation that mattered, not that of their past under a colonising power.

The capacity of these new nations to shape the common law to their own needs as independent states means that the shackles of history as postulated by La Porta and his colleagues are now illusory. To reiterate Sgard's observation cited above, they were not forever in the grips of a hard-core fixed identity, but rather in a new phase or cycle in their economic or political development. They were now the masters of their own destiny, albeit somewhat burdened by the excess baggage of colonialism, but nevertheless now with an independent capacity to shed this baggage in the future should they need or desire to do so.

Nonetheless, discontent has recently emerged in discussions as to the ongoing repercussions of past company law transplants amongst a growing assemblage of former colonies, all products of the post-independence era in Asia. The current state of corporate governance in many of these states is now blamed by indigenous commercial interests on the original colonial company law transplant, its inherent imperialism, and the lack of adaptability of such legislative provisions to peculiar needs arising from local conditions and business cultures. (On this issue see Mahy and Ramsay 2014.)

This argument is supported by, for instance, evidence of the mismatch between Asian family business practices and the particular understanding of 'agency' problems that Western company law is designed to regulate (McQueen 1995: 125). This mismatch is a result of differing views between cultures as to who or what should be regarded as having agency under law; in this case it is not a question of the age at which a human actor can be seen to be an adult, and thus able to exercise agency, nor is it to do with whether particular forms of artificial legal persons, such as corporations might or might not have agency and, if so, on what terms. It is more fundamental. For the Indians it was a question of cosmology as to who had legal standing, rather than a simple question of legalism. For them the crucial question in this case was 'can gods be constituted as legal actors?'.

Not surprisingly the colonised and, in particular, colonised populations involved in business activities, often saw the world through very different lenses to their colonisers, and thereby were often given to interpreting introduced areas of law, such as those pertaining to corporations, in ways which the colonising power would not have, nor could have, anticipated.

As Ritu Birla (2009: 96–99) has noted, Indians often chose to 'accommodate to their own cosmology' certain aspects of British law, the trust being one of the areas of law so affected. This local reinterpretation of the nature of the trust, for instance, arose in the case of 'rest houses', simple accommodations located along the routes of religious pilgrimages, the building costs of which were endowed by rich traders and other wealthy individuals for the use of pilgrims along the way during their pilgrimages.

However, such penitents were not the only travellers to undertake journeys along these routes, nor indeed to use the endowed rest houses. Bands of robbers and other undesirables were also given to using the rest houses – not whilst on pilgrimages, however – but rather for their own purposes as resorts from which to prey on those engaged in pilgrimages and any other lone travellers using these trade routes. As time wore on, particular endowed rest houses that had become known for these dangers were avoided by pilgrims and fell into dereliction and 'insanitation' (ibid: 99).

The British administration became concerned about these developments and sought to rid the rest houses and the pilgrimage trails on which they were located of these 'dacoit bands' (dacoits being, as the Merriam-Webster Dictionary states: 'one of a class of criminals in India and Burma who rob and murder in roving gangs'). Consequently, the British authorities attempted to have the rich Indians who had endowed the rest houses take responsibility as trustees for maintaining them and ridding them of 'undesirables'.

However, the authorities then discovered that the wealthy families who had endowed the rest houses in the first place were not actually the trustees of these endowments; rather, they had seen this trust in the context of an Indian as opposed to a British cosmological perspective, and had thus named as trustees of these rest houses various deities amongst the pantheon of gods existing in the Indian spiritual world. They had chosen to see the 'trust' as a mechanism for honouring a deity or late beloved, rather than as a legal means for determining a person or body responsible for maintaining the 'gift' over the ensuing years. As such, these rest houses often fell into dereliction and became unused for want of a trustee who could be legally required to maintain and police them. Thereby the British notion of an enduring trust was effectively subverted.

This 'deliberate' misreading of the purpose and nature of the trust is not unlike the manner in which Gilbert and Sullivan, in their satire of the corporate form, *Utopia Limited*, have the Utopians 'misinterpreting' the limited liability company as a legal mechanism for avoiding creditors and escaping personal responsibility for economic failure, rather than as an effective form of aggregating capital whilst at the same time providing a structure within which an economically efficient allocation of risk might occur.

Conclusions

In the foregoing we have examined in some detail the ongoing debate as to the manner in which the legacy of particular colonial laws may have affected the commercial prospects of specific states in the past and, in a number of cases, continues to dog their prospective post-colonial economic futures.

The form of corporate law adopted in such states, common or civil law in origin, has been suggested by a number of researchers as a key factor in the later development or lack thereof amongst the many new states that emerged from their colonial pasts after the Second World War.

Indeed, one body of research, that of Professor Emmanuel La Porta, has been particularly influential in regard to the influence such inherited legal systems may, even today, exert on the future economic prospects of a number of states that are now independent. Those states which inherited civil law systems are considered by La Porta and his colleagues as 'less efficient' than former colonial states that had inherited legal systems based on common law. This matters insofar as various forms of international aid and other funding provided to these now post-colonial states has, over the past few decades, been allocated on the basis of perceived differences in the 'efficiency' levels of the differing legal systems inherited by these formerly colonised states, as identified by La Porta, his co-researchers and a number of other researchers working in the field.

La Porta's research paradigm, however, tends to assume hard and fast lines of demarcation as fixed at the time of decolonisation as between these prior 'civil law' and 'common law' colonies. This seemingly ahistorical assumption appears to have recently lost its allure, particularly with a number of researchers working in the field, many of whom have come from very different social science backgrounds than that of La Porta and his colleagues.

A number of these new contributors to the field have pointedly challenged the fixed demarcations between 'common law' and 'civil law' colonies as identified by La Porta and his co-researchers, as well as noting the not infrequent contributions of pre-colonial systems of law to the emerging legal domain of such states after the cessation of colonisation.

In particular, they identify the manner in which the pre-colonial cosmologies in a number of these colonised locales have recently begun to inflect local understandings and the practice of the law into a number of former colonial outposts of such commercial activity. One scholar in this field, in respect of the contribution of existing populations and their cosmologies in reshaping the legal landscapes of these former locales of Empire in the wake of colonisation, has recently noted that:

> Postcolonial theory acknowledges and recovers the ongoing significance of colonized peoples in shaping the epistemologies, philosophies, practices, and shifting identities of dominant and taken-for-granted Western subjects and subjectivities. Postcolonial scholars bring to the foreground the cultural and psychological relations between the former colonized and colonizers, whom, they argue, cannot be understood except in conjunction with each other.

(Darian-Smith 2015: 647–8)

Given that it is now some considerable time since the decolonisation of many of these states it is not surprising that the assumed hard and fast line of demarcation between states as lying on different sides of a fixed boundary separating common and civil law has recently become somewhat blurred. This is particularly so in contexts where aspects of pre-colonial cosmologies and understandings as to the role of law have begun to exert their influence on the ongoing re-shaping of such post-colonial legal systems.

In this vein, writing of the usual, and generally uncontentious characterisation of India as a 'common law' state, Umakanth Varottil of the National University of Singapore has observed the following with regard to the manner in which contemporary Indian company law might best be characterised today:

> Decolonization has had a significant effect in radically altering the course of Indian corporate law . . . Current Indian corporate law not only represents a significant departure from its colonial origins, but the divergence between Indian law and English law as they have developed since independence has been increasing.
>
> . . .
>
> Corporate law in India has evolved in a fundamentally different fashion from that in England despite both countries being part of the 'common law' family and one being a former colony of the other. This raises doubt about the bolder and more free ranging claims made by the proponents of the 'legal origins' thesis as to the differences between the 'common law' systems and the 'civil law' systems. A more nuanced approach ought to be taken while considering the effect of dispersion in the law among systems that share the same legal family . . .
>
> *(Varottil 2015: 71)*

Varottil then continues his analysis by stating that such legal transplants become 'fragile' in the post-colonial environment, as they were initially only transplanted to suit the business interests of the colonising power and their representatives, not those of the colonised. He then concludes by observing that a comparison of the historical colonial experience in the functioning of the transplanted legal system and the more contemporary experience in the post-colonial period suggests 'fragility in the foundations of the transplant' (ibid: 73).

Such analysis is certainly a long way from that offered by La Porta, his collaborators and a number of other scholars who have long been providing advice to international funding agencies as to the efficient deployment of aid and other grant monies to 'developing countries'. Even though Varottil's assessment may seem somewhat speculative, it nonetheless does alert us to the fact that law does continue to 'matter', but not necessarily in the form in which debates respecting 'efficiency' of common law and civil legal systems have framed the debate in recent years.

One suspects that as many evolving legal systems become more hybrid, and thereby not so clearly identifiable as either civil or common law in nature, this area of analysis may become redundant. However, just as surely one might predict that other bases for allocating funds on the basis of 'efficiency' will arise in their place. These allocations will in all probability no longer be made on the basis of the relevant legal system in any given recipient country but, rather, will utilise other markers of economic efficiency, both less contentious in nature and perhaps better proxies for prospective future development than is the contended 'efficiency' or otherwise of a legal system involuntarily inherited by a post-colonial state from its colonial past.

Bibliography

Andersson, David E, Andersson, Martin, Bjuggren, Per-Olof and Högberg, Andreas (2014) 'Corporate Governance Structures, Legal Origin and Firm Performance', No 246, Ratio Working Papers http://www.snee.org/filer/papers/570.pdf (last accessed 26 May 2016).

Beck, Thorsten, (2002) 'Financial Development and International Trade: Is there a link?', *Journal of International Economics*, 57: 107–131.

Beck, Thorsten, Demirgüç-Kunt, Asli and Levine, Ross (2003) 'Law and Finance. Why Does Legal Origin Matter?', *Journal of Comparative Economics*, 31: 653–75.

Beck, Thorsten and Levine, Ross (2005) 'Legal Institutions and Financial Development', chapter 11, *Handbook of New Institutional Economics*.

Beck, Thorsten, Demirgüç-Kunt, Asli, Laeven, Luc and Levine, Ross (2008) 'Finance, Firm Size, and Growth', *Journal of Money, Credit and Banking*, 40: 1379–1405.

Birla, Ritu (2009) *Stages of Capital: Law, Culture, and Market Governance in Late Colonial India*, Duke University Press.

Coffee, John C, Jr. (1999) 'Privatization and Corporate Governance: The Lessons from Securities Market Failure', Center for Law and Economic Studies, Working Paper No 158, Columbia University School of Law.

Cooper, Russell and John, Andrew (2012) *Theory and Applications of Macroeconomics*, Creative Commons http://2012books.lardbucket.org/pdfs/theory-and-applications-of-macroeconomics.pdf (last accessed 26 May 2016).

Darian-Smith, Eve (2015) *International Encyclopedia of the Social and Behavioral Sciences*, 2nd edn, Elsevier.

Garoupa, Nuno and Ligüerre, Carlos Gómez (2011) 'The Syndrome of the Efficiency of the Common Law', *B.U. Int'l L.J.*, 29: 287–94.

Gugler, K., Mueller, D. C. and Yurtoglu, B. B. (2003) 'The Impact of Corporate Governance on Investment Returns in Developed and Developing Countries', *The Economic Journal*, 113 (November), 511–539.

Gugler, K, Mueller, D. C. and Yurtoglu, B.B., (2004) 'Marginal q, Tobin's q, cash flow and investment', *Southern Economic Journal* 70 (3), 512–531.

Klerman, Daniel M, Mahoney, Paul G, Spamann, Holger and Weinstein, Mark I (2011) 'Legal Origin or Colonial History', *J. Legal Analysis*, 3: 379–409.

La Porta, Rafael, Lopez-de-Silanes, Florencio, Shleifer, Andrei and Vishny, Robert (1998), 'Law and Finance', *Journal of Political Economy*, 106(6): 1113–55.

La Porta, Rafael., Lopez-de-Silanes, Florencio, Shleifer, Andrei, Vishny, Robert, (2002). 'Investor Protection and Corporate Valuation', *Journal of Finance*, 57, 1147–1170.

La Porta, Rafael, de Silanes, Florencio Lopez and Schleifer, Andrei (2008) 'The Economic Consequences of Legal Origins', 46(2) *Journal of Economic Literature*, 285–332.

Mahy, Petra and Ramsay, Ian (2014) 'Legal Transplants and Adaptation in a Colonial Setting: Company Law in British Malaya', *Singapore Journal of Legal Studies* (Issue 1, 2014) 123–50.

McQueen, Rob (1995) 'Company Law as Imperialism', 5 *Australian Journal of Corporate Law*, 187–213.

Nunn, Nathan (2009) 'The Importance of History for Economic Development', 1 *Annual Review of Economics*, 65–92.

Schultz, A (2012) 'Comparing British and French Colonial Legacies: A Discontinuity Analysis of Cameroon' (with Alexander Lee), 7 *Quarterly Journal of Political Science*, 356–410.

Sgard, Jérôme (2006) 'Do Legal Origins Matter? The Case of Bankruptcy Laws in Europe (1808–1914)', CEPII and Université de Paris-Dauphine (January 2006) http://basepub.dauphine.fr/bitstream/handle/123456789/13599/2006-05-18_sgard.pdf?sequence=1 (last accessed 26 May 2016).

Siems, Mathias M (2007) 'Legal Origins: Reconciling Law and Finance and Comparative Law', 52(1) *McGill Law Journal*, 55–81.

Varottil, Umakanth (2015) 'The Evolution of Corporate Law in Post-Colonial India: From Transplant to Autochthony', Faculty of Law, National University of Singapore, Working Paper 2015/001 http://law.nus.edu (last accessed 26 May 2016).

Part II
Corporate law principles and governance

5

Independence and diversity in board composition

Sally Wheeler

Introduction

The idea of boards of directors including members that are independent of the corporation on whose board they serve has been a feature of those corporate governance regimes characterised by dispersed ownership for over half a century. Dispersed ownership is taken in this context as a shorthand to mean the UK, the US and other jurisdictions that follow predominantly the Anglo–American model of corporate governance, notwithstanding the very considerable difference of approach within those regimes in respect of shareholder rights (Williams and Conley 2005) and the inaccuracy of assuming that there is not at least a minority of companies controlled by blockholders within those jurisdictions (Holderness 2009).

From the early part of this century, broadly the years 2000–2007, there has been a considerably more heightened focus on the importance of having independent directors without there being any uniformity as to how independence is defined or assessed (Clarke 2007). Requiring independent directors on boards, increasing the number of independent directors and changing the definition of 'independence' to ensure that directors are really 'independent' have all been standard prescriptions to cure perceived systemic inefficiencies or failures in the governance of the corporation (Gutiérrez and Sáez 2013).

Alongside the push for independence, and in some respects as part of the push for independence, there have been demands to redress the gender balance in boardrooms by appointing more women as independent directors. One of the outworkings of the global financial crisis (GFC) has been the superseding of the independence demand, in the UK and at EU level, with what I have termed previously the 'independence plus' drive (Wheeler 2012) to change the character of board composition so that it includes a 'diversity' element, interpreted to be the appointment of more women as independent directors.

The popularity of independent directors as a governance mechanism is clear from its inclusion in the list of the six practices that appear to be common features across the corporate governance codes of 46 countries (Crespí-Cladera and Pascual-Fuster 2014). This chapter looks at the rise of independent directors as a policy tool within national legislatures, supranational regulatory and governance bodies and listing authorities not just in jurisdictions with diversified ownership but also in European jurisdictions where concentrated ownership and, more importantly perhaps, boards of directors charged expressly with representing the interests of stakeholders other than shareholders, are often found.

The chapter looks at some of the variances in role and function ascribed to independent directors across these very different governance regimes. It considers the extent to which the GFC can be seen as a test of the success of directorial independence as a monitoring mechanism. The final part of the chapter examines the 'diversity plus' drive and the different approaches that states and regulators have taken to embedding the desire for diversity of board membership in their corporate governance regimes.

Embedding the concept of independence

(i) Dispersed ownership systems of corporate governance

The US Securities and Exchange Commission (SEC) first introduced the idea of independent directors as a component of corporate governance in the Investment Company Act of 1940, which required 40 per cent of the board to be comprised of independent directors, echoing a New York Stock Exchange (NYSE) listing rule of 1931 that required independent representation on the boards of investment trusts. The SEC definition of independence was initially that directors could not be 'affiliates' of the investment company. Over the years this definition hardened to equate independence with disinterest and finally ended in a legislative requirement in 2001 that in certain classes of investment company a majority of board members be disinterested with access to independent council. Further SEC intervention in 2004 inter alia pushed the required proportion of independent directors to 75 per cent and imposed an annual reporting requirement around board effectiveness and a consideration of whether directors were serving on too many boards (Karmel 2014).

Karmel situates the SEC's concern to introduce independent directors into the governance of investment trusts as being one of wanting to eliminate conflicts of interest and introduce ideas of facilitating greater investor protection. In wider terms, the drive towards independent directors was spurred on by Berle's work on the rise of managerialism and the decline of owner situated power (Berle 1932), thus identifying a managerial agency problem for shareholders (Rashid 2015). As Cheffins has pointed out, confidence in the correctness of Berle's findings has been subject to very little challenge in the last 80 years or so (Cheffins 2009). Gordon in his magisterial survey of the rise of the independent directors (Gordon 2007) broadly supports this view of Berle as the starting point and adds a further dimension to the idea of independent directors as guarantors of shareholder primacy in circumstances where inside directors might find themselves waylaid by concerns for other stakeholders.

In Gordon's view the elevation of publicly available market information over privately held information, achieved as a result of externally imposed disclosure requirements and changes in information capture, storage and retrieval technologies, as the most dependable and accurate source for corporate data gave independent directors advantages over inside directors as strategic advisers to the chief executive officer (CEO). Their advice was based on market observations and was not clouded by concerns about internal firm performance and policy dynamics. After the GFC, however, concerns have been raised about both the quality of information that reaches independent directors as opposed to executive directors and the ability of independent directors to understand that information.

In the US the 1970s saw the emergence of the board of directors as a monitoring device for shareholders (Rock 2013) to combat fraud, self-dealing and incompetence on the part of corporate managers (Eisenberg 1976; Mitchell 2013), rather than as an advisory resource for them. This monitoring occurred through the power to control the selection and remuneration of corporate managers. The desire to monitor managers was fuelled by concerns about corporate under-performance as evidenced by the collapse of 'blue chip' corporations, such as Penn Central, Ampex and Memorex. Boards were seen as passive, too close to management and affecting only a veneer of accountability for decisions.

The SEC under its activist chairman, Harold Williams, pushed for rules that that would require corporations subject to its jurisdiction to identify directors as independent or affiliated (Kripke 1980). Whilst ultimately unsuccessful in achieving this reform, the SEC continued to push for a significant role for independent directors throughout the 1980s, a decade in the history of US corporate law characterised by large-scale merger and takeover activity. The presence of independent directors on the board of target corporations was used as part of a defence strategy, not unsuccessfully (Mitchell 2005), to fend off unwelcome bids as a corrective to the idea that the market for corporate control was an effective response to perceived managerial inefficiency and underperformance supported by board acquiescence or incompetence (Kahan and Rock 2002).

Contemporaneous empirical studies point to the success or perceived success of the board-room presence of independent directors. For example, one reported that boards with a majority of independent directors were more likely to replace a corporation's CEO after a period of poor performance (Weisbach 1988) and another that the announcement of the appointment of an additional independent director increased share price (Rosenstein and Wyatt 1990). These were studies set in a particular economic context – that of frenzied takeover activity. The question of whether examined in a more stable context and over a longer period of time independent directors can be said to enhance corporate performance is looked at in more detail below.

Sustained campaigning by the SEC, changing listing requirements of the NYSE in favour of the adoption of particular board committee structures, in particular an audit committee comprising solely independent directors with access to independent audit advice, pressure from the American Law Institute (ALI) with the inclusion of a significant role for independent directors in its *Principles of Corporate Governance* (Bainbridge 1993) in addition to takeover defence strategies meant that by the end of the 1990s directorial independence was an accepted part of corporate life. Korn/Ferry International's 30th *Annual Board of Directors Study* in 2002 reported an average ratio, which had been constant since 1995, of nine independent directors to two non-independent directors (Korn/Ferry International 2003).

Bainbridge writing in 2012 described directorial independence 'as the corporate governance success story of the decade' (Bainbridge 2012: 78) and he was presumably thinking of the requirement imposed by the NYSE, the National Association of Securities Dealers Automated Quotations (Nasdaq) and the American Stock Exchange (AMEX) in 2007 in the wake of the Enron and World Com collapses and scandals and the reforms of the Sarbanes-Oxley legislation that the majority of directors of listed corporations be independent. This requirement was accompanied by more stringent definitions of 'independence', an expansion of the duties of independence (Rodrigues 2007) and a requirement that audit, compensation and nomination sub-committees of boards of directors be used as part of a corporation's governance structure. The Sarbanes-Oxley legislation is largely silent on the subject of main board membership and independence (Fogel and Geier 2007).

The listing bodies capitalised on the destabilising effect of Enron's collapse in particular to enhance the rules on director independence. However, somewhat ironically, Enron's collapse was mainly thought to be as a result of due diligence failings by gatekeepers in the professions (auditors, lawyers, credit rating agencies and securities analysts) rather than a failure of a sufficient number or capacity of independent directors (Coffee 2006). What an examination of Enron's governance arrangements does demonstrate is the degree of flex that existed previously in the different definitions of independence in relation to board membership employed by listing bodies and jurisdictions such as Delaware (Fairfax 2010). Enron's board comprised only two directors it employed as executives; however, when industry ties and other factors such as charitable donations were factored in, the board only had 43 per cent independent directors as opposed to 72 per cent in its peer corporations (Gillan and Martin 2007).

The picture painted above of directorial independence arriving in US corporate law by a process of osmosis based on listing rules accompanied by a desire from corporate governance professionals to avoid overt, prescriptive legislative intervention on the matter (Gordon 2007) is, in large part, echoed by the UK's journey to the same point on the enhanced role of independent directors. The UK experienced much of the corporate turmoil that the US experienced. In the 1980s there were a considerable number of contested takeover bids and a series of high-profile corporate collapses that were considered to be attributable to poor governance rather than market conditions. The highest profile corporate casualties included the media empire of Robert Maxwell and the bank, BCCI. There was also an outbreak of executive salary increases which were thought to be 'excessive', particularly as they often seemed to concern recently privatised formerly publicly owned utilities and disquiet about audit standards and the reliability of audit (Clarke 2004).

The response was the creation of a high-profile committee set up under the auspices of the accountancy profession, business representative groups and the banking sector, supported by a civil servant seconded from the relevant government department, with a self-designated remit to put forward a code of best practice for corporate governance (Spira and Slinn 2013). The result was the production of a voluntary regulatory code, known as the Cadbury Code, supported by the listing authority; corporations that do not either follow the voluntary code or explain why they are not following it will be denied a listing on the London Stock Exchange (Cadbury 1992). This is the cornerstone of the UK principles-based approach supported by a 'comply or explain' mechanism, as opposed to the US strategy of governance through a rules-based framework.

The concept of outside directorship was already part of UK corporate culture. Paragraph 4.12 of the Cadbury Code stressed the importance of independence of judgment as a characteristic of outside directors and the Principles themselves (2.2) suggested that a majority of non-executive directors 'should be independent of management and free from any business or other relationship which could . . . interfere with the exercise of their independent judgment apart from . . . their shareholding'. A majority of independent outside directors means, in the context of the Cadbury Code, at least two directors, as the recommendation is that to give effect to all the duties laid out in the code a corporation requires at least three outside directors.

This initial statement of best practice has been augmented by a succession of reports, recommendations and statements, each constructed using the same industry-based approach, seeking to improve the standards of corporate governance generally. The Higgs Report (Higgs 2003), commissioned by the UK's Department of Trade and Industry (DTI, as it then was), was the last in this series before the GFC and the changes to UK corporate governance principles that resulted from it and the Smith Report (Smith 2003) on audit reform should be seen as the UK governmental level response to the Sarbanes-Oxley legislation and the changed listing requirements across the US exchanges. The governance structure that was laid out for corporations listed in London from 2003 onwards, on a 'comply or explain' basis, was one which inter alia required half the board of directors to be independent, the chair of the board to be independent on appointment and independent directors to take on enhanced roles within the board committee structure around audit and nomination of directors.

A new role was created of 'senior' independent director, who was to facilitate communications between shareholders and the board, thus emphasising the role of independent directors in dealing with the agency problem. A more developed test for independence based around describing instances where independence was unlikely to be found (e.g. family ties, relevant cross-directorships or less than five years' post-employment) was set out, with the onus on the board to identify which of its directors it considered to be independent. Defining independence using a structural methodology is supposed, then, to lead to the exercise of the behavioural trait of 'dispassionate objectivity'.

In Australia the journey to directorial independence as the preferred board structure has been very similar; there have been concerns about corporate under-performance (Hilmer Report 1993, Ramsey and Hoad 1997) and more latterly a response to Sarbanes-Oxley, sparked by the collapses in Australia of One Tel and HIH Insurance (Clarke 2011; Monem 2011). The response to the Sarbanes-Oxley legislation was the release in 2003 by the newly formed Corporate Governance Council, underwritten, as it were, by the Australian Stock Exchange, of the Principles of Good Corporate Governance and Best Practice (Principles) (Matolcsy and others 2011). Those principles were broadly similar to those created in the UK on the role of independent directors; for example, a definition of independence supported by a declaration of independence in the Annual Report.

Once again, the test of independence is a structural one in relation to each particular corporation where office is held. Behavioural determinants, network independence and social ties between directors are not considered to be important. This is not surprising, given the focus of agency theory on shareholder protection and monitoring (Zattoni and Cuomo 2010) and the dominance, certainly in the years preceding the GFC, of the agency paradigm of corporate governance (Shapiro 2005).

The result of defining independence in this way meant that individuals who were executive directors of one listed company were often non-executive directors of another company. For example, Australia's largest corporations appointed few individuals without an established boardroom profile in the period 2004–2007 (Kang and others 2007; Chen 2009). A similar pattern for that time period can be found in the UK; 60 per cent of Financial Times Stock Exchange (FTSE) 100 companies had a non-executive director who was an executive director at another FTSE 100 and in excess of 40 FTSE 100 companies shared a non-executive director with another listed company (Froud and others 2008). The perceived sameness and staleness of boardroom participants, one of the drivers for boardroom diversity or independence after the GFC, became the norm in both the UK and Australia.

(ii) Concentrated ownership systems of corporate governance

La Porta and others (1999) identified the depth of concentrated ownership in corporate governance systems outside the large common law jurisdictions. In numerical terms, if not in asset value terms, it is the most common form of ownership in the corporate world. This generalisation masks some distinct jurisdictional differences; in some instances, for example China, the state is the controlling shareholder. In India, ownership is structured through family business groups and in other jurisdictions the degree of control held by the blockholders varies considerably. Germany and Italy are characterised by a significantly higher level of ownership concentration than the Netherlands, for example (Nowack 2013).

The agency problem is constructed rather differently in situations of concentrated ownership. Here the shareholders are not collectively looking for the cheapest and most effective way of ensuring that management pursue their interests. Typically in these systems the power to appoint and dismiss directors rests with the controlling shareholder. Additionally, there may be a two-tier board structure, either as a compulsory feature of corporate governance (for example Germany and China) or as an optional feature (France, the Netherlands and Norway for example) and representatives of stakeholders other than shareholders such as employees on those boards as non-executive appointments (Collier and Zaman 2005).

The monitoring issue in concentrated ownership systems arises between the controlling shareholder and the minority shareholders. Given the context of many concentrated ownership regimes, independent directors, on the face of it, look to be less useful as an intervention or protection device for minority shareholders than a well developed system for minority challenge around remuneration and other potential tunnelling activities and a robust structure for disclosure of third party related transactions in particular. There is an opportunity to view the drive towards requiring independent directors across different regimes of corporate law as one of the indicators in the much broader debate about the convergence of corporate law (Davies and Hopt 2013).

Nevertheless, independent directors have become a feature of the boards of listed companies in the major European jurisdictions. Independent directors are to be found in 35–40 per cent of board seats, with Germany as an outlier on 5 per cent (Cromme 2005). Given Germany's compulsory two-tier board structure and position on labour representation, this is not surprising (Ferreira and Kirchmaier 2013). The concept of independent directors is pushed into the corporate governance systems of the European jurisdictions by two interventions of the European Commission. The first, an Action Plan released in 2003, tied the reform of European corporate governance systems to the need to demonstrate parity of robustness with the US corporate governance system after the reforms of Sarbanes-Oxley. There was a need to bolster shareholder and investor confidence and ensure that corporate mobility could occur.

The Action Plan rejected the need for an EU level code in favour of supporting the subsidiarity of national approaches but did suggest that non-executive or supervisory directors, the majority of whom were to be independent, should be involved in remuneration, audit and nomination processes through a committee structure. The emphasis was placed on the need for audit committees and the role of independent directors within it. This was to be done on a 'comply or *explain* basis', with the EU Commission setting out in a later Recommendation the definition of independence to be applied and the minimum standards required for the committees (EU Commission 2003).

A later departure from the 'comply or explain' approach was the requirement of a 2006 Directive that there be at least one independent member on the audit committee (EU 2006). Audit is seen as a key area for accessing and controlling information about corporate performance and also corporate compliance with regulatory demands. Whatever the ownership structure of a corporation is, the audit committee can only be used in this way if independent directors are sufficiently knowledgeable to be able to understand and act upon information or request further information. The competence of those appointed as independent directors does not become an issue for comment until after the GFC.

The Recommendation appeared in 2005 (EU 2005) and suggested that there should be 'a sufficient number' of independent non-executive or supervisory directors on the board to ensure that conflicts of interest could be dealt with. It defined independence as being 'the absence of any material conflict of interest' and a director as 'independent' if there was freedom from any business, family or other relationship, with the company, its controlling shareholder or management. It also included an Annex in which it set out a number of possible threats to independence. Much of this material has been incorporated into national codes as the definitional context for independence (Davies and Hopt 2013) with the final decision on independence being made by the individual board. There are considerable national differences on the definition of independence that is employed (Aguilera and Cuervo-Cazurra 2009).

There are also differences around how independence from the controlling shareholder is dealt with (Ferrarini and Filippelli 2015). The Recommendation indicated that a representative of the controlling shareholder could not be considered to be independent. In Germany, a supervisory board member is considered as independent if he or she has no business or personal relationship with the corporation or its management board that causes a conflict of interest. In France, the Corporate Governance Code allows a representative of the major shareholder to be considered as independent if that shareholder does not take part in the control of the corporation (Menjucq 2005). To these national deviations from the Recommendation standard must be added the 'comply or explain' mechanism, which might allow for considerable inroads to be made into national definitions of independence (Pietrancosta, Dubois and Garçon 2013).

It is worth noting that the Organisation for Economic Co-operation and Development (OECD), in a similar timeframe to the EU and with similar underlying concerns about investor confidence and competitiveness endorsed, in its *Principles of Corporate Governance*, the importance of maintaining a plurality of approaches to corporate governance frameworks to accommodate different institutional environments, whilst encouraging the recognition of 'common elements' underlying 'good corporate governance' (OECD 2004b: 40–51). One of these common elements was the need for a sufficient number of directors to be independent of management to allow for the exercise of 'objective independent judgement' by the board (OECD 2004b: 63–65). The commitment of the OECD to the plurality of corporate governance forms is clear from its identification of the need for independent directors not only in the dispersed and concentrated shareholder models but also where there is the possibility of influence being exercised by a dominant creditor.

Independent directors and corporate performance

The idea of independent directors as the monitors of corporate managers on behalf of shareholders and the repeated enhancement of this model as a response to corporate failures (Hill 2005) suggests that the model delivers improved corporate performance and the end of corporate failures. However, it has been tested in numerous different ways: examining the return on assets, the return on equity, the return to shareholders and the return per share are just some of the operationalisations that have been used but a clear picture of success has not emerged. Rather, the picture is equivocal to say the least. Dalton and others (1998) use meta-analysis of 54 studies of board composition and 31 studies of board leadership structure to conclude that there is little evidence of a link between a corporation's governance structure and its financial performance. A later review by Bhagat and others (Bhagat, Bolton and Romano 2008) asserts that there is no relationship between director independence and firm performance.

However, alongside these studies there are some that offer a more positive account of the success of directorial independence. Dahya and others (2008) examined data from

22 countries and found that in jurisdictions where there was a relatively low level of shareholder protection there was a positive correlation between corporate value and the presence of independent directors. Krivogorsky (2006) makes a similar finding in relation to European listed firms using profitability ratios. For all that this suggests a positive correlation between firm performance and the presence of independent directors in systems of concentrated ownership, a study on Portuguese listed corporations suggested that independent directors were ineffective at controlling executive remuneration (Fernandes 2008). Dalton, the author of a number of studies on the relationship between directorial independence and firm performance, suggests that the inability to provide a definitive answer on whether there is a negative or a positive correlation relates to the absence of multilevel research, which connects together and evaluates a broader range of variables across the corporation (Dalton and Dalton 2011).

The scale of the failure of financial firms in the GFC presents a considerable challenge to the idea of independent directors as successful monitors of firm performance. Financial firms with a greater number of independent directors on their board performed more poorly in the crisis than those with more executive directors (Becht and others 2011; Hsu and Wu 2014) in the UK, the US and parts of the EU but not in Canada or India (Ferreira and others 2010).

Added to the results of the empirical studies referred to above it suggests that the model has failed to deliver the control for shareholders that it was thought it would. This might be for a variety of reasons. The simplest explanation is that the governance requirements of financial firms are intrinsically different from other commercial corporations. The risk profile of banks changes very quickly and financial trading is complex and not easily understood. Banks are highly leveraged and consequently a more accurate model of governance might be one that reflects their relationship to creditors. There is also the position of depositors whose protection with deposit insurance weakens their need for monitors and introduces into bank governance the taxpayer who underwrites failure because of the systemic importance of finance corporations to the wider economy (Laeven 2013).

It may be that board members can never be truly independent when independence is assessed solely by means of a director's relationship with the corporation to the exclusion of prohibiting social network ties. If social ties exist between independent directors and others in the corporate management structure they are likely to create a tension with the demands of active monitoring (Beecher-Monas 2007). Independent directors may be appointed because they are known, through social network ties, to be sympathetic to management (Cohen, Frazzini and Malloy 2012). Social connections have also been linked to a lower level of corporate reporting and a higher level of executive compensation (Tung 2011). A director may be free of social ties in addition to satisfying the relevant structural test on appointment only for his or her independence to melt away over the period of the appointment as working relationships evolve and develop (Bhagat and Black 1999; Dalton and others 2007).

Independent directors are dependent on managers for the information they require to provide either a monitoring or an advisory function (Brown 2015). The independent director model requires this information to be digested and used and, whilst independent directors, despite the absence of a requirement for evidenced knowledge or experience, are likely to have a strong business background, they lack knowledge about the particular corporation on whose board they sit (Fairfax 2010; Karmel 2014). They may also lack industry knowledge and expertise (Lorsch 2011). These deficits are unlikely to encourage them to exercise their monitoring function and question corporate management closely (Sharpe 2011).

Questions about the competence of independent directors are at the forefront of debates about corporate governance reform following the GFC (Kirkpatrick 2009). A caveat to this discussion is that most of the suggested reforms relate to the governance of financial firms and, as highlighted above, there are arguments that the governance of those firms raises different issues that any agency model that seeks to mediate between manager and shareholder conflicts through a monitoring function will struggle to address.

In the UK the Walker Review (Walker 2009) suggested that effective challenge in financial firms required non-executive directors with 'financial industry capability', availability and 'independence of mind' at the expense of 'formal independence' if this was necessary to get the right mix of skills. The European Commission, looking back in the wake of the GFC at the governance of financial firms, criticised board level governance in terms of the failure to recognise and control risk appropriately, the failure to exercise an effective challenge function to senior management and, consequent upon this, the lack of diversity in board membership (EU Commission 2010a). In its 2011 Green Paper the Commission posed a number of questions about board structures, including floating the idea of restricting the number of non-executive directorships that could be held to address the problem of the time required to act effectively as a director.

However, the 2012 Action Plan does not engage explicitly with the question of independence. Instead, the need for improved transparency and shareholder engagement is stressed. The key point in relation to board composition was the need for corporations to strive for greater diversity of membership. Only in asserting the importance of implementing national codes of corporate governance, which contain requirements for independent directors, could the Commission be seen to be advancing its earlier concern with structural independence (EU Commission 2011a, 2012a).

The Commission has not been the only actor to suggest that enhanced shareholder governance through closer direct shareholder engagement was a stronger policy imperative after the GFC than the reinforcement of directorial independence. In the UK the Financial Reporting Council published the Stewardship Code in 2010. Whilst the code was addressed primarily not to institutional investors themselves but to those who manage their share-based assets, its aim was to create a dialogue around active investment and in particular the use of proxy voting to direct and to effect comment on corporate policy (Roach 2011). Legislative reform in the UK, by means of a 2013 amendment to the Companies Act 2006 gives shareholders a binding vote on the appropriateness of a corporation's proposed remuneration policy. It is one of only three states to do this and the largest economy by some distance (Chui 2015).

Given that the setting and monitoring of executive remuneration was previously an area for independent directors to assert their authority, this might suggest that the reliance on independent directors as monitors was at least being tempered, if not replaced. It is important, however, to qualify this observation with two caveats: the UK was the first jurisdiction to introduce an advisory shareholder vote on remuneration in 2002 and the UK is considered, by some commentators, to offer a corporate governance regime that is somewhat context specific in its orientation towards shareholder rights (Hopt 2011). The introduction of a binding vote on remuneration might be the reinvigoration of earlier policy choices rather than signalling a loss of faith in the independent director model.

The US position on independent directors after the GFC provides something of a contrast to that of the UK. The legislative response to the GFC, the Dodd-Frank legislation, gave an increased role to independent directors, despite sustained media criticism of board performance, mandating that all corporations should have a risk committee comprised only of independent directors and that compensation committee members should fulfil an enhanced standard of independence (Karmel 2014; Ringe 2013). The importance of expertise was also emphasised by the requirement that every corporation should have a risk committee with an expert in risk appointed to it.

Diversity as an augmentation to independence

Whilst the Walker Review in the UK emphasised the importance of capturing expertise on the board, even if this sacrificed independence, the view taken by politicians, regulators and financial journalists (Tomasic 2008) was that directorial independence needed to be steered in a different direction: that of diversity of membership. This can be seen as an acknowledgement that structural tests of independence, no matter how detailed and formidable, had produced boards whose members were too similar or perhaps too familiar with each other, if not exactly tied by common prior experiences in educational and professional terms. Diversity of board membership was not an entirely new idea in the UK. It had been highlighted as a concern in the Higgs Report (Higgs 2003) and on the foot of that a further report – the Tyson Report – was set up in the same year to examine ways in which the recruitment base for non-executive directors could be broadened. The latter, in a manner not dissimilar to that of the Walker Review stressed the importance of diversity in appointments for locating different skill sets and attracting them to the board.

This push for diversity in board appointments occurred contemporaneously with a lobby for gender diversity in both business leadership (Brown 2015) and political life (Squires 2009). The EU, which had mentioned diversity as one criterion for selection as a director in its 2011 Green Paper on Corporate Governance (EU Commission 2011), used its equality strategy to focus on a drive to obtain a higher percentage of women participating in business life (EU Commission 2010b). It followed this up with a proposal in 2012 for boards of directors across the EU to include 40 per cent of the unrepresented gender, which will almost invariably be female (EU Commission 2012b; Stein and Van der Vlies 2014).

Whilst some EU Member States such as Norway and Spain had previously legislated in 2003 and 2007 respectively to introduce quota mechanisms to promote gender diversity, others acted on the threat of a potential quota imposition from the EU with their own arrangements to support diversity-based appointments, some through legislative intervention requiring inclusion, for example France and Italy, and others, such as the UK, through code amendment and 'comply or explain' mechanisms to support voluntary initiatives (Sweigart 2012; Hickman 2014). Each jurisdiction has its own contextual challenges, such as a large number of family controlled corporations, other forms of concentrated ownership or overseas registered corporations where less diversity pressure exists in their domestic exchanges (Vinnicombe and others 2008). Nevertheless positive progress on inclusion can be reported across the EU Member States.

The US, which does not have any measures in place to support diversity, although it began the push for female board membership much earlier than the EU and its Member States, in the 1990s through organisations such as Catalyst (Mattis 2000) reports a lower overall percentage of board seats held by women and a slower rate of growth in appointments (Hodigere and Bilimoria 2015).

The evidence of a positive link between female board appointments and firm financial performance is as unconvincing (Choudhury 2014) as is the link between independent directors and firm financial performance, without the disaggregation of gender (McCann and Wheeler 2011). Many of the studies that are available draw on US data because diversity has been an issue there for considerably longer. Using accounting data, Shrader and others (1997) find a negative impact and Francoeur and others (2008) are equivocal and, despite using both US and Canadian data over a four year period, these data point to the difficulty caused for extracting reliable data by the very low number of female directors. Campbell and Minguez-Vera (Campbell and Minguez-Vera 2008) uses Spanish data, which draws upon an even smaller sample to report that corporate performance is at worst not impaired.

Moving away from financial performance, Brammer and others (Brammer 2009) suggested a tentative link between numbers of female directors and particular industry sectors such as retail, on the basis that female directors attracted consumers to the corporation's products and female staff to the workplace. This is hardly an endorsement of the business case to appoint more women to the boardroom.

Rather than being supported by an economic or social justice argument it appears diversity-based appointments are considered attractive because the members of that group are unlikely to have been tainted by failure in the GFC. They are seen as a way around perceived 'psychological limitations' of the group dynamic of boardroom deliberations (O'Connor 2003) and inherent biases (Sharpe 2011), despite the lack of any real evidence from either the psychology literature or any of the extant studies on boardroom behaviours that their introduction can achieve the desired change of increased challenge and object-ivity (Wheeler 2012). Female appointments are being used as structural solution to the problem of seeing independence as a structural issue. There seems to be confusion between independent ideas and thinking and independence as some sort of identity (Beecher-Monas 2007).

Conclusion

Directorial independence is a tool of agency theory that has found its way from the Anglo–American paradigm of corporate governance to the corporate governance systems of concentrated ownership corporations, where it has a less obvious role. This perhaps tells us something about the perceived requirements of global investment capital in terms of familiar governance structures and assurances of credible domestic governance arrangements. Independence has been used as a policy response to corporate failure in several waves of corporate failure crises on both sides of the Atlantic Ocean, without ever demonstrating that it has been or can be successful. It has been rebuilt with enhanced structural definitions on each occasion, which consistently fail to deal with issues such as social ties and net-work power (Le Mire and Gilligan 2013). It is no longer clear just what directors should be independent of and adding diversity into this picture only renders this even more opaque.

Bibliography

Books and articles

R Aguilera and A Cuervo-Cazurra (2009) 'Codes of Good Governance' *Corp Gov* 17: 376–87.
S Bainbridge (1993) 'Independent Directors and the ALI Corporate Governance Project' *George Washington L R* 61: 1034–83.
S Bainbridge (2012) *Corporate Governance after the Financial Crisis* Oxford, OUP.
M Becht, P Bolton and A Röell (2011) 'Why Bank Governance is Different' *Oxford Review of Econ Pol* 27: 437–63.

E Beecher-Monas (2007) 'Marrying Diversity and Independence in the Boardroom: Just How Far Have You Come, Baby?' *Oregon Law R* 86: 373–412.

A Berle Jr (1932) 'For Whom Corporate Managers Are Trustees: A Note' *Harv L R* 45: 1365–72.

S Bhagat and B Black (1999) 'The Uncertain Relationship Between Board Composition and Firm Performance' *Business Lawyer* 54: 921–63.

S Bhagat, B Bolton and R Romano (2008) 'The Promise and Perils of Corporate Governance Indices' *Col L R* 108: 1803–882.

S Brammer, A Millington and S Pavelin (2009) 'Corporate Reputation and Women on the Board' *Brit J of Man* 20: 17–29.

J Brown (2015) 'The Demythification of the Board of Directors' *American Business Law Journal* 52: 131–200.

K Campbell and A Mínguez-Vera (2008) 'Gender Diversity in the Boardroom and Firm Financial Performance' *J Bus Eth* 83: 433–51.

B Cheffins (2009) 'Is Berle and Means Really a Myth' *Business History Review* 83: 443–74.

R Chen et al 'The Link Between Board Composition and Corporate Diversification in Australian Corporations' (2009) 17 *Corp Gov* 208–223.

B Choudhury (2014) 'New Rationales for Women on Boards' *Oxford Journal of Legal Studies* 34: 511–42.

I Chui (2015) 'Learning from the UK in the Proposed Shareholder Rights Directive 2014? European Corporate Governance Regulation from a UK Perspective' *Journal of Comparative Jurisprudence* 114: 121–57.

J Coffee, *Gatekeepers: The Role of the Professions and Corporate Governance* OUP Oxford 2006.

D Clarke (2007) 'Three Concepts of the Independent Director' *Del J Corp Law* 32: 73–111.

T Clarke (2004) 'Cycles of Crisis and Regulation: The Enduring Agency and Stewardship Problems of Corporate Governance' *Corporate Governance: An International Review* 12: 153–61.

T Clarke (2011) 'Corporate Governance and Corporate Reputation: A Disaster Story' in R Burke and others (eds) *Corporate Reputation* Farnham, Gower 267–80.

L Cohen, A Frazzini and C Malloy (2012) 'Hiring Cheerleaders: Board Appointments of "Independent" Directors' *Management Science* 58: 1039–58.

P Collier and M Zaman (2005) 'Convergence in European Corporate Governance: The Audit Committee Concept' *Corporate Governance* 13: 753–68.

R Crespí-Cladera and B Pascual-Fuster (2014) 'Does the Independence of Independent Directors Matter?' *J of Corp Fin* 28: 116–34.

G Cromme (2005) 'Corporate Governance in Germany and the German Corporate Governance Code' *Corporate Governance* 13: 362–67.

J Dahya, O Dimitrov and J McConnell (2008) 'Dominant Shareholders, Corporate Boards and Corporate Value: A Cross-country Analysis' *Journal of Financial Economics* 87: 73–100.

D Dalton, C Daily, A Ellstrand, and J Johnson (1998) 'Board Composition, Leadership Structure, and Financial Performance: Meta-analytic Reviews and Research Agenda' *Strategic Management Journal* 19: 269–90.

D Dalton, M Hilt, S Certo, C Dalton (2007) 'The Fundamental Agency Problem and its Mitigation' *Acad Man Annals* 1: 1–64.

D Dalton and C Dalton (2011) 'Integration of Micro and Macro Studies in Governance Research: CEO Duality, Board Composition, and Financial Performance' *J of Man* 37: 404–11.

P Davies and K Hopt (2013) 'Corporate Boards in Europe – Accountability and Convergence' *Am J of Comparative Law* 61: 301–75.

M Eisenberg (1976) *The Structure of the Corporation* Boston, Little Brown and Co.

L Fairfax (2010) 'The Uneasy Case for the Inside Director' *Iowa L R* 96: 127–93.

N Fernandes (2008) 'EC: Board Compensation and Firm Performance: The Role of "Independent" Board Members' *J of Multinational Fin Man* 18: 30–44.

G Ferrarini and Filippelli (2015) 'Independent Directors and Controlling Shareholders Around the World' in J Hill and R Thomas (eds) *Research Handbook on Shareholder Power* Edward Elgar: Cheltenham 269–93.

D Ferreira, T Kirchmaier, and D Metzger (2010) 'Boards of Banks' *ECGI—Finance Working Paper* No 289/2010 http://papers.ssrn.com/sol3/Papers.cfm?abstract_id=1620551 (last accessed 10 June 2016).

D Ferreira and T Kirchmaier (2013) 'Corporate Boards in Europe: Size, Independence and Gender Diversity' in M Belcredi and G Ferrarini (eds) *Boards and Shareholders in European Listed Companies* Cambridge, CUP 191–224.

E Fogel and A Geier (2007) 'Strangers in the House: Rethinking Sarbanes-Oxley and the Independent Board of Directors' *Delaware J of Corporate Law* 32: 33–72.

J Froud, A Leaver, K Williams, G Tampublon (2008) 'Everything for Sale: How Non-executive Directors Make a Difference' in M Savage and K Williams (eds) *Remembering Elites* Oxford Blackwell 162–86.

C Francoeur, R Labelle and B Sinclair-Desgagné (2008) 'Gender Diversity in Corporate Governance and Top Management' *Journal of Business Ethics* 81: 83–95.

S Gillan and J Martin "Corporate Governance Post-Enron: Effective Reforms or Closing the Stable Door" (2007) *Journal of Corporate Finance* 13.5, 929–958.

J Gordon (2007) 'The Rise of Independent Directors in the United States: of Shareholder Value and Stock Market Prices' *Stanford Law Review* 59: 1465–568.

M Gutiérrez and M Sáez (2013) 'Deconstructing Independent Directors' *J Corp L St* 13: 63–94.

E Hickman (2014) 'Boardroom Gender Diversity: A Behavioural Economics Analysis' *J Corp L S* 14: 385–418.

J Hill (2005) 'Regulatory Responses to Global Corporate Scandals' *Wis Int LJ* 23: 367–416.

R Hodigere and D Bilimoria (2015) 'Human Capital and Professional Network Effects on Women's Odds of Corporate Board Directorships' *Gender in Management* 30: 523–50.

C Holderness (2009) 'The Myth of Diffuse Ownership in the United States' *Review of Financial Studies* 22: 1377–408.

K Hopt (2011) 'Comparative Corporate Governance: The State of the Art and International Regulation' *Am J of Comp Law* 59: 1–73.

H Hsu and C Wu (2014) 'Board Composition, Grey Directors and Corporate Failure in the UK' *Brit Acc Rev* 46: 215–27.

M Kahan and E Rock (2002) 'How I Learned to Stop Worrying and Love the Pill: Adaptive Responses to Takeover Law' *U Chi L R* 69: 871–915.

H Kang et al 'Corporate Governance and Board Composition: Diversity and Independence of Australian Boards' (2007) 15 *Corp Gov* 194–207.

R Karmel (2014) 'Is the Independent Director Model Broken' *Seattle L R* 37: 775–811.

G Kirkpatrick (2009) 'The Corporate Governance Lessons from the Financial Crisis' *Financial Market Trends* 1: 61–87.

H Kripke (1980) 'The SEC, Corporate Governance, and the Real Issues' *The Business Lawyer* 173–206.

V Krivogorsky (2006) 'Ownership, Board Structure, and Performance in Continental Europe' *Int J Acc* 41: 176–96.

R La Porta, F Lopez-De-Silanes and A Schleifer (1999) 'Corporate Ownership Around the World' *J of Finance* 54: 471–517.

L Laeven (2013) 'Corporate Governance: What's Special About Banks?' *Annual Review of Financial Economics* 5: 63–92.

S Le Mire and G Gilligan (2013) 'Independence and Independent Company Directors' *J Corp L S* 13: 443–75.

J Lorsch (2011) 'Board Challenges 2009' in W Sun, J Stewart and D Pollard (eds) *Corporate Governance and the Global Financial Crisis* Cambridge, CUP 165–87.

Z Matolcsy and others (2011) 'The Impact of Quasi-Regulatory Reforms on Boards and their Committees During the Period 2001–2007' *Aus Acc Rev* 21: 352–64.

M Mattis (2000) 'Women Corporate Directors in the United States' in R Burke and M Mattis (eds) *Women on Corporate Boards of Directors* Kluwer, Dordrecht 43–56.

M McCann and S Wheeler (2011) 'Gender Diversity in the FTSE 100: The Business Case Claim Explored' *J L S* 38: 542–74.

M Menjucq (2005) 'Corporate Governance Issues in France' *Eu Bus L Rev* 16: 1003–1016.

L Mitchell (2005) 'Structural Holes, CEOs, and Informational Monopolies: The Missing Link in Corporate Governance' *Brook L R* 70: 1313–69.

L Mitchell (2013) 'The Trouble with Boards' in F Scott Kieff and T Paredes (eds) *Perspectives on Corporate Governance* Cambridge, CUP pp17–61.

R Monem (2011) 'The One.Tel Collapse: Lessons for Corporate Governance' *Aus Acc Rev* 21: 340–51.

R Nowack (2013) 'Corporate Boards in the Netherlands' in P Davies, K Hopt, R Nowak and G von Solinge (eds) *Corporate Boards in Law and Practice*, Oxford: Oxford University Press 429–510.

M O'Connor (2003) 'The Enron Board: The Perils of Groupthink' *U Cin L R* 71: 1233–320.

A Pietrancosta, P Dubois and R Garçon, (2013) 'Corporate boards in France' P Davies, K Hopt, R Nowak and G von Solinge (eds) *Corporate Boards in Law and Practice*, Oxford, Oxford University Press 175–251.

I Ramsey and R Hoad (1997) 'Disclosure of Corporate Governance Practices by Australian Companies' *Company and Securities Law Journal* 15: 454–70.

A Rashid (2015) 'Revisiting Agency Theory: Evidence of Board Independence and Agency Cost from Bangladesh' *Journal of Bus Eth* 130: 181–98.

W-G Ringe (2013) 'Independent Directors: After the Crisis' *Euro Bus Org L R* 14: 401–24.

L Roach (2011) 'The UK Stewardship Code' *J Corp L S* 11: 463–93.

E Rock (2013) 'Adapting to the New Shareholder-Centric Reality' *U Pa L Rev* 161: 1907–988.

U Rodrigues (2007) 'The Fetishization of Independence' *J Corp Law* 33: 447–95.

S Rosenstein and S Wyatt (1990) 'Outside Directors, Board Independence, and Shareholder Wealth' *Journal of Financial Economics* 26: 175–92.

S Shapiro (2005) 'Agency Theory' in K Cook and D Massey (eds.) *Annual Review of Sociology* 31: 263–84.

N Sharpe (2011) 'The Cosmetic Independence of Corporate Boards' *Seattle Univ L R* 1435–56.

N Sharpe (2013) 'Informational Autonomy in the Boardroom' *U Ill L R* 1089–130.

C Shrader, V Blackburn and P Iles (1997) 'Women in Management and Firm Financial Performance: An Exploratory Study' *J of Managerial Issues* 9: 355–72.

L Spira and J Slinn (2013) *The Cadbury Committee* Oxford, OUP.

J Squires (2009) 'Intersecting Inequalities: Britain's Equality Review' *International Feminist Journal of Politics* 11: 496–512.

A Stein and R Van der Vlies (2014) 'The Commission Proposal for Improving Gender Balance in Company Boards' in M De Vos and P Culliford (eds) *Gender Quotas for Company Boards* Cambridge: Intersentia 57–81.

A Sweigart (2012) 'Women on Board for Change: The Norway Model of Boardroom Quotas As a Tool For Progress in the United States and Canada' *Northwestern J of International Law and Business* 32: 81A–105A.

R Tomasic (2008) 'Corporate Rescue, Governance and Risk Taking in Northern Rock: Part 2' *Co Lawyer* 29: 330–37.

F Tung (2011) 'The Puzzle of Independent Directors: New Learning' *Boston University Law Review* 91: 1175–90.

S Vinnicombe, V Singh, R Burke, D Bilimoria and M Huse (2008) *Women on Corporate Boards of Directors: International Research and Practice*, Cheltenham: Edward Elgar.

M Weisbach (1988) 'Outside Directors and CEO Turnover' *Journal of Financial Economics* 20: 431–60.

S Wheeler (2012) 'Independent Directors and Corporate Governance' *Aus J Corp Law* 27: 168–87.

C Williams and J Conley (2005) 'An Emerging Third Way – The Erosion of the Anglo–American Shareholder Value Construct' *Cornell Int L J* 38: 493–551.

A Zattoni and F Cuomo 'How Independent, Competent and Incentivized Should Non-executive Directors Be? An Empirical Investigation of Good Governance Codes' (2010) 21 *British Journal of Management Man* 63–79.

Reports

Cadbury Report (1992) *The Financial Aspects of Corporate Governance* http://www.ecgi.org/codes/documents/cadbury.pdf (last accessed 27 May 2016).

EU Commission (2003) *Modernising Company Law and Enhancing Corporate Governance in the European Union — A Plan to Move Forward* COM(2003) 284 final.

EU Commission (2005) Recommendation of 15 February 2005 on the role of non-executive or supervisory directors of listed companies and on the committees of the (supervisory) board, OJ L52/51 of 2 February 2005

EU Commission (2006) Directive 2006/43/EC on Statutory Audits, 17 May 2006, L 157/87.

EU Commission (2010a) *Green Paper: Corporate Governance in Financial Institutions and Remuneration Policies* COM(2010) 284.

EU Commission (2010b) *Strategy for equality between women and men 2010–2015*, COM(2010) 491 final.

EU Commission, (2011a) *Green Paper: The EU Corporate Governance Framework* COM (2011) 164.

EU Commission, (2012a) *Action Plan: European Company Law and Corporate Governance*, COM(2012) 740 final (12 December 2012).

EU Commission, (2012b) *Proposal for a Directive on improving the gender balance among non-executive directors of companies listed on stock exchanges* COM(2012) 614 final.

Higgs Report (2003) *Review of the Role and Effectiveness of Non-Executive Directors* http://www.ecgi.org/codes/documents/higgsreport.pdf (last accessed 27 May 2016).

Hilmer Report (1993) *Strictly Boardroom: Improving Governance to Enhance Company Performance* Australian Print Group, Melbourne.

Korn Ferry Institute (2003) *30th Annual Board of Directors Study* http://www.kornferry.com/institute/166-30th-annual-board-of-directors-study (last accessed 27 May 2016).

OECD (2004a) *Corporate Governance: A Survey of OECD Countries* OECD Publications Service Paris.

OECD (2004b) *Principles of Good Governance* OECD Publications Service Paris.

Smith (2003) *Audit Committees Combined Code Guidance* http://www.ecgi.org/codes/documents/ac_report.pdf (last accessed 27 May 2016).

Tyson Report (2003) *The Tyson Report on the Recruitment and Development of Non-Executive Directors* http://www.london.edu/facultyandresearch/research/docs/TysonReport.pdf (last accessed 27 May 2016).

D Walker (2009), A Review of Corporate Governance in UK Banks and Other Financial Industry Entities: Final Recommendations http://webarchive.nationalarchives.gov.uk/+/http:/www.hm-treasury.gov.uk/d/walker_review_261109.pdf (last accessed 27 May 2016).

6

The fiduciary duties of institutional investors

Folarin Akinbami[1]

1 Introduction

In July 2012, Professor Kay published his final report entitled 'UK Equity Markets and Long-term Decision-making' (the Kay Review), a report that had been commissioned by the UK's Department for Business, Innovation and Skills (BIS). The Kay Review was tasked with examining the mechanisms of corporate control and accountability provided by UK equity markets and their impact on the long-term competitive performance of UK businesses (BIS 2011). This was borne out of the UK Government's concern that investors' behaviour has become misaligned with long-term interest in corporate performance, as well as the fragmentation of UK investment markets and the proliferation of intermediaries within those markets.

The Kay Review's overall conclusion was that short-termism is a problem in UK equity markets and the causes of short-termism are the decline in trust throughout the equity investment chain and the misalignment of incentives throughout the equity investment chain (Kay Review 2012: 9). The review noted that institutional investors (asset managers and other investment intermediaries) have become the dominant players in the investment chain as individual shareholding has declined over the years (ibid: 11). It focused on the distinction between institutional investors who 'invest', based on the their understanding of the fundamental value of the company and those who 'trade', based on their expectations of likely short-term movements in share price, and concluded that current levels of trading activity exceeded the level necessary to support the core purposes of equity markets (ibid). It therefore proposed a number of principles and recommendations aimed at addressing the problems identified.

1 The research in this chapter was carried out while on secondment to the Law Commission of England & Wales, working on the *Fiduciary Duties of Investment Intermediaries* project. I am indebted to David Hertzell, Tammy Goriely, Moeiz Farhan, Chris Stears and other colleagues at the Law Commission. I am also grateful for funding from the Leverhulme Trust (Tipping Points project) and to Professor Roman Tomasic, Professor Ranald Michie and my other colleagues on the Tipping Points project at Durham University. I am indebted to Professor Roger Masterman for being a supportive Head of School, and allowing me to take the opportunity of the secondment to the Law Commission.

One of the Kay Review's key findings was that, although fiduciary duty is a key component of the relationship between savers (equity owners) and the investment intermediaries through which they hold their equity holdings, there was considerable uncertainty and difference of opinion as to when fiduciary duties arise in these relationships and the content and extent of such fiduciary duties (Kay Review: para 9.2). Some of its stakeholders had suggested that pension trustees equated their fiduciary responsibilities with a narrow interpretation of the interests of their beneficiaries, which focused on maximising financial returns in the short term and thereby prevented the consideration of longer term factors that could have an effect on company performance, such as questions of sustainability or environmental and social impact (ibid: para 9.20). It therefore asked the Law Commission to review the legal concept of fiduciary duty as applicable to investment and thereby address the uncertainties and misunderstandings on the part of trustees and other investment intermediaries (ibid: 13). In June 2014 the Law Commission published its final report on the fiduciary duties of investment intermediaries, which clarified the concept of fiduciary duty with regard to investments and addressed the uncertainties surrounding it. This chapter discusses the Law Commission's report.

2 Definition of fiduciary duty

The Kay Review took the view that 'all participants in the equity investment chain should observe fiduciary standards in their relationships with their clients' and interpreted fiduciary duties as requiring that clients' interests are put first, conflicts of interest are avoided, all costs are disclosed to the client and fiduciary standards should not be capable of being overridden by contract (Kay Review 2012: 12).

The Law Commission clarified that the distinguishing feature of a fiduciary relationship is the duty of loyalty (Law Commission 2014: para 3.75). A fiduciary may owe other duties (such as a duty of care or a duty to exercise a power appropriately) alongside his or her fiduciary duties but this does not mean these other duties are fiduciary duties. It further explained that there are two main themes within fiduciary duty: the first is the 'no conflict rule', which requires a fiduciary to avoid acting where there is a conflict between their duty and their interest (duty–interest conflict) or where there is a conflict between duties owed to multiple parties (duty–duty conflict) (ibid: para 3.28). The second theme within fiduciary duty is the 'no profit rule', which forbids a fiduciary from making an unauthorised profit by reason or by virtue of their position as a fiduciary (ibid: para 3.28).

The Law Commission also clarified when fiduciary duties would apply and to whom. It began by explaining that fiduciary relationships arise in two main circumstances: status-based fiduciaries (where a relationship falls within a previously recognised category that is inherently fiduciary by its very nature, for example trustee and beneficiary or solicitor and client) and fact-based fiduciaries (where specific facts and circumstances of the relationship justify the imposition of fiduciary duties) (Law Commission 2014: paras 3.14–3.15). It did, however, acknowledge the difficulty in identifying the circumstances that justify the imposition of fiduciary duties with regard to fact-based fiduciaries.

It explained the differences in opinion on how to do this, beginning with its own previous interpretation, given in 1992, which was based on 'discretion, power to act and vulnerability' (Law Commission 1992: para 2.4.6). It acknowledged other views on the matter, for example the view that it is based on an undertaking to act for or on behalf of another person (Finn 1977: para 467; Scott 1948–49: 540; Sealy 1962: 72–79) in a relationship where the beneficiary has a legitimate expectation that the fiduciary will act in the beneficiary's interests (Finn 1989)[2] or where the beneficiary is vulnerable to the fiduciary and the fiduciary has scope for the exercise of some discretion or power.[3]

It has been argued that the courts are coalescing the factors of trust, vulnerability, confidence, power and discretion into a single test based on the legitimate expectations of the principal (Edelman 2010). Finally, it clarified that the key test is whether there is a legitimate expectation that one party will act in another's interest with discretion, power to act and vulnerability being indicators of such an expectation (Law Commission 2014: para 3.24).

On the issue of whether fiduciary duties should be capable of being contractually overridden, the Law Commission took the view that fiduciary duties can be modified; it is open to the parties to a contract to exclude or modify the operation of fiduciary duties (Law Commission 2014: para 3.38). The contract is the starting point,[4] and in such situations 'it is the contractual foundation which is all important because it is the contract that regulates the basic rights and liabilities of the parties' and the fiduciary relationship 'must accommodate itself to the terms of the contract so that it is consistent with, and conforms to, them' (Law Commission 2014: para 3.38; Frase 2011: para 8–069).

3 Applying fiduciary duties to investment intermediaries: pension trustees

A typical investment chain will have the investors (savers) at one end and the investee companies at the other end, but might have several investment intermediaries in between, such as pension funds, investment consultants, investment managers, collective investment schemes, brokers and custodians. The Law Commission focused on one particular type of investment intermediary: pension funds. Pensions are an important investment for many UK citizens and are an area where people are especially vulnerable to market failures and other failures of financial markets (Law Commission 2014: para 1.25). In addition, pension fund trustees control vast resources and the investment policies they adopt can have important macro-economic and social policy implications. Moreover, consultees of both the Kay Review and the Law Commission's Review specifically asked the Law Commission to answer the question of how far the law requires pension trustees to focus on maximising financial returns over a short timescale, as opposed to considering other longer term factors such as environmental and social impact (ibid: para 1.24).

The law governing occupational pension funds

The duties of pension trustees arise from a number of sources, including the trust deed, pensions legislation, fiduciary duties, the duty of care and duties attached to the exercise of a power (Law Commission 2014: para 6.4). The Goode Report of 1993 played a key role in shaping the law governing occupational pension funds (Goode 1993). It recommended maintaining the previously existing system of governance provided by trust law but also reinforcing it with a Pensions Act administered by a Pensions Regulator (ibid: para 1.1.13).

---

2 *Arklow Investments Ltd v Maclean* [2000] 1 WLR 594 at 598.
3 *Frame v Smith* [1987] 2 SCR 99 at 136; *Hospital Products v US Surgical Corp* (1984) 156 CLR 41 at 97.
4 *Fattal v Walbrook Trustees (Jersey) Ltd* [2010] EWHC 2767 (Ch) at [113].

This led to the enactment of the Pensions Act 1995, which specifies the functions of pension trustees, some of which include ensuring that there is a written statement of the principles governing investment decisions, paying due regard to the need for diversification of investments and ensuring that the investments are suitable for the pension fund.[5]

This statute also prevents pension trustees from excluding or restricting their liability for breach of their duty of care when performing their investment functions.[6] Moreover, it requires them to obtain and consider 'proper advice' when making their investment decisions.[7] It also requires them to prepare a statement of investment principles (SIP) and ensure that it is reviewed and amended if the need to amend it arises.[8] Trustees or investment managers to whom discretion has been delegated must exercise their powers of investment in accordance with the SIP.

The Pensions Act 2004 updated the obligations on pension trustees by, for example, requiring trustees to be 'conversant' with the trust deed and the rules of their pension scheme, as well as its SIP and any other trust scheme documentation.[9] It also required trustees to have knowledge and understanding of the law relating to pensions and trusts, as well as the principles relating to funding and investment of their trust scheme.[10] The Pensions Acts 2008 and 2011 also deal with other aspects of pensions not necessarily related to the duties of the pension trustees – the 2008 Act, for example, automatically enrols all employees into their employer's occupational pension scheme and it established the National Employment Savings Trust (NEST), a pension scheme to support the introduction of automatic enrolment.

The Occupational Pension Schemes (Investment) Regulations 2005 impose a duty on pension trustees to disclose the extent (if at all) to which social, environmental or ethical considerations are taken into account in the formulation and implementation of their investment decisions or investment strategies.[11] They require trustees to invest 'in the best interests of members and beneficiaries'.[12] This is broadly in line with the Trustee Act 2000, which requires trustees, when exercising their investment powers, to keep the portfolio under regular review and to have regard to the standard investment criteria (the suitability of the type of investment under consideration and the suitability of the specific asset in question).[13] The 2005 Regulations elaborate on what considerations should be included in the SIP: these include the kinds of investments to be held, the balance between different kinds of investments, risk, the expected return on investments and the exercise of the rights (including voting rights) associated with the investments.[14]

Although fairly comprehensive, the legislation does not give a conclusive explanation of whether pension trustees may take environmental and social impact into account when making investment decisions and we must turn to case law for further clarification. The decision in *Cowan v Scargill* is the starting point for an in-depth discussion of this issue, where

---

5 Pensions Act 1995 ss 32–39.
6 ibid s 33(1).
7 ibid s 36(3).
8 ibid s 35(1).
9 Pensions Act 2004 s 247(3).
10 ibid s 247(4).
11 Occupational Pension Schemes (Investment) Regulations 2005/3378 reg 2(3)(b)(vi). These regulations implement the requirements of the European Pensions Directive (2003/41/EC) and the Directive on Markets in Financial Instruments (2004/39/EC).
12 Occupational Pension Schemes (Investment) Regulations 2005/3378 (n 11) reg 2.
13 Trustee Act 2000 s 4(2) and 4(3).
14 Occupational Pension Schemes (Investment) Regulations 2005/3378 (n 11) reg 2(3).

it was held that trustees are duty-bound to exercise their powers in the best interests of present and future beneficiaries of the trust and to treat different classes of beneficiaries impartially.[15] It was also held that where the trust is for the provision of financial benefits (as most trusts are) the paramount duty of the trustees is to provide the greatest financial benefit for the beneficiaries, and this is the case even where the trust is a large pension fund.[16]

Other court decisions have affirmed this duty of pension trustees to exercise their powers in the best interests of the beneficiaries. In *Martin v City of Edinburgh District Council* the Court of Session held that, in adopting an 'apartheid-free' policy and thus deciding to disinvest its trust funds in South Africa during the apartheid regime, the council had not fully considered whether this was in the best interests of its beneficiaries nor had it sought professional advice, with the effect being that it had reached its decision in the wrong way.[17] In *Harries v Church Commissioners* it was held that trustees should not lose sight of the purpose of their investment powers.[18]

The 'best interests' of beneficiaries

The Law Commission explained the requirement to act in the best interests of beneficiaries as a bundle of duties (Law Commission 2014: para 6.15). Pension trustees must promote the purpose for which the trust was created (Nicholls 1996). For pension schemes this will be to generate adequate returns to provide the scheme members with retirement and other benefits (Law Commission 2014: para 6.6). Pension trustees must act within the confines of the legislation, exercise their own discretion and follow the correct procedure to reach their decision (ibid: paras 6.7–6.12). They must also exercise reasonable care and skill when carrying out their duties (ibid: paras 6.13–6.14).

Although the purpose of a pension fund is to provide a pension, the decisions of trustees may vary from fund to fund. In defined benefit (DB) schemes trustees' duties may include taking care not to imperil the continuity of the employer's business as the employer's insolvency could undermine the employer's guarantee of the member's benefits, thus yielding an outcome that is not in the best interests of the scheme members (Law Commission 2014: paras 5.28–5.35, para 5.45). In defined Contribution (DC) default schemes, they may be required to provide the best realistic returns over the long term while keeping costs low, whilst in defined Contribution chosen schemes the greater emphasis on allowing beneficiaries to 'choose' their investment means there is scope for allowing beneficiaries to follow their ethical preferences (ibid: para 5.46).

4 The investment considerations of pension trustees

The Kay Review suggested that, subject to the risk preferences and time horizons of ultimate beneficiaries, asset holders and asset managers should adopt investment policies that maximise absolute long-term investment returns, comply with generally prevailing ethical standards and take account of specific wishes of beneficiaries (Kay Review 2012: para 9.21).

---

15 *Cowan v Scargill* [1985] Ch 270, 287–88; the view that the paramount consideration must be what is in the best interests of the beneficiaries has been reaffirmed in *Martin v Edinburgh District Council* [1989] Pens LR 9, 1998 SLT 329.
16 *Cowan v Scargill* (n 15) 287–88, 290.
17 [1989] Pens LR 9 at [24], [32], 1988 SLT 329 at 331–32, 334.
18 [1992] 1 WLR 1241, 1247.

The Law Commission therefore had to consider the extent to which fiduciary duties require pension trustees to consider interests beyond the maximisation of financial return, factors relevant to long-term performance (such as questions of sustainability or environmental and social impact), ethical considerations and the views of their beneficiaries (Law Commission 2014: 241).

Interests beyond the maximisation of financial return

The Law Commission did not think it helpful to suggest that trustees should only maximise financial returns. Instead, it stressed the distinction between factors relevant to increasing returns or reducing risks (financial factors) and factors that were not relevant to increasing returns or reducing risks (non-financial factors) (Law Commission 2014: paras 6.22, 6.24 and 6.33). The primary aim of trustees' investment strategy should be to 'secure the best realistic return over the long term, given the need to control for risks' (ibid: para 6.23). The Law Commission therefore argued that trustees should take financially material factors into account (ibid: paras 6.30–6.32). Trustees can therefore take environmental, social and governance (ESG) factors into account if they are financially material to the performance of an investment (ibid: paras 6.27 and 6.29). They can also take into account risks to the long-term sustainability of a company's performance as such as risks are financially material (ibid: para 6.25).

Non-financial factors, on the other hand, may not be taken into account by trustees save for a few limited exceptions. Non-financial factors may only be taken into account if two tests are met: the trustees have good reason to think that scheme members would share the concern and the decision does not involve a risk of significant financial detriment to the fund (Law Commission 2014: para 6.34). Any decision based on non-financial grounds would be subject to both tests (ibid: para 6.77). The Law Commission did, however, outline two exceptions where the second test could be disregarded, i.e. significant financial detriment could be permitted: these are where the decision is expressly permitted by the trust deed and where members of DC chosen schemes choose to invest in a specific fund (ibid: para 6.85).

Factors relevant to long-term performance

The Law Commission argued that investment strategies that aim to produce higher returns in the short term, whilst endangering the financial viability of the scheme in the long term will have a disproportionate impact on younger scheme members, and it is therefore important that trustees adopt an appropriate timeframe over which they formulate their investment strategies (Law Commission 2014: para 7.17). Trustees have discretion with regard to picking a strategy they think is appropriate, but they should be impartial with regard to how they treat younger and older scheme members (ibid: para 7.17). The Law Commission also took the view that it is desirable for pension funds to promote the long-term success of the companies in which they invest and trustees should therefore be encouraged to consider when and how to engage with companies to promote their long-term success (ibid: para 5.98).

Ethical considerations

Taking ethical considerations into account when making investment decisions is not altogether unproblematic. The problem is that different people have different views on what they think is ethical. Taking ethics into account raises the question of whether trustees may deviate from the goal of securing the best realistic risk-adjusted returns, so as to further other aims and objectives (McCormack 1998: 39). There are, broadly speaking, three investment strategies relevant to a discussion on ethical investing (Thornton 2008; McCormack 1998). The first of these is a 'neutral policy', which is one that is solely focused on financial returns; this policy is compatible with the Law Commission's explanation of the law.

The second is an 'ethics sensitive' policy, which first considers financial returns, but then uses ethical or other non-financial criteria to choose among investments that generate equal financial returns. This policy is also unproblematic from a legal standpoint because, arguably, it ensures the best interests of the beneficiaries (Nicholls 1996). There is, however, the counter-argument that it is not possible to have two investments that are of exactly equal value or generate equal returns and therefore there can never be a situation where it is acceptable for trustees to use ethical considerations to choose between different investments (Thornton 2008: 405).

There is a further counter-argument that it is not possible for two different investments to pose the exact same amount of risk, and that since risk is a necessary consideration in determining the desirability of an investment in terms of financial returns it is undesirable to use non-financial considerations as the basis for deciding between different investments (Thornton 2008: 406). These arguments cast doubt on the legitimacy of 'ethics sensitive' investment policies. The Law Commission has, however, clarified that non-financial factors (such as ethics) can be used if they do not cause significant financial detriment (Law Commission 2014: paras 6.68–6.74).

The third investment policy is a 'socially dictated' policy, which is one that either sacrifices financial returns for ethical considerations or serves an objective unrelated to the interests of the beneficiaries in their capacity as such (Hutchinson and Cole 1980: 1345). This is problematic, as the subjective nature of 'ethics' makes it a difficult criterion to use as the basis for investment decisions (Thornton 2008: 418–19). Such policies are problematic because they run the risk of falling foul of the trustees' duty to act in the best interest of the beneficiaries.

The views of beneficiaries

The starting point on this issue is that non-financial factors may only be taken into account if two tests are met: the trustees have good reason to think that scheme members would share the concern and the decision does not involve a risk of significant financial detriment to the fund (Law Commission 2014: para 6.34). Trustees must not impose their own ethical views on the beneficiaries (Thornton 2008: 397);[19] however, they may reflect the views of their beneficiaries (or the views that beneficiaries would have if they addressed the question) (Law Commission 2014: para 6.59). It will often be difficult to do this where the views of some beneficiaries differ from the views of other beneficiaries.

The Law Commission refused to specify a set proportion of beneficiaries that would be required to support a particular view in order to allow the trustees to give effect to it; instead, it suggested that the courts would take into account all the circumstances, although the focus would be on whether the trustees applied their minds to the right question and sought an answer in a reasonable way (Law Commission 2014: para 6.63). In cases where the issue is

---

19 *Harries v Church Commissioners* (n 18) 1247; *Martin v City of Edinburgh* (n 17) 334.

controversial the courts would expect the trustees to focus on financial factors rather than getting involved in disagreements between the beneficiaries (ibid: para 6.67).

5 The investment considerations of other investment intermediaries

Although the Law Commission report focused on pension trustees it did also consider how the law applies to other investment intermediaries. Trustees are present in DB pension schemes and some DC pension schemes. There are, however, a large number of DC pension schemes where there are no trustees and instead the employer enlists an investment intermediary (pension provider) to administer the pension scheme. The pension provider offers a range of funds in which the member may choose to invest. Such schemes are not subject to trust law as there are no trustees to hold to account. They are, instead, contract-based; they are governed by the contract between the pension provider and each individual employee. The contributions from the employee and employer are specified, but the retirement benefits are uncertain, so that the employee's pension will depend not only on the level of contribution but also on the performance of the investments, the fees charged and the annuity rate obtained (Law Commission 2013: para 2.12). The employee bears the risk of poor performance, and for this reason DC pension schemes have become increasingly popular amongst employers, and many DB schemes have been replaced with DC ones.

The rules governing contract-based pension schemes

Contract-based schemes are subject to contract law and the regulatory rules of the Financial Conduct Authority (FCA). The FCA's normative framework consists of broad principles and detailed rules. There are 11 broad regulatory principles that apply, not just to contract-based pension providers but to all authorised persons, i.e. persons who have permission to carry on regulated activities.[20] Five of these principles are particularly relevant to the best interests of scheme members in contract-based pensions. These principles require firms to conduct business with due skill, care and diligence (Principle 2), to pay due regard to the interests of their customers and treat them fairly (Principle 6), to pay due regard to the information needs of their clients (Principle 7), to manage conflicts of interest fairly (Principle 8) and to ensure the suitability of the advice given and discretionary decisions made for customers (Principle 9).[21] Breaches of these principles could result in FCA enforcement action, but individuals have no right of action.[22]

In addition to the principles there are more detailed rules that cover different aspects of financial services business and provide guidance on how regulated firms should behave in order to comply with the regulation. The relevant detailed rules are the Conduct of Business (COBS) rules, which can be found in the FCA's Handbook. COBS 2.1.1R requires firms to act honestly, fairly and professionally in accordance with the best interests of their clients and provides the regulatory equivalent of the duty to act in the scheme members' 'best interests'. COBS 2.1.2R prevents firms from excluding or restricting their liability to their clients under the regulatory system, whilst COBS 2.2.1R and COBS 14.3.2R require

---

20 Financial Services and Markets Act 2000, s 31, Pt 4A.
21 FCA Handbook PRIN 2.1.1R.
22 ibid PRIN 3.4.4R.

appropriate disclosure of the relevant costs and risks associated with designated investments and investment strategies.

Two important detailed rules are the requirement, derived from the Markets in Financial Instruments Directive (MiFID), requiring clients to be categorised as retail, professional or eligible counterparty clients and treated accordingly (COBS 3) and the requirement that firms ensure that any personal recommendation they make or any decisions to trade are suitable for their clients (COBS 9.2.1R). Contract-based pension funds will often not be subject to the suitability rule in COBS 9.2.1R as that rule only applies to firms which make personal recommendations 'in relation to designated investments or that manage investments', and contract-based schemes typically own the assets of the scheme themselves rather than 'managing investments' on behalf of others (COBS 9.1.1R and COBS 9.1.3R). Independent financial advisers are, however, subject to the suitability requirements if they recommend contract-based schemes to clients (Law Commission 2014: para 8.30; Law Commission 2013: paras 11.65–11.68).[23]

Fiduciary duties and contract-based pensions

Although contract-based pension providers are in a position to affect the interests of vulnerable members they are not trustees and will not automatically be subject to fiduciary duties (Law Commission 2014: para 8.48). Whether or not a contract-based pension provider is subject to a fiduciary duty will depend on whether a member has a legitimate expectation that the provider will act in that member's interests; the Law Commission took the view that in many cases the contract terms will mean that such an expectation will not be legitimate, even if it arises at all (ibid: para 8.48).

Although contract-based pension providers will often not owe fiduciary duties, they will be subject to other 'fiduciary-like' duties, for example the duty to act honestly, fairly and professionally in accordance with the best interests of their clients, which is one that arises from the FCA's regulatory rules (COBS 2.1.1R; Law Commission 2014: para 8.49). Breach of this rule gives the client the right to bring an action under section 138D of the Financial Services and Markets Act 2000. In addition, contract-based providers are subject to the duty of care and skill when carrying out services they have undertaken to provide under the terms of the contract, as well as the duty to ensure that they do not fetter their discretion when making discretionary decisions that affect the scheme members (ibid: para 8.50).[24]

Problems with contract-based pensions

The Law Commission found there to be 'serious problems' with the law governing contract-based pensions. The contract-based nature of these pensions means that they are based on an assumption that savers are fully autonomous market participants, able to make rational and fully informed decisions on what is in their best interests – an assumption the Law Commission found to be erroneous (Law Commission 2014: para 8.51). It argued that, in truth, savers often do not engage with pensions. Even where savers are informed there is often very little they can do to alter the contract terms, as contract-based pensions are

---

23 See also *Loosemore v Financial Concepts* [2001] Lloyd's Rep 235; *Gorham v British Telecommunications plc* [2000] 1 WLR 2129.
24 See also *Paterson Arran Ltd Group Personal Pension Scheme* Ref 80843/1 (27 April 2011)

standard form contracts (contracts of adhesion), where the terms are set by the pension provider and offered on a 'take it or leave it' basis, so that the saver has no ability to negotiate for more favourable terms (ibid: para 8.6).

The contract-based nature of contract-based pensions was also found to lead to a governance gap because the contract-based model lacks the oversight that trustees provide in trust-based schemes. Although employers choose the pension provider and enrol their employees on the scheme, the employers have neither the incentive nor the capability effectively to oversee pension providers on behalf of the scheme members. In the absence of trustees, and with employers unwilling or unable to perform a governance function over pension providers, governance gaps can arise such as high, complex charges that lack transparency and insufficient review of investment strategies (Law Commission 2014: para 9.3). This had been recognised before by the Office of Fair Trading (OFT) and the Department for Work and Pensions (DWP) (OFT 2014: paras 7.33–7.34; DWP 2013: para 25), and had led the Association of British Insurers (ABI) to recommend the embedding of independent governance committees (IGCs) within all contract-based pension providers, as a way to address this governance gap (OFT 2014: para 7.52).

The Law Commission found the costs and charges in contract-based pensions to be excessively high and complex (Law Commission 2014: paras 9.8–9.12). This observation is in line with the findings of other reports (Pensions Institute 2012: 9, 17–19; Fabian Society 2013: 6). The problem with excessively high charges is that they have a significant effect on the amount a scheme member receives on retirement (Harrison, Blake and Dowd 2014: 13). Although the industry moved away from a wide variety of charges to an emphasis on levying a single charge (the annual management charge (AMC)), and this had increased competition within the industry, problems remained as there is no consistent way of calculating AMCs across the industry (OFT 2014: para 6.21). Moreover, AMCs do not include transaction costs such as brokers' commissions and taxes (ibid: para 6.28).

The Law Commission also found the regulation to be focused on point of sale rather than ongoing suitability and on product design rather than individual suitability; consultees explained to the Law Commission that the FCA Handbook is aimed at ensuring clients are fully aware of the costs and risks of products at the point of sale rather than ongoing suitability over time (Law Commission 2014: paras 8.31–8.34). Furthermore, where there is recognition of the importance of reviewing products the emphasis is on the overall suitability of the product for its target market, rather than its suitability for an individual member (ibid: para 8.35).

Measures designed to address the problems with contract-based pensions

In light of the problems with contract-based pensions the Law Commission discussed some of the measures being adopted in the UK, in order to address them. With regard to the governance gap, the DWP proposed a set of overarching standards across all schemes, aimed at ensuring that all schemes are governed by a body obligated to act in members' interests, with the majority of the members of such a governing body being independent of the pension provider (DWP 2014: 11). DWP also took up the idea of IGCs and set out the areas that IGCs would be required to focus on including whether DC default investment strategies are designed in the interests of members and whether they are regularly reviewed, the levels of charges borne by scheme members and the costs incurred through investments and whether core scheme financial transactions are processed promptly and accurately (DWP 2014: 18).

These have been incorporated into FCA rules, which also require providers to consider and act on all recommendations received from IGC unless there are justifiable reasons for not doing so (FCA COBS 19.5.7). The Law Commission welcomed these changes but also recommended that IGCs should owe a statutory duty to scheme members to act, with reasonable care and skill, in members' interests, and that this duty should not be excludable by contract (Law Commission 2014: paras 9.53, 9.87). It also recommended that pension providers be required to indemnify members of their IGCs for any liabilities incurred in the course of their duties (ibid: paras 9.53, 9.88).

To tackle the issue of costs and charges in contract-based pensions the DWP brought in a charge cap of 0.75 per cent of funds under management. This cap applies to member-borne deductions (costs and charges relating to scheme and investment administration) but does not apply to transaction costs (variable costs associated with buying, holding and selling the underlying investment instruments) (DWP 2014: 58–60). Transaction costs were excluded from the cap in order not to create incentives for investment managers to avoid carrying out transactions where such transactions would be beneficial for scheme members. This contrasts with the view, in the Kay Review, that trading should be discouraged in favour of long-term investing and engagement with investment companies. The Law Commission therefore recommended, as part of its review of the cap in April 2017, that the government should specifically consider whether the design of the cap has incentivised trading over long-term investment and, if so, what measures can be taken to reduce this effect (Law Commission 2014: paras 9.72, 9.89).

Another problem with the exclusion of transaction costs from the charge cap is that it could lead to a 'water-bed effect' whereby pension providers increase transaction costs in order to make up for lower management charges (Law Commission 2014: para 9.59). The Law Commission therefore recommended that IGC members be given training and support in carrying out their functions, as well as a central source for tracking what level of fees might represent good value for money (ibid: para 9.71).

With regard to the problem that the regulation focused on the point of sale rather than ongoing suitability, the Law Commission recognised that contract-based pension providers may be constrained in their ability to make changes to contract terms or to move savers to other funds without their express agreement (Law Commission 2014: para 9.80). It therefore suggested allowing specified changes, on an opt-out basis, where the changes meet clearly defined standards of savers' best interests, although it did not go as far as making this a recommendation (ibid: para 9.81).

6 Fiduciary duties along the investment chain

The Kay Review took the view that all participants in financial markets should apply fiduciary standards in their dealings with each other whenever they give investment advice or exercise discretion over the investments of others (Kay Review 2012: 12). The Law Commission, however, took a different view on this issue. It argued that whether market participants will be found to owe fiduciary duties always depends on the facts of each particular case, and that the courts often take a different view from that advanced by the Kay Review (Law Commission 2014: paras 10.4–10.8). For this reason it suggested that fiduciary duties were not an effective way to achieve the Kay Review's policy aims on this issue (ibid: para 10.8).

For courts the starting point is always the contract and the relevant regulatory rules, and courts are often reluctant to impose fiduciary duties in contracts where both parties are sophisticated commercial parties (Law Commission 2014: paras 10.6–10.8). Much will depend on the function the intermediary performs and the nature of his or her relationship with the client: in the Australian case of *Daly v Sydney Stock Exchange Ltd* it was held that giving advice was sufficient to bring about a fiduciary relationship and thus that those who provide investment advice or other financial advice may owe fiduciary duties to their clients.[25] In the Canadian case of *Hodgkinson v Simms* it was held that fiduciary duties could apply to financial advisers if there was vulnerability, trust, reliance, discretion and the relevant professional rules or codes of conduct supported such a finding.[26] The position appears to be a little clearer with regard to actuaries; it has been argued that they will usually be in a fiduciary relationship with their clients (Jackson and others 2011: para 18–017).

For investment managers, again much will depend on the investment mandate. The mandate will set out the scope of the manager's discretion, and it has been argued there is a 'clear basis' for investment managers to owe fiduciary duties to their clients (Frase 2012: 6; Penner 2002: 245). Such duties will usually be owed to the manager's principal, such that if there is another intermediary (such as a pension fund) between the manager and the ultimate saver or investor then the manager's duties will be owed to that other beneficiary rather than to the ultimate investor or saver (Law Commission 2014: paras 10.25–10.26). There is Australian authority suggesting that, in exceptional cases, an agent of a trustee may have a direct fiduciary relationship with the beneficiaries of the trust, but this appears to be so only in rare cases.[27]

There is also authority that brokers may be subject to fiduciary duties. The relationship between a broker and his or her client is not automatically a fiduciary relationship, and whether or not the broker owes a fiduciary duty to the client will depend on the nature of the services provided to the client. Where the client has a discretionary account and the broker makes all the decisions, there will be great trust and reliance reposed in the broker and this will probably give rise to a fiduciary duty, whereas where the client has an 'execution only' account and the broker is merely an 'order taker' for the client, the relationship will 'lack the elements of a fiduciary relationship'.[28]

With custodians the existence of fiduciary duties to their clients will also depend on the facts of the case. Although commercial banking relationships will not generally give rise to fiduciary duties, a bank may nevertheless be subject to fiduciary duties in relation to custodial activities or in relation to its activities as a stock lending agent.[29] This is the case with regard to its relationship with its immediate client in the investment chain. Where there is a chain of investors this will be seen as a chain of sub-trusts, and the 'no-look-through' principle operates to limit fiduciary duties to the next intermediary along the chain, thus precluding the finding of fiduciary duties to the ultimate investor or saver (Law Commission 2014: paras 10.36–10.37). There is academic support for this argument that fiduciary duties are owed only to the immediate client (Austen-Peters 2000: para 4.32). The only instance where custodians might owe fiduciary duties to the end-investor appears to be in a situation where the end-investor in fact appointed the custodian (ibid: para 10.40).

25 *Daly v Sydney Stock Exchange Ltd* (1986) 160 CLR 371.
26 [1994] 3 SCR 377.
27 *Australian Securities Commission v AS Nominees Limited* (1995) 62 FCR 504.
28 *Kent v May* (2001) 298 AR 71 at [51]–[53], affirmed (2002) 317 AR 381 (CA). For a good discussion of industry practice see the judgment of Hamblen J in *Redmayne Bentley Stockbrokers v Isaacs* [2010] EWHC 1504 (Comm) at [35]–[40].
29 *Forsta AP-Fonden v Bank of New York Mellon* [2013] EWHC 3127 (Comm) at [173].

The difference of opinion between the Kay Review and the Law Commission on this issue is instructive of the different terms of reference given to each review, as well as differences in the approaches taken in the two reviews. The Kay Review had a much wider remit, and was therefore free to consider and propose any options that achieved the objectives set for it. In addition, it was able to take a more normative approach and reach conclusions aimed at improving the UK economy. The Law Commission, on the other hand, had a much narrower remit, i.e. to clarify the law, and was also limited to having to rely on legal sources and what was actually contained in those legal sources rather than on a more normative conception of what the law ought to be.

7 Shareholder engagement, macro-economic considerations and tackling short-termism

Before concluding this chapter it is worth considering the extent to which the Law Commission's report addresses the central concerns in the Kay Review, namely the problem of short-termism in UK equity markets and the lack of shareholder engagement with the managements of their investee companies.

Short-termism in UK equity markets

The Law Commission addressed the issue of short-termism in a number of ways. Its consultees expressed strong views in favour of investment intermediaries paying greater attention to long-term considerations when making their investment decisions (Law Commission 2014: paras 5.47–5.51, 7.13–7.16 and 7.29–7.32), and it agreed with them that long-term risks should be one of the risks that trustees consider when making investment decisions (ibid: para 5.52). In describing the primary purpose of the investment powers given to trustees it highlighted long-term concerns as it emphasised that the primary purpose of their investment power is to secure the best realistic return over the longer term, given the need to control for risks (ibid: para 5.56). The importance of trustees adopting an appropriate timeframe over which they formulate their investment strategies was also emphasised (ibid: para 7.17).

Lack of shareholder engagement with the managements of their investee companies

The Law Commission addressed this issue in a number of ways. It first explained that in a situation where a trust's shareholding confers complete or substantial control over an investee company it is possible for trustees to be subject to a duty to engage with the management of that company (Law Commission 2014: paras 3.85–3.88; Rennie and others 2006: paras 34–49, 34–50). This decision has support in the law.[30] It then referred to the UK Stewardship Code, which is aimed at enhancing the quality of engagement between investment intermediaries and the companies in which they invest, in order to improve long-term risk-adjusted returns to the ultimate investor or saver (ibid: paras 5.80–5.83).

The problem of inadequate shareholder engagement generated strong responses from the Law Commission's consultees, who disagreed with the Law Commission's earlier position,

---

30 *Bartlett v Barclays Bank Trust Co Ltd* [1980] Ch 515 at 532.

in its Consultation Paper, on the practicalities of carrying out engagement. Consultees disagreed with the statement in the Consultation Paper that, apart from the very largest pension schemes, most pension schemes lacked the internal resources or the financial clout to carry out effective shareholder engagement (Law Commission 2014: para 5.84). Consultees argued that, in practice, engagement was often delegated to investment managers, a point which was confirmed by the Financial Reporting Council (FRC) (ibid: para 5.85).[31]

The Law Commission accepted these criticisms and broadened its analysis of engagement; it concluded that trustees, like other institutional investors, can outsource or delegate engagement to agents such as investment managers, and therefore even small and medium-sized schemes can carry out engagement (Law Commission 2014: para 5.89). It also recommended that SIPs should contain a statement of trustees' policy (if any) on stewardship (ibid: para 5.98). It was, however, keen to point out that there is no duty to undertake engagement and trustees have discretion over the extent to which they engage with their investee companies or exercise their shareholder voting rights (ibid: paras 5.96–5.97).

Transaction costs: trading over investing

This was one of the Kay Review's central concerns as short-termism often goes hand in hand with investment strategies that focus on trading rather than long-term investment. The Law Commission discussed the difference in views between the Kay Review, which was concerned with inappropriate incentives for institutional investors to trade excessively, and the OFT Review, which was concerned that if transaction costs were included in the single 'framework' charge this could discourage institutional investors from carrying out transactions even where those transactions were in the interests of savers (Law Commission 2014: para 9.62). The Law Commission did not wholly endorse either view, commenting instead that there were no ideal answers (ibid: para 9.63).

8 Conclusion

In concluding, an important point to note is that although the Law Commission did make some recommendations it focused to a large extent on clarifying the law, rather than proposing changes to the law. This was largely in keeping with the terms of reference set out by the Kay Review and also because the Law Commission was reluctant to interfere with the flexibility that currently exists in the area of fiduciary duties – a flexibility that is regarded by many as desirable.

The Law Commission did a good job of explaining fiduciary duties and how they operate with regard to investment, and its report will undoubtedly be of great use to pension trustees, contract-based pension providers and other investment intermediaries. Nevertheless, the Law Commission's clarification and recommendations are only one part of the overall strategy to tackle the problems identified by the Kay Review. This is, largely, because fiduciary duties are more concerned with the relationship between the investment intermediary and the

---

31 The FRC did, however, note that although institutional investors are allowed to outsource engagement to external service providers, the responsibility for engagement ultimately remains with the investor.

ultimate investor or saver, rather than the relationship between the investment intermediary and the investee company. Fiduciary duties are focused on the duty to the client and are therefore not the most effective way of enforcing duties between the intermediary and the investee company. The Law Commission was therefore able to explain fiduciary duties but not to resolve the problems of short-termism and lack of engagement between owners and investee companies in the UK. This is something that some of the other recommendations in the Kay Review are better suited to address.

Bibliography

Austen-Peters, A. (2000) *Custody of Investments: Law and Practice*, Oxford: OUP.

Department for Work and Pensions (DWP) (2013) *Quality Standards in Workplace Defined Contribution Pension Schemes: Call for Evidence* (July 2013).

Department for Work and Pensions (DWP) (2014) *Better Workplace Pensions: Further Measures for Savers*, Cm 8840.

Department for Business, Innovation and Skills (BIS) (2011) *The Kay Review: Terms of Reference* (June 2011) https://www.gov.uk/government/consultations/the-kay-review-of-uk-equity-markets-and-long-term-decision-making (last accessed 27 May 2016).

Edelman, J. (2010) 'When do Fiduciary Duties Arise?' *Law Quarterly Review*, 126, p 302.

Fabian Society (2013) *Pensions at Work, that Work: Completing the Unfinished Pensions Revolution* (May 2013) http://www.fabians.org.uk/publications/pensions-at-work-that-work/ (last accessed 27 May 2016).

Finn, P. (1977) *Fiduciary Obligations*, Law Book Company.

Finn, P. (1989) 'The Fiduciary Principle' in T. Youdan (ed), *Equity, Fiduciaries and Trusts*, Toronto: Carswell.

Frase, D. (2011) *Law and Regulation of Investment Management*, 2nd edn, London: Sweet & Maxwell.

Frase, D. (2012) 'Conflicts of Interest', *Compliance Officer Bulletin* 97 (June), p 1.

Goode, R. (1993) *The Report of the Pension Law Review Committee* (Pensions Law Reform (CM 2342, 1993)).

Harrison, D., Blake D. and Dowd, K. (2014) *VfM: Assessing Value for Money in Defined Contribution Default Funds* (January 2014) http://openaccess.city.ac.uk/6808/ (last accessed 27 May 2016).

Hutchinson, J. and Cole, G. (1980) 'Legal Standards Governing Investment of Pension Assets for Social and Political Goals', *University of Pennsylvania Law Review*, 128, p 1340.

Jackson, R., Cannon, M., Powell, J. and Stewart, R. (2011) *Jackson & Powell on Professional Liability*, 7th edn, London: Sweet & Maxwell.

Kay, J. (2012) *The Kay Review of UK Equity Markets and Long-term Decision-making: Final Report* (July 2012) https://www.gov.uk/government/consultations/the-kay-review-of-uk-equity-markets-and-long-term-decision-making (last accessed 27 May 2016).

Law Commission (1992) *Fiduciary Duties and Regulatory Rules*, Law Com Consultation Paper 124, London: HMSO.

Law Commission (2013) *Fiduciary Duties of Investment Intermediaries*, Law Com Consultation Paper 215, London: HMSO.

Law Commission (2014) *Fiduciary Duties of Investment Intermediaries*, Law Com 350 HC 368 2014–15.

McCormack, G. (1998) 'Sexy But Not Sleazy: Trustee Investments and Ethical Considerations', *Company Lawyer*, 19(2), p 39.

Nicholls, D. (1996) 'Trustees and Their Broader Community: Where Duty, Morality and Ethics Converge', *Australian Law Journal*, 70, pp 205.

Office of Fair Trading (OFT) (2014) *Defined Contribution Workplace Pension Market Study* (September 2013, revised February 2014) http://webarchive.nationalarchives.gov.uk/20140402142426/http://www.oft.gov.uk/OFTwork/markets-work/pensions/ (last accessed 27 May 2016).

Penner, J. (2002) 'Exemptions' in Birks, P. and Pretto-Sakmann, A. (eds), *A Breach of Trust*, 1st edn, Cambridge: Hart Publishing.

Pensions Institute (2012) *Caveat Venditor: The Brave New World of Auto-Enrolment should be governed by the principle of seller not buyer beware* (October 2012) http://www.pensions-institute.org/reports/CaveatVenditor.pdf (last accessed 27 May 2016).

Rennie, R., Brymer, S., Cabrelli, D., Mowbray, J., Tucker, L., Le Poidevin, N. and Simpson, E. (2006) *Lewin on Trusts*, 18th rev edn, London: Sweet & Maxwell.

Scott, A. (1948–49) 'The Fiduciary Principle', *California Law Review*, 37(4), pp 53.

Sealy, L. (1962) 'Fiduciary Relationships', *Cambridge Law Journal*, 20, pp 69–81.

Thornton, R. (2008) 'Ethical Investments: A Case of Disjointed Thinking', *Cambridge Law Journal*, 67(2), pp 396.

7

Corporate law and the phoenix company

Helen Anderson[1]

1 Introduction

Phoenix activity is a product of the two most basic and well accepted characteristics of corporate law – the limited liability of shareholders and the separate legal entity of the company. These place a 'corporate veil' between the company and its investors. A phoenix company, however named, is one that arises from the ashes of its former self, taking advantage of these corporate characteristics, which have remained largely intact since *Salomon*'s case.[2] The term phoenix activity is generally pejorative and describes debt-laden 'Oldco' entering into liquidation where its controllers continue the business debt-free through 'Newco'. Externally, the conduct might appear to be a legitimate business rescue. Where the use of successor companies breaches directors' duties because of an improper motivation, it is described as illegal phoenix activity. Corporate law rarely provides an official definition nor a specific offence capturing phoenix activity.

This chapter considers many aspects of phoenix activity – why and how people engage in the behaviour, who these people are and who its victims are; how it is tackled both in Australia and other jurisdictions around the globe; and a critique on these measures. First, the chapter explains how corporate law allows it to happen and, from this, the other questions are answered. Whilst drawing upon Australian material, the chapter also seeks to compare how different corporate law systems have sought to deal with the problem of phoenix companies and engages with international theoretical debates in this area.

1 Associate Professor, Melbourne Law School. This research is part of a project funded by the Australian Research Council (ARC) and the author thanks the ARC for its generous support: DP140102277, 'Phoenix Activity: Regulating Fraudulent Use of the Corporate Form'. Her co-investigators on the project are Professors Ian Ramsay and Ann O'Connell, also of Melbourne Law School, and Associate Professor Michelle Welsh, Monash Business School, Monash University. A detailed analysis of international measures and recommendations to combat phoenix activity will be forthcoming in 2016 or 2017. See further http://law.unimelb.edu.au/cclsr/centre-activities/research/major-research-projects/regulating-fraudulent-phoenix-activity (last accessed 29 May 2016).
2 *Salomon v A Salomon & Co Ltd* [1896] UKHL 1.

2 How corporate law facilitates phoenix activity

Limited liability is one of the default rules making up the standard form contract between the company and the parties with which it deals. This default rule lowers the cost of transacting with the company for all parties because it saves them the cost of having to negotiate such a term expressly (Easterbrook and Fischel 1989: 1444). Those who wish to contract out of the rule, such as a strong creditor obtaining a personal guarantee from a director or shareholder, must incur the costs of doing so and will effectively pierce the corporate veil.

Whilst limited liability provides cheaper contracting and certainty to creditors, it is primarily of benefit to shareholders. It encourages them to invest in risky projects by externalising some of the risk of loss to creditors. The shareholders do not jeopardise their personal assets, yet reap the rewards of the investment should it succeed (Bainbridge 2001: 489). The amount of each shareholder's potential loss is finite and known, giving the shares a stable price and aiding their transferability (Halpern, Trebilcock and Turnbull 1980). If shareholders were concerned about losing their personal assets in the event of the company's default, the risk could be disproportionate to the return. A small investment could render the shareholder liable for a large corporate debt, yet the return, should the company be successful, would remain small.

Unlimited liability would prompt shareholders to monitor the board's and the company's behaviour, and because monitoring is time-consuming and costly, shareholders would either demand large returns on their investments to compensate, or would confine their investing to a small number of low-risk companies. This would effectively constrain investors' ability to reduce their risk through the diversification of their portfolio of investments, and would stifle investment in new or innovative enterprises. Boards of large companies, separated from the shareholder body, would be encouraged to avoid risk, and would probably be risk averse anyway because of close scrutiny by nervous shareholders.

In addition, shareholders would need to monitor their fellow investors, to ensure that they were not left bearing the debt alone, causing considerable problems with large corporations with extensive and changing membership. Share trading would also suffer, as incoming investors would need to make sure they are investing in an entity with an acceptable risk profile, adequate capitalisation and well resourced fellow shareholders. The different appetite for risk amongst shareholders is reflected in the price they are willing to pay for their shares, and this can adversely affect achieving a stable price for shares.

Whilst limited liability shifts some of the risk of loss to creditors, they are considered to be the 'cheapest cost avoider' (Bainbridge 2001: 501–502) because of their capacity, at least in theory, to protect ex ante against it. One way is by charging more for their goods. Easterbrook and Fischel (1991: 50) assert that: '[a]s long as these risks are known, the firm pays for the freedom to engage in risky activities . . . The firm must offer a better risk–return combination to attract investment'. In addition to the capacity to price-protect, some creditors can also be protected by devices such as loan covenants, restricting the company's ability to sell or further pledge its assets, security over the corporation's major assets, retention of title clauses or personal guarantees from the directors (Posner 1976: 504). Creditors are also expected to diversify away their risk by dealing with many different debtor companies.

However, these theoretical justifications for shifting the risk of loss to creditors do not hold up except in relation to the most powerful creditors. Often there is not full or timely information to enable creditors to make an accurate assessment and pricing of risk. The contention that creditors can self-protect is based on the theoretical 'efficient markets' hypothesis, which assumes that all relevant information is available and digested by the market (Gordon and Kornhauser 1985: 770).

Unforeseen ex post opportunism by directors and managers interferes with creditors' ability to price-protect (Eisenberg 1989: 1465). Importantly, creditors vary in their ability to protect themselves, as some creditors, such as small trade creditors, cannot make their own bargains. This may be because of lack of bargaining power, lack of incentive to bargain owing to the small size of the contract, or lack of skill and knowledge of the bargaining process. With small debts, the cost of obtaining information about the risk may be prohibitive. Some creditors, such as taxation authorities and tort victims, are involuntary (Lipson 2003). Others, including employees, have the difficult choice between unemployment or working for a company that may not pay their wages.

It should then come as no surprise that the victims of phoenix activity are those very creditors for whom the theoretical underpinnings of limited liability are the least convincing. This is explored in the next section.

3 The who, how and why of phoenix activity

It is important at this stage to differentiate phoenix activity from illegal phoenix activity. The limited liability of shareholders and a company's separate legal entity allows companies of any size or nature to close down when burdened by debt without those debts having an impact on shareholders. Indeed, in Australia and many other jurisdictions around the world, insolvency – the inability to pay debts as and when they fall due – *requires* directors to cause their companies to cease business, or risk facing personal liability for their debts.[3]

The liquidation or administration could involve some or all of the company's assets to be sold to the company's former controllers. The business as a whole could be sold to them as a going concern. Provided the process is conducted independently and transparently and in the absence of improper motives on the part of the controllers, the resurrection of the business through a new corporate entity is legal and, in some cases, even desirable. Jobs may be saved and returns to creditors of Oldco maximised if the controllers pay a better price for the business purchased 'lock, stock and barrel', rather than as individual assets, broken up and sold piecemeal.

The creditor victims of this kind of legal phoenix activity, better described as 'business rescue' to differentiate it from its evil twin, will generally lose their money. As a result, business rescue still generates comments that the transaction involving Newco's controllers is 'suspicious'. Some creditors with special vulnerability have individual legislative schemes to allow recovery, and these are considered in the next section. Others, mainly unsecured trade creditors, must rely on whatever self-protection mechanisms they put in place ex ante, and eventually write off any unpaid amounts against their own taxation liability. It is important to recognise that these innocent victims of legitimate business rescue are the necessary collateral damage of maintaining limited liability for shareholders. To allow them to recover from Newco's controllers simply because the business was rescued by its previous operators would be counter-productive. In the end, the risk of creditors sustaining losses is the price of dealing with a limited liability company.

The success of illegal phoenix activity, by its nature, depends upon the company controllers being able to dress up the closure of Oldco and sale of assets to Newco as a proper business

---

3 For example Corporations Act 2001 (Aus) s 588G, Insolvency Act 1986 (UK) s 214.

rescue and to conceal their own improper behaviour. The smaller the company, the more likely it is that there is little or no external interest in its affairs and that the debts are comparatively small. The controllers have no public reputations to jeopardise and can surface running the business in a different location without new customers being any the wiser. Where the very act of illegal phoenixing involves the company being stripped of its assets for token consideration, creditors have to decide whether to invest further money to fund a liquidator to investigate or to write the debt off. Typically, therefore, illegal phoenix activity occurs in micro or small businesses.

There is another version of illegal phoenix activity, however, that can occur in larger enterprises. Labelled in Australia as 'sophisticated' phoenix activity, this occurs in corporate groups where a subsidiary might lack assets but be used to accrue liabilities such as taxes and employee entitlements by being a 'labour hire' entity for the group (Australian Government Treasury 2009: 2). Once these creditors start pressing for payment, the subsidiary is placed into liquidation and the labour hire function is taken over by an existing or newly created entity within the group. This creates special problems for regulators attempting to tackle the behaviour because of the limited liability of the parent company shareholders, the separate legal entity status of the insolvent subsidiary and the general reluctance of courts to pierce the corporate veil. The lack of an undervalue asset transfer or some other evidence of breach of directors' duties makes an attack on the subsidiary's directors problematic.

Certain industries lend themselves to illegal phoenix activity, whether through successor companies or corporate groups. The building and construction industry is notorious for it in Australia.[4] Whilst the head contractor might be a reputable large company with proper business practices, there may be multiple layers of sub-contractors beneath it engaging in illegal phoenix activity. The sub-contractors themselves may operate through multiple companies with one entity hiring the workers and another owning the necessary equipment. There may be a change of the sub-contractor's name on workers' payslips, but those workers are unaware that their employment is now with a new labour hire company within the group that has no liability for wages or other entitlements accrued previously.

Temporary migrant workers may be hired and then threatened with the loss of their jobs and revocation of their visas if they complain. Many such workers are unaware of the full extent of their entitlements in the first place. However, the problem is not confined to construction or blue collar employment. In Australia, personal services businesses such as security and financial advising are also commonly identified industries where illegal phoenix activity is suspected to take place. In such industries, there is little investment required in premises or equipment, and therefore any improper transfer of assets between businesses is indiscernible. This highlights the often opportunistic nature of illegal phoenix activity.

Employees are not the only victims of illegal phoenix activity, whether of the successor company or sophisticated kind. In Australia it is common for both federal and state revenue authorities to be deliberate targets. It might seem surprising that apparently powerful, well resourced and highly motivated creditors such as these would become victims to illegal phoenix activity. They are because of the confluence of a number of factors: the difficulty of knowing what amounts are owing until companies report their earnings and what taxes they have withheld; problems in detecting whether this non-payment is as a result of a

---

4 See for example The Hon Terrence Cole, *Final Report of the Royal Commission into the Building and Construction Industry* (February 2003) (Cole Royal Commission) ch 12; Australian Government, Senate Economics References Committee, *Insolvency in the Australian Construction Industry* (2015).

legitimate corporate failure (involving a business rescue or otherwise) or something more sinister; the fact that these non-payments are amongst millions of transactions that come to their attention; a shortage of resources; and a relative lack of legislative powers to attack the company's controllers directly when the company becomes insolvent and enters external administration.

Detection is often problematic because of the sleight of hand practised by the company controllers. A company might be placed into liquidation one day but its Newco, phoenixed version, opens the next day in the same premises. Other people – family members or close associates – might be appointed to Newco as its 'official' directors. In some cases, the registered trading name stays the same or similar so that customers are oblivious to the change. Necessary employees and suppliers might continue to be paid to ensure the continuity of the business, with the result that only the revenue authority misses out on payment. The combinations and permutations of illegal phoenix activity are such that a great deal of data, plus hours of detective work, are sometimes needed to trace these transactions and *then* to discern whether the new arrangements are evidence of impropriety in the finalisation of Oldco's affairs.

4 Tackling phoenix activity

The difficulties identified above affect the way that legislatures around the globe have dealt with phoenix activity and its victims. The present examination concentrates on a limited number of jurisdictions, although the critique of these measures in section 5 below can be applied more broadly. There are a range of measures that exist which help victims of phoenix activity, expressly or incidentally, and these fall into broad categories.

(a) No need to establish a phoenix company

The first category relates to company insolvencies whether or not a new company is created – in other words, regardless of phoenix activity, legal or not. This avoids the difficulties of detecting the transfer at an undervalue of assets to Newco or the illegal intention of company controllers to avoid paying creditors. Into this category fall schemes such as Australia's Fair Entitlements Guarantee (FEG),[5] which is available for employees of insolvent companies placed into liquidation, or of insolvent unincorporated businesses. Schemes such as these are funded by consolidated revenue and thus place a significant burden on government. On the other hand, by not relying on employee or industry contributions or on court proceedings to establish blame, they are comparatively cheap and straightforward to administer.

In contrast, Canada imposes personal liability on directors of companies incorporated federally for up to six months' unpaid wages in certain circumstances.[6] The UK's National Insurance scheme is different again, not being dependent on the insolvency of the employer. It is more in the nature of a pension scheme funded by employees themselves through contributions deducted from wages and remitted to the government.

---

5 See https://employment.gov.au/fair-entitlements-guarantee-feg (last accessed 29 May 2016).
6 For example Canada Business Corporations Act RSC 1985 (c C-44) s 119; Ontario Business Corporations Act s 131(1). Recently, the Ontario Superior Court has held that the director of a closely-held corporation can be held liable for unpaid wages and termination pay under the oppression remedy: *El Ashiri v Pembroke Residence Ltd* 2015 ONSC 1172 (Boswell J).

Australia also has the director penalty notice (DPN) regime,[7] which imposes personal liability on directors for unremitted taxation deductions from workers' wages. Unpaid superannuation contributions – mandated by the government at 9.5 per cent of employees' gross wages – are also covered by the regime. Again, this liability does not depend upon proof that a later company was created or that any impropriety occurred in relation to the non-payment. Personal liability is avoided by reporting amounts owing to the Australian Taxation Office (ATO) and promptly placing the company into external administration if these debts cannot be met.

(b) Director is associated with a prior failed company

The second category of measures recognises phoenix activity in its broad sense more explicitly. These measures broadly fall into two sub-categories. The first has no requirement to prove impropriety on the part of the director; the second involves an implication that the director has not performed adequately but falls short of requiring any proof of breach of directors' duties.

In the first sub-category lie the UK and New Zealand 'similar names' legislation. According to the UK's Insolvency Act 1986, without leave of the court or unless other prescribed circumstances apply,[8] a person who was a director of Oldco within 12 months prior to its insolvent liquidation is prohibited from being a director of another company with the same or similar name as the first within five years of the first company's liquidation. Breach of the prohibition attracts a term of imprisonment or a fine.[9] As a strict liability offence, there is no requirement for a fraudulent intention or bad faith.[10] Personal liability for the debts of the second company is imposed by section 217, and action may be brought by individual creditors. New Zealand's legislation expressly uses the word 'phoenix' in its similar names legislation,[11] although it defines a phoenix company to be one with the same or similar name as the previous failed company.[12] As in the UK, there is no requirement of impropriety.

The second sub-category covers circumstances where there is a justification either for restricting the director from acting in the future or for requiring a bond to safeguard against future non-payment of company debts. For example, in Australia, a director who has been an officer of two or more failed companies in the past seven years may be disqualified for up to five years by the corporate regulator, the Australian Securities and Investments Commission (ASIC) if it is satisfied that the disqualification is justified.[13] A longer period of disqualification may be given by the court.[14]

In the UK, a more stringent provision is section 6 of the Company Directors Disqualification Act 1986 (UK) (CDDA). The court must disqualify a person who is or has been a director of a company that becomes insolvent, where 'his conduct as a director of that company (either taken alone or taken together with his conduct as a director of any other company or companies) makes him unfit to be concerned in the management of a company'. Action is taken by the

---

7 Taxation Administration Act 1953 (Aus) Sched 1 s 269-15.
8 Insolvency Rules 1986 (UK) IR 4.228–30.
9 Insolvency Act 1986 (UK) s 216(4).
10 *Ricketts v Ad Valorem Factors Ltd* [2004] 1 All ER 894.
11 Companies Act 1993 (NZ) s 386A.
12 ibid s 386B(1).
13 Corporations Act 2001 (Aus) s 206F.
14 ibid s 206D.

Insolvency Service, although information forming the basis of the application may come from insolvency practitioners.[15] In addition, the court may disqualify a director under section 8 of the CDDA on the application of the Secretary of State in similar circumstances. In 2015, some small changes were made to tighten up directors' disqualification processes.[16]

Ireland has taken an interesting approach to mandatory capital and the restriction of directors. Courts can make declarations that directors of insolvent companies should not be appointed or act as a director or be involved in forming or promoting a company.[17] However, the court is not obliged to make this declaration in one of two circumstances. The first is that the person has acted honestly and responsibly in the insolvent company's affairs, assisted the liquidator where possible and there are no other reasons that it would be just and equitable to restrict the director in this way.[18] The second is that the new company pays up a share capital of €500,000 if it is a public company or €100,000 if it is any other type of company.[19] The court may grant relief from the restriction if it deems it just and equitable.[20]

The liquidator is obliged to apply for this restriction unless relieved from doing so,[21] and penalties apply to the liquidator for failing to do so.[22] Other officers of the new company may find themselves personally liable for the debts of the new company, if it becomes insolvent, where the new company had received a notice relating to the restriction of the director and the required capital noted above had not been paid.[23] Ireland also has provisions for disqualification generally.[24]

There is also scope for requiring a security bond against future liabilities, rather than a mandatory capital contribution, in Australia. The ATO can obtain security from a taxpayer for any existing or future tax liability, including the superannuation guarantee charge, if the Commissioner considers that the taxpayer intends to carry on an enterprise for a limited time only, or if it is otherwise appropriate.[25]

(c) Director is alleged to have behaved improperly

The third category of approach targets the improper behaviour of the director. Whilst for the purpose of the present discussion this behaviour is occurring in the context of phoenix activity, these laws go beyond that situation. Examples include breaches of directors' duties[26] and fraud offences[27] under both corporations law and taxation law.[28] There is a vast array of statutory provisions or general law precedents around the world allowing for civil action,

---

15 Company Directors Disqualification Act 1986 (UK) s 7(3) and (4).
16 Small Business, Enterprise and Employment Act 2015 (UK) Pt 9.
17 Companies Act 2014 (Ireland) s 819(1).
18 ibid s 819(2).
19 ibid s 819(3).
20 ibid s 822(1).
21 ibid s 683(2).
22 ibid s 683(5).
23 ibid s 836(2).
24 ibid Pt 14, ch 4.
25 TAA Sched 1 s 255-100. Failure to pay the security is an offence, punishable by a fine: s 255-110.
26 Examples in Australia include *Corporations Act* ss 180–184, s 588G and s 596AB.
27 ibid s 590, s 592 and s 596.
28 For example, being knowingly concerned in the defrauding of the Commonwealth in respect of unremitted group tax: Crimes Act 1914 (Aus) s 29D.

civil penalty action or criminal proceedings, whether brought by the company or a regulator, against directors behaving improperly.

(d) The corporate veil is pierced

The fourth category of measures looks past the actions of the directors and focuses on recovering from shareholders. Because these involve piercing the corporate veil, there needs to be some particular justification for doing so. The United States has a 'laundry list' attitude to the identification of relevant factors that justify shareholder liability[29] and Easterbrook and Fischel (1985: 89) famously commented that: "[p]iercing' seems to happen freakishly. Like lightning, it is rare, severe and unprincipled'. It occurs, for example, where the shares are all held by one or few holders, or in cases of fraud, or where the company is an alter ego of the shareholder, or where there is a failure to observe corporate formalities, or where there is an intermingling or absence of corporate records (Millon 2007: 1325–36).

New Zealand provides one of the clearest examples of comprehensive legislation[30] to allow both pooling of the affairs of an insolvent group of companies, as well as contribution orders to be made against solvent companies in aid of related insolvent companies. The legislation provides wide powers to the courts to order related companies to contribute to the payment of a related company's debts or for their liquidation to take place as though they were one company, where it is just and equitable to do so.[31] This is determined in accordance with specified factors.[32] Whilst these factors are widely expressed and include 'such other matters as the Court thinks fit', it is significant that they expressly exclude '[t]he fact that creditors of a company in liquidation relied on the fact that another company is, or was, related to it'[33] as a ground for making an order.

According to Farrar (1998: 195), section 315C was inserted to allay fears that creditors would base their claim on the fact that they had invested because of their debtor company's relationship with another company. It is noteworthy that the definition of a related company[34] covers the intermingling of corporate affairs, by including in the definition: '(d) [t]he businesses of the companies have been so carried on that the separate business of each company, or a substantial part of it, is not readily identifiable'. This echoes one of the pooling grounds, which looks at: '[t]he extent to which the businesses of the companies have been combined'.[35]

Ireland also allows pooling of assets of related companies. A court may order that a contribution be made only where it 'is satisfied that the circumstances that gave rise to the

---

29 This has been discussed by many authors. See, for example, Robert Thompson, 'Piercing the Corporate Veil: An Empirical Study' (1991) 76 *Cornell Law Review* 1036,1063; Stephen Bainbridge, 'Abolishing Veil Piercing' (2001) 26 *Journal of Corporation Law* 479, 510; S Ottolenghi, 'From Peeping Behind the Corporate Veil, to Ignoring it Completely' (1990) 53(3) *Modern Law Review* 338, 353; Franklin Gevurtz, 'Piercing Piercing: An Attempt to Lift the Veil of Confusion Surrounding the Doctrine of Piercing the Corporate Veil' (1997) 76 *Oregon Law Review* 853, 861–70.

30 Companies Amendment Act 1980 (NZ) ss 315A, 315B and 315C, amending Companies Act 1955 (NZ).

31 Companies Act 1993 (NZ) s 271.

32 The factors are specified under Companies Act 1993 (NZ) s 272(1)(a) (for contribution orders) and (b) (for pooling orders).

33 Companies Act 1993 (NZ) s 272(3).

34 ibid s 2(3).

35 ibid s 272(2)(d).

winding up of the company are attributable to the acts or omissions of the related company'.[36] A court may also order the pooling of the assets of two or more insolvent-related companies where it is just and equitable to do so.[37] American bankruptcy courts use the equity powers provided in section 105 of the Bankruptcy Code to order substantive consolidation, as pooling is known there (Widen 2007). This provision allows courts to 'issue any order, process, or judgment that is necessary or appropriate to carry out the provisions of this title'. Generally, all the companies to be consolidated are insolvent,[38] although it is possible, depending on the particular consolidation, for certain companies within the group or certain debts to be excluded (Blumberg and others 2005: 88.04).

Another approach is to subordinate debt provided by a parent company behind the repayment of debt to non-related parties. This deprives the shareholding parent of any advantage gained from its choice to fund the subsidiary with debt capital rather than equity. In the US, the equitable subordination doctrine was codified in 1978.[39] It allows a court to subordinate the claim or interest of a creditor, being a shareholder or affiliated entity, who has acted inequitably.[40] In addition, US courts have the power to recharacterise debt as equity in certain circumstances, even where the shareholder has not acted inequitably (Skeel and Krause-Vilmar 2006: 265).

Germany has substantially overhauled its subordination laws (Verse 2008: 1112–21).[41] Prior to 2008, loans by shareholders to GmbH companies were deemed to be 'substitutes for equity' and treated as equity if they were granted in the course of a 'crisis' of a company or, if granted before the crisis began, they were not immediately withdrawn when it did begin.[42] After 2008, the subordination rules have been moved from the GmbH legislation to the Insolvency Act (Germany),[43] thus extending it to stock corporations. In addition, the subordination rules apply to all loans by shareholders to the company made within one year prior to, or after filing for insolvency,[44] and not just those given or maintained during the company's financial crisis. Certain exceptions apply.[45]

---

36 *Companies Act 2014* (Ireland) s 599(5).
37 ibid s 600(1).
38 With some exceptions: see *In re 1438 Meridian Place, NW, Inc.*, 15 Bankr 89 (Bankr DDC 1981); *In re Crabtree*, 39 Bankr 718 (Bankr ED Tenn 1984).
39 11 USC § 510 (2012); Bankruptcy Reform Act 1978, Pub L No 95-598, 92 Stat 2549.
40 The National Bankruptcy Review Commission had proposed that insider claims be automatically subordinated: National Bankruptcy Review Commission, *Report of the Commission on the Bankruptcy Laws of the United States*, HR DOC No 93-137 (1973). This proposal was not adopted.
41 Gesetz zur Modernisierung des GmbH-Rechts und zur Bekämpfung von Missbräuchen (known as MoMiG).
42 The relevant provisions were: Gesetz betreffend die Gesellschaften mit beschränkter Haftung [Act concerning Companies with Limited Liability] (Germany) 20 April 1892, RGBl, 1892, 477, §§ 32a–32b; Insolvenzordnung [Insolvency Act] (Germany) 5 October 1994, BGBl I, 1994, 2886, § 135; Gesetz über die Anfechtung von Rechtshandlungen eines Schuldners außerhalb des Insolvenzverfahrens [Law concerning the Contestability of Legal Acts of a Debtor outside of Insolvency Proceedings] (Germany) 21 July 1879, RGBl, 1879, 277 § 6.
43 Insolvency Act (Germany) 1999 §§ 39(1) n 5, (4)–(5) (as amended by the Gesetz zur weiteren Erleichterung der Sanierung von Unternehmen, known as ESUG (Further Facilitation of the Restructuring of Companies) which largely came into force as of 1 March 2012).
44 ibid §135(1) n 2.
45 The rules do not apply to shareholders who are not directors and who do not hold more than 10 per cent of the company's registered capital; or new investors who are attempting to rescue the company. These exceptions also applied under the old rules.

5 Critique

Section 2 above showed how corporate law facilitates phoenix activity. The fundamental characteristics of most companies – the company as a separate legal entity with shareholders enjoying limited liability – allow a business to be transferred from an insolvent corporate entity to a new one, minus troublesome debt. Whilst this process may cause consternation to unpaid creditors, the ability to quarantine unpaid debt is usually essential to giving businesses a second chance.[46] The process has both economic benefits and detriments, and the challenge is to achieve the former and minimise the latter. This section will evaluate the various measures outlined in section 4 and consider how to achieve a balance between deterring improper conduct whilst allowing legitimate entrepreneurs to try again.

The distinction between legal and illegal phoenix activity is reminiscent of the language of tax planning, aggressive tax planning, profit shifting, tax minimisation, tax avoidance and tax evasion. In the tax context, the activities undertaken by the taxpayer in each of these situations are essentially motivated by the same desire to pay as little tax as possible but fall on either side of lawful, depending on where the legislators chose to draw the line. This is a matter of public policy, to be decided after an evaluation of the advantages and disadvantages of drawing the line at any particular point. The same considerations of public policy need to be undertaken with phoenix activity. In terms of achieving an appropriate legislative balance, the starting point is to articulate precisely the evil which the government wants to eliminate or reduce.

(a) Overcoming wrongdoing and fraud

If the legislature wishes to ensure that the corporate form is not used to shed debts under 'improper' circumstances, this involves an ex post examination of the circumstances under which the insolvent company closed and its business was transferred to the new company. Such an evaluation inevitably requires external scrutiny by courts, external administrators or regulators, or all three to ensure detection of improper behaviour, followed by prosecution or civil action by a liquidator. This can be costly and time-consuming, and necessitate judgments about subjectively held beliefs and intentions. Damage can be done to the resurrected business while this scrutiny is taking place. To be done effectively, the process requires complete and timely information. None of this is easy.

Detection is the first step. In this, it might be preferable to have a specialist insolvency regulator such as the Insolvency Service in the UK, rather than a generalist corporate regulator such as ASIC in Australia. A specialist service builds expertise and its resources are dedicated to insolvency issues, whereas a generalist corporate regulator may be tempted or instructed by government to prioritise detection and enforcement action against ongoing companies. Insolvency issues do not appear to be a priority for Australia's regulator, ASIC. Private external administrators such as liquidators are expected to be 'gatekeepers',[47] both in

---

46 Some companies restructure without becoming insolvent. The detailed consideration of the circumstances of solvent corporate restructure is beyond the scope of this chapter. In addition, many countries have processes for the formal restructure or the continued operation of insolvent companies. In Australia, for example, it is voluntary administration under Pt 5.3A. In the UK, it is administration under Sched B1 of the Insolvency Act 1986 or company voluntary arrangement under Pt I of the Insolvency Act 1986 (UK).

47 See, for example, http://asic.gov.au/about-asic/media-centre/find-a-media-release/2013-releases/13-332mr-asic-enforces-liquidators-fiduciary-duties/ (last accessed 29 May 2016).

detecting wrongdoing and reporting it to ASIC, and in bringing recovery actions on behalf of creditors. However, unlike the official receiver in the UK, Australia has no government-funded liquidator to undertake investigations where no private practitioner has been appointed. Australian external administrators are generally expected to make investigations at their own expense, with payment to be had from the corporate estate. Only limited government funding is available to these private practitioners.[48]

One of the most troubling aspects of phoenix activity is that the very act of illegally stripping companies of assets takes money away from payment of liquidators, with the result that their investigation could be cursory.[49] Alternatively, the company may not be externally administered at all, becoming dormant and resulting in a later deregistration by ASIC for failing to pay fees and supply documents.[50] Adding insult to injury for Australian liquidators is the fact that, in conducting their investigations of failed companies, they must pay ASIC for access to lodged documents such as directors' personal details. This is not the case in the UK, for example, where searches may be made without charge.

The UK takes an apparently more open-minded approach to business rescues through the facilitation of prepackaged administrations. These involve the sale of the business prior to the formal appointment of the administrator and without creditor approvals. This is meant to preserve corporate goodwill. In 2014, the UK's Graham Report into prepacks, as they are known, found that they have the capacity to save jobs, they are cheaper than formal procedures and that, generally, deferred consideration payable by the purchaser of the business is paid. However, Graham (2014: 59) found that prepacks lacked transparency and adequate marketing, which might result in a better price for the assets and a better return to creditors. She made a number of recommendations, including that transactions with 'connected parties' are subject to the opinions of a 'prepack pool' to whom details have been disclosed. This is a useful balancing device against prepacks being used as a screen for illegal phoenix activity.

The second step is enforcement. For example, in the UK, the Criminal Investigations and Prosecutions team of the Department of Business, Innovations and Skills prosecute wrongdoers in the context of insolvency. Recently, two directors were sentenced to lengthy disqualifications and jail terms for fraudulently removing company property in anticipation of the winding up of the company, failing to keep adequate accounting records and reusing a prohibited company name.[51] By way of contrast, ASIC rarely brings any actions against alleged phoenix operators, generally only disqualifying them for short periods of time. Discharging the criminal burden of proof is understandably difficult, especially where the directors' actions are capable of an innocent explanation.

---

48 ASIC administers the Assetless Administration Fund, which provides limited funding to investigate and report wrongdoing. See http://asic.gov.au/for-finance-professionals/registered-liquidators/your-ongoing-obligations-as-a-registered-liquidator/assetless-administration-fund/ (last accessed 29 May 2016). In 2015, Australia's Department of Employment announced the Fair Entitlements Guarantee Recovery Fund: https://employment.gov.au/FEGRecoveryProgramme (last accessed 29 May 2016).

49 It is clear from s 545 of the Corporations Act 2001 (Aus) that liquidators are not obliged to conduct work, beyond preparation of their statutory report, for which they will not be paid.

50 Corporations Act 2001 (Aus) s 601AB.

51 See for example https://www.gov.uk/government/news/jail-and-disqualification-for-middles brough-taxi-hire-directors (last accessed 29 May 2016).

Similar names legislation overcomes this difficulty. As a strict liability offence, there is no requirement for a fraudulent intention or bad faith.[52] However whilst it has the advantage of targeting those seeking to hoodwink customers, employees or suppliers who think they are dealing with a previous corporate incarnation, it has the potential to over-reach, and the section has been interpreted widely in the UK.[53] It may capture innocent directors who seek to utilise the remaining goodwill and brand recognition associated with the failed company, even where its debts have been paid in full. On the other hand, the provision only captures liquidated companies and not those who are in another form of administration or are simply deregistered (Milman 1997: 228). In addition, these laws do nothing to prevent the incorporation of a new entity with a similar name to the failed company where a related party of a director of the failed company, for example an associate, spouse, son or daughter, is appointed director instead. The issue of phoenixing within corporate groups is also not addressed.[54]

To assist ex post detection, there are some limited ex ante measures that can be undertaken. For example, regulators need to be easily able to identify and track possible offenders. This includes being able to trace certain individuals from one company to the next, so that their pattern of behaviour is detected, and also to identify dummy and fictitious directors who mask the true controllers of companies that have been phoenixed. Requiring all directors to establish their identity through verification processes – for example, a current passport, drivers' licence, bank account or birth certificate – would assist in eliminating fictitious directors. Directors could be issued with a director identity number (DIN) that must be quoted when dealing with regulators, lenders and parties with whom their companies contract.

(b) Preventing or deterring creditor losses caused by serial entrepreneurs

If the evil to be prevented is to stop the incurring of debts by inept entrepreneurs creating company after company, the solutions are different. Evidence of wrongdoing is not required. This means that measures such as director penalty notices, security bonds, mandatory capitalisation, disqualifications for being involved in multiple failed companies and other forms of restriction are useful. They work in different ways. Some of these can be sought before a new company is established; others impose personal liability on directors or else limit their capacity to begin another business. Here, the challenge is to calibrate the particular mechanism so that it eliminates those who should not be running businesses but allows those who have learnt their lessons to try again. However, such calibration requires consideration of the particular circumstances of the person and the relevant failed companies, and this adds to the cost and complexity of using these mechanisms.

---

52 Insolvency Act 1986 (UK) s 216.

53 See for example *Ad Valorem Factors Ltd v Ricketts* (n 10) at [18], where Mummery LJ said: 'the legal position is that, if the name of Air Equipment is a prohibited name within the natural and ordinary meaning of the language of s 216(2), this case is caught by the restrictions, even if this is not a 'Phoenix Syndrome' case and even if the sanctions of criminal liability seem to be harsh'.

54 In the UK, an exception to liability exists where the successor company has been known by its prohibited name for the whole of the 12 month period prior to the liquidation of the failed company. See Insolvency Rules r 4.230. This would frequently be the situation for related companies within corporate groups. The UK legislation thus provides no impediment to phoenix activity within groups.

(c) Protecting especially vulnerable creditors

If the evil to be prevented is damage to creditors, particularly vulnerable creditors such as employees and taxation authorities, the task of identifying some illegal or improper behaviour is again removed. These two groups require separate treatment. Government funds to cover unpaid wages and other entitlements are useful in ensuring that employees are not severely disadvantaged by working for an insolvent employer. However, they potentially create a moral hazard if they encourage employers not to make adequate provision for their workers in the event of insolvency. Arguably, they also remove the incentive for regulators and external administrators to seek recovery from errant companies and their directors, on the basis that the employees have been taken care of.

Special provisions for taxation authorities are based on their status as protectors of the public revenue. Unlike trade creditors, taxation authorities are involuntary creditors. These two factors arguably justify fairly draconian measures, such as Australia's director penalty notice regime, to recover amounts owed by companies from their controllers in the event of business failure.[55] A useful mechanism in these circumstances is automated reporting of payroll deductions, such as the 'single touch' payroll device proposed in Australia. This enables the Australian Taxation Office to chase up those companies where payments have not been made in a timely manner. These measures, however, have the potential of discouraging legitimate entrepreneurs from establishing companies, and may also penalise directors who have overlooked their taxation payment responsibilities during their fight to keep their companies alive.

6 Conclusion

Any mechanism that seeks to impose liability on directors for the non-payment of company debts where the business might prosper through a new corporate entity runs the risk of doing more harm than good. The rhetoric becomes one of honest, risk-averse business people being reluctant to start again whilst their more reckless or morally compromised counterparts are undeterred. That said, it is imperative that fraudulent directors are held accountable for their actions and others are deterred from trying similar manoeuvres.

In addition, any suggestion that shareholders, rather than managers, should be liable for corporate debts is met with apocalyptic predictions that no-one will ever invest in companies again. The particular concern in piercing the corporate veil is line-drawing. This includes whether any imposition of liability can be known ex ante, so that risk can be priced and behaviour adjusted, or ex post by the court based on tests such as the 'just and equitable' test or according to 'laundry list' factors.

If holding companies are only to be liable for the debts of wholly-owned subsidiaries in specified circumstances, there is an avoidance incentive to have some shares owned by another person or company. If holding companies might be liable for the debts of partly owned subsidiaries, it becomes an issue of fairness if the human holders of the other shares are not liable. If those human holders are to be liable, the principle of limited liability comes directly under threat. The justification for imposing liability on holding companies could therefore be because of their behaviour in wielding control over the subsidiary. That

---

55 Taxation authorities are not priority creditors in Australia (Taxation Debts (Abolition of Crown Priority) Act 1980 and Insolvency (Tax Priorities) Legislation Amendment Act 1993) nor the UK (Enterprise Act 2002 (UK) s 251.

said, it might be preferable to characterise these holding companies as shadow directors because of their degree of involvement in the affairs of the subsidiary, thus side-stepping the language of veil piercing if not its outcome.

Allowing courts to make these sorts of determinations, for example, to order contribution from a solvent parent company or subordination of its debt, based on a 'just and equitable' test is always likely to lead to a conservative approach to piercing the corporate veil. This is because the limited liability of shareholders is such a fundamental corporate law concept. At the same time, it is galling for creditors and regulators alike when the repeated use of insolvent subsidiaries within a corporate group allows the group to escape substantial liabilities for taxes, employee entitlements and other debts. A balance needs to be struck between measures that facilitate the resuscitation of businesses with potential to thrive in a new corporate home, and those that properly deter or prevent fraudulent or ill-advised business rescues occurring.

Bibliography

Australian Government, Treasury (2009) *Action Against Fraudulent Phoenix Activity Proposals Paper*.

Bainbridge, S. (2001) 'Abolishing Veil Piercing' *Journal of Corporation Law*, 26: 479.

Blumberg, P. I. and others (2005) *Blumberg on Corporate Groups*, vol 2, New York, Aspen Publishers.

Easterbrook, F. and Fischel, D. (1985) 'Limited Liability and the Corporation' *Chicago Law Review*, 52: 89.

Easterbrook, F. and Fischel, D. (1989) 'The Corporate Contract' *Columbia Law Review*, 89: 1416.

Easterbrook, F. and Fischel, D. (1991) *The Economic Structure of Corporate Law*, Cambridge MA: Harvard University Press.

Eisenberg, M. (1989) 'The Structure of Corporation Law' *Columbia Law Review*, 89: 1461.

Farrar, J. (1998) 'Legal Issues Involving Corporate Groups' *Company and Securities Law Journal*, 16: 184.

Graham Review into Prepack Administration (2014) Report to The Rt Hon Vince Cable MP.

Gordon, J. and Kornhauser, L. (1985) 'Efficient Markets, Costly Information and Securities Research' *New York University Law*, 60: 761

Halpern, P., Trebilcock, M. and Turnbull, S. (1980) 'An Economic Analysis of Limited Liability in Corporation Law' *University of Toronto Law Journal*, 30: 117.

Lipson, J. (2003) 'Directors' Duties to Creditors: Power Imbalance and the Financially Distressed Corporation' *UCLA Law*, 50: 1189.

Millon, D. (2007) 'Piercing the Corporate Veil, Financial Responsibility, and the Limits of Limited Liability' *Emory Law Journal*, 56(5): 1308.

Milman, M. (1997) 'Curbing the Phoenix Syndrome' *Journal of Business Law*, 224.

Posner, R. (1976) 'The Rights of Creditors of Affiliated Corporations' *University of Chicago Law Review*, 43: 499.

Skeel, D. A. and Krause-Vilmar, G. (2006) 'Recharacterization and the Nonhindrance of Creditors' *European Business Organization Law Review*, 7: 259.

Verse, D. A. (2008) 'Shareholder Loans in Corporate Insolvency – A New Approach to an Old Problem' *German Law Journal*, 9: 1109.

Widen, W. (2007) 'Corporate Form and Substantive Consolidation' *The George Washington Law Review*, 237.

8

Trust is good but control is better?

A critical introduction to remuneration governance in Germany and the United Kingdom

Philipp Kanzow

Introduction[1]

One of the most contentious aspects of corporate governance is the remuneration of managers. Flawed remuneration structures and inefficient governance mechanisms have been related to several major corporate scandals (Ferrarini and others 2009: 3). However, remuneration is also an important instrument for incentivising managers.

This chapter compares the three main mechanisms to set and monitor executive remuneration in Germany and the United Kingdom (UK). The aim is to identify similarities and differences as well as advantages and disadvantages and to suggest improvements. Both remuneration governance frameworks have been subject to reform in recent years. Say-on-pay supported by effective disclosure was recently the 'réforme du jour' (Ferrarini and others 2010: 86). The latest wave of reforms aimed at making the say-on-pay vote partially binding. Thus, control rather than trust appears to be the watchword.

The focus of this chapter lies, first, on 'remuneration governance' (Kanzow 2014: 1), meaning the setting and monitoring of executive remuneration. Second, the focus is on listed public companies, since in both countries special remuneration governance rules exist for this type of company. The topical remuneration governance of banks is excluded because of banks' particular corporate governance, which differs from that of 'generic firms', as a consequence of bank-specific executive remuneration problems and special regulations (cf Mülbert 2009: 411).

Theoretical foundations

Executive remuneration is the total material compensation an executive receives within a company. Its purpose can best be explained on the basis of the agency theory. Executive

---

1 This chapter draws on the findings in P Kanzow *Remuneration Governance in Germany and the United Kingdom* (Thesis, University of Durham 2014).

remuneration will alleviate the agency problem (Bebchuk and Fried 2004: 15). The dominant view is that well drafted remuneration contracts can offer powerful means for aligning managers' and shareholders' interests (cf Jensen and Murphy 1990a: 225 ff; Jensen and Murphy 1990b: 36 ff). However, managers cannot be trusted to set their own pay owing to their interest in receiving more pay for less work. Therefore, in arm's length bargaining, the board, defending the interests of the company and the shareholders, will try to conclude the best contract possible (Bebchuk and Fried 2004: 18). Following this 'optimal contracting' approach, executive remuneration provides an ex ante incentive for executives to maximise shareholder value by offering them the opportunity to share the gains achieved ex post (Sheehan 2012: 257).

The 'managerial power' approach, however, doubts that remuneration contracts solve the agency problem (Bebchuk and Fried 2004: 61 ff). Following this approach, optimal remuneration contracts are possible in theory only. In reality, the managers have power over the board, inter alia because the directors' reappointment depends on them (Bebchuk and Fried 2004: 25 ff). Therefore, in the negotiations the board does not focus on the shareholders' interests and allows managerial rent extraction (Bebchuk and Fried 2004: 62). Negative reactions by outsiders ('outrage') and the costs these may generate are identified as the only constraint (ibid: 64). Managers try to 'camouflage' the true remuneration to avoid 'outrage' (ibid: 4).

Whilst the 'optimal contract' approach regards the purpose of executive remuneration as solving the agency problem, the 'managerial theory' approach does not consider it as a remedy but as an 'amplifier' (Geiler and Renneboog 2010: 263) and an 'agency problem in itself' (Bebchuk and Fried 2004: 62).

The question of which approach is preferable is not easily answered. Remuneration is certainly an effective incentive, and one which aligns interests. However, shortcomings exist, which need to be addressed through remuneration governance instruments. Effective monitoring and control through shareholders (and other stakeholders) is needed to avoid managerial rent extraction.

Remuneration governance

The regulation of executive remuneration is multi-layered (cf Döll 2010: 103). Over the next pages the three main layers, namely remuneration-setting by the (supervisory) board, disclosure of executive remuneration and shareholder voting on executive remuneration are examined. The layers are inter-linked and share the aim of reducing agency costs.

(1) The first layer: the (supervisory) board

The rules regarding the setting of executive remuneration, including the competence to determine the remuneration and procedural and material rules, constitute the first layer (cf Döll 2010: 103). Public discontent about the high level of managers' remuneration has led to several reforms in this field in both countries throughout the last two decades. Whilst the focus in the UK was predominantly on self-regulatory corporate governance codes and binding legislation only as a last resort, German public company law has traditionally offered a high degree of regulation (cf Aktiengesetz §§ 76ff) and provisions on the procedure for setting levels of remuneration have existed for decades.

This, in conjunction with the – theoretically – high degree of independence of the remuneration-setting supervisory board, necessitated only minor changes to the existing regulatory framework. A 'comply or explain' best practice code – the German Corporate Governance Code[2] (GCGC) – was introduced. The UK system, in contrast, leaves the organisation of the procedure of executive remuneration-setting entirely up to the private parties involved. More detailed and strict provisions are made by 'comply or explain' best practice codes. Enforcement is left to the market and especially institutional investors (Rode 2009: 71).

(a) Board structure

The board structure is the 'most obvious' (Davies 2002: 435) difference between the two systems. German companies are characterised by a mandatory two-tier structure, whilst UK companies usually have unitary boards.

Prima facie the German separation of those who determine the remuneration and those who receive it seems advantageous. Not separating these roles causes conflicts of interest and a lack of external and internal independence. However, the low level of regulation in UK company law allows flexibility. The establishment of remuneration committees consisting of independent non-executive directors (NEDs) is possible and best practice. Hence, both systems now entrust a separate, independent body with the remuneration-setting process.

(b) Appointment of executives

The appointment of management board members is regulated in great detail in the German Aktiengesetz (Public Companies Act). Candidates cannot be members of the company's supervisory board at the same time. Apart from that, the Aktiengesetz provides only a few general and easy to fulfil criteria. The supervisory board is exclusively competent to appoint management board members. Also, one has to distinguish between the appointment *stricto sensu* and the service contract.

The Companies Act (CA) 2006 does not provide many rules regarding the appointment of board members. It does not regulate the procedure of appointment at all. Generally, it is left to the company's articles of association to lay down rules. The UK Corporate Governance Code[3] (UKCGC) recommends the use of a remuneration committee consisting of independent NEDs. Finally, a distinction needs to be made between the appointment to the office of director and the service contract for management services.

Thus, both systems entrust the appointment of executives and the setting of their remuneration to bodies that are separate from the recipients of the remuneration. Using independent individuals assures investors that the managers are not using the company's assets for their own benefit. However, despite convergence – especially in the best practice codes – the independence requirements' substance still differs (Ringe 2013: 15). Another commonality is the significant influence that the management board and executive directors each has in practice on the appointment of new (supervisory) board members.

---

2 http://www.dcgk.de/en/code.html (last accessed 31 May 2016).
3 https://www.frc.org.uk/Our-Work/Codes-Standards/Corporate-governance/UK-Corporate-Governance-Code.aspx (last accessed 31 May 2016).

(c) Powers and duties

In German companies the management board is competent to direct the company and manage its business. The supervisory board is entrusted with the managers' appointment and removal, their remuneration and their supervision.

The CA 2006 by comparison does not stipulate rules on the division of powers but leaves this to the company's articles of association. Usually the board has all powers except those that are statutorily required to remain with the general meeting. The more detailed UKCGC provides that the board's function is to 'provide entrepreneurial leadership of the company'.[4] Consequently, as to powers, the UK board and the German management board are similar.

The independent NEDs recommended by the UKCGC resemble the supervisory board. The description of NEDs' tasks in A.1 UKCGC is almost identical to that of the supervisory board's task in 5.1.1 GCGC. An important difference is that NEDs participate in the management of the company, whilst supervisory board members do not. Taking part in more meetings offers the former better information than their German counterparts receive, who struggle with information asymmetry. However, NEDs' dual role may leave insufficient time for the supervisory work and may affect their independence negatively.

(d) Setting and controlling executive remuneration

(AA) COMPETENCE

Following detailed statutory provisions in Germany the full supervisory board has exclusive competence to determine management remuneration.[5] Delegation to a committee is no longer permitted.[6] The situation in the UK is diametrically opposed. The CA 2006 neither stipulates the exclusive competence of one organ nor a specific mode. Owing to concerns over conflicts of interest and independence, the best practice is to entrust independent NEDs that form a remuneration committee with this task.

The remuneration committee in UK companies has been created in order to ensure that executive directors cannot directly decide on their own remuneration. The driving concerns were the apparent issues of self-dealing, the required antagonism of interests and internal and external independence of the decision-makers.

In Germany, owing to the supervisory board's exclusive competence, management board members should – theoretically – have no influence on the remuneration decision anyway. The reasons for creating remuneration committees here were different: (1) delegating the decision to specialists should deliver more efficient outcomes; (2) supervisory boards with up to 21 members can be too large and unwieldy (Thüsing 2009a: 524); (3) committees could relieve the full supervisory board of some of its work load (Hoffmann-Becking and others 2009: 23), so that the supervisory board does not neglect its primary task of monitoring the management board's actions (Kremer 2009: 1); and (4) small committees allowed for confidentiality in the remuneration negotiations (Strieder 2005: 107). Therefore, open, objective and confidential negotiations in a small group were recommended.[7]

---

4 UKCGC s A.1 Supporting Principle at 7.
5 Aktiengesetz § 84 (1).
6 ibid § 107 (3) sentence 3.
7 See 4.2.2 GCGC 2008.

What led to the prohibition of the delegation to a remuneration committee in Germany? Probably the main motive for it was strengthening the supervisory board's responsibility for the managers' remuneration. Moreover, if not all members of the supervisory board were involved in the remuneration decision it would be difficult to justify that the extended liability of § 116 Aktiengesetz should apply to all members. Furthermore, it could be argued that the remuneration decision is of such significance that the full supervisory board should legitimise it. Another objective was increased transparency of the process (Lingemann 2009: 1922). This reason is not entirely convincing as the managers' remuneration has to be disclosed individually anyway. However, it may improve the transparency of the procedure as such.

Thus, owing to the different starting points the rationales for introducing remuneration committees in Germany and the UK differed. The German move back to decisions by the full supervisory board may seem surprising. However, discussions can still take place in an expert committee; it is just that the decision has to be taken by the full board.

(BB) LEGAL FRAME OF THE DECISION

The legal framework of the remuneration decision shows commonalities. It is the entrepreneurial and organisational task of the German supervisory board and the UK remuneration committee respectively to decide on the amount and the structure of the remuneration package. Both deciding bodies have a large margin of discretion (Germany: Dauner-Lieb 2009: 586; Cannivé and Seebach 2009: 599; UK: Morse and Worthington 2011: 8.913; *Burland v Earle*;[8] *Normandy v Ind Coope & Co*[9]). Both jurisdictions provide that the remuneration should be sufficient to attract and motivate talented personnel, but not more. They also share an emphasis on the company's long-term success and performance-related pay.

However, the German rules are stricter and more detailed. By establishing an adequacy requirement,[10] the legislator limits the freedom of contract. It is explicitly aimed at preventing excessive remuneration. The German law also offers another, even more incisive instrument: the subsequent reduction of management remuneration if the situation for the company deteriorates and the agreed remuneration would be inequitable.[11]

The UK system refrains from limiting private autonomy and upholds the principle of *pacta sunt servanda*. The committee is free to decide on remuneration as long as it is within the legal boundaries and does not violate any of the determining directors' duties.

(e) Strengths and weaknesses

One of the central functions of comparative law is to enable one jurisdiction to learn from the experiences of another (Zweigert and Kötz 1996: 15). However, 'legal transplants' are only possible within the boundaries of path dependence (Bebchuk and Roe 1999: 127 ff). With this in mind, the strengths and weaknesses of the two approaches and how they strike a balance between opposing axioms will be analysed.

---

8 [1902] AC 83.
9 [1908] 1 Ch 84.
10 Aktiengesetz § 87(1).
11 ibid § 87(2).

(AA) INDEPENDENCE VERSUS PROFESSIONALISM

Conflicting regulatory aims can be identified. On the one hand, the decision-making body is supposed to be uninfluenced by the remuneration recipients. In addition to being independent of mind, the body's members must appear independent to an outside observer. Potential conflicts of interest of the decision-makers will be avoided by ensuring that their interests are not congruent with those of the recipients. Ideally, the individuals making the decision would have no links with the company or its managers and be organisationally separate.

On the other hand, owing to the complex nature of remuneration-setting it is necessary that those making the remuneration decision are highly qualified and have sufficient expertise. They are supposed to be informed, critical and sufficiently engaged. They require a profound understanding of the firm and inside knowledge. The obvious solution would be to appoint former managers of the company or executives of other listed companies to determine executive remuneration.

The German legislator opted for a focus on independence by using the clear and mandatory separation of supervisory and management boards. Thereby a high degree of neutrality and independence should be ensured. In theory, managers have no influence on the determination of their remuneration. Conflicts of interest should be avoided as the supervisory board members' re-election depends on satisfactory performance.

This focus on independence is contrasted by the low statutory requirements regarding the qualification of supervisory board members. Almost any adult fulfils the Aktiengesetz's requirements. Higher requirements are set by the courts and the GCGC. Having realised this problem, the legislator allows the use of remuneration committees which can draft the service contract but cannot make a decision on it.

However, the remuneration committees, too, need individuals with sufficient expertise. One solution that is widespread is the appointment of the company's former management board members or managers of other companies as supervisory board members. They possess the necessary skills and knowledge to assess the performance of present managers and the market value of candidates. However, their appointment compromises the supervisory board's independence, owing to social cohesion and solidarity between these supervisory board members and the management.

Therefore, 5.4.2. GCGC recommends truly independent members on the supervisory board and sets more concrete provisions to safeguard supervisory board independence. However, whether the recommendations can improve independence without limiting professionalism is doubtful.

The focus on independence and simultaneous negligence regarding professionalism of both Aktiengesetz and GCGC was counteracted in practice. The management having influence on the supervisory board member's nomination and the fact that most supervisory board members belong to a network of successful managers allows the appointment of highly qualified individuals. In addition, it hinders arm's length bargaining on remuneration.

The UK approach faces a similar dilemma. The CA 2006 remains generally silent regarding both independence and professionalism. That led to procedures being established by the companies' articles of association, which caused a stark conflict of interest. Therefore, the UKCGC recommends entrusting independent NEDs with this task. They should form a remuneration committee. Thereby a separation of remuneration setters and recipients is established, as in the German model. Additionally, independence is defined very narrowly by the UKCGC. Companies adhering to its recommendations should seldom face conflicts of interest. However, a new problem arises: the independence criteria are so strict that finding independent but sufficiently qualified NEDs becomes difficult.

An advantage of NEDs over supervisory board members could be the fact that they are involved in the day-to-day management of the business. This could allow for a better flow of information, which is indispensable for efficient remuneration decisions. In addition, being in frequent meetings with the executive directors can lead to collegiality and loyalty between NEDs and executives. As a result, the desired and vaunted independence could be forfeited.

To summarise, both systems struggle to reconcile the requirements of independence and professionalism. An additional problem is that the law in the books and the law in action differ. Neither approach can ensure sufficient expertise and knowledge of the decision-makers, whilst at the same time ensuring their independence.

(BB) PRACTICABILITY VERSUS TRANSPARENCY

Another problem is the balance between practicability and transparency of the procedure. Practicability is best ensured if a small group of specialists deals with the issue of executive remuneration. In a small group decisions can be made more swiftly. Members of a specialist group have greater expertise so that their decisions are likely to be more efficient. Transparency is best ensured if the remuneration-setting process is public and easily rationalised. It seems advantageous if a wider group can inspect the service contract prior to signing, and can assess the quantum and structure of the remuneration. As 'sunlight helps to disinfect', this greater publicity and the scrutiny by the full board helps to avoid self-serving behaviour.

The difficulty in striking the right balance between the two axioms can be illustrated by the changes to the German rules. Traditionally, delegation of the remuneration decision to a committee was possible[12] and recommended.[13] A 2009 reform prohibited this practice. The then legislator strove for increased transparency by making the full supervisory board responsible for the decision. However, the change also has disadvantages. Now the complex issue of remuneration is decided by a group of up to 21 people. Needless to say, not all supervisory board members have the necessary expertise nor will their number allow for swift decisions. Also, confidentiality is difficult to achieve.

Has the German legislator therefore opted for an increase in procedural transparency at the cost of a decrease in practicability? It is important to note that the *decision* has to be made by the full board. It is still possible for a committee to negotiate with the candidate and draft a service contract. Specialists can discuss the issue but a wider group scrutinises the remuneration agreement before accepting it and taking responsibility for it. The practicability remains almost the same but the transparency is increased.

In the UK the balance between transparency and practicability is different. The best practice involving delegation of the decision to a remuneration committee emphasises practicability. Remuneration committees are small groups of specialists who are experienced in assessing management performances and can ensure efficient remuneration. Is sufficient transparency ensured? The committee has to make available its terms of reference. In addition, the process of remuneration-setting involves only a very limited number of people. Limited publicity increases the risk of collusion and may foster inefficiencies.

12 BGHZ 65, 190, 191.
13 Cf 5.1.2 GCGC 2008.

Thus, the UK focuses on practicability, whilst the German procedure emphasises transparency, although it allows *modi operandi* that ensure the procedure's practicability. The German solution seems advantageous. However, it cannot be 'transplanted' into the UK system owing to the absence of a separate supervisory board in the latter.

(2) The second layer: disclosure

Reverting to the layer model mentioned above, the second layer will now be examined. Remuneration disclosure means the publication of information regarding the remuneration paid to executives by companies and the publication of the company's remuneration policy in the company's financial statement or another relevant medium.

However, disclosure on its own is merely a weak form of accountability (Bottomley 2007: 77 ff). Disclosure 'only serves a purpose if the shareholders or other stakeholders can act on the information' (Sorensen 2009: 272). Disclosure 'may enable shareholders to exercise control and to re-align shareholder and agent interests' (Ward 1998: 48). It will reduce information asymmetries to ensure 'stronger' (Bottomley 2007: 78) accountability of the (supervisory) board vis-à-vis the shareholders (Bahar 2005: 23) and facilitate the 'monitoring of the monitors' (Baums 2005: 301). Hence, based on the information disclosed, enhanced control by the shareholders, e.g. through say-on-pay or exit, and improved prevention, e.g. through 'outrage' and stricter remuneration-setters, will avoid excessive executive remuneration and reduce agency costs (Villiers 2006: 2 ff).

(a) Regulation of disclosure

In both jurisdictions the company legislation is surprisingly silent on the issue of remuneration disclosure. The Aktiengesetz contains hardly any rules on this matter. The Handelsgesetzbuch (commercial code) is the place to find disclosure provisions. Likewise, in the UK the CA 2006 provides sparse information. The details are left to the Large and Medium-sized Companies and Groups (Accounts and Reports) Regulations 2013.

(b) Personal scope

In both systems the law prescribes different remuneration disclosure requirements for listed and non-listed public companies. Comparing the definitions of German listed and UK quoted companies reveals a striking similarity. Moreover, both legislators intend to prevent companies from escaping the disclosure requirements easily by including certain foreign listings, too. A further similarity is that for non-listed companies less extensive disclosure rules apply, e.g. individualised remuneration disclosure is not required.

(c) Duties

Listed companies in both countries have the duty to provide two kinds of information. First, the remuneration of members of the (management) board has to be disclosed in an individualised and detailed way. Second, a statement on the remuneration policy has to be published. However, there are several differences as to what exactly has to be disclosed.

Under German disclosure law the remuneration of each member of the management board has to be disclosed, giving the managers' full names and classified into three categories. The categories are non-performance-related remuneration, performance-related remuneration and long-term incentive components. Payments on termination of a management contract have to be disclosed, as well as benefits received from third parties outside the company.

Quoted UK companies have to give more information and this is also more detailed information. The requirements for the 'Annual Remuneration Report' are similar to the ones for German listed companies. For each director the remuneration, share options, long-term incentive plans (LTIPs), pension payments etc have to be disclosed, identifying the individual by name.

The 'Remuneration Policy Report' requires the disclosure of the remuneration committees' composition, names of advisers and other services they provide, performance criteria for share options and LTIPs, including the methods for assessing them. Also, the relative importance of each remuneration component has to be explained and details on the service contracts with directors have to be disclosed. It also contains a statement on the company's remuneration policy. Comparing this report with the German report on the main features of the remuneration system, it becomes evident that the latter provides less information. Moreover, it is not clear what should be considered 'main features', in contrast to details in the first place.

(d) Exemption

Another significant difference exists with respect to the option to decide not to disclose executive remuneration in an individualised manner. Only the German regulation offers the possibility for the general meeting to opt out of individualised disclosure and to decide to disclose minimal information only, or a level in between.

(e) Sanctions

In both systems the sanction for not fulfilling the duty to disclose executive remuneration as required is a fine, although only the German rules provide a specific amount, namely up to €50,000.

(f) Strengths and weaknesses

A common feature of the two approaches is the restriction of individualised disclosure to listed companies. This limitation avoids unnecessary and costly burdens on non-listed companies as, in their case, there is no need of the capital market for information. It could be argued that it is not the information of the capital market but improved monitoring by the shareholders that is the main objective of the regulations – at least in Germany. Shareholders of non-listed companies should also have the necessary tools to monitor satisfactorily. However, shareholdings of non-listed companies are usually less dispersed, so that other forms of shareholder information should be possible. The inclusion of domestic companies that are listed at certain stock exchanges abroad is also useful to avoid evasion.

The German rules require a classification of remuneration in three groups, whereas the UK rules provide a more detailed breakdown. For certain parties it might be desirable to receive a very detailed breakdown. However, the slightly simplifying German approach offers greater clarity and comprehensibility. The German legislator successfully tried to avoid overloading the annual accounts, whilst providing all necessary information for a rational and well informed investment decision. The completeness of the information and its usefulness seems to be well balanced. However, further standardisation, especially regarding the presentation, is necessary.

Another strength of the German disclosure provisions is that they require the publication of benefits a manager received from or was promised by a third party with regard to his work as a management board member. This is a sensible measure to elucidate potential conflicts of interest. Unfortunately, the UK disclosure regime reveals a gap in this respect.

However, German disclosure rules are unconvincing when it comes to other aspects. Under German law it is possible not to disclose information in an individualised and detailed manner. It may be consistent to argue that, because the main objective of individualised disclosure is the empowerment of shareholders, disclosure should be at the shareholders' discretion and not forced upon them against their will. Similarly, the argument may hold that it should be for the shareholders to decide whether they are willing to accept a potential decrease in share value for making less information available to the capital market. Nevertheless, a mandatory requirement of individualised disclosure without exemptions, as in the UK, is preferable. Entering the capital market entails a wide range of duties, including publicity. Hence, disclosure should not be at the disposition of current shareholders. Investors can never be certain that the company will continue to disclose all the information the investor would like to receive in the future. The only remaining option would be exit at a loss. Hence, minority shareholders are less well protected when the opt-out option exists. The opt-out option is flawed and one of the main weaknesses of the German approach.

A second point on which the UK solution is more convincing is the disclosure of remuneration consultants and other contracts these consultants have with the company. Under German law such a provision does not exist, despite calls for such a disclosure requirement (Kramarsch 2005: 115). Its merits are evident. Potential conflicts of interest of remuneration consultants who would like to receive further contracts from the company would be elucidated. Convincing arguments for non-disclosure are not apparent. The UK regulation is exemplary in this respect. It remains unclear why the German legislator neither followed this example nor took up similar recommendations by the EU.

Both systems offer relatively mild sanctions. Stricter sanctions would be advisable. A good invention by the UK legislator is the idea of requiring the auditor to provide missing information insofar as it is reasonable to expect him to do this. This 'sanction' is a more effective remedy with respect to the aim of shareholder information and protection than a fine.

It should be noted that both regimes have significant weaknesses. The main weakness is a lack of clarity, comprehensibility and usefulness of the information disclosed owing to an overload of information, its unsatisfactory and non-uniform presentation and the complexity of the data disclosed. Neither approach fulfils the objectives set, namely the informing and protecting of shareholders, as well as improved monitoring. To some extent this may be the result of shareholder apathy, although enhanced, standardised disclosure could improve the situation. The 2013 reform in the UK represents movement in the right direction. Finally, neither approach has been able to prevent executive remuneration from rising.

(3) The third layer: say-on-pay

The third layer of remuneration governance – the so-called say-on-pay, meaning shareholder voting on executive remuneration – links remuneration-setting and remuneration-disclosure (cf Döll 2010: 103). It enables shareholders who have gained the necessary information through disclosure effectively to monitor the remuneration system set by the (supervisory) board.

Say-on-pay is the remuneration governance instrument that has been the subject of considerable public discussion in recent years. One may recall the reporting on the 2012 'shareholder spring' in the UK, which coincided with the government's deliberations on reforming the vote, e.g. making it binding (BIS 2012: 1 ff). The reform entered into force in 2013. In Germany, too, there have been interesting developments. Inspired by a Swiss measure, a reform was initiated to make the vote binding.[14] However, it failed to pass the Bundesrat in 2013.

(a) Personal scope

In both countries the say-on-pay rules apply only to public companies that have access to the capital market. The reason lies in part in the difference in size and relevance for the overall economy of these companies, in the particularities of capital markets such as greater transparency needs and, finally, in the higher-level complexity and publicity of the executive remuneration agreements of these companies. Both approaches include domestic companies that are listed in a comparable foreign market in order to prevent avoidance strategies.

(b) (Non-)mandatoriness

The 'most important difference' (Lieder and Fischer 2011: 407) is that the shareholder vote under German law is optional, whereas under UK law it is mandatory. At first glance this difference is astounding. The German *travaux préparatoires* do not explain this deviation from the UK model.[15] It probably results from the different board structures. The one-tier structure may necessitate a mandatory vote, whilst it might be less necessary in the two-tier system of German companies with a (co-determined) supervisory board (ibid).

In practice the difference is less distinctive – at least when it comes to the largest companies. Only two years after the vote's introduction the shareholders of all DAX30-companies had already voted pursuant to § 120 (4) Aktiengesetz. Usually the administration had put the vote on the agenda.

(c) Subject-matter of the resolution

Another aspect where the two say-on-pay regulations differ is the resolution's subject-matter.

In Germany, the resolution's subject-matter is the 'system for the remuneration of management board members'. The term 'remuneration system' is unclear and needs interpretation. It can be defined as the 'abstract and general overall concept', which guides the supervisory board when setting the management board members' individual and precise remuneration (Deilmann and Otte 2010: 546; Fleischer and Bedkowski 2009: 682). The resolution is related to the past as the *existing* remuneration system is the subject-matter under consideration. Thus, the supervisory board's remuneration decision is not anticipated. In practice it has a future-related aspect as well, since the supervisory board is likely to consult (major) shareholders prior to the resolution and shareholders consider future developments too when voting on the 'old' remuneration system.

---

14 *Gesetz zur Verbesserung der Kontrolle der Vorstandsvergütung und zur Änderung weiterer aktienrechtlicher Vorschriften (VorstKoG), BT-Drucks 17/14214.*
15 Cf *BT-Drucks* 16/13433, 12.

The subject-matter of the resolutions in the UK are the parts of the Directors' Remuneration Report (DRR). The resolution on the remuneration policy report is future-related. The resolution on the annual remuneration report, which contains the payments actually made to the directors in that financial year, is related to the past.

The German legislator has followed the UK model in that the resolution concerns the whole remuneration concept rather than individual remuneration agreements (Hupka 2012: 280). Nevertheless, the subject-matters clearly differ. Whilst the UK regulation refers to the statutorily defined DRR, the term 'remuneration system' used by the German legislator needs interpretation (Hupka 2012: 286). The German regulation emphasises the past aspects as future-related decisions would conflict with the supervisory board's exclusive remuneration-setting competence. The UK regulation is clearly future-related, with its explicit reference to the remuneration policy for the following years. Also, the aspect related to the past differs from the German resolution's subject-matter, as it concerns the concrete payments actually made rather than merely the abstract remuneration system.

However, in both countries the dissent is often detached from the resolution's actual subject-matter, since frequently the absolute level of management remuneration or the remuneration package of a particular manager causes concern (Döll 2010: 108; Fleischer and Bedkowski 2009: 682). Irrespective of the exact subject-matter, both resolutions serve as an outlet for dissatisfaction with executive remuneration.

(d) Consequences

(AA) (NON-)BINDING

Initially, the regulations concurred regarding the lack of legal consequences. Both favoured a non-binding vote. In Germany, the main concern was that a binding vote would infringe the supervisory board's exclusive remuneration-setting competence. Also, trade unions opposed the introduction of the say-on-pay vote, as it would increase the influence of shareholders at the expense of the workers. In the UK, mainly practical reasons were mentioned.

Since 2013 the CA 2006 provides a binding vote – at least every three years – on the remuneration policy. Regarding implementation the vote remains advisory. If this advisory vote is lost, the policy must be brought to a binding vote at the next annual general meeting (AGM). Thus, the differences from the German regulation have become more significant. The vote's character and the distribution of powers within UK companies have been changed. Owing to the strict allocation of powers and concerns regarding systematic inconsistencies, even with respect to a merely advisory vote, it seemed very unlikely that the German system would take a similar development. However, surprisingly, a corresponding reform was almost enacted in 2013.

(BB) FACTUAL CONSEQUENCES

Both regulations rely (to some extent) on factual consequences revolving around the threat of reputational damage and improved contact between (supervisory) boards and shareholders. In practice, in both countries factual consequences are already noticeable if less than 50 per cent of the votes – which would be the threshold for a disapproval – are dissenting. Dissent is already considered 'high' if more than 20 per cent of the shareholders fail to back the resolution. This 'high' level of dissent is considered in both countries to require a reaction by the (supervisory) board.

(e) Strengths and weaknesses

The similarities between the two say-on-pay instruments are not surprising, since the German regulation used the UK one as a model. Therefore, the differences are of particular interest.

(AA) MANDATORY VERSUS NON-MANDATORY

The 'most important difference' (Lieder and Fischer 2011: 407) between the regulations is that the vote is optional in Germany, whilst in the UK it is mandatory. The German legislator did not give any explanation for the non-mandatory vote, despite prominent voices in the legislative process (Thüsing 2009b: 20) being in favour of a mandatory vote. A reason for the preference for a non-mandatory vote could be the opposition of influential trade unions. The question arises as to which approach is more advantageous.

The mandatory annual vote offers the advantage of maintaining constant pressure on the board to monitor and deal with executive remuneration and to engage with the shareholders regularly. The shareholders have to deal with executive remuneration details at least annually. This should lead to greater expertise, experience and better board accountability. If the vote is recurring 'automatically', it lifts the burden of action from the shareholders. Moreover, even if the true character of a remuneration contract or policy becomes evident only over a period of time, the shareholders can voice their concerns promptly (Döll 2010: 108). Also, the (supervisory) board will be more careful to leave room for possible contractual amendments in order to react to negative votes if the vote is frequent (Döll 2010: 108).

However, a mandatory annual vote faces the risk of being unnecessary if the remuneration has not been changed since the last vote. This would be a time-consuming exercise without any useful effect. Furthermore, a vote can be costly (Lieder and Fischer 2011: 404). If the vote is merely optional, these costs would only have to be incurred if strictly necessary. Moreover, the (supervisory) board might be more inclined to draft remuneration policies with a longer-term focus. Correspondingly, the 2013 UK regulation provides that a vote is not necessary for three years. This indicates the conclusion that a mandatory annual vote is too strict and potentially inefficient.

The non-mandatory vote offers greater flexibility. Shareholders vote only if it is considered necessary. This can be beneficial for smaller listed companies in particular. Often their shareholder structure differs significantly from that of DAX30 or FTSE 100 companies. They have different and potentially more efficient ways to communicate with their shareholders. A mandatory vote would be unnecessary and inefficient. Finally, a non-mandatory vote is also a less intrusive regulation of companies' internal affairs than a mandatory vote. Regulations should not be more intrusive than necessary to achieve their aim.

However, criticism could arise on the basis that, owing to the optional nature, the effectiveness of the entire say-on-pay regulation depends largely on the companies' administrations. Shareholders may be insufficiently inclined to initiate the vote because of collective action and rational apathy problems (Döll 2010: 108). Moreover, they have to fulfil a relatively high quorum. However, in practice DAX30 companies treat the vote as a standard item, despite its optional nature and smaller companies who do not put the vote on the agenda regularly may not need to do so.

Thus, the optional vote's advantages seem to outweigh those of the mandatory vote. However, the decision as to whether the vote should be mandatory or optional depends largely on one's view regarding the vote's regulatory purpose (Hupka 2012: 324). If the vote is considered to be primarily a monitoring tool for shareholders to prevent excessive remuneration, an optional vote is sufficient since the shareholders can use it if they see the need to do so (ibid). If the vote is regarded as a measure to inform the (supervisory) board about the shareholders' view on the company's executive remuneration arrangements, a mandatory solution is preferable so that the board receives 'feedback' regularly. The first view is the one taken here. The divergence of the German approach from its model regarding the level of the mandatoriness has proven itself to be positive.

The 2013 reform indicates that the UK regulation is converging towards the German one to some extent. However, different board structures may require different solutions. The supervisory board, which is (at least partially) elected by the shareholders and which separates remuneration-setting from managing the company decreases the need for additional shareholder influence, compared with the one-tier system (similar: Lieder and Fischer 2011: 408). Differences in the company organisation and the absence of an adequacy requirement may increase the need for more shareholder involvement. A mandatory vote may be more indicated in the UK than it is in Germany.

(BB) BINDING VERSUS NON-BINDING

Initially both jurisdictions opted for an advisory vote but the 2013 regulation in the UK favours a binding vote on the policy report. The question therefore arises whether the advisory vote is a failed experiment.

The main argument why a non-binding character could be a weakness is lack of effectiveness. Strong (supervisory) boards and managers can ignore the vote. However, there are factual consequences which can be almost as 'binding' as a binding vote. Furthermore, the advisory vote is not designed to be a coercive instrument; rather, it is an outlet for shareholder dissent, which is supposed to lead to more discussions on and publicity around executive remuneration.

A binding vote can lead to practical difficulties. However, if the factual consequences are as compelling as intended, then the difference should be marginal. Also, binding votes bear the risk of either being too prescriptive, and thus hindering recruiting and retaining the best personnel possible, or leaving too much leeway and hence being ineffective. An advisory vote may concern a very detailed policy but if the board has to diverge from it in order to retain or recruit a manager it considers important to the company, it can do so – albeit at the risk of a negative vote at the next AGM.

However, since a binding vote increases the costs and the potential loss of time if a vote is lost, it may be a more effective deterrent vis-à-vis both boards and managers. Similarly, it may be more effective in encouraging shareholders and boards to engage in setting the remuneration from an early stage and on communicating with each other.

Hence, a binding vote may indeed have advantages and further (especially empirical) research should be conducted.

(CC) REMUNERATION SYSTEM VERSUS DRR

In addition, the resolutions' subject-matter differs. The main criticism regarding the German subject-matter 'remuneration system' is a lack of clarity (inter alia Hohenstatt 2009: 1356; Annuß and Theusinger 2009: 2439; Schick 2011: 596). The term is not legally defined. Its meaning has to be deduced from Handelsgesetzbuch and GCGC disclosure rules. The reference to the disclosure provisions, however, is of limited use as their details are not entirely clear either (Thüsing 2009a: 525). Regarding the GCGC rules, one can criticise that the legislator referred to a private organisation's regulation in order to define a statutory term. Furthermore, the GCGC provisions are merely recommendations and § 389 (2) no 5 Handelsgesetzbuch is merely a 'shall'-provision (Reger 2014: 21). The shareholders are not necessarily provided with information about the remuneration system (Reger 2014: 21). Some have even have doubted whether there should be a remuneration system at all (Spindler 2009: 3209; Annuß and Theusinger 2009: 2439; Thüsing 2009a: 524).

In practice, the issues mentioned above are less problematic. According to empirical studies the vast majority of German public limited companies (AGs) present a remuneration report which outlines the management board members' remuneration system (Talaulicar and von Werder 2010: 858). Following other research, the resolution's subject-matter is usually clarified by a reference to the content of the remuneration report (Deilmann and Otte 2010: 564). The invitation to the AGM usually contains a reference to the remuneration report, stating that the report will form the basis for the resolution (von Falkenhausen and Kocher 2010: 625; Deilmann and Otte 2010: 564). Nevertheless, the resolution remains not self-explanatory (similar: Deilmann and Otte 2010: 564). Also, the remuneration report's content is defined neither by statute nor by the GCGC itself (Hupka 2012: 282).

In contrast to that, in the UK the subject-matter of the resolution is the approval of one of the parts of the DRR. Their content is defined by statute. Finally, the subject-matter of the say-on-pay resolution under UK law seems advantageous owing to its superior precision and clarity.

Conclusion

The current remuneration governance regulation in Germany and the UK is not satisfactory. Using effectiveness and agency costs reduction as a yardstick, all three layers are – to varying degrees – not satisfactory in their current form. The setting and monitoring of executive remuneration by (supervisory) boards is not satisfactory and should be improved in both countries. Common problems are remuneration-setters' lack of independence in practice, insufficient commitment and unsatisfactory qualification. The remuneration-setting process also lacks transparency. Several options exist for enhancing this remuneration governance instrument. However, improving one aspect such as independence can negatively affect other aspects such as professionalism. The same applies to transparency and practicability. The right balance between these axioms is difficult to strike and the two systems have opted for different solutions. Neither can overcome the (supervisory) board's inherent shortcomings.

The current disclosure rules go in the right direction. Both jurisdictions provide adequate rules on the content of the disclosure. Despite the failure to curb the absolute level of remuneration, the current regulation has been effective in enabling the control of managerial agency costs, especially if one takes pay increases unrelated to performance and 'rewards for failure' as indicators for managerial agency costs. Nevertheless, both systems should be improved. The main shortcomings both systems have are the lack of force of the sanctions for incorrect or incomplete information, the inability to help to curb the level of remuneration and the lack of requirements regarding the form of the information disclosed.

Recent reforms in both systems are moving in the right direction. They discovered standardisation as a possible solution to the problem of opaque disclosure on remuneration. Clarity and comparability of the information disclosed could be ensured by rules on the substance and form of the information to be disclosed. Shareholders' monitoring of executive remuneration should be facilitated and, consequently, agency costs reduced. Ideally, binding provisions should require standardised disclosure.

The current say-on-pay mechanisms in Germany and the UK are useful instruments but need further improvement. Both regulations have been effective in preventing outliers in the form of extortionate executive remuneration, sudden rises of executive remuneration in a company and remuneration unrelated to performance. A focal point for concerns regarding executive remuneration has been created, awareness regarding executive remuneration has been increased and smaller shareholders have been given a voice. However, the mechanisms were not able to prevent significant increases in executive remuneration levels in both countries. Both systems' say-on-pay rules are not satisfactory and the German vote in particular lacks 'teeth'. The resolutions' consequences should be increased. The (supervisory) board should not be able to deviate from a remuneration policy accepted by the shareholders. Importantly, the subject-matter of the say-on-pay vote in Germany and the UK differ. The former also lacks clarity. The subject-matter should be harmonised to ensure comparability. A standardised remuneration report would be an ideal subject-matter.

The combination of standardised disclosure and standardised say-on-pay is the key to improved remuneration governance and reduced agency costs. To return to the initial question: indeed, trust is good – but control is better.

Bibliography

Annuß, G. and Theusinger, I. (2009) 'Das VorstAG – Praktische Hinweise zum Umgang mit dem neuen Recht' *Betriebs-Berater*, 64: 2434–42.

Bahar, R. (2005) 'Executive Compensation: Is Disclosure Enough?' *Centre de droit bancaire et financier, Université de Genève Working Paper.*

Baums, T. (2005) 'Zur Offenlegung von Vorstandsvergütungen' *Zeitschrift für das gesamte Handelsrecht und Wirtschaftsrecht*, 169: 299–309.

Bebchuk, L. and Roe, M. J. (1999) 'A Theory of Path-Dependence in Corporate Ownership and Governance' *Stanford Law Review*, 52: 127–70.

Bebchuk L.M. and Fried J.A. (2003) 'Executive Compensation as an Agency Problem' *Harvard John M Olin Discussion Paper 04/2003* http://ssrn.com/abstract=364220 (last accessed 31 May 2016).

Bebchuk L.M. and Fried J.A. (2004) *Pay without Performance: The Unfulfilled Promise of Executive Compensation*, Cambridge, MA: Harvard University Press.

BIS (2012) 'Executive Remuneration: Discussion Paper: Summary of Responses' http://www.bis.gov.uk/assets/biscore/business-law/docs/e/12-564-executive-remuneration-discussion-paper-summary-responses.pdf (last accessed 31 May 2016).

Bottomley, S. (2007) *The Constitutional Corporation: Rethinking Corporate Governance*, Aldershot: Ashgate Publishing.

Cannivé, K. and Seebach, D. (2009) 'Vorstandsvergütung als neue Haftungsfalle für Aufsichtsratsmitglieder? – Haftung und Verhaltenspflichten der Aufsichtsratsmitglieder nach Inkrafttreten des VorstAG' *Der Konzern*, 38: 593–601.

Dauner-Lieb, B. (2009) 'Die Verrechtlichung der Vorstandsvergütung durch das VorstAG – Methodische Probleme im Umgang mit Rechtsunsicherheiten' *Der Konzern*, 38: 583–93.

Davies, P.L. (2002) 'Board Structures in the UK and Germany: Convergence or Continuing Divergence?' *International Comparative Corporate Law Journal*, 2: 435–56.

Deilmann, B. and Otte, S. (2010) 'Say on Pay – erste Erfahrungen der Hauptversammlungspraxis' *Der Betrieb*, 63: 545–47.

Döll, M. (2010) 'Das Votum zum Vergütungssystem nach § 120 Abs. 4 AktG' *Wertpapier-Mitteilungen*, 64: 103–112.

Falkenhausen, J. v. and Kocher, D. (2010) 'Erste Erfahrungen mit dem Vergütungsvotum der Hauptversammlung' *Die Aktiengesellschaft*, 55: 623–29.

Ferrarini, G., Moloney, N. and Ungureanu, M.C. (2009) 'Understanding Directors' Pay in Europe: A Comparative and Empirical Analysis' *ECGI Law Working Paper No 126/2009* http://ssrn.com/abstract=1418463 (last accessed 31 May 2016).

Ferrarini, G., Moloney, N. and Ungureanu, M.C. (2010) 'Executive Remuneration in Crisis: A Critical Assessment of Reforms in Europe' *Journal of Corporate Law Studies*, 10: 73–118.

Fleischer, H. and Bedkowski, D. (2009) 'Say on Pay im deutschen Aktienrecht: Das Vergütungsvotum der Hauptversammlung nach § 120 Abs. 4 AktG' *Die Aktiengesellschaft*, 54: 677–86.

Geiler, P. and Renneboog, L. (2010) 'Executive Compensation: Incentives and Externalities' in Baker, H.K. and Anderson, R. (eds) (2010) *Corporate Governance: A Synthesis of Theory, Research and Practice*, Hoboken, NJ: Wiley: 263.

Hoffmann-Becking, M. and others (2009) 'Stellungnahme des Deutschen Anwaltvereins – Handelsrechtsausschuss zum Entwurf eines Gesetzes zur Angemessenheit der Vorstandsvergütung (VorstAG)' http://anwaltverein.de/downloads/Stellungnahmen-09/DAV-Stellungnahme-32-2009. pdf (last accessed 31 May 2016).

Hohenstatt, K.S. (2009) 'Das Gesetz zur Angemessenheit der Vorstandsvergütung' *ZIP – Zeitschrift für Wirtschaftsrecht*, 30: 1349–58.

Hupka, J. (2012) *Das Vergütungsvotum der Hauptversammlung*, Cologne: Heymanns.

Jensen, M. and Murphy, K. (1990a) 'Performance Pay and Top Management Incentives' *Journal of Political Economy*, 98: 225–64.

Jensen, M. and Murphy, K. (1990b) 'CEO Incentives: It's Not How Much You Pay But How' *Journal of Applied Corporate Finance*, 3: 36–49.

Kanzow, P. (2014) 'Remuneration Governance in Germany and the United Kingdom', Thesis, University of Durham.

Kramarsch, M.H. (2005) 'Organvergütung' *Zeitschrift für das gesamte Handelsrecht und Wirtschaftsrecht*, 169: 112–23.

Kremer, T. (2009) 'Stellungnahme zur öffentlichen Anhörung des Rechtsausschusses des Deutschen Bundestages am 25 Mai 2009' http://www.kapitalmarktrecht-im-internet.eu/de/Rechtsgebiete/ Gesellschaftsrecht/Artikelgesetze/85/VorstAG.htm (last accessed 31 May 2016).

Lieder, J. and Fischer, P. (2011) 'The Say-on-Pay Movement – Evidence From a Comparative Perspective' *European Company and Financial Law Review*, 8: 376-421.

Lingemann, S. (2009) 'Angemessenheit der Vorstandsvergütung – Das VorstAG ist in Kraft' *Betriebs-Berater*, 36: 1918–24.

Morse, G. and Worthington, S. (eds) (2011) *Palmer's Company Law*, London: Sweet & Maxwell.

Mülbert, P.O. (2009) 'Corporate Governance of Banks' *European Business Organization Law Review*, 10: 411–36.

Reger, G. (2014) '§ 120' in Bürgers, T. and Körber, T. (eds) (2014) *Heidelberger Kommentar zum Aktiengesetz*, 3rd edn, Heidelberg: C.F. Müller.

Ringe, W.G. (2013) 'Independent Directors: After the Crisis' *University of Oxford Legal Research Paper Series, Paper No 72/2013* http://ssrn.com/abstract=2293394 (last accessed 31 May 2016).

Rode, O. (2009) *Der deutsche Corporate Governance Kodex: Funktionen und Durchsetzungsmechanismen im Vergleich zum britischen Combined Code*, Frankfurt: Peter Lang.

Schick, W.P. (2011) 'Praxisfragen zum Vergütungsvotum der Hauptversammlung nach § 120 Abs. 4 AktG' *ZIP – Zeitschrift für Wirtschaftsrecht*, 32: 593–601.

Sheehan, K. (2012) 'Say on Pay and the Outrage Constraint' in Thomas, R.S. and Hill J.G. (eds) (2012) *Research Handbook on Executive Pay*, Cheltenham: Edward Elgar, 255–83.

Sorensen, K.E. (2009) 'Disclosure in EU Corporate Governance – a Remedy in Need of Adjustment?' *European Business Organization Law Review*, 10: 255–83.

Spindler, G. (2009) 'Vorstandsgehälter auf dem Prüfstand' *Neue Juristische Online-Zeitschrift*, 9: 3282–91.

Strieder, T. (2005) *DCGK Praxiskommentar*, Berlin: Erich Schmidt.

Talaulicar, T. and Werder, A. v. (2010) 'Kodex Report 2010: Die Akzeptanz der Empfehlungen und Anregungen des Deutschen Corporate Governance Kodex' *Der Betrieb*, 16: 853–61.

Thüsing, G. (2009a) 'Das Gesetz zur Angemessenheit der Vorstandsvergütung' *Die Aktiengesellschaft*, 54: 517–29.

Thüsing, G. (2009b) 'Stellungnahme zum Entwurf eines Gesetzes zur Angemessenheit der Vorstandsvergütung (VorstAG) (BT-Drucks. 16/12278)' http://webarchiv.bundestag.de/cgi/show. php?fileToLoad=1373&id=1136 (last accessed 31 May 2016).

Villiers, C. (2006) *Company Reporting and Company Law*, Cambridge, UK: Cambridge University Press.

Ward, M. (1998) 'Director Remuneration: A Gap in the Disclosure Rules' *Corporate Governance*, 6: 48–51.

Zweigert, K. and Kötz, H. (1996) *Einführung in die Rechtsvergleichung*, 3rd edn, Tübingen: Mohr.

9

State capitalism and corporate law

The governance of state-owned enterprises in China

Jenny Fu

1 Introduction

China has announced a new round of reform initiatives to improve corporate governance of state-owned enterprises (SOEs). At the Third Plenum of the Eighteenth Congress of the Communist Party, President Xi Jinping called for the adoption of a capital management-based approach to the management of China's massive state investments in enterprises.[1] This (and a variety of other strategies unveiled by the Party) has been widely reported in the media as a major shake-up of the state sector, as well as China's greater embrace of the Temasek model for managing government investments in Singapore.

The last round of Chinese SOE governance reforms began in the early 2000s and saw the establishment of the State-owned Assets Supervision and Administration Commission (SASAC) under State Council to take control of over 100 large central government-affiliated SOEs. A high watermark of that round of reforms was the 2005 corporate law revision,[2] which was followed by various steps taken by SASAC to improve the governance of central SOEs under its control.

This chapter examines this recent history in the Chinese legal and regulatory reforms of SOE governance from the perspective of China's state-led approach to economic development. In doing so, the term 'corporate law' is used in its broadest sense to include not only corporations legislation, but also relevant administrative regulations and guidelines, as well as Party/government policy documents, as these form an integral part of the regulatory framework for SOE governance in China.

---

1 《中共中央关于全面深化改革若干重大问题的决定》 [Decision on Several Major Issues Concerning Comprehensively Deepening Reforms], adopted at the Third Plenum of the 18th Central Committee of the Chinese Communist Party, 12 November 2013 (Decision on Deepening Reforms).

2 《中华人民共和国公司法》 [Company Law of the People's Republic of China] (People's Republic of China) National People's Congress Standing Committee, 27 October 2005 (2005 PRC Company Law); 《中华人民共和国证券法》 [Securities Law of the People's Republic of China] (People's Republic of China) National People's Congress Standing Committee, 27 October 2005.

This chapter was inspired by a perceived disjuncture between two strands of literature on China. On the one hand, consistent with the predominance of the Anglo–American outsider-based model of corporate governance at least until the Global Financial Crisis (GFC), research on Chinese corporate governance has mainly focused on how the mechanisms of that model can be emulated to improve Chinese corporate governance, primarily the governance of listed SOEs. On the other hand, in contrast with this ongoing primacy of the Anglo–American corporate governance model, there have been some signs of change in the literature on the model of economic development employed in China.

Until the early 2000s, the Chinese approach to economic growth and development had been widely considered an incremental approach, in contrast to the various 'big bang' strategies adopted by the former Soviet Union and Eastern European countries in their transformation from a planned state to market economy (Pei 2006: 25–27). However, in more recent years, China has been increasingly viewed as 'state-led capitalism' or its short form 'state capitalism' (Bacon 2012; Bremmer 2010; Ikenberry 2011: 57). Despite their nuanced differences, the various terms (from 'state capitalism', 'state-directed capitalism'[3] to 'centrally-managed capitalism'[4]) used by different researchers point to a system in which the state plays a significant and visible role in promoting economic development through intervention in or association with businesses, particularly large businesses.

How might this perceived role shift of the state in economic development influence China's post-2005 regulation of corporate governance in SOEs (including listed SOEs) as the chief embodiment of the Chinese form of state capitalism? Indeed, the nexus between state capitalism, corporate law and corporate governance is not entirely new. In their 2001 seminal work *The End of History for Corporate Law*, Hansmann and Kraakman identified a state-oriented model of corporate governance in post-Second World War state-led economies such as France and some East Asian countries, including Japan and South Korea (Hansmann and Kraakman 2001: 446–7).

Scholarship on comparative capitalism has lent support to this observation. For example, based on a number of comparative capitalism studies that had identified state capitalism as a distinct capitalist prototype (in addition to the liberal market economies represented by the US and the UK and the coordinated market economies exemplified by Germany and post-1980s Japan), Kang (2010: 533) postulated that state capitalism is associated with a particular model of corporate governance, namely, the state-led model. Rather than maximising financial return to shareholders, the state-oriented or state-led model of corporate governance is fundamentally an instrument of the state to maintain control over corporate affairs. As Hansmann and Kraakman (2001: 446–7) put it:

> The principal instruments of state control over corporate affairs in corporatist economies generally lie outside of corporate law . . . Nevertheless, corporate law also plays a role by, for example, weakening shareholder control over corporate managers (*to reduce pressures on managers that might operate counter to the preferences of the state*) and employing state-administered criminal sanctions rather than shareholder-controlled civil lawsuits as the principal sanction for managerial malfeasance (*to give the state strong authority over managers that could be exercised at the government's discretion*).

---

3 Stefan Halper, *The Beijing Consensus* (Basic Books, 2010) 113; Yasheng Huang, *Capitalism with the Chinese Characteristics* (Cambridge University Press) xvii.
4 Nan Lin, 'Capitalism in China: A Centrally Managed Capitalism (CMC) and Its Future' (2010) 7 *Management and Organisation Review* 63.

This statement suggests that close state association with corporate managers lies at the heart of state-led corporate governance. However, one would doubt that this singular focused relationship-based approach (hereafter referred to as the 'post-war state-led model') would have much application to the regulation of corporate governance in SOEs in China today. Indeed, the Chinese state-led economic development takes place in dramatically different international and domestic environments from the early post-war state-led economies. With increased globalisation, competition and the pluralisation of interests within Chinese society, there are multiple strong forces that propel the policy-makers to move away from this model.

Through examining the changes and continuities in China's post-2005 reforms of corporate governance, particularly state-manager relations in SOEs, this chapter will suggest that China's post-2005 regulatory framework for SOE governance has significantly moved away from the old post-war state-led model. As the Party/state intensified efforts on strengthening the monitoring of corporate managers in listed SOEs and their state-owned parent entities by borrowing from Western, particularly Anglo–American, corporate governance, this framework has taken on a more market-oriented aspect. However, with ongoing state involvement in the appointment of top executives and management decision-making in the parent SOEs, and the high level of commingling senior executives in the listed companies and their state-owned parents, these market-based changes have not led to a fundamental systemic transformation.

Nor is this new 'reform, but without losing Party/state control' approach likely to solve the dual governance problem that has long been associated with the listed SOEs and their state-owned parents, namely excessive administrative interference and insider control by top executives at the same time. This is especially so with the persistent lack of authority and independence of SOE boards in performing their oversight functions over senior corporate executives, including the chair of the board of directors. However, owing in part to its general congruence with the Chinese model of state-led economic development, future change to this regulatory approach is likely to be incremental.

This chapter is set out as follows. Section 2 examines China's pre-2005 regulation of state-manager relations in listed SOEs and the dual governance problem associated with these companies. Sections 3 and 4 provide an overview of the various market-based mechanisms of corporate governance that have been brought into the listed SOEs and their parent companies through the 2005 corporate law revision, SASAC, as well as the current round of SOE governance reform. Section 5 considers the two main continuities in the regulation of state-managers' relations in SOEs as indicated above and their impact on corporate governance. Section 6 concludes with the broader implications of China's current approach to the regulation of state-manager relations in SOEs, given the rapid expansion of these companies overseas.

2 The pre-2005 regulatory framework and the dual SOE governance problem

China began mass corporatisation and partial privatisation of SOEs in the early 1990s. The governance of listed SOEs in China has been described as 'a control-based model, in which the controlling shareholders – in most cases, the state – employ all feasible governance mechanisms to tightly control the listed firms' (Liu 2006: 418). Whilst consistent with a state-led approach to economic development and corporate governance, this statement may have exaggerated the degree of effective state control over senior SOE executives, at least prior to the 2005 corporate law reform.

The governance structure for joint stock companies, including listed SOEs, prescribed in the 1993 Company Law (the first PRC company law) was fairly hierarchical. The structure consisted of a general meeting and two parallel boards elected by it,[5] namely the board of directors as the 'executive organ' of the company and a board of supervisors as the 'watchdog' (Zhang 2012: 40). As the state was envisaged to remain the controlling shareholder in most corporatised SOEs at the early stage of the corporatisation reform, the 1993 Company Law conferred on the general meeting a long list of powers that are usually considered as management powers in Anglo–American jurisdictions, such as the power to make decisions on the company's operational guidelines, and to approve annual budget plans and profit distribution plans (Article 103).

Where the state is the controlling shareholder, another avenue for the state to influence corporate affairs was the board of directors, primarily the chair of the board (commonly referred to as the 'chairman' in China). Unlike a typical non-executive chairman role in some other jurisdictions such as Australia, the chairman in a Chinese company enjoyed a broad range of management powers under the 1993 *Company Law*. This often allowed the chairman to overshadow the general manager (another senior management role responsible for the day-to-day management of a company) to become the company's de facto chief executive officer. For example, the chairman was responsible for convening and presiding over shareholders' and board meetings and examining the implementation of board resolutions (Article 114), as well as carrying out the functions of the board outside board meetings (Article 120(1)).

As the company's designated 'statutory legal representative', the chairman also had the sole authority to represent the company in executing contracts and undertaking legal proceedings (Article 113(2)). In addition, the chairman's position was (and is) often associated with significant political influence. As will be discussed in section 5, the chairman role is fundamentally a political appointment. The dual identity of the chairman as both a senior SOE executive and a ministerial or vice-ministerial-ranking government official allows the chairman to rotate between senior government and enterprise positions.

State involvement in corporate affairs was, however, a double-edged sword. Whilst it facilitated state-manager association to promote economic-oriented goals of the state, it paradoxically endorsed a dual corporate governance problem, namely the simultaneous lack of independence of SOE boards and the weakening of state control by corporate executives from within. This is particularly so with the high level of commingling of senior executives in listed SOEs and their state-owned parent companies. As most listed SOEs in China were established as fundraising vehicles for their parent SOEs, they often maintain substantial personnel and business connections with the latter. Indeed, a survey of 109 listed companies controlled by central SOEs in 2010 found that 80 per cent of the chairman positions in these companies were held by senior executives of the companies' state-owned parents.[6]

One major consequence of this regulatory framework was the lack of authority and independence of SOE boards to perform their oversight functions over the management, particularly the chairman. Board independence and authority is generally considered an essential mechanism of corporate governance for not only private sector but also public sector

---

5 This is with the exception of supervisory board members acted by employee representatives. The percentage of employee representatives was specified as no less than one-third in the 2005 revision of the PRC Company Law.

6 卢福才 [Lu Fucai] (ed.), 《中央企业公司治理报告》 [Report on Corporate Governance of Central State-owned Enterprises] (China Economic Publishing House, 2011) 55.

companies. For example, the OECD Guidelines on Corporate Governance of State-owned Enterprises (OECD Guidelines) provide that 'boards of SOEs should have the necessary authority, competencies and objectivity to carry out their functions of strategic guidance and monitoring of management'.

However, deprived of substantial management powers, including the power to appoint and evaluate top corporate executives, boards in Chinese SOEs were not strong monitors of their legally powerful and politically well connected chairmen. Compared with the board of directors, the board of supervisors was an even weaker form of monitoring. Whilst lacking the power to appoint and remove directors including the chairman, the supervisors, typically nominated by the controlling shareholders/parent SOEs and the listed companies' management, faced the problem of 'hav[ing] to bite the hand that feeds them' (Tomasic and Andrews 2007: 112).

Some changes to this weak regulatory framework took place towards the end of the 1990s. As the concept of 'corporate governance' was officially endorsed by the Party in 1999,[7] the China Securities Regulatory Commission (CSRC, China's central government authority for the regulation of the stock market) was given the leading role of improving corporate governance of listed companies, including listed SOEs.

Since the early 2000s, the CSRC has sought to introduce checks and balances into the governance of listed companies by borrowing from advanced market economies. For example, drawing upon the system of independent directors in Anglo–American jurisdictions, the CSRC required all listed company boards to be composed of at least one-third independent directors, with at least one of these with an accounting background.[8] The CSRC also issued the Code of Corporate Governance for Listed Companies modelled on the OECD Principles of Corporate Governance. The code, among other things, recommends that all listed companies adopt specialised board committees (including the audit committee, the nomination committee and the remuneration and appraisal committee) comprising a majority of independent directors. However, these measures led to more formal than substantive changes. The new independent directors did not play an important role in enhancing corporate governance. This was, in part, owing to the lack of independence of these directors from the parent SOEs and the listed companies' management to whom they owed their appointments (Andrews and Tomasic 2005: 291–92).

With the lax internal, as well as external monitoring environment (as discussed below), the problem of insider control in SOEs was prevalent, and was reflected in a number of high-profile corporate scandals in the early to mid-2000s. For example, the 2004 China Aviation Oil saga led to the collapse of the group's Singapore-listed subsidiary. In another case, a former chairman of Sinopec was sentenced to a suspended death penalty for taking bribes of RMB 196 million (approximately AUS$ 40 million).

Faced with the poor management of SOEs, including listed SOEs, Chinese policy-makers resorted to further governance reforms. As discussed below, through the 2005 corporate law revision, various SASAC-led initiatives, as well as China's current round of SOE reforms,

---

7 《中共中央关于国有企业改革和发展若干重大问题的决定》 [Decision of the Central Committee of the Chinese Communist Party on Several Major Issues Concerning the Reform and Development of State-owned Enterprises], Adopted at the Fourth Plenum of the 15th Central Committee of the Chinese Communist Party, 22 September 1999.

8 《关于在上市公司建立独立董事制度的指导意见》 [Guidelines for the Introduction of Independent Directors into Listed Companies] (People's Republic of China) China Securities Regulatory Commission, 16 August 2001.

and many more Anglo–American market-based mechanisms have been introduced to strengthen corporate governance, particularly the monitoring of senior executives. Whilst some of these changes put into place more internal checks and balances on the exercise of management powers, others sought to enlist market-based institutions, such as foreign institutional investors and stock market regulators, in the disciplining of managers.

At the same time, the problem of insider control of SOEs by managers was also tackled at the level of state assets management, with various institutional reforms carried out to enhance China's system for managing state investment in enterprises. However, as will be considered below, the introduction of these wide-ranging market-based changes have not caused China's post-2005 regulation of state-manager relations in SOEs fundamentally to shift away from a state-led approach. On the other hand, the problem of insider control of SOEs by managers has also continued.

3 The 2005 corporate law reform and SASAC-led reforms of SOE governance

China's SOE governance reform efforts have undergone some significant changes since the early 2000s. Two major regulatory events underlined this period of reform prior to the Third Plenum of the Eighteenth Party Congress. The first was the 2005 major revision of the Chinese 1993 Company Law and 1998 Securities Law. Commentators suggest that, with the adoption of 'more traditional corporate governance objectives' (Tomasic 2010: 195), the 2005 corporate law amendments have significantly modernised or Westernised the Chinese systems of corporate law and corporate governance, particularly the governance of listed SOEs (Feinerman 2008: 57).

Another event during this period was the Party's announced reform of China's system for managing state assets in enterprises, which occurred in November 2002. This was followed by the establishment of SASAC in early 2003. The creation of SASAC, amongst other objectives, was intended to address the lack of a single uniform representation of the interests of the state in corporatised SOEs. Until the early 2000s, the administration of corporatised SOEs was scattered amongst different central and local government agencies. This not only led to the phenomenon of 'no entity responsible for SOEs' bottom line' (The World Bank 1997: xii), but also exacerbated the problem of insider control in corporatised SOEs.

To end this situation, at the Sixteenth Party Congress the Party put forward two guiding principles for the reform of China's system for managing state investments in SOEs. The first was the separation of state investor functions in SOEs among different levels of government to 'give full play to the initiative of both central and local authorities'.[9] Second, a specialised state-owned assets authority was to be established at each government level to centralise the regulation and management of state assets in enterprises, as well as to serve as a leading government agency for the further reform of SOEs at various government levels. Consequently, SASAC was established as a special commission of the State Council. Upon its creation, SASAC was initially bestowed with a portfolio of then 196 large industrial and commercial enterprises previously administered by the central government under its

---

9 Full Text of Jiang Zemin's Report at the 16th Congress of the Chinese Communist Party (18 November 2002) http://english.people.com.cn/200211/18/eng20021118_106983.shtml (last accessed 3 June 2016).

control.[10] As discussed below, and echoing the 2005 corporate law reform, the creation of SASAC led to many Anglo–American market-based mechanisms of corporate governance being introduced into SOEs, particularly central SOEs as the state-owned parents of over 300 listed SOEs.

Changes to corporate governance in SOEs brought by the 2005 corporate law reform

The 2005 Company Law did not alter the basic structure for corporate governance in listed SOEs established by the 1993 Law (thereby preserving the avenues for state intervention in corporate affairs). However, drawing upon Anglo–American jurisdictions, the revised Company Law has made some efforts to improve the authority of the board by readjusting the roles and responsibilities of different corporate organs. In the meantime, the new Company Law has sought to improve the accountability of directors and managers through strengthening directors' duties and shareholders' remedies.

First, the 2005 Company Law strengthened the role of the board of directors in management decision-making. As mentioned earlier, under the 1993 Company Law, the power to convene meetings of the board of directors was solely vested in the chairman. The new Company Law made it clear that where the chairman failed to perform any of his responsibilities, including those of convening and chairing a board meeting, such responsibilities must be performed by the deputy chairman or, if this is not possible, by a director nominated by more than half of the directors (Article 110(2)). To ensure equal decision-making power is enjoyed by all directors, the new Company Law also specified the principle of 'one director one vote' for board resolutions (Article 112(2)). As a further effort to strengthen the role of the board, the new Company Law formally endorsed the system of independent directors for listed companies introduced by the CSRC (Article 123).

As a corollary to empowering the board of directors, the new Company Law also removed some provisions from the 1993 Law that granted excessive powers to the chairman. For example, the revised Company Law deleted the provision that gave the board of directors the power to delegate part of its functions to the chairman. The 2005 Law also allowed companies to appoint their legal representatives from a broader range of executives, including the chairman, executive directors and the general manager (Article 13). Consequently, a former provision in the 1993 Law that conferred on the chairman the power to sign for the issue of shares and corporate bonds has been removed. Nevertheless, it should be noted that as the new Company Law does not specifically prohibit companies from conferring such powers on their chairmen, the real impact of these legislative changes on the chairman's role can be quite limited.

In addition to empowering the board of directors, the 2005 Company Law sought to strengthen the role of the supervisory board by granting it more powers to monitor and discipline directors. Thus, apart from its routine powers to inspect a company's financial affairs and audit directors' meetings, the supervisory board was granted the power to raise questions and make suggestions at meetings of the board of directors (Articles 119(1), 55(1)). The supervisory board was also granted the power to investigate any irregularities in company

---

10 For enterprises in the financial sector that fell outside SASAC's purview, Central Huijin Investment Limited was established by the Ministry of Finance to hold and manage state shares in major financial institutions, including China's four largest commercial banks.

operations. In doing so, it may seek assistance from professional advisers such as accountants, at the expense of the company (Articles 119(1); 55(2)).

Where a director or senior manager fails to rectify an alleged wrongdoing at request, the supervisory board has more options at its disposal. These include convening and presiding over an extraordinary general meeting to report its findings to the shareholders (Articles 119(1), 54). The supervisory board may also launch a derivative action against the wrongdoer at the request of shareholders who meet certain thresholds (Article 152(1)). Of course, with the ongoing lack of independence of the supervisors from the management and the parent SOEs, the extent to which these newly acquired supervisory powers can be put into practice remains questionable.

With respect to directors' duties, the 1993 Company Law only broadly required directors, supervisors and the general manager to 'perform their functions and responsibilities loyally', and omitted the directors' duty of care and diligence. Under a new chapter entitled 'Qualifications and Duties of Directors, Supervisors and Senior Managers', the 2005 Company Law specifically subjects directors, supervisors and senior managers to both the duty of loyalty and the duty of care and diligence (Article 148(1)). The new Company Law also expands the circumstances that would constitute a breach of directors' duty of loyalty. Thus, various conflict of interest situations arising in the Anglo–American jurisdictions, including usurping corporate opportunity and accepting secret commissions, have been included (Article 149). In the meantime, some changes have also been introduced by the 2005 Securities Law to strengthen information disclosure by listed companies.[11]

Last but not least, this revamped regime of directors' duties has been complemented by a new regime of shareholders' rights and remedies. Indeed, strengthening legal protection of investors was one of the most pronounced objectives of the 2005 corporate law amendments. Many new relevant provisions have been introduced through drawing upon experiences of the Anglo–American jurisdictions. Whilst some of these provisions provide minority share-holders with more opportunities to participate in corporate decision-making (for example, the introduction of cumulative voting for joint stock companies subject to the company's constitution), others afford them better protection from abuse of power by controlling share-holders and other corporate insiders. Particularly, the introduction of several Anglo–American style shareholder remedies, including derivative and direct lawsuits, has been considered as 'arguably the single most important rule of law development in China's corporate law system' (Wang 2008), and represents 'a broader formal shift in the Company Law towards a greater emphasis on judicial power and the ex post remedies instead of ex ante supervision by administrative agencies' (Clarke and Howson 2012: 243).

Needless to say, the passage of the 2005 Company Law and the 2005 Securities Law has also generated a new round of administrative rule-making. Whilst some of these rules have mainly concerned the implementation of legislative changes, others introduced new measures for further modernising the governance of China's listed companies, including listed SOEs. One particular set of rules of this latter category has been the Basic Standards for Enterprise Internal Control (the Basic Standards) made by the CSRC in conjunction with four other

11 For example, art 68 of the 2005 Securities Law requires directors, supervisors and senior managers of listed companies to issue their written opinions on company periodical reports and guarantee the truthfulness, accuracy and completeness of any information disclosed by their companies. Article 67 extends the definition of 'major events' that are subject to continuous disclosure by listed companies to include pending judicial investigation into company crimes.

central government authorities.[12] Widely referred to in the media as the 'Chinese version of the Sarbanes-Oxley Act', the Basic Standards require all listed companies in China to establish an internal control system in line with the framework adopted in the US Sarbanes-Oxley Act by July 2009.

Listed companies are further required to undertake self-evaluation of their internal controls, publish annual self-evaluation reports and appoint accounting firms to audit and report on the effectiveness of their internal controls. In addition, to motivate directors and managers to maximise the financial performance of their companies, the CSRC has allowed listed companies that satisfy certain prescribed conditions to adopt equity-based incentive plans to remunerate their directors and managers.[13] The implementation of these plans has become possible with the 2005 'split share structure' reform, which converted non-tradable state shares into tradable shares.[14]

SASAC-led reforms

Whilst China's post-2005 legal and regulatory reforms outlined above mainly concern listed SOEs, the various governance reforms initiated by SASAC towards central SOEs deserve some special attention. As large enterprises in strategically important sectors and key fields,[15] the combined assets of central SOEs account for about one-third of China's total state investments in enterprises.[16] Further, as wholly state-owned parents of over 300, generally the largest listed companies in China, corporate governance in central SOEs also shapes the governance of the latter.

Governance reform in the central SOEs had lagged behind their listed subsidiaries prior to the creation of SASAC. Notwithstanding the passage of the first PRC Company Law in

---

12 《关于印发《企业内部控制基本规范》的通知》 [Circular on Release of the Basic Standards for Enterprise Internal Control] (People's Republic of China) Ministry of Finance, China Securities Regulatory Commission, National Audit Office, China Banking Regulatory Commission and China Insurance Regulatory Commission, 22 May 2008; Basic Standards art 10.

13 《上市公司股权激励管理办法 (试行)) [Measures for the Administration of Equity Incentive Plans of Listed Companies (For Trial Implementation)] (People's Republic of China) China Securities Regulatory Commission, 31 December 2005; 《国有控股上市公司（境外）实施股权激励试行办法》 [Trial Measures for the Implementation of Equity Incentive Plans by State-controlled Companies Listed Overseas] (People's Republic of China) State-owned Assets Supervision and Administration, 27 January 2006; 《国有控股上市公司 (境内) 实施股权激励试行办法》 [Trial Measures for the Implementation of Equity Incentive Plans by Domestically Listed State-controlled Companies] State-owned Assets Supervision and Administration Commission and Ministry of Finance, 30 September 2006.

14 《关于上市公司股权分置改革试点有关问题的通知》 [Notice on Relevant Issues concerning the Pilot Reform of Split Share Structure in Listed Companies] (People's Republic of China) China Securities Regulatory Commission, 29 April 2005, s 3(4); 《关于上市公司股权分置改革的指导意见》 [Guiding Opinion on Reforming the Split Share Structure in Listed companies] (People's Republic of China) China Securities Regulatory Commission, State-owned Assets Supervision and Administration Commission, Ministry of Finance, People's Bank of China and Ministry of Commerce, 23 August 2005.

15 《中华人民共和国企业国有资产法》 [Law of Enterprise State-owned Assets of the People's Republic of China] (People's Republic of China) National People's Congress, 28 October 2008, art 4.

16 '财政部公布 2013 年全国国有企业财务决算情况' [2013 SOE Financial Statements released by Ministry of Finance] Chinese Central Government Website (28 July 2014) http://www.gov.cn/xinwen/2014-07/28/content_2725636.htm (last accessed 3 June 2016).

1993, many central SOEs remained registered under the 1988 Law on Industrial Enterprises Owned by the Whole People.[17] In relation to governance arrangements, these enterprises followed a 'factory head responsibility system' prescribed by the 1998 law (Article 7). This one-man-in-control system also had a strong hold in the central SOEs that were converted into wholly state-owned companies, and registered under the 1993 Company Law. This was despite the Company Law requirement for the establishment of a board structure in all companies, including wholly state-owned companies. With overlapping senior executives in the parent SOEs and their listed subsidiaries, this one-man-in-control model also contributed to the problem of insider control in listed SOEs.

SASAC has undertaken two main steps as part of its overall strategy to transform its central SOEs into internationally competitive large businesses. Given the role of SASAC in guiding and supervising the operations of its local equivalents, these steps may also be expected to have been followed to various extents at local government levels.[18]

The first of these steps was the 'standardised board' reform seeking to improve the effectiveness of the board of directors in corporatised central SOEs. SASAC initiated a pilot programme in June 2004 and selected seven central SOEs to participate in the experiment of the 'standardised board'. By the end of 2014, 52 of the then 121 SASAC-controlled SOEs had undergone such reform.

The structure of the 'standardised board' as promoted by SASAC seems to be consistent with the OECD Guidelines on Corporate Governance of State-owned Enterprises in many aspects. According to a regulatory document released by SASAC,[19] the 'standardised board' should have seven to thirteen directors, with the majority being external directors nominated by SASAC (indeed, the introduction of SASAC-nominated majority external directors into central SOE boards has been widely considered the centrepiece of the standardised board reform).

SASAC has also set out detailed rules concerning the desirable mixture of skills among the external directors. For example, the majority of outside directors should have experience in managing large enterprises, and at least one should have a background in accounting. Appointment of external directors from foreigners is also encouraged for companies with substantial operations overseas. The 'standardised board' should also establish several board committees, including the nomination committee, the remuneration and evaluation committee and the audit committee, to act as advisory bodies to the board. Whilst the majority members of the nomination committee should be external directors, the latter two committees should only be formed by external directors.

To further reduce the concentration of management powers in central SOEs, SASAC has required that the standardised board display a clear separation of the role of the chairman from that of the general manager and the role of the board from senior managers involved in the day-to-day operations of the company. The chairman should be responsible for the

---

17 《全民所有制工业企业法》 [Law on Industrial Enterprises Owned by the Whole People] (People's Republic of China) National People's Congress, 13 April 1988.

18 《企业国有资产监督管理暂行条例》 [Interim Regulations on the Supervision and Administration of Enterprise State-owned Assets] (People's Republic of China) State Council, 13 May 2003, art 13.

19 《董事会试点中央企业董事会规范运作暂行办法》 [Interim Measures for the Standard Operation of the Board of Directors of Central State-owned Enterprises under the Pilot Program on Board of Directors] (People's Republic of China) State-owned Assets Supervision and Administration Commission, 20 March 2009, art 22.

oversight of the proper functioning of the board, and the general manager for the organisation of company day-to-day business operations. The two positions should, where possible, be separate.

To limit the management powers of the chairman, SASAC encourages central SOEs to appoint their chairman from external directors and their legal representatives from general managers. To separate the role of the board from senior managers, managers other than the general manager (such as the deputy general manager and chief accountant) should not act as directors. In the meantime, to empower the standardised board, SASAC also delegated the central SOE boards that have completed this transformation, the power to appoint, evaluate and remunerate some of their senior management positions, such as the general manager, chief accountant and the board secretary.

Relevant to corporate governance, another step undertaken by SASAC has been the promotion of full listing of the typically wholly state-owned central SOEs on domestic and international stock markets. There are, of course, many reasons for SASAC to pursue this goal. For example, with additional funds raised from the market, full-listing will help central SOEs to increase their economies of scale, and thereby their international competitiveness. For SASAC, full listing would also lead to better liquidity of state-owned assets held by enterprises, which means greater flexibility and efficiency in the management of state assets.

The improvement of the governance of central SOEs was, however, one of SASAC's chief concerns. According to Shao Ning, a former deputy director of SASAC, overseas listing would not only force central SOEs to undergo thorough restructuring, but would also expose them to scrutiny by foreign stock market regulators and international investors, including sophisticated institutional investors. By the end of 2011, 40 central SOEs had listed the whole, or substantially the whole, of their main business on Chinese mainland and overseas (primarily Hong Kong) stock markets.[20] Few of these giant groups have, however, achieved the full listing of the parent central SOEs for various reasons, including resistance from central SOE leaders.[21]

4 China's search for a version of Singapore's Temasek model: SOE reform plans announced at the Eighteenth Party Congress

This trend in favour of market-based reform of SOE governance has continued as a new generation of Chinese leaders came into power. This is despite some signs of a reversal in certain respects, as considered below. The various reform plans released by the Party under its current round of SOE reform efforts run from the adoption of a capital management-based approach to the management of state investments in enterprises; it has included the development of mixed ownership and professional management in SOEs, as well as the

---

20 '国资委再推央企整体上市, 已上市央企融资超 9000 亿' [SASAC Continues to Promote the Full Listing of Central SOEs, Funds Raised by Listed Central SOEs Exceeded RMB900 Billion], *China Venture* 18 May, 2012 http://news.chinaventure.com.cn/2/20120518/86119.shtml (last accessed 3 June 2016).

21 Two main factors have contributed to the slow process in full listing of central SOEs. First, many of these parent SOEs have some non-performing assets or welfare functions that are difficult to incorporate into the listed companies. This is despite the fact that, in order to improve the efficiency of central SOEs, SASAC has, since its establishment in 2003, helped these enterprises to divest from their non-core businesses and social welfare functions. Second, the full listing plans have to be devised and implemented by parent SOEs, who naturally have a strong disincentive to go to full listing by forcing themselves to be integrated into their listed subsidiaries.

classification of SOEs based on their functions (e.g. commercial and public interest SOEs) so as to achieve more streamlined regulation and supervision.[22]

Amongst these strategies, the Party's call for the adoption of a capital-management approach to the management of state investments in enterprise has been widely considered as inspired by the Temasek model in Singapore. As outlined by the Party, a capital management-based approach would enhance the efficiency of the management of state assets by enabling the state to focus on maintaining and steadily increasing the overall value of state assets. Through separating capital management from the day-to-day operations of the SOEs, this approach would also help to improve corporate governance.

Nevertheless, the decision to move towards a capital management-based approach also reflects the Party/government's rethinking of the role of SASAC in the management of state assets and central SOEs. SASAC has played a crucial role in transforming central SOEs from traditional SOEs into large internationally competitive businesses. As discussed earlier, the consolidation of state powers over SOEs in SASAC has enabled the Commission to carry out a broad range of reforms, including corporate governance reforms of these large companies.

However, the inherent conflict between the regulatory and state shareholder roles of SASAC (and its local equivalents) has led to some unintended consequences. Particularly in relation to corporate governance, it has exacerbated, rather than solved, the dual governance problem associated with the central SOEs. On the one hand, the dual role of SASAC as both a regulator of state assets and state shareholder has led SASAC to be heavily involved in the management of the central SOEs. This is especially so because, at the time of its creation, SASAC had been mandated to 'combine its management of state assets with the management of executives and (major) corporate affairs'.[23]

On the other hand, since its creation, SASAC has prioritised fostering larger and stronger central SOEs, and the relentless pursuit of business growth and expansion has rendered its regulatory role largely subsidiary to its state investor function (Liu and Huang 2014: 42). This has further meant that SASAC has failed to exercise effective monitoring and discipline of central SOE executives, thereby perpetuating the problem of insider control within these large companies. Indeed, as the large number of disciplinary actions taken by the Party Central Commission for Discipline Inspection against central SOEs and their executives over the past year suggest, the various SASAC-led reforms of corporate governance have resulted in very limited success.

The adoption of a capital management-based approach by drawing upon Singapore's Temasek model would help to address the Party/government's objectives as stated above, including the objective to separate the regulatory role of SASAC (and their local equivalents) from its investor function. Arguably, the adoption of this approach will also be complemented by other reform strategies announced at the Eighteenth Party Congress, such as the development of mixed ownership and professional management in SOEs. However, as considered below, it remains questionable whether this raft of new strategies would lead to a fundamental shift in the Chinese approach to the regulation of state-managers in SOEs, as well as provide an effective solution to the dual problem of corporate governance associated with these companies.

22 Decision on Deepening Reforms (n 1).
23 Full Text of Jiang Zemin's Report at the 16th Congress of the Chinese Communist Party (18 November 2002) http://english.people.com.cn/200211/18/eng20021118_106983.shtml (last accessed 3 June 2016).

5 China's post-2005 regulation of state-managers in SOEs: continuities and implications

The wide-ranging changes in China's post-2005 regulation of state-manager relations reviewed above beg the question of 'what has not changed?' First and foremost, the ultimate control of the Party-state over senior personnel appointments in the parent SOEs, including central SOEs, has not changed and has, arguably, been strengthened with more recent regulations.

Indeed, Party appointment and evaluation of corporate executives has remained a chief instrument for the Party-state to retain its control over large SOEs. In relation to the central SOEs, the top three leadership positions, namely the chairman, the Party secretary and the general manager, in 53 of the largest central SOEs are still appointed and evaluated by the Organisational Department of the Central Party Committee. For the remaining 68 central SOEs, as noted earlier, SASAC has authorised those with a standardised board structure to appoint some of their senior management positions, such as the general manager and the deputy general manager. SASAC, however, retains its power over the appointment, evaluation and remuneration of the top two leadership positions in these enterprises, namely the chairman and the Party secretary. Moreover, SASAC also appoints, evaluates and decides the remuneration of other directors, including external directors and supervisors (except those acted by employee representatives) in these central SOEs.

Personnel decisions in local SOEs at provincial, municipal and county levels are managed by the local branches of the Organisation Department of the Party Central Committee and the local equivalents of SASAC (Szamosszegi and Kyle 2011: 75). There is no suggestion that Party appointment of senior SOE executives in central SOEs extends to their listed subsidiaries. However, this might not, in reality, lead to significantly different practice in the listed SOEs, given the high level of commingling of top executives in the central SOEs and their listed subsidiaries.

This system of Party/government appointment and evaluation of parent SOE executives is unlikely to be affected by the current round of SOE reforms. First, although the Party called for 'increasing the proportion of market-oriented recruitment' to promote professional management of SOEs,[24] it has expressed no intention to relinquish Party/government control over the appointment of top executives, including the chairmen in SOEs. Nor is the mixed ownership reform of SOEs likely to have any significant impact on the continuation of this system. Whilst the mixed ownership reform has generated a great deal of excitement amongst investors on the Chinese stock market, there is no evidence that this reform will fundamentally alter the controlling shareholder position of the state in large and strategically important SOEs, including the central SOEs. As President Xi pointed out, public ownership will remain the mainstay of China's socialist market economy, and China will 'unwaveringly consolidate and develop the public sector' to 'enhance its vitality' and 'capacity to leverage and influence the economy'.[25]

Further, under the current 'strengthening the Party role' approach adopted in China, Party control of central SOEs is likely to be tightened rather than loosened. In June 2015, the Party Central Committee released the Temporary Regulations on the Work of the

---

24 Decision on Deepening Reforms (n 1).
25 ibid.

Chinese Communist Party Committee (Temporary Regulations).[26] The Temporary Regulations require that a Party Committee be established in a wide range of state and non-state organisations, including all SOEs affiliated to the central government, which include but are not limited to SASAC-controlled central SOEs (Article 5). Given the unitary Party/government system followed in China, these regulations are likely to be mirrored to various extents at local levels.

According to the Temporary Regulations, the Party Committee of a central government-affiliated SOE should consist of three to nine members, drawn from Party members from the board of directors, the board of supervisors, senior management and the leader of the enterprise-based Party Disciplinary Inspection Committee. The position of secretary of the Party Committee should be assumed by the chairman (which signifies the ongoing prominence of the chairman's role in the management of SOEs) or the general manager, where a board of directors has not yet been established in a SOE (Article 7).

The presence of a Party Committee in Chinese companies has long been facilitated by the Chinese Company Law.[27] The Temporary Regulations, however, for the first time, grant the Party Committee the 'core leadership' position in enterprises in which it has a presence (Article 2).[28]

It is not clear how the enhanced position of the Party Committee will fit into existing governance structures in central SOEs, particularly the board of directors. Nevertheless, in elevating the Party Committee to the core leadership status in central SOEs, the governance of these companies seems to have moved away from the board-centred approach to corporate governance adopted in Anglo–American jurisdictions. This approach also seems to contradict the 'standardised board' reform initiated by SASAC, which, to a limited extent, aims to strengthen the authority and independence of central SOE boards along the lines of the OECD Guidelines.

The involvement of the state in the appointment of top corporate executives aside, nor is the Party/government's influence over business decision-making in parent SOEs, including the central SOEs, likely to be subject to fundamental change under the current round of SOE reforms. According to a document released by the State Council in November 2015,[29] China's new capital management-based approach to the management of state assets will be implemented through the establishment of a three-tiered regulatory structure. At the central government level, this structure will, first, consist of SASAC as the regulator of state assets; second, a mid-tier of state capital operating and investment companies[30] to be established by

---

26 《中国共产党党组工作条例（试行）》 Temporary Regulations on the Work of the Chinese Community Party Committee (Temporary Regulations), Centre Committee of the Chinese Communist Party, effective from 11 June 2015.

27 The 1993 Company Law provided that a grassroots organisation of the Party shall be established in all companies to carry out its activities according to the Party's Constitution (art 17). The 2005 Company Law retains this provision, and goes further to require that 'companies shall provide necessary conditions to assist the activities of the Chinese Communist Party' (art 19).

28 The 'core leadership' of the Party Committee is also specified in 《关于在深化国有企业改革中坚持党的领导加强党的建设的若干意见》 (Several Opinions on Upholding the Party's Leadership and Strengthening Party Construction in Deepening the Reform of State-owned Enterprises), The Chinese Communist Party Central Committee, 20 September 2015.

29 《关于改革和完善国有资产管理体制的若干意见》 [Several Opinions on Reforming and Perfecting the System for State-owned Assets Management], State Council, 4 November 2015.

30 State capital operating companies are state holding companies that hold and manage shares in a portfolio of unrelated SOEs, while state capital investment companies are state-owned industrial

SASAC or transformed from certain existing central SOEs as the investment arm of SASAC; and, third, a lower tier of central SOEs and/or their subsidiaries.

This three-tiered structure may, at least in form, share some of the characteristics of the Temasek model. This is because the latter also involves the establishment of a state holding company (Temasek Holdings) as the investment arm of government. However, the Ministry of Finance of Singapore has very little power over Temasek Holdings beyond its role as the state shareholder.[31] By contrast, SASAC and its local equivalents, in their role as both a state shareholder and regulator of state assets in enterprises, have been accustomed to be involved in the management of SOEs under their control. This relationship is unlikely to be severed with the insertion of a layer of state investment companies wholly-owned by SASAC. After all, as the regulator of state assets and the ultimate controller of central SOEs, SASAC is still responsible for preserving and increasing the value of state investments in these enterprises.

This 'reform, but without losing Party/government control' approach adopted in China's post-2005 regulation of state-manager relations in SOEs is difficult to understand from the perspective of Anglo–American corporate governance. Nor does it sit comfortably with the type of state shareholder-manager relationships recommended in the OECD Guidelines. Whilst the state is projected as 'an informed and active owner' in the Guidelines, it is suggested that it not to be 'involved in the day-to-day management of SOEs'.

However, this approach can be explained from the perspective of China's state-led model of economic development, in which state control of large and strategically important SOEs is a chief component. As indicated earlier, state-led corporate governance is primarily a tool of the state for promoting economic-oriented policy goals through state intervention in corporate affairs. Viewed in this light, none of the corporate governance mechanisms, market or non-marked-based, adopted by Chinese policy-makers post-2005 has been an end in itself. Put together, they form an integral part of the policy tools of the state that have been used to maintain effective control and coordination of SOEs, whilst grappling with the need to improve their management and performance amidst changing international and domestic expectations.[32]

This 'policy tool' function of corporate governance mechanisms has indeed under-lined China's recent move in strengthening the Party's role in central SOEs, which is otherwise inconsistent with the market-based changes discussed above. Where the Anglo–American corporate board structure was not seen as particularly effective in achieving the Party/state's policy goals, it was quickly modified with non-market-based means adopted by the Party.

Arguably, China's post-2005 regulation of state-manager relations in SOEs is also consistent with an important feature of the Chinese form of state capitalism, as illustrated by commentators. This reflects the remarkable ability of the Party-state to combine administrative with market-based means to achieve economic development-oriented policy goals. Indeed, this feature has led Bremmer to define state capitalism as 'a system in which the state functions as the leading economic actor and uses markets primarily for political gain' (Bremmer 2009: 41).

holding companies converted from parent SOEs of certain state-owned or controlled corporate groups.
31 The Tamasek Charter.
32 Indeed, this objective is also reflected in the Temporary Regulations, which seek to 'enhance the governing capacity of the Party and ensure the Party's command of the overall situation and coordination of the core functions of all aspects of leadership'.

However, this new regulatory approach relying upon a combination of market and non-market-based means is unlikely to provide an effective solution to the dual governance problem associated with Chinese SOEs, including the problem of insider control by top corporate executives. The strengthening of the role of the Party in central and local parent SOEs may potentially provide some rather intrusive means of imposing discipline upon Party-appointed managers, given the pervasive reward and sanction systems at the Party's disposal (Naughton 2010: 456). However, as with SASAC, the Party is not immune from the inherent conflict entailed in its multiple political, economic and social goals in managing Chinese SOEs.

More fundamentally, strengthening the Party's role in the parent SOEs further marginalises the role of their boards in monitoring and disciplining top corporate executives. Under the current framework for the governance of central SOEs, the chairman is entrusted with three prominent roles, namely as SOE chairman, as de facto chief executive officer and as secretary of the Party Committee, which is bestowed with the top authority in corporate management decision-making. As a consequence, board oversight of the chairman's role is likely to be further diminished. Indeed, with the ongoing involvement of the state in the appointment of top executives and management decision-making in parent SOEs, and overlapping senior executives in the listed companies and their state-owned parents, the various legal and regulatory reforms aimed at strengthening the governance of listed SOEs could, in reality, lead to very limited progress.

6 Conclusion

This chapter has reviewed China's post-2005 developments in the regulation of state-manager relations in large state-controlled listed companies. By examining the changes and continuities, the chapter has shown the emergence of a new state-led approach to the regulation of state-manager relations in these companies. On the one hand, this approach has significantly moved away from the old post-war state-led model (as discussed by Hansmann and Kraakman and comparative capitalism researchers) by applying extensive market-based governance mechanisms to both listed companies and their state-owned parents. On the other hand, ongoing state control in the appointment of senior SOE executives and management decision-making suggest that this approach has been adopted so as to strengthen, rather than to weaken, the effectiveness of state control over these large enterprises.

This new state-led approach to the regulation of state-managers relations in Chinese SOEs is difficult to reconcile with the Anglo–American shareholder-oriented model of corporate governance. It cannot, however, be separated from China's efforts to maintain its state-led model of economic development amid international and domestic pressures for change and the poor governance of these SOEs.

The long-term viability of this approach is likely to hinge on the balance between the will and capacity of the state to adjust its competing roles over its SOEs and the risk of lax internal controls that persists at the corporate level. As this chapter has suggested, Chinese policy-makers will continue to face the battle between retaining ultimate state control over the country's large SOEs and improving their management (and efficiency). Nevertheless, as long as this regulatory approach continues to serve state policy goals, it is unlikely to be subject to significant changes in any near future.

In light of the situation discussed above, foreign regulators and corporations dealing with Chinese SOEs should reassess the somewhat optimistic convergence models that have been so widely articulated in the corporate law literature, given the ongoing dominant position of the Chinese state in the governance of its SOEs.

Bibliography

Books and articles

Andrews, N. and Tomasic, R. (2005), 'Directing China's Top 100 Listed Companies: Corporate Governance in an Emerging Market Economy' *The Corporate Governance Law Review* 2, 245–309.

Bacon, D. (2012), 'Emerging-market Multinationals: The Rise of State Capitalism' *The Economist* (online) (21 January) <http://www.economist.com/node/21542930>.

Bremmer, I. (2009), 'State Capitalism Comes of Age' *Foreign Affairs* 88, 40–41.

Bremmer, I. (2010), *The End of the Free Market: Who Wins the War between States and Corporations?*, Portfolio.

Clarke, D. and Howson, N. (2012), 'Pathway to Minority Shareholder Protection: Derivative Actions in the People's Republic of China' in D. Puchniak and others (eds), *The Derivative Action in Asia: A Comparative and Functional Approach*, Cambridge University Press.

Derek, B. (2012), 'Emerging-market Multinationals: The Rise of State Capitalism', *The Economist* (online) (21 January 2012) http://www.economist.com/node/21542930 (last accessed 3 June 2016).

Feinerman, J. V. (2008), 'New Hope for Corporate Governance in China?' in Donald Clarke (ed.) *China's Legal System: New Developments, New Challenges*, Cambridge University Press.

Hansmann, H. and Kraakman, R. (2001), 'The End of History for Corporate Law' (2001) *Georgetown Law Journal* 89, 439–68.

Howson, N. (2010), 'Corporate Law in the Shanghai People's Courts, 1992–2008: Judicial Autonomy in a Contemporary Authoritarian State' *East Asia Law Review* 5, 303–442.

Ikenberry, G. J. (2011), 'The Future of the Liberal World Order' *Foreign Affairs* 90, 56–62.

Kang, N. (2010), 'Globalisation and Institutional Change in the State-led Model: The Case of Corporate Governance in South Korea' *New Political Economy* 15: 519–42.

Liu, J. P. and Huang, X.W. (2014), '组建国有资本运营公司–国资改革突破口' [Establishing State Capital Operating Companies as a Breakthrough for Reform of State Assets Management] 首都经贸大学学报 *Capital Economic and Trade University Review* 1, 41–44.

Liu, Q. (2006), 'Corporate Governance in China: Current Practices, Economic Effects and Institutional Determinants' *CESifo Economic Studies* 52, 415–53.

Lu, F.C. (ed.) (2011), 《中央企业公司治理报告》 [Report on Corporate Governance of Central State-owned Enterprises], 中国经济出版社 [China Economic Publishing House].

Naughton, B. (2010), 'China's Distinctive System: Can it be a Model for Others?' *Journal of Contemporary China* 19, 437–60.

Pei, M. X. (2006), *China's Trapped Transition: the Limits of Developmental Autocracy* Harvard University Press.

Szamosszegi, A. and Kyle, C. (2011), 'An Analysis of State-owned Enterprises and State Capitalism in China' US–China Economic and Security Review Commission.

Tomasic, R. and Andrews, N. (2007), 'Minority Shareholder Protection in China's Top 100 Listed Companies' *Australian Journal of Asian Law* 9, 88–119.

Tomasic, R. (2010), 'Looking at Corporate Governance in China's Large Companies: Is the Glass Half Full or Half Empty?' in Guanghua Yu (ed.) *The Development of the Chinese Legal System Change and Challenges*, Routledge.

Wang, J. Y. (2008), 'Rule of Law and Rule of Officials: Shareholder Litigation and Anti-Dumping Investigation in China' (The Foundation for Law, Justice and Society in collaboration with The Centre for Socio-Legal Studies, University of Oxford) 24 January 2008 http://www.fljs.org/uploads/documents/Jiangyu%231%23.pdf (last accessed 3 June 2016).

The World Bank (1997), *China's Management of Enterprise Assets: The State as Shareholder*, The World Bank.

Zhang, X. Ch. (2012), 'Company Law Reform in China' in Garrick, J. (ed.), *Law and Policy for China's Market Socialism*, Routledge.

Legislation, administrative regulations and policy documents

《中华人民共和国企业国有资产法》 [Law of Enterprise State-owned Assets of the People's Republic of China] (People's Republic of China) National People's Congress, 28 October 2008, art 4.

'财政部公布 2013 年全国国有企业财务决算情况' [2013 SOE Financial Statements released by Ministry of Finance] Chinese Central Government Website (28 July 2014) http://www.gov.cn/xinwen/2014-07/28/content_2725636.htm (last accessed 3 June 2016).

'国资委再推央企整体上市, 已上市央金融资超 9000 亿' [SASAC Continues to Promote the Full Listing of Central SOEs, Funds Raised by Listed Central SOEs Exceeded RMB900 Billion], China Venture 18 May, 2012 http://news.chinaventure.com.cn/2/20120518/86119.shtml (last accessed 3 June 2016).

《关于改革和完善国有资产管理体制的若干意见》 [Several Opinions on Reforming and Perfecting the System for State-owned Assets Management], State Council, 4 November 2015.

《关于上市公司股权分置改革试点有关问题的通知》 [Notice on Relevant Issues concerning the Pilot Reform of Split Share Structure in Listed Companies] (People's Republic of China)China Securities Regulatory Commission, 29 April 2005.

《关于印发《企业内部控制基本规范》的通知》 [Circular on Release of the Basic Standards for Enterprise Internal Control] (People's Republic of China) Ministry of Finance, China Securities Regulatory Commission, National Audit Office, China Banking Regulatory Commission and China Insurance Regulatory Commission, 22 May 2008; Basic Standards art 10.

《关于在上市公司建立独立董事制度的指导意见》 [Guidelines for the Introduction of Independent Directors into Listed Companies] (People's Republic of China) China Securities Regulatory Commission, 16 August 2001.

《关于在深化国有企业改革中坚持党的领导加强党的建设的若干意见》 [Several Opinions on Upholding the Party's Leadership and Strengthening Party Construction in Deepening the Reform of State-owned Enterprises], The Chinese Communist Party Central Committee, 20 September 2015.

《企业国有资产监督管理暂行条例》 [Interim Regulations on the Supervision and Administration of Enterprise State-owned Assets] (People's Republic of China) State Council, 13 May 2003, art 13.

《全民所有制工业企业法》 [Law on Industrial Enterprises Owned by the Whole People] (People's Republic of China) National People's Congress, 13 April 1988.

《上市公司股权激励管理办法（试行)) [Measures for the Administration of Equity Incentive Plans of Listed Companies (For Trial Implementation)] (People's Republic of China) China Securities Regulatory Commission, 31 December 2005.

《中共中央关于国有企业改革和发展若干重大问题的决定》 [Decision of the Central Committee of the Chinese Communist Party on Several Major Issues Concerning the Reform and Development of State-owned Enterprises], Adopted at the Fourth Plenum of the 15th Central Committee of the Chinese Communist Party, 22 September 1999.

《中共中央国务院关于深化国有企业改革的指导意见》 [Guiding Opinion on Deepening State-owned Enterprise Reform], Central Committee of the Chinese Communist Party and State Council, 24 August 2015).

《中国共产党党组工作条例（试行）》 [Temporary Regulations on the Work of the Chinese Community Party Committee (Temporary Regulations)], Centre Committee of the Chinese Communist Party, effective from 11 June 2015.

《中华人民共和国公司法》 [Company Law of the People's Republic of China] (People's Republic of China) National People's Congress Standing Committee, 29 December 1993.

《中华人民共和国证券法》 [Securities Law of the People's Republic of China] (People's Republic of China) National People's Congress Standing Committee, 29 December 1998.

《中华人民共和国公司法》 [Company Law of the People's Republic of China] (People's Republic of China) National People's Congress Standing Committee, 27 October 2005 (2005 PRC Company Law).

《中华人民共和国证券法》 [Securities Law of the People's Republic of China] (People's Republic of China) National People's Congress Standing Committee, 27 October 2005.

Full Text of Jiang Zemin's Report at the 16th Congress of the Chinese Communist Party (18 November 2002) http://english.people.com.cn/200211/18/eng20021118_106983.shtml (last accessed 3 June 2016).

10

The limits of institutional shareholder activism in China and the United Kingdom

Some comparisons

Bo Gong

1 Understanding individual shareholder activism

Is activism by shareholders rational? What factors determine the extent of institutional shareholder activism? Before looking closely at institutional shareholder activism in the UK and China, this chapter seeks to deal with some fundamental issues by identifying the factors that explain when shareholder activism will occur. In other words, it intends to show how individual shareholders might go about deciding whether they ought to be active. Whether individual action is likely to happen depends upon the motivations that drive individual investor action.

Perhaps the dominant explanation for individual action in recent years has been an economic one. On this approach, an individual investor (including institutional shareholders) will take part in some shareholder action where it is in their own interests to do so. Since institutional shareholders are assumed to be essentially financial institutions, this becomes a question of whether it is in the shareholder's financial interests to undertake activism of some kind. The individual shareholder will calculate the costs and the likely benefits of its acting, and will act according to this calculation.

A shareholder will calculate the total benefits to the company as a whole of some collective action. It will then work out what proportion of that total benefit the individual shareholder will secure, where that proportion is the same as the proportion of the company's shares the shareholder holds (so an institution holding, say, 5 per cent of the company's shares will thereby keep 5 per cent of the total corporate benefit earned by some collective action). Finally, the shareholder will then calculate its individual costs of participating in the collective action. Only if its share of the total collective benefits outweighs its own individual costs of action will the institutional shareholder bother to act.

However, the position is even more complex than this, for it raises the 'problem' of collective action (sometimes also called the 'free-rider' problem). The core motivation that encourages institutional shareholders to act is whether the free-rider problem facing any collective action can be overcome. This chapter suggests four factors that can, in some circumstances, undermine the likelihood of free-riding. They are: (i) the significance of large individual institutional holdings; (ii) the possibility of concerted action; (iii) the existence of so-called 'in process' benefits; and (iv) whether there is a normative obligation to act. This chapter will discuss these four factors and then seek to apply them to UK and Chinese institutional investors.

The logic of collective action

The so-called collective action problem was famously identified by Olson in his classic work, *The Logic of Collective Action: Public Goods and the Theory of Groups* (Olson 1965: 14). The problem that Olson identified was not just that the individual shareholder will capture only a small fraction (equivalent to the proportion of the company's total share capital the shareholder owns) of the total gains accruing to the company from the collective action, but that this small fraction may be less than the individual shareholder's costs of action. Furthermore, an individual shareholder's own contribution to the success of collective action is unlikely to be *decisive*.

Accordingly, each shareholder will reason as follows. *Either* enough other shareholders will participate in the collective action to ensure it is successful, so that my contribution is unnecessary. *Or* so few others will participate that, even if I join in the action, it will still fail. Moreover, any positive return from monitoring/activism will go to all shareholders regardless of whether or not they have participated, or contributed to the monitoring/activism. My own participation, then, will either be unnecessary or it will be ineffective. Either way, logically, I should not join in. Another way of expressing this seems to be that whatever the likely benefits of the collective action, *the benefits of my own participation* will be minor. On this view, it does not really matter what the costs of the shareholder's actions may be: given a zero benefit from my action, then *any* costs, *however small*, make my own action irrational, economically speaking.

How can we explain any individual institutional activism in the face of the free-rider problem that is inherent in the logic of collective action? This chapter argues that this logic can indeed (sometimes) be overcome for individual shareholders, but that it entails a more complex analysis of shareholder activism. In particular, we must show that, for an individual investor, that individual investor's own activism will indeed make a difference to the outcome of a collective action. Thus, it will conclude that 'free-riding' is not an option for institutional shareholders; were one to sit back and do nothing, then it would either mean that some collective action would fail (meaning that no-one would benefit), or that the inactive shareholder would be denied some individual benefits – that some individual benefits would be secured only if it individually took action.

When is free-riding not an option, so that a shareholder would think it must act in order to gain some individual benefits? Four factors need to be considered so as to make free-riding an individually irrational policy for some shareholders: (i) the decisiveness of large individual institutional holdings; (ii) the possibility of concerted action; (iii) what so-called 'in process' benefits are there; and (iv) the existence of a normative obligation to act.

Overcoming free-riding

The decisiveness of large individual institutional holdings

It should first be noted that voting in a company differs fundamentally from voting in a political election, where no one voter is ever likely to make a difference to the outcome of the election. The size of some shareholders' holdings may be sufficiently large so as to 'tip the balance' between failure and success. Of course, a shareholder, even one with 3 or 4 or 5 (or more) per cent of the company's shares, cannot be *sure* that its own holding will be sufficient to change the outcome of, say, a contested vote, or a private meeting where a change in corporate policy is demanded. However, the larger the shareholder's holding, *the greater the chance* that its votes may be decisive (a likelihood that never really arises in a one person-one vote political election).

This is one reason (but not the only reason) why we would expect to find that the larger a shareholder's holding of shares, the greater the likelihood that it will indeed be active. Mallin, for example, notes that there should be a positive correlation between the proportion of shares held in a company and the propensity to vote those shares (Mallin 1997: 160). Taking the institutional shareholder Prudential as an example, of its total disclosable interests,[1] only 5.6 per cent are in companies with the lowest level of voting, whilst the largest proportion of Prudential's disclosable interests (28 per cent) are in companies with voting levels of 35–40 per cent (Mallin 1997: 161). That suggests that institutional investors will vote their shares in the companies in which they have sufficiently large shareholdings.

The possibility of concerted action

Olsen's logic of collective action also assumes that those who decide whether to act will do so 'in isolation'. A potential actor (shareholder) is assumed not to agree with others that she will act *if they will also do so*. In that respect, it is modelled as a 'prisoner's dilemma' (Hardin 1993: 23). However, if shareholders can explicitly agree with others that each will join in an action if the others will do likewise, then together they may have enough votes to tip the balance. The practicality of such coalitions by agreement are, as we shall see below, significantly increased by the extent that share ownership is more concentrated, so that fewer shareholders need to agree to act together in order to constitute a decisive bloc of shares (Crespi and Renneboog 2010: 274).

Generally, one or more large institutional investors will take the lead to organise other institutional shareholders to join the collective action. This was well illustrated in the jettisoning of Michael Green, who had been earmarked as the chairman of the new ITV plc, a merger of broadcast companies Carlton and Granada. Fidelity International took the lead and effectively mobilised other institutional investors and signalled that 35 per cent of Carlton's shareholders wanted Green out. Consequently, this coalition blocked Green's appointment by resolutely arguing against it (Randall 2003).

Moreover, collective action is often organised by representative associations, such as the Association of British Issuers. In these cases, other institutional investors, even where they do not join a formal coalition, are likely to act in the same way as those taking the lead. Both of these two factors – the decisiveness of individual holdings and the possibility of concerted action – depend, clearly, upon the pattern of share ownership amongst institutional holders. We can ask, do individual institutions acquire sufficiently large holdings in some companies where, individually, they perceive they can make a difference? We can also ask, do small groups of institutions, acting collectively, hold enough shares in some companies to allow them to believe that they are likely to make a difference by joining together? As we will see

---

1 A substantial holding of 3% or 5% in a company is required to be disclosed in the company's annual report, in the UK and in China, respectively. See UK Financial Services Authority Handbook, Disclosure and Transparency Rules 5.1.2.R. and Chinese Securities Law 2005 s 86.

later, over recent decades, institutional ownership of stock has indeed rapidly increased in many countries, including both the UK and China.

One might argue that, although institutional shareholding as a whole has increased in listed companies, few institutions still do not have sufficient shares to counterbalance the power of the incumbent management. However, they will have such power if small groups of them collectively constitute a significant bloc. With regard specifically to the possibility of 'concerted action', or what has been termed 'control through a constellation of interests' (Scott 1985: 49), Scott argued over two decades ago that the growth of institutional holdings had led to 20–30 per cent of shares typically being concentrated into the hands of the top 20 or so shareholders (Scott 1985: 81).

A more recent study conducted by Mallin (1997) found that 88 per cent of the Top 250 companies in 1994 had disclosable interests, that is, had a shareholder owning 3 per cent or more of their shareholdings. (Indeed, 50 per cent of the companies had disclosable interests totalling 13.5 per cent or less.) The mean disclosable interest was about 18.5 per cent. As some data have suggested, few if any individuals or groups hold sufficient shares to exercise control; however, the largest shareholders have substantial shares and, collectively, they represent an important group that the board cannot easily disregard.

'In process' benefits

Yet another factor that affects free-riding is that some benefits to individual institutional investors may come from *the process of engagement* itself and not from improvements to the company's own performance. Activism, for example, may be a marketing policy for the institutional shareholder that makes its own fund more attractive to *its own* potential beneficiaries/investors. This possibility is confirmed by the study undertaken by Hendry and others, in which they found that institutional investors are sometimes motivated by the need to maintain their own competitive position to take action (Hendry and others 2004: 8). As they suggested, clients of institutions expected them to exercise a certain level of responsibility in respect of governance matters, and that fund managers had had to 'follow suit in order to pitch for, gain and retain their business'. As such, some institutions might actively engage in activism just in order to promote their brand image and receive *reputational* benefits.

Moreover, MacNeil and Macey both observed that shareholder intervention in one investee company has the potential to provide some level of deterrence against potential managerial abuses in the *other* companies of the institutional investor's portfolio (MacNeil 2010: 10; Macey 2008: 250). The other companies, even if they are not the target of shareholder activism, will feel that they are under attack in much the same way as they would be if they were performing badly in corporate governance. This, in turn, creates strong incentives for institutional shareholders to engage in activism as a way of improving *overall* portfolio values.

Finally, 'in-process' benefit is perhaps more important, and evident for those funds whose business strategy is precisely to profit by engaging with underperforming investee companies. They rely heavily on an engagement investment strategy to attract clients. One of the leading examples of this in the UK is that of Hermes, which we shall address in section 3 below.

A normative obligation to act?

Moving beyond the previous strictly 'economic' analysis, it may be argued that there may be demands for action that compel shareholders to entertain action *without strictly calculating* whether they need to do so to ensure success. Here one can differentiate between demands that emanate from legal requirements to act, through to codes of practice that seek to encourage action, and even beyond to a more general 'cultural' expectation that institutions 'do their bit' towards a collective endeavour. The extent to which they force institutional shareholders to take action will vary as between different types of activism. However, it might still be helpful to give a brief illustration of this here.

For example, legally, the UK Companies Act 2006 (CA 2006) grants reserve power to the UK Government to make rules requiring certain types of institutional shareholders to disclose how they have voted shares which they own or in which they have an indirect interest (CA 2006: ss 1277–80). A desire to avoid intervention by compulsion prompted major institutional investors to increase the level of engagement with their investee companies (Cheffins 2008: 386). Moreover, regulatory guidelines often generate a normative obligation on institutional shareholders to vote their shares and accordingly, the voting levels of UK listed companies have been steadily increasing over the last decade (Goergen, Renneboog and Zhang 2008: 56). Driven by these normative demands, as will be seen below, in many cases shareholders' propensity for active engagement does not rely solely on a precise calculation of whether or not they *need* to act to ensure success.

Nevertheless, even where some shareholders do perceive that there is a positive obligation to join in a collective action, it seems unlikely that such financial institutions would act on this obligation entirely regardless of the balance between the benefits and the costs of action. One might suggest, for example, that some shareholders will feel that it is wrong to free-ride on the efforts of others, and that they should contribute towards a collective action (regardless of whether they *need* to do so in order to enjoy its benefits); however, these institutions may feel that this obligation exists only in so far as the institution's own benefits will still outweigh its own costs.

There is evidence to show that the level of institutional shareholder activism is positively linked to a country's legal and political environment (Ameer 2010: 133). For example, institutional investors are much more willing to invest in companies when information disclosure is more apparent, with the consequence that the resulting legal and economic cost of such activism is reduced.

So far, we have seen how the 'free-rider' problem can be overcome amongst institutional shareholders, for at least four reasons – the decisiveness of (sizeable) institutional holdings, the possibility of concerted action, the existence of 'in process' benefits and a normative obligation to join in collective actions. Moreover, the analysis above suggests that many factors are relevant to understanding when and why shareholder activism is likely to take place. So, activism seems to depend upon the ownership structure of stock markets, the total amount of institutional investment, the type of institutional shareholder concerned, the type of activism that is being contemplated and the governance or regulatory environment. The following sections draw upon such empirical knowledge as can currently be reasonably gathered about these three variables, both in the UK and in China, and explore the likelihood of institutional shareholder activism in these two countries.

2 The institutional shareholder investment in the UK and in China

In the UK, equity ownership in listed companies has experienced two notable changes over recent decades. First, share ownership has moved away from individual investors to become concentrated in the hands of a relatively few powerful institutional shareholders. By 2012, according to the data compiled by the Office of National Statistics, domestic institutional shareholders (including insurance companies, pension funds, unit trusts, investment trusts, banks and other financial institutions) accounted for 36.1 per cent of the UK ordinary shares.

Individuals, who once held the greatest proportion of total equity in the 1960s, fell to only about 10.7 per cent of the total ownership (Office for National Statistics 2015). Second, the rise of foreign ownership accounts for an estimated 53.2 per cent of the value of the UK stock market. Considering overseas ownership is mainly controlled by institutions, despite likely differences when they determine to take action, they are essentially similar to UK institutional shareholders. This chapter will examine their influences on UK institutional investor activism where this is appropriate.

In China, the stock market had a late start in the early 1990s following the establishment of stock exchanges in Shanghai and Shenzhen. Institutional investors, including mutual funds, insurance companies, pension funds, qualified foreign institutional investors and other financial institutions, however, have now risen to become an important group of shareholders in Chinese listed companies. The level of institutional investor ownership had increased from 10 per cent in 2003 to 30 per cent in 2007. It later dropped gradually to 14.22 per cent in 2014 (CSRC 2015).

The greater presence of institutional investors has not only resulted from the development of stock markets, but has also benefited from substantial support from government. Institutional investors are believed to be beneficial to the long-term development of the Chinese stock market, as it is believed that this will promote market integrity, stability and innovation. Hence, the Chinese Government has cultivated institutional investor ownership in Chinese firms to take advantage of an increasingly important external control mechanism for monitoring of firm management. For example, the government has gradually lowered the investment threshold for institutional investors and transferred some state-owned shares in IPOs to the national social security pension fund. Meanwhile, the rapid expansion of the Chinese stock market has also fuelled the growth of the institutional shareholder industry.

The growth of institutional investors has promoted greater shareholder engagement in Chinese listed companies. Data from the China Stock Market & Accounting Research (CSMAR) database suggests that the attendance of shareholders at company meetings is positively linked to the level of institutional ownership (Cai and Yu 2015: 78). As the following table shows, for companies without institutional investors, 47 per cent of shareholders attend shareholders' general meetings when there is no institutional investor in the companies. The attendance of shareholders' meetings increases as the institutional ownership becomes larger. When institutional investors hold more than 10 per cent of securities, the average attendance of shareholders has grown to 55 per cent. This suggests that institutional shareholders are more willing to attend shareholders' meetings than individual shareholders, possibly leading to a better corporate governance system in those investee companies.

However, as we can see, the total level of institutional ownership in China is far smaller than that in the UK. The positive governance effect discussed above, which was brought about by the rise in the proportion of institutional investors is, however, rather limited because of the investment restrictions imposed on institutions. Despite the existence of portfolio regulation in the UK and other countries, institutional shareholders in China also have to cope with stricter investment limitations.

An institutional shareholder is not only limited in how much stock it can own in a single company, as is also the case in the UK, but the collective shareholdings of institutional shareholders are also limited. For example, a Chinese mutual fund is not allowed to hold more than 10 per cent of its net assets in the shares of a single issuer (Chinese Securities Fund Law: s 31). Nor is it permitted to hold more than a total of 10 per cent of one company's

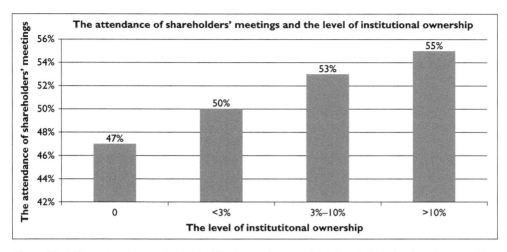

Figure 10.1 The attendance of shareholders' meetings and the level of institutional ownership

share in the fund managed by the same fund manager. China's biggest pension fund, the National Social Security Fund, is even not allowed to buy shares in Chinese listed companies. The hope that institutional shareholders might play a greater role in corporate governance relies heavily on their increasingly large shareholdings and, if their growth is limited, it is less likely for them to be able to overcome the problems associated with concentrated state ownership, as discussed further below.

3 Equity ownership in the UK and Chinese stock markets

The different equity share ownership patterns found in the UK and China should be seen as the primary reason for variations in the level of institutional shareholder engagement between the two countries. The basic characteristics of company share structure in listed companies can determine both the context within which activism can occur and the role that activism can play within companies. The UK listed company sector and the Chinese listed company sector each differ fundamentally in the way that shares are controlled. The UK is generally described as a system with a diffused shareholder base, suggesting that listed companies do not normally have a single large individual investor who is capable of exercising influential control over its management (Shleifer and Vishny 1997: 731). The danger that selfish managers will pursue their own agendas rather than seek to promote corporate success is the principal concern of investors in UK companies.

Whilst by no means universal, it is not uncommon for individual institutional shareholders to hold more than 3 per cent of any given listed company's issued shares. In this regard, we can consider the ownership structure of a UK company like Marks & Spencer Plc, as set out in its 2015 annual report. This data reveals that, whilst the number of retail investors accounts for a super-majority of the total number of shareholders, they own comparatively few shares: 15.71 per cent retail investor ownership as against 84.29 per cent institutional investor ownership (including corporate shareholders). As such, equities are concentrated in a relatively small group of institutional investors. Elsewhere, Marks & Spencer Plc's 2015 annual report reveals that there are seven shareholders with greater than 2 per cent shareholdings: one of them has 5 per cent or above (*Financial Times* 2015).

In contrast, the corporate sector in China is well known for its 'insider/control-oriented' system of ownership and control, where listed companies typically have a 'block holder' – the state, which owns a sufficiently sizeable fraction of the voting shares to control the corporation.[2] Recent research in 2012 shows that in the top 100 Chinese listed companies, 84 are highly concentrated with a single, large owner associated with the Chinese Government or are a government-run and related enterprise (Institute of World Economic and Political in Chinese Academy of Social Science 2012). By 2012, state shares accounted for 51.4 per cent of the total A share market in China.

Where the state acts as the controlling shareholder, the way it pursues its own interests differs from the way that other investors would act. The state has multiple strategic goals, and many of these are social and political, which need not coincide with those of other investors in the company. For example, a major objective of the Communist Party of China (CPC) – the ruling party – has been to maintain 'social stability' or today's 'China dream' by maintaining social equity, ensuring full employment and refraining from taking such profit enhancing measures as asset divestiture and job cuts (Su, Xu and Phan 2008: 19).

In pursuit of these interests, the state could make rules in its own favour; in other words, it could potentially legitimate its expropriating behaviours or political interests since the state serves a dual role as both major shareholder and as regulator (Shanghai Stock Exchange 2003: 14). Moreover, the managerial personnel, who are often appointed by the controlling shareholder, are likely to interpret their fiduciary duty towards the state, instead of the company as a whole (Tomasic and Fu 2006: 245).

As a consequence of the concentrated shareholding in most Chinese listed companies, holding the controlling shareholder accountable has become the primary concern of Chinese institutional shareholders. The manager–shareholder agency problem, whilst certainly being a worry for investors, is less threatening than it is in UK companies.

This contrast regarding equity ownership in UK and Chinese companies suggests that the context within which activism will occur is different in these two countries. It also has significant implications for the level of institutional investor involvement in corporate governance. The collective action problem (also called the 'free-rider' problem) that faces any institutional shareholder's engagement efforts is easier to overcome in the UK where shares are dispersed, than it is in China where shares are concentrated. The individual shareholder engaging in action against controllers will incur significant costs but will capture only a small fraction of the total gains accruing to the company from the collective action. Moreover, where the individual shareholder makes a contribution to the success of the collective action it is unlikely to be *decisive*.

In the UK, the collective action problem can be overcome when any given institution's shareholdings are sufficiently large to 'tip the balance' between success and failure, or institutional shareholders are willing to engage in various forms of collective action so as to make their holding decisive. In China, however, the problem is much more complicated. Because of the presence of large shareholders, institutional shareholders have both fewer incentives and less ability to overcome collective action problems.

---

2 It is important to make clear here, that the State does not fall into the category of institutional investor. The role of the State in a company is significantly different from that of an institutional investor. They have very different objectives to each other. Institutional investors are normally bound by various fiduciary duties towards their clients while the State is not but it is always oriented by political purposes.

To illustrate this point, we can compare the likelihood of institutional shareholder activism in two companies, one UK listed company: Marks & Spencer Plc and one Chinese listed company: Sichuan Changhong Electric Co. The equity held in Marks & Spencer is dominated by institutional shareholders, with 84 per cent of shares owned by institutional investors. The top 10 institutional shareholders collectively hold about 25.71 per cent of the total equity (*Financial Times* 2015). If we then calculate their actual significance on the basis that the average voting level in the UK is 60 per cent (Myners 2005: 1), these top five shareholders, if they work jointly, actually control 40 per cent of the votes cast at shareholders' meetings. In the absence of a large shareholder who can influence the remaining 60 per cent of votes at a meeting, the coalition of the top five shareholders can be decisive in shareholder meetings held by Marks & Spencer.

This is not the case in Sichuan Changhong, however. Sichuan Changhong is in the top 10 Chinese listed companies in terms of the level of shareholding held by investment funds (East Money 2015). In this company, 12.24 per cent of tradable shares are collectively controlled by institutional investment funds, or so-called mutual funds. In spite of that, institutional shareholders are unlikely to play a decisive role in Sichuan Changhong, even if it were feasible for them to form an alliance comprising all institutional shareholders in the company, because the largest shareholder controls 24 per cent of the total equity.

If we have a further look at equity share ownership patterns in other UK and Chinese listed companies, it can be seen that the ownership structures of Marks & Spencer and Sichuan Changhong are representative in both countries. In the UK, for example, Prudential and Vodafone both have a similar shareholder structure to Marks & Spencer, involving a significant number of individual investors and a small number of institutional investors owning most of the shares in the company. Prudential has four shareholders with a shareholding of greater than 4 per cent: one with 5.81 per cent; one with 4.99 per cent; another holding 4.08 per cent and another with 4.07 per cent (Prudential Plc 2015). There are two shareholders with a disclosable shareholding in Vodafone: one with 3.33 per cent and the other with 3.32 per cent (Vodafone Plc 2015).

In China, for instance, China Citic Bank Co and Shanghai International Port (Group) Co, which are both ranked as the top 10 companies with best corporate governance amongst the top 100 largest Chinese listed companies (Institute of World Economic and Political in Chinese Academy of Social Science 2012), each has a largest shareholder who holds 67.13 per cent and 34.56 per cent of the total equity, respectively. The levels of institutional shareholding in these two companies, however, are only 0.19 per cent and 16.91 per cent, respectively.

These studies support the view that state-controlled ownership has reduced institutional investors' motivation to engage. Chinese shareholder activism, such as through voting practices, submitting shareholder resolutions and appointing directors proposed by institutional shareholders occurred more often in companies where shares are more dispersed (Cai and Yu 2015: 82).

Obviously, institutional shareholders in Chinese listed companies, both individually and collectively, are unlikely to have a decisive shareholding in their portfolio companies to challenge large shareholders. In the context of institutional shareholder activism this fact leads to collective action problems in China, constituting a more difficult obstacle than they do in the UK. Moreover, shareholder collective actions in the UK are often facilitated by industry representative associations, such as the Association of British Insurers. Those associations will organise their institutional members and use their combined weight to bring pressure to bear on companies to follow corporate governance good practice.

When institutional investors realise that their participation may not make much of a difference in their investee companies, they are less willing to act together to engage in collective action, resulting in the low level of institutional shareholder participation in China.

4 In process benefits for institutional investors

The ultimate purpose of institutional shareholder engagement is to obtain benefits from the improvement of the company's performance. However, some types of institutional investors do not expect a return from a long-term holding. This feature of institutional investment matters significantly in the context of shareholders, as institutional shareholders' incentives for activism are associated with their investment horizon. Pension funds and life insurance companies' investments tend to be longer term, as the objectives of a pension fund's asset management is to attain a high replacement ratio at retirement and insurance companies aim to pay their policy-holders a specified sum only if an insured event occurs. In contrast, mutual funds, in particular actively managed funds, tend to be short-term investors as they make profits by trading securities (Davis and Steil 2001: 58).

Long-term institutional investors have more incentives to participate in monitoring because, first, many benefits of activism take a longer time to be realised and, second, the length of time that an investment is held by institutions is positively related to the size of the benefits secured from activism. Many changes promoted by shareholder activism, for example, to increase the independence of the board by appointing more independent directors to the company, will not have an immediate impact on a company share price. The well known UK activist fund, Hermes, which adopts shareholder engagement as its investment strategy, has said that it can take two to three years for its activism to result in a sufficient increase in the company's stock price (Becht and others 2009: 3093). Engaging in activism to wait for slow returns may therefore be at odds with the investment strategies of some short-term institutions who rely on market forces to improve fund performance, often on a quarterly or shorter term basis.

Moreover, institutional shareholders with long-term investment horizons will receive more benefits from activism than those with shorter-term investment. First, longer-term investments offer a good opportunity for institutions to develop long-term relationships with investee companies to increase those institutions' influence over the company and to secure more accountability from its board (Millstein 1991: 68). Second, a close relationship between institutional investors and corporate management is found to be helpful in reducing the possibility of managerial short-termism through facilitating the board's adoption of a longer-term investment strategy in their companies (Robert 2004: 271).

The main institutional investors in both the UK and China comprise pension funds, insurance companies and mutual funds. It is necessary to point out in advance that investments by different types of institution are not separate but often overlapping. Insurance companies both hold shares in their own right and also manage the investment of other institutions, such as pension funds. Pension funds and insurers are often the largest clients of mutual funds.

In the UK, pension funds used to be the largest institutional investor in the 1990s; they held an estimated 4.7 per cent of total domestic shares by value at the end of 2012, down from 5.6 per cent in 2010 and, significantly, lower than the levels seen in recent years (Office for National Statistics 2005). Unit trusts now formed the largest group of institutional shareholders, holding an estimated 9.6 per cent by value at the end of 2012, continuing the strong growth seen in recent years. Insurance companies held an estimated 6.2 per cent by value at the end of 2012, continuing the fall witnessed in recent years. Other financial institutions held an estimated 6.6 per cent by value at the end of 2012, which was significantly lower than the levels in 2010, following strong growth in earlier years. It is therefore reasonable to predict that the level of institutional shareholder activism might decrease if UK securities are dominated by the short-termism of unit trusts.

In addition to these 'mainstream' institutional investors, one recently emerging type of institution – the hedge fund – has, as Amour and Cheffins, and MacNeil show, the potential to be an important player in the UK corporate governance arena. As of March 2010, total assets under management by global hedge funds were estimated to be US$1.5 trillion. Some hedge funds may regard engagement itself as a way of gaining profits and thus have incentives to forgo free-riding so as to gain these 'in process' benefits.

Perhaps the leading example of this in the UK is that of Hermes. Hermes has actively engaged in shareholder activism to improve the corporate governance of investee companies. To be sure, part of the benefit of doing this is an anticipated rise in the value of its investee companies. Recently, researchers from the London Business School examined the investment and shareholder engagement approaches adopted by the Hermes UK Focus Fund (HUKFF) over the period 1998–2004 and found that its engagement is ultimately value-increasing (Becht and others 2009: 3093).

During that period, the HUKFF invested in 41 companies, and engaged with 30 of them. It had meetings with chairmen, CEOs, divisional managers, heads of investor relations and with non-executive board members (ibid: 3095). It also contacted other institutional share-holders to seek their support for its efforts. The research found that the fund's engagement approach was highly successful. It generated annual raw returns net of fees of 8.2 per cent, or 4.9 per cent if measured by the abnormal returns against the FTSE All-Share Index over the period 1998–2004. Thus, 90 per cent of such returns were attributable to engagement activities.

In China, the composition of institutional investment differs sharply from that in the UK owing to the much greater presence of mutual funds. The equity held by mutual funds, or so-called securities investment funds, prevails in the institutional investor industry with mutual funds holding more than 60 per cent of total Chinese institutional shares. Insurance companies accounted for around 22.65 per cent of total institutional shareholdings (Cai and Yu 2015: 79). The remaining institutional shareholders in China are banks and other financial institutions.

Despite considerable growth potential, Chinese pension funds and insurance companies are still at an embryonic stage of development, as noted earlier, subject to strict quantitative investment limits in the stock market. Qualified foreign investment institutions (QFIIs), which are foreign institutions that meet certain conditions, have invested directly in the Chinese A share market since December 2001 under the quota granted by the Chinese Government. There are high expectations that QFIIs will improve corporate governance standards in Chinese listed companies.

However, when examining some activities of QFIIs in one Chinese listed company, Xia and Tomasic found that the present role of QFIIs in improving corporate governance is somewhat limited. This seems to result from the fact that their shareholdings are generally small, compared with the dominant controlling shareholder. By mid-2014, QFIIs share-holdings only accounted for 1.1 per cent of the stock market. Meanwhile, research by Chen, Liu and Guan suggest that the activism of QFIIs is largely in the nature of the herd effect, which means that QFIIs tend to follow the actions of other large domestic institutional investors (Chen, Liu and Guan 2014: 110).

Therefore, since the majority of Chinese institutional shareholders tend to be relatively short-term in their focus, the likelihood of institutional shareholder activism is lower in China than in the UK, which has a larger long-term institutional investor base. Institutional shareholder ineffectiveness in China in part, therefore, results from this feature of the composition of institutional investment.

5 Normative obligations

As noted in section 1, there may be occasions when shareholders do not make economic calculations and, instead, accept an obligation to act regardless of whether they could free-ride on the efforts of others. This obligation arises in two ways as a result of a regulatory norm: the first is to facilitate shareholder activism arising through strengthening shareholder rights and, second, as a result of regulatory calls.

Shareholder rights

Shareholders' rights are a key determinant of the extent of institutional shareholder activism. This is because the influence of institutional investors on corporate governance rests critically on the powers that the background rules of legislation grant them. The UK corporate law regime, as noted by scholars such as Nolan, Davies, Rickford and MacNeil, has a shareholder-oriented base, reserving a wide range of powers to shareholders to act collectively as controllers and monitors of the company (Nolan 2003: 75; Davies and Rickford 2008: 248). Shareholder decision-making powers include the power to change the company's constitution (CA 2006: s 21(1)), to remove directors (ibid: s 168), to call a special meeting and to submit proposals (ibid: ss 303, 314) and, in a number of circumstances, to approve certain managerial actions, including the award of long-term service contracts to directors (ibid: s 188) and the power to approve substantial property transactions with directors (ibid: ss 190–96). All these rights are important in the context of shareholder activism, as they offer institutional investors the necessary means to participate in corporate affairs.

However, whilst the powers enjoyed by UK shareholders are considered as 'amongst the most significant powers of investors in the world', they are still dwarfed by those reserved to shareholders under China's corporate law. In China, the shareholders' meeting is explicitly referred to as an 'organ of power' in company law, with the absolute decision-making authority in the company (Chinese Company Law 2014: s 36). In addition to the above rights, as in the UK, some rights that are vested exclusively within the authority of directors in the UK (such as the right to examine and approve the company's plan for the distribution of profits and recovery of losses, to decide the company's management policy and its investment plan), are also subject to the approval of shareholders in China.

The extensive shareholder powers granted by Chinese company law seem, in theory at least, to provide institutional shareholders with a good opportunity to have a greater role in the companies in which they invest. However, it does not follow that Chinese institutional shareholders have greater incentives to make use of these rights. Since the power to determine corporate affairs is granted to shareholders as a whole, most decision-making rights, such as the right to remove a director, require a majority or even super-majority approval from shareholders attending the shareholders' general meeting. This indicates that the larger the shareholding, the greater the chance that exercise of these rights will be decisive in the company. Therefore, although institutional shareholders are offered a chance to have a say on a wide range of issues, their efforts can easily be overridden by large shareholders.

In practice, the shareholders' meeting in Chinese listed companies is often controlled by the majority shareholder, who is able to demand such changes in the company as it wishes (Yang 2007: 17). Research conducted by Tomasic and Andrews found that, where a single shareholder controls more than half of the company's shares, 'they pass resolutions at AGMs without the presence of other shareholders and small shareholders have no chance to be involved in corporate governance' (Tomasic and Andrews 2009: 98). Yang drew a similar conclusion in his study, finding that in some cases only one shareholder attended the shareholders' meeting and his presence was sufficient to amend the articles of association of the company by passing a special resolution (Yang 2007: 7).

In fact, the extensive powers accorded to shareholders under the PRC Company Law are consistent with the Chinese Government's desire not to relinquish ownership or lose ultimate control over companies. By assigning management authority to the board of directors and by holding a majority of shares as a strong owner, the state can retain a significant level of control through the exercise of extensive powers, as provided in Chinese company law. The interests of the dominant state shareholder, who is sometimes influenced by political or social needs, as explained earlier, can take priority over those of minority shareholders.

In order to strengthen the power of minority shareholders, the 2005 Chinese Company Law introduced a permissive rule, allowing listed companies to choose whether to adopt a cumulative voting method in the election of directors and supervisors. In cases where cumulative voting is applied, shareholders can multiply their votes by the number of directors and supervisors to be elected and can cast all their votes for a single nominee for the board of directors when the company has multiple candidates on its board.[3] Scholars such as Vittas and Gordon argued that the cumulative voting system is the most powerful tool for allowing institutional shareholders to elect directors that are truly independent and to play an active role in protecting the interests of minority investors (Vittas 1998: 15; Gordon 1994: 170–74).

However, the impact of cumulative voting is dependent upon, and varies with, the size of institutional shareholdings and the number of directors to be elected. The cumulative voting system will only benefit those that own a certain percentage of shares alone or with others in an effort to win a board seat. Moreover, the larger the number of directors proposed in the shareholders' meeting, the greater the chance that minority shareholders will win a board seat. By law, the Chinese board of directors can consist of 5 to 19 directors elected by the shareholders' meeting (Company Law 2014: s 108).

It has been found that that the average size of the board in the top 100 Chinese listed companies is 11, which indicates that only shareholders individually or collectively holding 9.09 per cent or more of shares have the possibility of winning a seat on the board (Institute of World Economic and Political in Chinese Academy of Social Science 2012). Even though there is a lack of good data concerning the average level of institutional shareholding in Chinese listed companies, the total institutional shareholding is only around 14 per cent. It is therefore reasonable to conclude that in many companies cumulative voting cannot secure institutional shareholders a board position.

---

3 Chinese Company Law 2014 s 105, for example, if an election is for five directors and a shareholder holds 100 votes, under a straight voting system he has a maximum of 100 shares for any one nominee (500 votes total, 100 votes for each of the five nominees). With cumulative voting, he could cast all 500 for one candidate, 250 each to two candidates, or otherwise divided whichever way he chooses.

In terms of whether and how institutional shareholders have used cumulative voting to advance their interests in practice, regrettably there is currently an absence of research in this regard. However, if we consider the difficulty of overcoming collective action problems in forming a coalition in Chinese listed companies, as discussed earlier, the actual impact of the cumulative voting system on generating more institutional shareholder participation is likely to be limited.

In sum, the passivity of institutional shareholders in Chinese listed companies does not result from the lack of sufficient legal rights allowing institutional shareholders to exercise control over companies. The problem lies in the fact that the exercise of these rights by institutional shareholders is not decisive in the company owing to the presence of controlling shareholders, usually a state agency.

Regulatory calls

The higher level of institutional shareholder activism in the UK has resulted from the existence of a more sophisticated regulatory framework regarding the role of institutional shareholder in corporate governance. Institutional shareholder engagement has long been seen to have a vital role in the UK's system of corporate governance. In contrast, China lacks sufficient recognition of the role that the institutional shareholder can play in promoting improved corporate governance.

In the UK, the Companies Act 2006 gives the UK Government the power to require institutional investors to disclose how they voted their shares (CA 2006: ss 1277–80). Whilst it is stated that the UK Government will use this power only if a voluntary regime fails to improve disclosure, this threat forces institutional investors to consider their responsibilities as owners of investee companies for the interests of their beneficiaries. In response to this reserve power, as noted, more UK institutional investors have raised the level of their engagement with their investee companies. In contrast to the UK, Chinese company law has not recognised the potential influence of institutional shareholders and their potential role in corporate governance.

Moreover, in the UK, successive corporate governance guidance, from the Cadbury Report in 1992, through to the Greenbury, Hampel, Turnbull and Higgs reviews in the mid-1990s to early 2000s, to the current UK Corporate Governance Code (UK Code), has placed significant emphasis on institutional shareholder monitoring as a discipline on corporate management. The newly-issued Stewardship Code demonstrates well the UK government's consistent willingness to promote shareholder engagement in the UK. Although it has not gone without criticism, the UK Stewardship Code sets out good practice on engagement with portfolio companies to which the government believes institutional investors should aspire (Reisberg 2015: 217–53; Cheffins 2012: 1004–1025).

By contrast, the role of institutional shareholders has not attracted sufficient attention from Chinese regulators, which can be seen in China's Code of Corporate Governance for Listed Companies (Chinese Code). Whilst the role of institutional shareholders is indeed mentioned in the Chinese Code, reference to it is somewhat vague. Paragraph 11 of the Chinese Code states that: 'institutional shareholders shall play a role in the appointment of company directors, the compensation and supervision of management and major decision-making processes'.

Such a broad provision cannot be easily implemented in practice. It does not make the case justifying why institutional shareholders should consider active engagement in their own interests and consistent with their duty to their beneficial owners. Nor does it give sufficient guidance to those institutions that are seeking to play a role in corporate governance. These shortcomings give rise to the lack of awareness amongst institutional shareholders about why and how they can make constructive use of the ownership influences that they undoubtedly have. It is perhaps not surprising then, that although some institutional shareholders in China have made commendable efforts to influence companies in positive directions, cases of such activism in this area have regrettably been rare.

6 Conclusion

This chapter has first developed a 'model' that sought to explain when and why activism by shareholders is rational, both collectively and individually, and then explored and compared the nature and extent of institutional shareholder activism in both countries by applying this model. Generally, UK institutional shareholders demonstrate a more active level of involvement in corporate governance than their Chinese counterparts. Some lessons can be drawn from the UK experiences to promote achieving greater institutional monitoring in China.

The greatest obstacle to institutional investor activism in China is the dominance of the state as a shareholder in listed companies and the first and foremost reform to promote more shareholder activism is to the reduction of the level of state ownership, albeit in a gradual way. In the meantime, the Chinese Government should develop a stronger institutional investor base, including relaxing institutional investment restrictions, tax relief for institutional investors and a liberalisation of investment opportunities for foreign institutional investors; this should be done not solely for the purpose of an increase of shareholder activism, but also for the long-term development of the Chinese securities market.

Second, in light of the facilitative role played by trade industry associations in the UK, establishing similar organisations in China will make a significant contribution to the increase in the level of institutional shareholder engagement. The third approach is to enhance normative obligations via shareholder engagement guidance. China can learn from the newly-issued UK Stewardship Code with a full account of its specific conditions and needs, to build a set of benchmarks and principles relating to the responsibilities of institutional shareholders in corporate governance.

However, the UK's experience is by no means perfect. The drop in the level of long-term institutional investor numbers over recent years brings the risk that motivations aiming at improving corporate governance in listed companies have been reduced. Moreover, it is worth exploring whether regulatory calls urging activism do indeed result in more involvement or merely lead to passive compliance. These remain questions that need to be answered.

Bibliography

Ameer, R. (2010) 'The Role of Institutional Investors in the Inventory and Cash Management Practices of Firms in Asia', *Journal of Multinational Financial Management*, 20: 126–43.

Andrews, N. and Tomasic, R. (2006) 'Directing China's Top 100 Listed Companies: Corporate Governance in an Emerging Market Economy', *The Corporate Governance Law Review*, 2: 245–309.

Becht, M. and others (2009) 'Returns to Shareholder Activism: Evidence from a Clinical Study of the Hermes UK Focus Fund', *Review of Financial Studies*, 23: 3093–129.

Cai, Y. and Yu, Z. B. (2015) 'Legal Suggestions on Promoting Chinese Institutional Investor Activism', *Financial Law Forum*, 90: 74–91.

Cheffins, B. (2008) *Corporate Ownership and Control: British Business Transformed*, Oxford: Oxford University Press.

Cheffins, B.R. (2012) 'The Stewardship Code's Achilles Heel', *Modern Law Review*, 72: 1004–1025.

Chen, T. X., Liu, L.Y. and Guan Y. Z. (2014) 'Empirical Research on Herd Effects of QFII and Domestic Institutional Investors', *Management Science*, 4, 110–118.

China Securities Regulatory Committee (2015), '2014 Annual Report' http://www.csrc.gov.cn/pub/newsite/zjhjs/zjhnb/ (last accessed 3 June 2016).

Crespi, R. and Renneboog, L. (2010) 'Is (Institutional) Shareholder Activism New? Evidence from UK Shareholder Coalitions in the Pre-Cadbury Era', *Corporate Governance: An International Review*, 18: 274–95.

Davies, P. and Rickford, J.(2008) 'An Introduction to the New UK Companies Act: Part 1', *European Company and Financial Law Review*, 5: 239–79.

Davis, E.P. and Steil, B.(2001) *Institutional Investors*, Cambridge: MIT Press.

East Money (2015), 'Sichuan Changhong', <http://quote.eastmoney.com/sh600839.html?=600839> accessed 14 November 2015.

Financial Times (2015), 'Market Data, Marks and Spencer Plc' <http://markets.ft.com/research/Markets/Tearsheets/Business-profile?s=MKS:LSE.>accessed 14 November 2015.

Goergen, M., Renneboog, L.D.R. and Zhang, C. (2008) 'Do UK Institutional Investors Monitor Their Investee Firms', *Journal of Corporate Studies*, 8: 39–56.

Gordon, J.(1994) 'Institutions as Relational Investors: A New Look at Cumulative Voting', *Columbia Law Review*, 94: 124–92.

Hardin, R. (1993) *Collective Action*, Baltimore: Johns Hopkins University Press.

Hendry, J. and others (2004) 'Responsible Ownership, Shareholder Value and the New Shareholder Activism', ESRC Centre for Business Research, University of Cambridge Working Paper No 297.

Institute of World Economic and Political in Chinese Academy of Social Science, 'Corporate Governance Assessment Report on the Top 100 Chinese Listed Companies For 2012' http://www.iwep.org.cn/ (last accessed 3 June 2016).

Keasey, K. and Wright, M. (1997) *Corporate Governance: Responsibilities, Risks and Remuneration*, Chichester: John Wiley and Sons.

MacNeil, I. (2010) 'Activism and Collaboration Among Shareholders in UK Listed Companies', *Capital Markets Law Journal*, 5: 419–38.

Macey, J. (2008) *Corporate Governance: Promises Kept, Promises Broken*, Princeton: Princeton University Press.

Mallin, C. (1997) 'Investors' Voting Rights' in Keasey, K. and Wright, M. *Corporate Governance:Responsibilities, Risks and Remuneration*, Chichester: John Wiley and Sons.

Market Data, *Financial Times*, Marks and Spencer http://markets.ft.com/research/Markets/Tearsheets/Business-profile?s=MKS:LSE (last accessed 3 June 2016).

Millstein, I.A. (1991) 'The Responsibility of the Institutional Investor in Corporate Management' in Sametz, A.W. and Bicksler, J.L. (eds) *The Battle for Corporate Control: Shareholder Rights, Stakeholder Interests and Managerial Responsibilities*, Homewood: Business One Irwin, 67–76.

Myners, P. (2005) *Review of the Impediments to Voting UK Shares* (2005), London: Shareholder Voting Working Group.

Nolan, R.C. (2003) 'Indirect Investors: A Greater Say in the Company?' *Journal of Corporate Law Studies*, 3: 73–121.

Office for National Statistics (2015), 'Share Ownership Survey 2014', http://www.statistics.gov.uk/pdfdir/share0110.pdf (last accessed 3 June 2016).

Olson, M. (1965) *The Logic of Collective Action: Public Goods and the Theory of Groups*, Cambridge: Harvard University Press.

Prudential Plc, 2015 Financial Report http://markets.ft.com/research/Markets/Tearsheets/Business-profile?s=PRU:NYQ (last accessed 3 June 2016).

Randall, J. (2003) 'Why Michael Green Had to Go', BBC News http://news.bbc.co.uk/1/hi/business/3210372.stm (last accessed 3 June 2016).

Reisberg, A. (2015) 'The UK Stewardship Code: On the Road to Nowhere?', *Journal of Corporate Law Studies*, 15: 217–53.

Robert, J. (2004) *The Modern Firm: Organizational Design for Performance and Growth*, Oxford: Oxford University Press.

Scott, J. (1985) *Corporations, Classes and Capitalism*, London: Hutchinson.

Shanghai Stock Exchange (2003), *Gongsi Zhili Baogao [Corporate Governance Report]*, Shanghai: Fudan University Press.

Shleifer, A. and Vishny R. (1997) 'A Survey of Corporate Governance', *Journal of Finance*, 52:737–83.

Su, Y.Y., Xu, D. and Phan, P.H. (2008) 'Principle-principle Conflict in the Governance of the Chinese Public Companies', Management and Organization Review, 4: 17–38.

Tomasic, R and Andrews, N. (2009) 'Minority Shareholder Protection in China's Top 100 Listed Companies' *Australian Journal of Asian Law*, 9: 88–119.

Tomasic, R. and Fu, J. (2006) 'Legal Regulation and Corporate Governance in China's Top 100 Listed Companies', *The Company Lawyer*, 27: 278–87.

Vittas, D. (1998) 'Institutional Investors and Securities Markets: Which Comes First?', Paper presented at the Annual Bank Conference on Development Economics Latin American and Caribbean Conference, June 28–30, World Bank, Washington, D.C.

Vodafone Plc, 2015 Annual Reporthttps://www.vodafone.com/content/annualreport/annualreport15/assets/pdf/full_annual_report_2015.pdf (last accessed 13 June 2016).

Yang, J.Z. (2007) 'Shareholder Meetings and Voting Rights in China: Some Empirical Evidence', *International Company and Commercial Law Review*, 18: 4–17.

Part III
Some cross-cultural comparisons

11

Corporate governance in China

The law and its political logic

Jiangyu Wang

1 Introduction

Corporate governance is defined as a response to the agency problems resulting from the separation of ownership and control or the asymmetry of powers amongst the different participants in a company. The classic agency problems include the conflict between the company's shareholders/owners and its hired managers, and the conflict between the majority/controlling shareholders and the minority or non-controlling shareholders.[1]

It has been argued optimistically that corporate law – or company law – across the world is marching toward the same direction – or a universal framework: 'Notwithstanding the very real differences across jurisdictions . . . [in corporate governance, share ownership, capital markets, and business culture], the underlying uniformity of the corporate form is at least as impressive'.[2] As such, 'Business corporations have a fundamentally similar set of legal characteristics – and face a fundamentally similar set of legal problems – in all jurisdictions'.[3]

Corporate law in China demonstrates similar characteristics, although the details may be different. In 1993, the People's Republic of China (PRC or China) enacted its first national Company Law, or Gongsi Fa, one that adopted a generally Westernised legal framework for business enterprises.[4] The Gongsi Fa sets up a corporate governance structure featuring a shareholders' meeting, a board of directors, a supervisory board and a manager (chief executive officer) for almost all business companies in China. All the key players are bound by legal responsibilities and liabilities such as fiduciary duties, which are indeed not very different from their counterparts in other jurisdictions, especially Anglo–American countries.

---

1 Kraakman and others (2009) 36.
2 Kraakman and others (n 1) 1. See also generally Hansmann and Kraakman (2004).
3 ibid.
4 Company Law of the People's Republic of China [Zhonghua Renmin Gongheguo Gongsi Fa] (2013 Amendment), adopted by the Standing Committee of the National People's Congress on 29 December 1993; amended, respectively, in December 1999, August 2004, October 2005 and December 2013 (hereinafter Gongsi Fa).

In the traditional corporate marketplace of Anglo–American jurisdictions, 'great reliance was placed on the power of a market place of independent investors and their advisors and intermediaries to restrain corporations from undertaking actions that the market might perceive to be contrary to its interests'.[5] Only about a decade ago did the balance of power shift to more government intervention in the United States, which was spread also to the rest of the world, because of corporate failures including the bankruptcy cases of Enron, Global Crossing, Adelphia and WorldCom, amongst others. As a result, the Sarbanes-Oxley Act of 2002 introduced a wide range of regulatory measures relating to internal corporate governance and external monitoring and control of companies.[6]

Corporate governance has become a highly fashionable topic in China since the outset of the twenty-first century, when a listed company, popularly known as YinGuangXia, was disclosed by the media to have committed a RMB 745 million fraud through massive fabrication of sales receipts and false disclosures perpetrated by a few 'core' insiders. This case caused losses to thousands of minority shareholders and is considered one of the biggest corporate scandals in the recent decade of the PRC history.[7] It revealed some fundamental weaknesses in the management, regulation and supervision of the country's enterprises. As a Standard & Poor's report noted: '[c]orporate governance since then has been placed at the very top of the government's agenda', and 'the mandate to improve corporate governance is a top priority amongst all sectors, including government bodies, regulators, intermediaries, corporations, and investors'.[8] In the following years, various government agencies have issued numerous laws and normative documents to standardise the corporate governance practice of Chinese enterprises.

Several 'Chinese characteristics' of corporate governance will be pointed out. First, China has set up a hybrid system of corporate governance institutions, borrowed from both the Anglo–American model and Germanic–Japanese model. In terms of internal governance, the typical organisational structure of a company comprises three tiers of control, namely the shareholders' meeting, the board of directors and the supervisory board. In addition, a joint stock limited company (JSLC) is legally required to have a management team. Partially as a solution to the agency problem stemming from the separation of ownership and control in modern corporations, Anglo–American jurisdictions install independent directors on the board, Germanic–Japanese jurisdictions set a supervisory board to monitor the management board, but listed companies in China must have both. As observed in Tan and Wang (2007):[9]

> The coexistence of the supervisory board and the independent directors demonstrates a strong feature in the mentality of China's corporate reform, namely, an approach of 'crossing the river by feeling the stone', because, although the reformers were eager to learn from foreign experience, they were unsure as to which model was suitable to China. As such, legal institutions from both the 'insider' model and the 'outsider' model were transplanted into Chinese soil without a proper evaluation of their suitability.

5 Smith and Walter (2006) 217.
6 ibid 231–33.
7 Standard & Poor's (2003) 1.
8 ibid 1.
9 Tan and Wang (2007) 147.

A second feature is the political impact of dominant state ownership on the governance of companies. Most of those companies were converted from traditional state-owned enterprises (SOEs) and are said to have been suffering from political control by the government or even the Chinese Communist Party. One commentator thus concludes that: 'the corporate governance system adopted by the Chinese listed firms can be best described as a control-based model, in which the controlling shareholders – in most cases, the state – tightly control the listed companies through concentrated ownership and management friendly boards'.[10]

Indeed, the 'grabbing hand theory' suggests that the government uses SOEs 'to serve political and social objectives, which has a negative impact on the firm's economic performance'.[11] One could of course argue that this theory is overly simplistic, as the state might have a larger stake in converting the SOEs into normal, commercial entities. Another strand of literature, the 'helping hand theory', however, maintains that the government may 'generate a positive effect on firm performance because [it helps] secure scarce resources in the quasi-market economy and mitigate agency problems in firms with poor corporate governance'.[12]

Thirdly, culture also plays an important role in the corporate governance of Chinese companies. Hamilton (2006) points out that it is fundamentally wrong to characterise Chinese private firms by holding them up against similar firms of Western capitalism without considering the cultural aspects. Embedded in its own hierarchical and harmonious cultural tradition, 'the Chinese family firms is [sic] in fact . . . a "political infrastructure" in which "power differentials" . . . lie behind the disparities in economic roles and rewards in the family business'.[13]

In short, although the relevant Chinese law on paper produces the seemingly same kind of companies, the very different political, economic and social contexts in China, respectively and collectively, make corporate governance of Chinese companies fundamentally distinctive in many respects. It is of course too early to conclude that a Chinese model of corporate governance is emerging, but it is still very important conceptually to differentiate the Chinese practices of corporate governance from other models in the world, to explore the underlying rationale of Chinese corporate governance and to look at its future prospects.

On this basis, it is fair to say the governance practice of Chinese enterprises is an evolving process, the direction of which has been shaped by many factors. This chapter not only outlines the general allocation of corporate powers amongst various governance and management institutions in a company, including the shareholders' meeting, the board of directors, the supervisory board and the management, but also places the legal framework of corporate governance in China in its political, economic and social contexts.

10 Liu, Qiao (2006) 429.
11 Chang and Wong (2004) 618.
12 ibid.
13 Hamilton (2006) 224.

2 The political-economical context of corporate governance in China

Defining corporate governance in China

Corporate governance is traditionally defined as 'the system by which companies are directed and controlled'.[14] In such a system:[15]

> Boards of directors are responsible for the governance of their companies. The shareholders' role in governance is to appoint the directors and the auditors and to satisfy themselves that an appropriate governance structure is in place. The responsibilities of the board include setting the company's strategic aims, providing the leadership to put them into effect, supervising the management of the business and reporting to shareholders on their stewardship. The board's actions are subject to laws, regulations and the shareholder in general meeting.

As will be seen below, the rules on corporate governance embodied in the Chinese Company Law and Securities Law almost perfectly conform to the principles outlined in the definition above. However, the 'legal governance' structure is only part of the corporate governance regime in China. Apart from the boards and management defined in the Gongsi Fa, a number of other players, including, most importantly, the Chinese Communist Party (CCP), are directly or indirectly involved in the management of companies. In this sense, the G20/OECD Principles of Corporate Governance offer a more inclusive definition:[16]

> Corporate Governance involves a set of relationship between a company's management, its board, its shareholders and other stakeholders. Corporate governance also provides the structure through which the objectives of the company are set, and the means of attaining those objectives and monitoring performance are determined.

That is to say, we treat the formal – and informal, if necessary – rules enacted by the CCP and other Party-state apparatuses as regulatory rules of corporate governance in China, although they may fall outside the formal laws adopted by the legislative bodies of the Chinese state.

The role of the Party-state in governing China and Chinese corporations

China is a one-party state, in which the CCP is defined in the preamble of the PRC Constitution as the single ruling party for mainland China. The CCP has ruled China since 1949 when it defeated the Nationalist Government and drove it to Taiwan.

Although state institutions, such as the State Council (the executive branch, or the Central Government), the National People's Congress (NPC, the legislature and the parliament), the Supreme People's Court and the Supreme People's, as well as their counterparts at the various local levels, were established from the very beginning of the PRC, the Party, through the cells it sets up at all levels of the government and all state, state-related and even private organisations, controls firmly that government. That is, China's political governance

---

14 Cadbury Report (1992) para 2.5.
15 ibid.
16 G20/OECD (2015) 9.

consists of two parallel systems: the *dangwu xitong* (Party affairs system) and *Zhengwu xitong* (state affairs system), whereby the latter is subordinated to the former, resulting in the 'Party domination of the state', as observed by Zheng Yongnian:[17]

> The relationship between Party and the state (government) is the most important aspect of the Chinese political system. This analogy of the relationship between the owner and the manager to that between the Party and the state is heuristic in our understanding of the domination of the Party over the state in the contemporary era. The domination of the Party (property rights owner) over the state seems quite natural and logical.

Treating the CCP as the owner of China seems somewhat hilarious, but it does tell a truth in China today. That is, it makes no sense to separate the Party from the state. The Party is the state, and vice versa. In that sense, the Party-state accurately denotes the nature of the Chinese Government and captures the country's political reality.

The Party, through its organisations at various levels, directly exercises power to make decisions for all state-related institutions, including state-owned enterprises (SOEs). In this respect, one of the most significant powers held by the Party is embodied in the *nomenklatura* system, known as 'Party management of cadres' (*dangguan ganbu*). Put simply, it is a system of maintaining lists of leadership positions through which the Party monopolistically exercises the power to make appointments, promotions, demotions and dismissals. It is 'the most important organizational pillar [in the Chinese political system], which gives the CCP a dominant say over personnel decisions of all important positions'.[18]

As will be discussed in detail later on, the Party's powers, including personnel powers, reach to all SOEs. In addition, it can influence privately-owned enterprises through party-organisations established in them, although direct influence on decision-making and personnel appointment does not seem to exist.

In any event, the place of the CCP in business companies in China is stipulated in Article 19 of the Gongsi Fa, which reads:

> The Chinese Communist Party may, according to the Constitution of the Chinese Communist Party, establish its branches in companies to carry out activities of the Chinese Communist Party. The company shall provide necessary conditions to facilitate the activities of the Party.

3 The legal framework of corporate governance

Like most jurisdictions that have a company law, the PRC Gongsi Fa provides a common structure for business corporations.[19] In particular, the 2005 Gongsi Fa has abandoned most of the restrictive rules on company incorporation and operation, which were originated in China's planned economy, and has instead introduced new rules in line with international practice.[20]

---

17 Zheng (2010) 99.
18 Zheng (2010) 103–104.
19 Kraakman and others (n 1) at 1 (noting 'corporate law everywhere must, of necessity, provide for [these characteristics]').
20 CSRC (2011) at 16 notes that the 2005 Gongsi Fa has the following improvements: [It] improved companies' governance structure and mechanisms to protect lawful shareholders' rights and public

In addition to the Gongsi Fa, business companies are also subject to a wide range of other laws, including the PRC Securities Law (Zhengquan Fa),[21] the PRC Law on State-owned Assets in Enterprises (Guoyou Zichan Fa), the Accounting Law, a number of administrative regulations issued by the State Council (which is China's Central Government), a voluminous body of ministerial rules formulated by the various ministries under the State Council, as well as the rules of the self-regulatory rules of the stock exchanges.

Under the Gongsi Fa, a business company can take either of two legal forms: a limited liability company (*Youxian Zeren Gongsi*, or LLC) or a joint stock limited company (*Gufen Youxian Gongsi*, or JSLC). An LLC is a functional equivalent of the 'private company' under English law or the 'closely held corporation' in the United States. Its capital, however, is not divided into equal units in the form of shares (*Gupiao*). That is, although members of the LLC are also called 'shareholders' (*gudong*), the company does not issue shares to the shareholders. Instead, the percentage of ownership of a shareholder in the LLC is provided in the shareholders' agreement and the company's articles of association. In addition, an LLC cannot have more than 50 shareholders.[22] For these reasons, an LLC cannot offer shares to the public and become a listed company. In comparison, the JSLC is the business form for public companies. Its capital is divided into equal units in the form of shares, which can be offered to the general public, and listed on a stock exchange.[23]

The corporate governance structure of a typical Chinese company adopts a two-tier board system and comprises the general shareholders' meeting (also known as the general assembly), a board of directors, a supervisory board and a (general) manager (chief executive officer). The general shareholders' meeting is called the 'power organ' (*quanli jigou*) of the company,[24] indicating that the shareholders in China are more powerful than their counterparts in some other jurisdictions. Indeed, in addition to the usual power of electing directors and supervisors, the general meeting can also decide on the company's business strategies and investment plans, although the aforesaid 'strategies' and 'plans' were never defined in any law. It has also the authority to hear reports from the board of directors and the supervisory board, and to adopt resolutions as to whether to approve such reports. It has similar authorities with respect to issues concerning the company's financial budgets, profit distribution or the make-up of losses, amending the company's articles of association, increasing or decreasing of the company's registered capital, the issuance of corporate bonds and fundamental corporate changes such as merger, division, dissolution and liquidation.[25]

interests. It highlighted the legal obligations and responsibilities of those in actual control of the company – the directors, senior management and supervisors. It improved companies' financing and financial accounting systems of companies and the systems governing corporate mergers, divisions and liquidation. While ensuring the lawful rights and interests of the creditors are well protected, it facilitated the reorganisation of companies.

21 The Securities Law of the People's Republic of China, first adopted in 1998 and most recently amended in 2013, is another umbrella law governing corporate activities in China.

22 Gongsi Fa, arts 23, 24 and 25.

23 ibid arts 77, 126, 127, 130, 135, 145.

24 ibid art 37.

25 ibid art 38.

4 The role of the shareholders in corporate governance

The shareholders' meeting

Shareholders, as the electorate of the 'corporate republic',[26] play an important role in corporate governance. Although shareholders do not participate in the day-to-day management of the company neither can they act on behalf of the company; they are entitled to elect directors and supervisors, vote on major corporate transactions and decisions and amend the corporate charter and other bye-laws. The exercise of all these powers depends almost entirely on the proper functioning of the shareholders' meetings.

Voting at shareholders' meetings is the only direct way for shareholders to exercise the right of 'participation in major decision-making and selection of management personnel' provided in Article 4 of the Company Law. A shareholder has a right to attend and vote at a shareholders' general meeting, which can be either a regular (annual) general meeting or an extraordinary general meeting.[27] It is up to the corporate charter of an LLC to stipulate the frequency of general meetings, but a JSLC must have an annual general meeting.[28]

In an LLC, the general meetings should be convened regularly in accordance with its charter. An extraordinary general meeting of the LLC may be called by shareholders holding more than one-tenth or more of the voting rights, by one-third of the directors, or by the supervisory board or the supervisor in the event that the company does not have a supervisory board.[29] A JSLC must hold an annual general meeting. The extraordinary general meeting of a JSLC can be convened within two months of any of the following events:

* the number of directors falls below two-thirds of the quorum prescribed in the Company Law or the corporate charter
* uncovered losses reach one-third of the paid-up capital of the company
* the meeting is requested by shareholders who aggregately hold 10 per cent or more of the company's shares
* a meeting is deemed necessary by the board of directors
* a meeting is proposed by the supervisory board
* other events provided in the corporate charter.[30]

In both LLCs and JSLCs, the general meetings should first of all be convened by the board of directors and chaired by the chairperson of the board.[31] If the chairperson is unable or fails to perform his duties, the vice chairperson should take over to chair the meeting. In the event that the vice chairperson also is unable or fails to perform his or her duties, a director appointed by more than half of the board of directors shall take over to chair the meeting.[32] In LLCs without a board, the executive director shall perform the relevant duties.[33] Further,

---

26 English Jurist William Blackstone once described the company as the 'little republic'.
27 Gongsi Fa art 40.
28 ibid art 101.
29 ibid art 40.
30 ibid art 101.
31 One exception is that the first meeting after the establishment of an LLC should be convened by the shareholder who has made the largest amount of capital contribution. See Company Law art 39.
32 Gongsi Fa art 41 para 1; art 102 para 1.
33 ibid art 41 para 2.

if the board or executive director is not able to or fails to convene a meeting, the supervisory board (or the supervisor in LLCs that have not established a supervisory board) should take over the responsibility. If the supervisory board or supervisor does not act, the Company Law then empowers shareholders holding 10 per cent or more of the voting rights to do-it-yourself – convening and chairing the meeting directly.[34] However, there is a contemporaneous ownership requirement imposed on those JSLC shareholders, who must have held the shares for 90 or more consecutives days.[35]

These mechanisms were established in the Company Law with a view to ensuring that the general meetings are not delayed or spoiled by the insiders of the company. In contrast, the 1993 Company Law had a 25 per cent shareholding threshold for LLC shareholders to call a special meeting, and such a right was not even enjoyed at all by JSLC shareholders. Further, shareholders did not have any power to convene a meeting themselves under the 1993 law.[36]

The powers of the general meeting

In the law at face value, the Company Law provides 'shareholder centralism' in allocating corporate decisional powers.[37] Articles 37 and 99 define the shareholders' meeting as the company's *quanli jigou*, or organ of power. Serving as the 'parliament' or general assembly of the corporate republic, the shareholders' meeting has the following powers:[38]

- to decide on the company's business strategy and investment plans
- to elect and remove directors and supervisors who are not representatives of the employees
- to decide on the remuneration of directors and supervisors
- to review and approve the reports of the board of directors
- to review and approve the reports of the supervisory board or the supervisor
- to review and approve the annual financial budget and financial accounting plans of the company
- to review and approve the profit distribution plans or loss recovery plans of the company
- to pass resolutions on increase or reduction of the registered capital of the company
- to pass resolutions on the issuance of corporate bonds
- to pass resolutions on company merger, division, dissolution, liquidation or change of the corporate form
- to amend the corporate charter
- to exercise any other powers given to the shareholders' meeting by the corporate charter.

In addition, several special powers are given to the shareholders' meeting of a listed company. When the company, within one year, buys or sells major assets, or provides guarantees to outsiders, if the transactional value exceeds 30 per cent or more of the company's total assets, the Company Law requires the transaction to be approved by a two-thirds absolute majority

---

34 ibid art 41 para 3.
35 ibid art 102 para 2.
36 1993 Company Law art 43, 104 and 105.
37 Liu, Junhai (2011) 468–69.
38 Gongsi Fa arts 38 and 100.

of the voting rights of the shareholders present at the meeting.[39] Further, in line with Article 38(12) of the Company Law, the CSRC Model Corporate Charter confers upon the general meeting the powers, first, to pass resolutions on the hiring or dismissal of the accounting firms for the company, second to review and approve plans to change the usage of the funds raised and, third, to review (but not approve) the company's stock incentive plans.[40] The annotation following this Model Charter provision indicates that all these are exclusive powers of the general meeting and may not be delegated to the board of directors or any organs or individuals.[41]

The wide range of powers given to the general meeting of shareholders is remarkable in a comparative light. Calling the general meeting the 'highest body' of the company is not uncommon in civil law jurisdictions:[42] very few modern legal systems will actually treat it as the 'supreme' decision-making organ of the company. In Germany, it was permissible for the general meeting to give instructions on matters relating to the conduct of business until 1937, but it 'has . . . since 1937 lacked the general power to decide on competences within the company, so that the prevailing opinion no longer regards the general meeting as the "highest body"'.[43]

In the US, the separation of powers is tilted significantly towards the management. In contrast, the powers possessed by the general meeting of Chinese companies are more real and meaningful. As observed by Mathias Siems: '[b]y contrast with this internationally predominant legal position [of downgrading the status of the general meeting in the corporate structure], in China the general meeting shares responsibility for the conduct of business'.[44] The separation of power between the general meeting and the management will be further examined in the part on the powers and duties of the board of directors.

Voting in the general meeting

Decision-making in the general meeting is generally dominated by capital, not by heads. In an LLC, the default rule is that the amount of voting rights exercisable by a shareholder at a meeting is based on his percentage in the capital contribution.[45] The Company Law, however, permits LLC shareholders to make a different voting rule in the corporate charter.[46] Shareholders' meetings in a JSLC follow the principle of 'one share, one vote'.[47] Treasury shares – namely those held by the company – are not entitled to vote.[48] In addition, as JSLCs only issue common shares at this stage, realistically only common shares carry voting rights.[49]

As a general rule, resolutions of a general meeting in a JSLC will be passed by a simple majority of votes cast by shareholders present at the meeting. A mandatory two-thirds

---

39 Gongsi Fa art 122.
40 CSRC Model Corporate Charter art 40(11), 40(14) and 40(15).
41 ibid annotation to art 40.
42 Siems (2008) 151 (noting that 'in France, Japan and China the "highest body" terminology is quite common').
43 ibid.
44 ibid 154.
45 Gongsi Fa art 43.
46 ibid art 43.
47 ibid art 104.
48 ibid art 104.
49 Note that the Company Law does not prohibit the establishment of other classes of shares in a JSLC.

majority of votes is required for amending the corporate charter, an increase or reduction of the registered capital, corporate mergers, division, dissolution or change of corporate form.[50] Further, under Article 122 of the Company Law, major transactions, in which a listed company buys or sells major assets or provides security to others in excess of 30 per cent of the total assets within one year, must also be approved by two-thirds or more of the voting rights. There is, however, no such requirement for LLCs, who are permitted to freely specify the methods of deliberation and voting procedures of the meeting in their corporate charters, as long as an absolute majority – that is, two-thirds – voting requirement is imposed for approval of charter amendments, increase or reduction of the registered capital and merger, division, dissolution or change of corporate form.[51]

Shareholders are allowed to vote in person or in absentia, to a limited extent. A shareholder may attend the meeting in person, and may also send an authorised representative to vote on his behalf, as long as a proper power of attorney stating the scope of authorisation is submitted to the company.[52] However, no shareholder is allowed to post a proxy note to the company. Whilst this may make it logistically difficult for some shareholders to cast their votes, the difficulty can be alleviated by the increasingly popular online voting system, which was formally introduced by the CSRC in 2004 to enable shareholders to participate in meetings by means of remote communication. Both the Shenzhen Stock Exchange (SZSE) and Shanghai Stock Exchange (SSE) have established networks with thousands of securities companies for shareholders to vote on matters that bear upon major rights and interests of shareholders.[53]

Two voting methods are provided in the Company Law for JSLC shareholders. Straight voting, being the default voting method, is based on a traditional and rigid understanding of the 'one share, one vote' principle, which unreservedly favours the majority shareholders. For minority shareholders, this is not the end of the world, as the law offers an alternative voting mechanism, the cumulative voting method, which redresses the imbalance to a certain extent. Article 106 of the Company Law defines cumulative voting as a system in which the number of voting rights attached to each share is the same as the number of directors or supervisors to be elected and the voting rights of a shareholder can be pooled and used together. Plainly speaking, it is 'the privilege of multiplying the number of shares held by the number of directors [and supervisors in the Chinese context] to be elected and casting for a single candidate or distributing the product among two or more candidates'.[54] In doing so, the minority shareholders will have a better chance to secure representation on the board of directors and the supervisory board:

> Without cumulative voting, holders of a bare majority of the shares may elect the full board and thus control the corporation without any representative of other interests being present at board meetings.[55]

A controversial question is whether cumulative voting is mandatory or should be made mandatory for companies in China. Stating that 'the cumulative voting system may be

50 Gongsi Fa art 104.
51 ibid art 44.
52 ibid art 107.
53 Details on online voting can be found at www.sse.com.cn and www.szse.cn (both last accessed 4 June 2016).
54 Cox and Hazen (2003) 348.
55 ibid 349.

adopted in accordance with the corporate charter or shareholders' resolution when the shareholders' meeting elect directors and supervisors', Article 106 does not seem to be imposing a mandatory method but rather suggesting an opt-in approach, namely that companies may choose to adopt cumulative voting through the corporate charter or a shareholders' resolution. The Code of Corporate Governance for Listed Companies in China requires, in light of the spirit that 'the election of directors should fully reflect the opinions of minority shareholders', that 'cumulative voting should be adopted in listed companies that are more than 30 per cent owned by controlling shareholders'.[56] Fortunately for listed companies in China, the Code has not been regarded as an enforceable law and, as such, only '[c]ertain Chinese listed companies have already included the cumulative voting system in their articles of association'.[57]

5 The board of directors

As noted, China's hybrid regime of corporate governance features a two-tier board system, comprising a board of directors with decision-making functions and a supervisory board, which monitors the directors and managers. The functions and powers of the two boards are examined in this and the immediately following sections.

Board composition

All companies, even including wholly state-owned companies, are required by the Company Law to have a board of directors,[58] unless it is an LLC of few shareholders or small size, which could set up an executive director (*zhixing dongshi*) instead of a full board.[59]

The Company Law stipulates the range of the number of directors as from 3 to 13 for LLCs and 5 to 19 for JSLCs.[60] Under normal circumstances, these directors are to be elected by the general meeting of the shareholders. However, if the LLC is established by two or more state-owned enterprises (SOEs) or state investment entities, there should be employee representatives on the board. Employee representatives on the board are encouraged but not required for other types of LLCs and JSLCs.[61] Any board must have a chairperson director and may have one or more vice chairpersons.[62]

The term of appointment of the directors is a matter for the corporate charter to decide, provided that each term does not exceed three years. However, as there is no limit on the re-election of directors, in theory one could serve as a director indefinitely.[63] Further, a director whose term of office has expired could continue his directorship until a new director is appointed under the following circumstances: first, no election was held in time upon expiration of the term of office of the director; or, second, a director resigned

---

56 Code of Corporate Governance for Listed Companies, issued by the CSRC and then State Economic and Trade Commission (7 January 2001) art 31.
57 OECD (2011) 43.
58 Gongsi Fa art 45 para 1; art 109 para 1.
59 ibid art 51.
60 Gongsi Fa arts 45 and 109 respectively.
61 ibid art 45 para 2; art 109 para 2.
62 ibid art 45 para 3; art 110 para 1.
63 ibid art 46 para 1; art 109 para 2.

during his term of office, resulting in the number of directors falling below the statutory quorum.[64]

The Company Law does not define 'director'. Implicitly, a person becomes a director according to the formal procedures of appointment, and there is no explicit legal basis for de facto directors. Thus, under the Company Law a person is either a director or not a director. This clear position apparently denies the existence of 'shadow directors' who control the company's business to a significant extent by virtue of their position in the investment relations of the company, without letting their names appear in all corporate records and legal documents.

In terms of the appointment and removal of directors, normally directors are elected by the shareholders' general meeting. There is not much guidance in the Company Law as to how the directors should be elected, indicating that the legislators wisely wished to leave this a matter for the corporate charter to decide. The Code of Corporate Governance for Listed Companies ('Code of Corporate Governance) requires the charter to ensure a formal and transparent board nomination and election process.[65] In particular:[66]

1. The listed company should disclose detailed information of the candidates for directorship prior to the general meeting to ensure shareholders have adequate knowledge of the candidates.
2. The candidates should provide a written undertaking to accept the nomination and warrant the truthfulness and completeness of the disclosed information about the candidate, as well as to promise to perform their duties in earnest once elected.
3. The election process should thoroughly reflect the opinions of minority shareholders. Listed companies are encouraged to adopt the cumulative voting system, and they are obligated to adopt cumulative voting if over 30 per cent of the shares are owned by controlling shareholders.
4. Once directors are elected the company should sign appointment agreements with them to prescribe the respective rights and duties of both the company and the directors.

Regarding the removal of directors, one of the concerns has been whether a director can be removed with or without cause. On this point the Company Law is not clear. The 1993 Company Law contained a provision stating 'the shareholders' meeting may not remove a director before the expiration of his period of office without cause'.[67] This provision was deleted by the current 2005 Company Law. The deletion could arguably be understood as that the law-makers no longer wanted to prohibit the general meeting from removing a director without cause, or that the law-makers would rather leave this matter for the corporate charter to decide. It seems the latter understanding has prevailed, at least insofar as listed companies are concerned, as nothing has changed for them to date. Indeed, as Article 95 of the Model Charter still provides, the general meeting may not remove a director before his term of office expires. Of course, pursuant to Article 147 of the Company Law and the relevant CSRC and stock exchange rules, if a director falls under a circumstance enumerated in the above-mentioned negative qualifications of directors, his directorship must be terminated by the company and this is considered as a removal 'with cause'.

---

64 ibid art 46 para 2; Art. 109 para 2.
65 Code of Corporate Governance art 28.
66 ibid arts 29, 30, 31 and 32.
67 1993 Gongsi Fa art 47 para 2.

Board meeting and voting

The responsibilities of the various parties are similar to those they face in the case of a shareholders' meeting. Namely, the vice chairperson of the board shall act to convene and chair the meeting if the chairperson is unable or refuses to perform his or her own duties in this regard. In addition, a director authorised jointly by more than half of all the directors shall in his or her turn call and chair the meeting when the vice chairperson fails to do so.[68] These emergency plans are designed in the 2005 Company Law in response to the deadlocks created by the 1993 Company Law, which vested the power to convene a board meeting exclusively in the hands of the chairperson. Only when the chairperson cannot perform his duties because of some unexplained 'special reason' will he authorise the vice chairperson or another director to call and chair the meeting. One-third or more of the directors may propose a meeting of the board but may not have the power actually to convene one.[69] One can reasonably deduce from these provisions what the chairperson would do if he is faced with the resentment of the majority of the directors and a meeting is expected to result in board resolutions not in his favour. However, under the 2005 Company Law, the chairperson is not able unduly to delay a meeting.

Certain players in a JSLC have additional powers to have a board meeting called. In short, the Company Law mandates two regular board meetings for a JSLC, but shareholders holding one-tenth or more of the voting shares, one-third or more of the directors or the supervisory board may propose a special board meeting. The chairperson of the board is then obligated to respond within 10 days of receipt of the proposal to convene and chair such a meeting.[70]

It is an implicit requirement that the board of directors exercises its powers collectively by meeting. A director must join this collective decision-making process to perform his duties. In the Chinese context, he has no power of his own to act on the company's behalf. A JSLC director could attend the meeting in person or authorise someone to represent him at the meeting, but his representative must be another director.[71] In this digital age, a board meeting could be held in the form of a teleconference or videoconference, so that the directors do not have to travel to the same location for the meeting. A resolution could also be adopted by way of a circular instead of convening a meeting, which requires the directors to sign and return the circular within a given period of time.[72]

The right of voting comes with an important restriction for directors in listed companies. In brief, a director is prohibited from voting on a resolution if he is affiliated with – or a related party to – an enterprise involved in the subject-matter of the resolution. He may also not be represented by another director on this matter. 'Affiliation' or 'related-party relationship' is defined as 'the relationship between the controlling shareholder, *de facto* controlling person, director, supervisor or senior management executive of a company and an enterprise under their director or indirect control, or any other relationship that may lead to the transfer of any interest of the company'.[73] In this event, a valid board meeting may be held if attended by more than half of the directors without any such affiliation, and a resolution can only be passed by more than half of the unaffiliated directors. The company

---

68 Gongsi Fa arts 48 and 110.
69 1993 Gongsi Fa arts 48 and 114.
70 Gongsi Fa art 111 para 2.
71 ibid art 113 para 1.
72 Liu Junhai (n 37) 488.
73 Gongsi Fa art 217(4).

will have to submit the subject-matter of the resolution to the shareholders' general meeting when the number of unaffiliated directors is less than three.[74]

Powers of the board of directors

We now come to probably the most important aspect of the system of boards of directors in China, which concerns the key functions and powers of the board of directors. Under the Company Law, the board 'is accountable to the shareholders' meeting'. As a collegiate body, it is granted the following statutory powers:

- to convene the shareholders' general meeting and report on its work to the general meeting
- to implement the resolutions of the general meeting
- to decide on the company's business operation plans and investment proposals
- to formulate the company's annual financial budget and financial accounting plan
- to formulate the company's profit distribution plan and loss recovery plan
- to formulate the plans for increase or reduction of the company's registered capital and issuance of corporate bonds
- to formulate the plans for merger, division, dissolution or change of the corporate structure
- to decide on the establishment of the company's international management organs
- to appoint and remove the general manager (also known as the chief executive officer or CEO in some situations) of the company and decide on his remuneration
- to decide, based on the recommendations of the general manager, on the appointment and dismissal of the company's deputy general managers and chief financial officer, as well as on their remuneration
- to formulate the basic management system of the company
- to execute any other duties and powers granted by the corporate charter.

Indeed, in line with the last bullet point (12 above, the Model Charter gives the following additional powers for the board of listed companies:

- to formulate plans for major acquisitions and share repurchase
- decide, within the authorisation of the shareholders' general meeting, on the company's external investment, buying and selling assets, mortgage of assets, external guarantee, related party transactions etc.
- to appoint and dismiss the board secretary and decide on his remuneration
- to manage the company's information management
- to recommend to the general meeting for hiring or dismissing the company's outside auditor
- to listen to the general manager's work report and inspect his work performance
- to execute any other duties and powers given by the corporate charter.

Conceptually, these powers can be categorised into three groups: decisional powers, appointment powers and oversight powers. The decisional powers make the board of

74 ibid art 125.

directors a 'management board' to some extent, by virtue of which the board has the power to set the course of the company by determining its business operation plans and investment plans, to make the company's financial budget and accounting plans and to formulate plans concerning profit distribution and loss recovery, change in the registered capital, issuance of corporate bonds and fundamental changes of corporate form and structure. The appointment powers entitle the board to select corporate officers and to determine their compensation, amongst which the most important function of the board is to choose the company's general manager (chief executive officer). In addition, it is the duty of the board to determine the company's management structure and overall management system. The oversight authority subjects the general manager – and implicitly the entire management team – to the supervisory power of the board.

Separation of powers between the board and the general meeting

Looking at the allocation of decisional power in Chinese companies with a critical eye, one may not find a clear separation of powers between the board of directors and the general meeting. In contrast, the shareholder-centred nature of corporate governance in China has produced a 'mixture of competences' in the allocation of functions and powers between the board and the general meeting.[75] For example, the general meeting is in charge of 'determining the company's business strategy (*jingying fangzhen*) and investment plans (*touzi jihua*),[76] whilst the board has the power to 'decide on the company's business operation plans (*jingying jihua*) and investment proposals (*touzi fangan*)'. It is not absolutely clear where to draw a line between 'business strategy and investment plans' and 'business operation plans and investment proposals'. The authority to decide on the distribution of profits lies exclusively in the hands of the general meeting, although the board has the power to initiate dividend distribution plans.

Giving shareholders' general meetings so much power to intervene in running the company's business is a distinctive feature of corporate governance in China, especially in light of the international trend of vesting the management of the business and control of the company in the directors.[77] What explains this far-reaching statutory power granted to the general meeting? It is submitted that the purpose behind these powers is to favour the majority shareholder which, in the Chinese context, is often the state. The powers of the general meeting may only be exercised collectively through voting by the shareholders, and the passage of a resolution must be supported by at least a simple majority of the eligible voting rights, based on the percentage of the equity interest held by the shareholders.

Where the state is the single or largest shareholder in an SOE, giving some key decisional powers to the shareholders' meeting, which is usually controlled by the majority shareholders, could presumably undermine the independence of the board to prevent the latter from making decisions that are not in the interest of the state. On the other hand, since the state as a shareholder retains only the most important powers on fundamental corporate decisions, it does not need to involve itself in making trivial decisions for the day-to-day management

75 See Siems (2008) 154.
76 Company Law art 38(1).
77 Siems (2008) 152–54 at 153 (noting that: 'In most countries, it is accordingly taken as a basic tenet that the conduct of business is incumbent on the board of directors and other members of the management').

of the company.[78] However, the general meeting's possession of such comprehensive powers does not necessarily entail better protection of the minority shareholders; in fact, the interests of minority shareholders are often overlooked in such a system.

6 The independent directors

The original design of the two-tier board structure in the 1993 Company Law was meant to establish checks and balances within the company by having the supervisory board monitoring the management board (the board of directors). As will be examined below, the supervisory board system appeared to be a failure, at least from the perspective of the 1993 Company Law. Disappointed by the poor corporate governance of China's listed companies and the ineffectiveness of the supervisory boards, the CSRC issued, in August 2001, the Guidelines on the Introduction of the Independent Directors System in Listed Companies.[79]

Although it is not the CSRC's first mention of independent directors in its regulations,[80] the major change here is that, for the first time, the Guidelines mandate that: '[a]ll domestically listed companies shall amend their articles of association and . . . appoint qualified persons to be independent directors'.[81] Specifically, 'By June 30th, 2002, at least two members of the board of directors shall be independent directors; and by June 30th, 2003, at least one-third of [the] board shall be independent directors'.[82] The installation of independent directors to the board of directors of listed companies was further required by the Code of Corporate Governance issued on 7 January 2002 and the amended 2005 Company Law.[83]

The independence requirements

The Guidelines define an independent director as one 'who holds no posts in the company other than the position of director, and who maintains no relations with the listed company and its major shareholder that might prevent him from making objective judgment independently'.[84]

An independent director is to be nominated by the board of directors, the supervisory board or a shareholder or shareholders who independently or jointly have more than a 1 per cent stake in the company. The nominee, before the election at the shareholders' meeting, shall issue a public statement that she or he has no relationship with the listed company that may affect her/his independent objective judgment. The CSRC intervenes before the election, as it requires listed companies to submit the nomination for examination and approval by the CSRC. A nominee objected by the CSRC can only serve as candidate for

78 ibid 154.
79 Zhongguo Zhengquan Jiandu Guanli Weiyuanhui Guanyu Fabu 'Guanyu Zai Shangshi Gongsi Jianli Duli Dongshi Zhidu De Zhidao Yijian' De Tongzhi [China Securities Regulatory Commission Notice on Issuing the Guidelines for Introducing Independent Directors Listed Companies], Zhengjianfa [2001] No 102, 16 August 2001, Chinese text available at http://www.csrc.gov.cn/pub/newsite/flb/flfg/bmgf/ssgs/gszl/201012/t20101231_189696.html (last accessed 12 June 2016) (Guidelines on Independent Directors).
80 The CSRC indicated in its Guidelines on Articles of Associations of Companies issued in 1997 that 'companies may set independent directors according to their needs'.
81 Guidelines on Independent Directors art I:3.
82 ibid.
83 Article 123 of the Company Law stipulates that: 'Listed companies shall appoint independent directors; the specific measures shall be provided by the State Council'.
84 Guidelines on Independent Directors art I:1.

ordinary directorship but not independent directorship. If elected, an independent director may not occupy the position for more than six years. He or she may be removed by the shareholders' meeting, upon request of the board of directors, if failing to attend the board meeting in person three times consecutively. The independent director may also resign before the term expires, but the notice of resignation is to take effect only 'after the subsequently appointed independent director fills the vacancy', indicating that 'forced labour' is possibly intended in the Guidelines.[85]

The Guidelines grant a variety of powers to independent directors. A proposed related-party transaction (defined as a transaction concluded between the listed company and related parties, which is in excess of RMB 3 million or five per cent of the company's net assets) should be approved by independent directors before it is submitted to the board of directors for discussion. The independent directors may also appoint outside auditors and consultants and solicit proxies before the shareholders' meeting. They can also propose that the board of directors call an extraordinary shareholders' meeting or a meeting of the board of directors, as well as to hire or dismiss the company's accounting firm.[86]

In addition, the independent directors may issue 'independent opinions' with regard to matters relating to appointment and replacement of directors and senior management executives, remuneration for directors and senior managers, and any significant existing or new loans or funds transfer between the listed company and its shareholders, actual controllers and affiliated enterprises, as well as any other events that the independent directors consider detrimental to the interests of the minority shareholders.[87]

The independent directors are also assigned a number of rights and duties by the Guidelines. From a legal perspective, rights and duties must be associated with liabilities; in other words, directors should face certain legal consequences if they fail to perform their duties. With regard to duties, the Guidelines require that:

> The independent directors shall bear the duties of good faith and due diligence and care towards the listed company and all the shareholders. They shall earnestly perform their duties in accordance with laws, regulations and the company's articles of association, shall protect the overall interests of the company, and shall be especially concerned with protecting the interests of minority shareholders from being infringed. Independent directors shall carry out their duties independently and shall not subject themselves to the influence of the company's major shareholders, actual controllers, or other entities or persons who are interested parties of the listed company.[88]

But what are the legal consequences if the independent directors fail to fulfil their duties? The Guidelines, again, do not specify the consequences of violation, except that an independent director shall be removed if he or she fails to attend a board meeting in person three consecutive times.[89] Of course, an independent director is also subject to the legal liabilities imposed by the Company Law on any director who violates his duty of good faith and loyalty.[90]

---

85 CSRC Guidelines on Independent Directors (n 27) art IV.
86 ibid art V.
87 ibid art VI.
88 CSRC Guidelines for Independent Directors (n 27) art I:2.
89 ibid art IV:5.
90 Company Law arts 147–53.

A judicial case decided in 2002 revealed that if an independent director fails to perform the necessary legal duties, he might be subject to the disciplinary action of the CSRC. Lu Jiahao, a formal independent director of a listed company named Zhengbaiwen, was fined by the CSRC in the sum of RMB 100,000 because he did not take corrective action when the company made false disclosures to the public. Lu brought the CSRC to the Beijing Number One Intermediate Court. Although the court rejected Lu's claim on the ground of procedural error, the case still serves as an alarm bell to independent directors, reminding them of the high risks involved in this job.[91]

The current question for China's independent directors is, however, not how harsh the punishment should be. If harsh liability is not associated with proper institutions to support independent directors to perform their duties, e.g. ensuring that administrative and judicial remedies are available to independent directors or shareholders if the corporate management refuses to provide independent directors with access to corporate information and facilities, it will only prevent more able persons from entering into the pool of independent directors, which badly needs more able individuals. In fact, if anything, there has been a race towards early resignation by independent directors after the *Lu Jiahao* case was decided in 2002.[92]

In conclusion, the creation of independent directors for China's listed companies was a direct response of the CSRC in respect of the virtually complete failure of the supervisory board system. Empirical studies, rudimentary as they are, still suggest that independent directors have contributed to the improvement of corporate governance. One has to attribute this to the extremely poor quality of corporate governance in China's listed companies prior to the establishment of the independent director system in 2001. Independent directors are able to exercise some checks and balances to the power of the manager or the representative of the controlling shareholder.

As the independent director system has been in place in China for only a decade, it is still too early to assess the effectiveness of this institution, especially because it was imported into China from the origin countries (mainly the US and UK), which have a very different legal and cultural environment from the transplant country. Although the institution has achieved limited success, it is not easy for observers to be very optimistic about the role of independent directors in respect of corporate governance in China, unless certain fundamental defects, which are deeply rooted in the economic, political and legal environment surrounding China's enterprise sectors, are cured. Those problems include, most notably, a lack of true independence of the independent directors and the weak enforcement measures in relation to violation of the legal rules giving powers and privileges to independent directors.

7 The supervisory board

It is a statutory requirement that a company must have a supervisory board or at least a supervisor. An LLC with relatively fewer shareholders or one of smaller scale may appoint one or two supervisors instead of a supervisory board.[93] The supervisory board should be

---

91 Gu (2003) 70–71.
92 ibid 71.
93 Gongsi Fa art 118.

composed of not less than three supervisors.[94] The chairperson of the supervisory board, who has the authority to convene and preside over the supervisory board meetings will be elected by a majority of all the supervisors. The supervisory board of a JSLC may also have a vice chairperson.

To prevent the chairperson from abusing his position, the law mandates that, in a JSLC, when the chairperson fails or is unable to perform his duties, the vice chairperson shall take over the duty to convene and chair the meeting. If the vice chairperson suffers the same problem, a supervisor jointly designated by more than half of all directors shall take over to ensure the supervisory board meeting is smoothly convened and chaired.[95] For the supervisory board meeting in an LLC, if the chairperson is unable to or fails to perform his duties, a supervisor jointly appointed by a majority of the supervisors will immediately take over to convene and chair the meeting.[96]

Supervisors, like directors, serve three years for each term but may be re-elected upon the expiration of his office. Even after his term is expired, a supervisor may continue to hold his position until his replacement assumes duty.[97] Supervisors, like directors, exercise their supervisory powers collectively. That is, a supervisory board of an LLC must meet at least once a year, and a JSLC board must meet every six months. In addition, any supervisor may call for a special supervisory board meeting.[98] Resolutions will be adopted by a simple majority, unless the corporate charter of an LLC provides otherwise.[99]

The co-determination feature is more obvious in the supervisory board. The composition of the supervisory board must include representatives of shareholders, who are elected by the shareholders' general meeting, and 'an appropriate percentage of employee representatives', which means at least one-third of the supervisors should be democratically elected by the employees of the company.[100] Supervisors, like directors and the manager, must meet the negative qualifications stipulated in Article 147 of the Company Law. Directors and senior management executives are explicitly prohibited from serving as supervisors.[101]

The supervisory board in wholly state-owned companies (WSOCs) is subject to a separate regulatory regime. The number of supervisors on the supervisory board in a WSOC must not be fewer than five, with one-third of the supervisors being employee representatives. The normal supervisors and the supervisory board chairperson are appointed by the SASAC, but the employee supervisors will be elected democratically by the employees.

The supervisory board was intended to be the only internal watchdog over the management. The supervisory board oversees the board of directors and managers to assure that they comply with state laws and company policies. Specifically, PRC Company Law 1993, before it was amended in 2005, granted the supervisory board the following powers:

- examining the financial affairs of the company
- supervising the conduct of directors and managers in their performance of duties that is in violation of laws, administrative regulations or the corporate charter

---

94 ibid arts 52, 118.
95 ibid art 118 para 3.
96 ibid art 52 para 3.
97 ibid art 53.
98 Gongsi Fa arts 56 and 120.
99 ibid art 120 para 3; Art. 56 para 2.
100 ibid art 52 para 2.
101 ibid art 52 para 4; Art. 118 para 4.

- demanding the directors and senior manager correct their wrongdoings that injure corporate interest and
- proposing to convene extraordinary shareholders' meeting.[102]

The 2005 revisions to the Company Law have added or clarified the following substantial powers to the arsenal of the supervisory board:[103]

- proposing, to the general meeting, to remove directors or senior management executives who have violated any laws, administrative regulations, the corporate charter, or resolutions of the shareholders' meetings
- convening and presiding over the general meeting as required by the law if the board of directors fails to fulfil this duty
- making proposals to the general meeting
- conducting investigations or, when necessary, hiring an outside intermediary (such as an accounting firm or law firm) at the expense of the company to conduct investigation, if it discovers any irregularities in the company's business
- bringing legal actions against directors and senior management executives pursuant to Art. 152 of the Company Law and
- attending the board meeting, asking questions and providing advice to the board in relation to the resolution matters.

Is the supervisory board an effective institution? It is common knowledge that the Chinese system of the supervisory board was inspired by the two-tier board structure in Germany. However, it is essentially important to note that the supervisory boards in Chinese companies are significantly different from their counterparts in Germany in terms of both the statutory powers and the supervisory practice. According to Schneider and Heidenhain (1996) in their discussion of the German Stock Corporation Act:[104]

> The supervisory board is responsible for appointing and dismissing members of the management board (§ 84(1)) and representing the corporation in its dealings with such board (§90), including entering into employment agreements with its members (§112). The management board reports to the supervisory board, though the latter is independently entitled to inspect the books, records and properties of the corporation (§111(2)). The supervisory board must consent to certain business decisions of the management board if required by the articles or the supervisory board's rules. The supervisory board may not, however, encumber the management board's ability to manage the corporation with excessive consent requirements. If the supervisory board withholds consent, the management board may nevertheless act if it can obtain a three quarters majority of votes cast at the shareholders' meeting (§111(4)).[105]

Clearly, compared with its counterpart in China, the supervisory board in public corporations in Germany has a much broader power base, albeit that it is also expected to refrain from

---

102 Gongsi Fa (1993) art 54.
103 ibid arts 54 and 55.
104 Schneider and Heidenhain (1996).
105 ibid 10.

excessively interfering with the board of directors (the 'management board'), which is vested with the authority to manage the day-to-day operation of the business. In essence, the management board in a German stock corporation is legally accountable to the supervisory board to a very large extent as the directors of the management board have, first, to be appointed and removed by the supervisory board and, second, seek consent from the supervisory board regarding important business decisions.

China's supervisory board apparently does not possess such a wide range of powers. For instance, a Chinese supervisory board's statutory powers do not include any authority to control the appointment or business decision-making of the management board. Hence, as a matter of law, it is impossible for the supervisory board to act 'as supervisory organ in the sense of checks and balances, which appoints, controls, advises – and where necessary also dismisses – the Management Board',[106] as prescribed in the German corporate governance structure.

In practice, the effectiveness of a typical supervisory board is, first of all, undermined by its composition. The membership of the supervisory board consists of 'political officers', leaders of the non-functional trade union or close friends and allies of the senior management executives.[107] According to a survey of the Shanghai Stock Exchange Research Centre on the educational background of corporations listed in the Shanghai Stock Exchange, the overall professional quality of supervisors was inferior to the members of the board of directors.[108] Furthermore, supervisors, appointed by the executives who also determine the supervisors' compensation, had virtually no independence from the management.[109] In addition, the supervisory board had limited access to corporation information, rendering it impossible to make informed decisions. Last but not least, because of the highly concentrated leadership (in the hands of either the state or other controlling shareholders), many supervisory boards were at best a 'censored watchdog', not allowed to speak against the management controlled by the controlling shareholder or the government.[110]

The old supervisory board system provided under the 1993 Company Law was widely regarded as a failure. This was publicly admitted by one senior official of the China Securities Regulatory Commission (CSRC), which is China's chief watchdog on the capital markets:[111]

> It is sometimes argued that more authority should then be given to the supervisory boards, which sit on top of the boards of our listed companies. However, experience has shown that this system of supervision is not effective as it is often unclear whose interest is being represented by the supervisory board. In many cases, the supervisory board duplicates the authority of the board itself but without corresponding responsibilities. In fact, the presence of a supervisory board may give the illusion of certain checks and balance in the listed company when none existed.

Given that the new Company Law has tremendously strengthened the power base of the supervisory board, the new supervisory board has of course been expected to help improve

---

106 Berlin Initiative Group, 'German Code of Corporate Governance' Berlin: 2 June 2006, part I:6 http://www.ecgi.org/codes/documents/gccg_e.pdf (GCCG).
107 Tenev and Zhang (2002) 100; Dahya and others (2003) 313–316; SSE (2004) 44.
108 SSE (2003) 160.
109 SSE (2004) 44.
110 Dahya and others 315. See also SSE (2004)44.
111 Cha (2001).

corporate governance of Chinese companies. Professor Zhao Xudong has, however, pointed out that even the new supervisory board is 'xingtong xushe' (performing practically no function), and he radically – maybe wisely – suggested abolishing the supervisory board system and making the board of directors a direct and more effective supervisory body to oversee the management.[112]

Finally, it is useful to note the different roles played by the independent directors and the supervisory board in China's corporate governance system. They are of course expected to complement each other – otherwise why would the law-makers codify both of them? In the Chinese discourse of corporate law, the independent directors oversee the board of directors and the management by voting at board meetings, and thus provide 'ex ante supervision' in the company. In contrast, the supervisory board, because it has no right to participate in the decision-making process, is believed to be able to benefit from 'ex post supervision'.[113] One could easily differentiate the two roles by comparing the respective powers of the two governance organs.

8 The manager and senior management executives

The 'manager' (jingli) as mentioned in the Company Law is often known as the 'general manager' or even 'chief executive officer' (CEO) in practice. He is the person who has the authority to implement board resolutions and carry on the day-to-day operations of the company. The manager is appointed by and accountable to the board of directors.[114] He is subject to the same negative qualifications as set out in Article 147 of the Company Law.

The Company Law has also introduced the frequently mentioned concept of 'gaoji guanli renyuan' or senior management executives, which is akin to the concept of 'officers' in English and American corporate law. Senior management executives include the manager, deputy manager(s), chief financial officer and board secretary, as well as any other person as provided in the corporate charter.[115]

Notably, there is no clear separation of the chairperson of the board and the general manager. Arguably, the Company Law might even encourage a convergence of the two roles. Article 115 provides that the board of a JSLC can decide to appoint a director (including the chairperson) as the manager. Article 69 permits the SASAC to appoint a director as the manager. Finally, Article 51 provides that the executive director of an LLC with relatively few shareholders and on a small scale can serve as the company manager.

9 Fiduciary duties of directors, supervisors and executives

In 2005, the National People's Congress of the People's Republic of China adopted a set of amendments that were seen as the most important revision to China's Company Law in history. The PRC Company Law, originally adopted in 1993, was regarded as a law merely serving the interest of state-owned enterprises (SOEs). The 2005 revision, which rewrote

---

112 'Zhao Xudong Jiaoshou Dadan Jianyi quxiao Jianshihui' ['Professor Zhao Xudong boldly suggested to abolish the supervisory board'], *Legal Daily* (11 March 2011) http://www.legaldaily.com.cn/bm/content/2010-03/11/content_2079635.htm (last accessed 4 June 2016).

113 See CSRC (2011) 79. The supervisors may attend board meetings and ask questions or provide advice to the board, but may not vote on resolutions. See Gongsi Fa art 55.

114 Gongsi Fa arts 50 and 114.

115 Gongsi Fa art 217(1); Model Charter art 124 para 3 and the annotation thereto.

about two-thirds of the provisions, is so significant that the current corporate law statute is often referred to as the '2005 Company Law'.[116]

One of the major changes in the 2005 Company Law is the adoption of a framework of fiduciary duties 'resembling common law fiduciary duties'.[117] As is the case in major origin jurisdictions, China has now adopted in its corporate law a mixture of rules and standards, under the umbrella of 'fiduciary duties', to minimise the 'agency costs' arising out of the separation of ownership and control.[118] Not surprisingly, this has been regarded as a successful move to transplant an Anglo–American doctrine into Chinese law, as remarked upon by Nicholas Howson:[119]

> [I]n October 2005 China introduced Anglo-American-style corporate fiduciary duties into the nation's corporate law. In addition, and as in the 1994 Company Law (but in a different article), the 2005 Company Law sets forth in accompanying Article 149 a number of bright-line prohibitions, violation of which would constitute breach of loyalty-type obligations.

With Articles 147, 148, 149, 151 and 152 in the PRC Company Law, China appeared to be one of the first major jurisdictions that have systematically – not yet entirely – codified the contents and enforcement of fiduciary duties.[120] Article 147 of the Company Law requires senior personnel in a company to act in accordance of due care and loyalty:

> Directors, supervisors and senior management executives shall abide by laws, administrative regulations and the corporate charter, and have a duty of loyalty (*zhongshi yiwu*) and duty of care (*qinmian yifu*) to the company.[121]

This provision sets forth a general, statutory, standard of corporate fiduciary duties in China. Other than this, there are no general principles or guidelines to elaborate upon the contents the standards of fiduciary duties. As Nicholas Howson observes, with respect to the duty of care: 'the 2005 statutory formulation passes upon the opportunity to . . . articulate a specific *standard* for the duty of care prong, or any instruction to regulators or judges who might be employed as a "business judgment rule" for newly authorized duty of care inquiries'.[122]

---

116 The Company Law was most recently revised in December 2013 to abolish the rules on compulsory minimum registered capital.
117 Anderson and Guo (2006a and 2006b) (noting that 'the Chinese framework [of management duties] appears to be patterned on common law concepts').
118 For analytical purposes, it is useful here to distinguish between 'rules' and 'standards'. As Kraakman and others (n 1) at 39) point out: 'The most familiar pair of regulatory strategies [in addressing agency problems] constrains agents by commanding them not to make decisions, or undertake transactions, that would harm the interests of their principles. Lawmakers can frame such constraints as *rules*, which require or prohibit specific behaviors, or as general *standards*, which leave the precise determination of compliance to adjudicators after the fact'.
119 Howson (2008) 198.
120 After the 2005 PRC Company Law, the United Kingdom codified its body of directors' duties in Part 10 of the Companies Act 2006.
121 Gongsi Fa art 148 para 1 (Chinese pinxin *Zhongshi yiwu* and *qinmian yifu* added). There is a similar general standard of fiduciary duty in art 33 of the Code of Corporate Governance, which states that: 'Directors should act in the best interest of the company and all the shareholders, performing their duties loyally, in good faith and diligently'.
122 Howson (2008) 198.

An interesting comparison is the articulation of the general standard for directors' 'duty to promote the success of the company' in the UK Companies Act 2006, which, as mentioned above, requires the directors of a company to 'act in the way he considers, in good faith, would be most likely to promote the success of the company for the benefit of its members as a whole'.[123]

Noticeably, words such as 'good faith', 'benefit', 'success' etc., which feature a high degree of flexibility and uncertainties, all require clarification and interpretation whenever they are applied to specific facts. Similarly, the duty of loyalty in the US requires a director to act 'in the good faith belief that her actions are in the corporation's best interest'.[124] Flexible terminology such as 'good faith', 'best interests', 'fair', 'reasonable', 'adequate' etc also compels judicial interpretation; that is to say, in applying a standard of fiduciary duties, courts everywhere will always have to interpret the doctrine and terminology to determine, on the facts and context of each case, whether the standard was met.[125] China in theory is not an exception, but it is very questionable whether the Chinese judiciary is able to undertake such a task to understand the original meaning of corporate fiduciary duties as they are in the American or English common law context.[126]

Although it is overwhelmingly agreed that the doctrine of fiduciary duties in Chinese corporate law has Anglo–American origins, it can also find part of its roots in Chinese civil law, which was styled after the Continental legal family. The majority view is that the relationship between the company and its directors, supervisors and executives is built upon an agency based upon a 'contract of mandate' (*weiren hetong*, officially called *weituo hetong* in the PRC Contract Law), in which the principal and the agent agree that the agent will handle the principal's affairs.[127] Leading civil law textbooks in China have suggested that: 'the mandatory [agent] shall perform the duty of care of a good manager [*shangliang guanli ren*] in contracts of mandate with remunerations'.[128]

Since the modern civil law system on the Chinese mainland is, to a large extent, built upon the civil law of Republic of China (ROC), which is still applicable in Taiwan now, Chinese academic writing is accustomed to using laws, judicial decisions and scholarly opinions from Taiwan to interpret concepts in contemporary PRC civil law. This treatment of the mandatory/agent as a 'good manager' with the duty of care in Chinese textbooks on civil law is one such example. Article 535 of the ROC Civil Code states: 'The mandatory who deals with the affair commissioned, shall be [acting] in accordance with the instructions of the principal and with the same care as he would deal with his own affairs. If he has received the remuneration, he shall do so with the care of a good administrator'.[129] Article 192 of the ROC Company Law, which governs the legal relationship between the company

123 UK Companies Act 2006 art 172(1).
124 *Stone, ex rel. AmSouth Bancorporation v. Ritter*, 911 A 2d 362, 370 (2006), cited in Cahn and Donald (2010) 344.
125 Cahn and Donald (2010) 343.
126 See Howson (2008) 202 (noting 'the application of fiduciary duties requires extraordinary flexibility and complex fact analysis, and thus a demanding level of technical competence among the judicial corps (or state regulator) wielding the doctrine').
127 PRC Contract Law art 396. Leading text books on civil law in China suggest that *weiren* and *weituo* mean the same and can be used interchangeably. See Wang Liming (2010) 483; Guo Mingrui (2007) 507.
128 See eg Wang Liming (2010) 485; Guo Mingrui (2007) 508.
129 The bilingual versions of the ROC Civil Code were provided at the website of the ROC Ministry of Justice; see (http://mojlaw.moj.gov.tw (last accessed 4 June 2016).

and its directors, was largely derived from Article 535 of the Civil Code. It provides that: 'The relationship between a company and its directors, unless otherwise stipulated in this law, shall be [understood] in accordance with the civil code stipulations for mandate (*weiren*)'.[130]

Since the doctrine of fiduciary duties has been formally introduced but the traditional doctrine of 'mandate' is here to stay, how the Chinese courts will reconcile the two in disputes on director/management duties is an interesting question. Some pragmatic academics and judges in China have optimistically – but probably mistakenly – understood the two as having the same result. After the much hailed but rarely used PRC Trust Law was adopted in April 2001, they now have further reason to believe that the two doctrines can co-exist in China's corporate law regime. Article 25 of the Trust Law requires the trustee to 'be attentive to duties and perform his obligations honestly, trustworthily, prudently and effectively'. Liu Junhai, one of the leading corporate law scholars in China, thus concludes:[131]

> The generally agreed view in our country is that the relationship between the company and its directors, supervisors and senior management executives is one of contractual relations based on *weituo* (*weiren*). The directors, supervisors and senior management executives should perform both the obligations conferred upon him by the Contract Law and the contract of mandate, and the obligations arising from the provisions in the Company Law and its special laws. Although the respective duties of the directors, supervisors and senior management executives are a bit different, they share the common duty of being honest, trustworthy, and diligent.

The Anglo–American legal family usually relies on the concept of fiduciary duties to interpret the legal relationship between the company and its directors and senior executives. As China adopted the Trust Law in April 2001 and the trust obligations stipulated in the Trust Law are higher than the obligations in the contract of mandate under the Contract Law, we could also use trust obligations to describe the relationship between the company and its directors, supervisors and senior executives in China. Of course, it does not matter whether one uses the contract of mandate or the trust obligations to explain the relationship between the company and its directors, supervisors and senior executives; in any event, it will lead to the same result, although from different paths. In this sense, the two paths have no fundamental differences.

The zeal to embrace fiduciary duties in Chinese corporate law, however, ignores a basic fact in the development of the duties in their origin countries: these duties are not simply some plain and basic rules that could be easily copied from the statute book of one jurisdiction onto that of another. In fact, these rules and standards of great longevity were developed by courts over several centuries in Anglo–American jurisdictions and embedded in a vast body of cases, which is impossible to copy entirely in a civil law jurisdiction. As Paul Davies has remarked: 'These rules for directors were developed by the courts at an early stage, often on the basis of analogy with the rules applying to trustees. The substantial corpus of learning on the nature and scope of these general fiduciary duties and duties of skill and care has remained until now largely within the common law'.[132]

130 Translation provided in Howson (2008) 203.
131 Liu, Junhai (n 37) 506–7.
132 Davies (2008) 477.

It is still an open question whether Chinese courts could apply these duties in a way that is roughly in line with both the fundamental principles and legal reasoning for applying such duties in their origin countries. As will be seen below, Chinese courts, because of a lack of understanding of the common law in which the fiduciary duties are embodied, must resort to the traditional doctrines and legal reasoning in their own civil law system to interpret and apply the newly established 'fiduciary duties' in the PRC Company Law. Of course, there is probably nothing wrong with this per se, but eventually there will be a Chinese doctrine of fiduciary duties with distinctive Chinese characteristics. We look at how the fiduciary duties provided in the 2005 Company Law are understood and applied in Chinese courts in the following section.

10 Concluding remarks: convergence, divergence and Chinese characteristics of corporate governance

Corporate law in China developed from scratch in the 1980s. In the beginning, there were only a few provisions mainly dealing with the registration of state-owned enterprises. Today, Chinese corporate law has become a body of increasingly sophisticated and complicated rules. Of course, corporate law in China is a result of legal transplants and receptions, but its journey of taking root in China has generated certain strong Chinese characteristics. In short, the developmental path of corporate law in China demonstrates signs of both convergence and divergence, which are evident in the legal framework on corporate governance.

The corporate governance framework in China probably tends to be more eclectic than in other jurisdictions. The 1993 Company Law borrowed extensively from the German model, with respect to, in particular, the supervisory system. In the following years, it has been steadily marching towards the Anglo–American model by adopting the independent director system and codifying fiduciary duties, as well as regulating listed companies with American style securities regulation. One may argue that this change is driven by the search for economic efficiency, as the mainstream literature of corporate and financial law advocates that corporate law rules in Anglo–American jurisdictions are more conducive to financial market development and eventually economic growth. Of course, it might also be because more and more Chinese scholars – many of them involved in law-making in China – studied corporate law in Anglo–American jurisdictions and then returned to China with the knowledge they had acquired overseas. In short, the Americanisation of corporate governance rules in China seems to be apparent, but it is an open question whether this trend is sustainable.

For example, the codification of fiduciary duties in the PRC Company Law has raised the question of whether and to what extent Anglo–American fiduciary duties can be exported to other countries thorough legal transplantation. An empirical examination of the judgments and scholarly writing by Chinese judges suggests that the courts have been proactively using enforcement of fiduciary duties to protect minority shareholders' rights in China. This, however, is not necessarily a successful example of legal transplantation. In fact, Chinese courts and judges have almost totally disregarded the relevant overseas jurisprudence. Instead, they have relied on the traditional civil law doctrine of liability in tort to interpret fiduciary duties. In other words, fiduciary duties have been given substance, content and effect by Chinese courts and judges, not through the careful learning of relevant case law in Anglo–American countries, but through the application of domestic legal resources with which the Chinese judges are familiar.

The results are almost equally good, as investor protection in China is also thereby improved. So, the Chinese case of transplanting fiduciary duties probably proves again the non-transplantability of open-ended foreign institutions such as fiduciary duties. On the other hand, the codification of the name and a few principles of fiduciary duties have achieved an unexpected result, which has equally enhanced the quality of Chinese corporate law. This is a phenomenon that is worthy of further study in comparative law.

In conclusion, in corporate governance – and probably in many other areas, China appears to be an interesting legal laboratory for the experiments of borrowed foreign institutions – and occasionally for home-grown rules. For this reason, despite the many years of development, corporate governance law in China is still an immature child in search of a soul with which it can settle down somewhere.

Bibliography

Anderson, Braig and Bingna Guo (2006a). 'Corporate Governance under the New Company Law (Part 1): Fiduciary Duties and Minority Shareholder Protection', *China Law & Practice*, April 2006.
_____ (2006b). 'Corporate Governance under the New Company Law (Part 2): Shareholder Lawsuits and Enforcement', *China Law & Practice*, May 2006.
Berle, Adolf and Gardiner C. Means (1968). *The Modern Corporation and Private Property* (Revised Edition). New York: Harcourt, Brace & World, Inc.
Browne, Andrew (2015). 'Beijing's Response to Stock selloff Reveals Deep Insecurity', *Wall Street Journal* http://www.wsj.com/articles/stocks-and-insecuritiesbeijing-digs-in-to-avert-a-threat-1436253152 (last accessed 4 June 2016).
Cadbury Report (1992). *Report of the Committee on the Financial Aspects of Corporate Governance (Cadbury Report)* (1 December 1992), London: Gee and Co. Ltd.
Cahn, Andreas and David C Donald (2010). *Comparative Company Law: Text and Cases on the Laws Governing Corporations in Germany, the UK and the USA,* Cambridge, Cambridge University Press.
Cha, Laura M. (2001). 'The Future of China's Capital Markets and the Role of Corporate Governance'. Luncheon Speech at China Business Summit by Laura M. Cha, Vice Chairman of the China Securities Regulatory Commission (18 April 2001).
Chang, Eric C. and Sonia M.L. Wong (2004). 'Political Control and Performance in China's Listed Companies' (2004). 32 *Journal of Comparative Economics* 617–36.
Chen, Bin, She Jian, Wang Xiaojin and Lai Jianqing (2008). 我国民营上市公司发展实证研究。深圳证券交易所综合研究所研究报告, 深证综研字第0160号。
Chen, Jia-gui and Huang Qun-Hui (2001). 'Comparison of Governance Structures of Chinese Enterprises with Different Types of Ownership', 6 *China & World Economy* http://unpan1.un.org (last accessed 4 June 2016) .
(China International Capital Corporation) CICC (2014). 市场制度研究之六: 公司治理在中国。(2 December 2014) www.cicc.com.cn (last accessed 4 June 2016).
China Insurance Daily (2012). 'Zhongzubu Xuanbu Zhongguo Renbao Zhongguo Renshou Gaoceng Renshi Biandong' ['Central Organization Department Announces the Change of Top Personnel in PICC and China Life'] (20 March 2012) *Zhongguo Baoxian Bao* [*China Insurance Daily*] http://finance.sina.com.cn/money/insurance/bxyx/20120320/085411630947.shtml (last accessed 4 June 2016).
China Newsweek (2012). 'Fubuji Yangqi Laozong Huo Tiba Shengqian Cheng Changtai' ['It's Becoming Increasingly Normal for the Top Leaders of Central SOEs to Get Promoted in Their Political Career'] (9 April 2012) *Zhongguo Xinwen Zhoukan* [*China Newsweek*] http://district.ce.cn/newarea/sddy/201204/09/t20120409_23224122.shtml (last accessed 4 June 2016).
Coase, Ronald and Ning Wang (2013). *How China Became Capitalist.* New York: Palgrave MacMillan.
Cox, James D. and Thomas Lee Hazen (2003). *Corporations* (2nd edn). New York: Aspen Publishers.
Creemers, Rogier (2015). 'China's Rule of Law Plan is for Real'. East Asian Forum (10 May 2015) http://www.eastasiaforum.org/2015/05/10/chinas-rule-of-law-plan-is-for-real/ (last accessed 12 June 2016).
CSRC (China Securities Regulatory Commission) (2011). *Corporate Governance of Listed Companies in China – Self-assessment by the China Securities Regulatory Commission*, Paris: OECD.
Dahya, Jay and others (2003). 'The Usefulness of the Supervisory Board Report in China', 11:4 (2003) *Corporate Governance* 308–321.

Davies, Paul (2008). *Principles of Modern Company Law, 8th Edition,* London, Sweet & Maxwell.

G20/OECD (2015). Principles of Corporate Governance: OECD Report to G20 Finance Ministers and Central Bank Governors. Paris: OECD.

Gu, Minkang (2003). 'Will an Independent Director Perform Better than a Supervisory?' 6 *Journal of Chinese and Comparative Law* 59–76.

Guo, Mingrui (ed.) (2007). *Minfa [Civil Law],* Beijing: Higher Education Press.

Hamilton, Gary G. (2006). *Commerce and Capitalism in Chinese Societies.* London and New York: Routledge.

Hansmann, Henry and Reinier Kraakman (2004). 'The End of History for Corporate Law', in Jeffrey N. Gordon and Mark J. Roe (2004), *Convergence and Persistence in Corporate Governance* (pp 33–68). Cambridge: Cambridge University Press.

HKU Research Team (香港大学课题组) (2003). 'Business Performance and Governance Structures of Privately owned Listed Companies in China' [《民营上市公司的经营绩效和治理结构研究》], 上证联合研究计划第八期课题报告。

Howson, Nicholas C. (2008). 'The Doctrine that Dared Not Speak Its Name: Anglo-American Fiduciary Duties in China's 2005 Company Law and Case Intimations of Prior Convergence', in Hideki Kanda, Kon-Sik Kim and Curtis J. Milhaupt (eds), *Transforming Corporate Governance in East Asia.* London and New York: Routledge, 193–254.

Huang, Yasheng (2008). *Capitalism with Chinese Characteristics: Entrepreneurship and the State.* Cambridge: Cambridge University Press.

Kraakman, Reinier and others (2004). *The Anatomy of Corporate Law.* Oxford: Oxford University Press.

―――― (2009). *The Anatomy of Corporate Law: A Comparative and Functional Approach* (2nd edn) Oxford: Oxford University Press.

Li, Weiao (2015). '小米有了'党委书记''。《南方周末》, (2 July 2015) http://infzm.media.baidu.com/article/9887010567291664704 (last accessed 4 June 2016).

Lieberthal, Kenneth (2004). *Governing China: From Revolution Through Reform.* New York: W. W. Norton & Company.

Lin, Li-Wen and Curtis J. Milhaupt (2013). 'We are the (National) Champions: Understanding the Mechanisms of State Capitalism in China'. 65 *Stanford Law Review,* pp 697–759.

Liu, Junhai (2011). *Xiandai Gongsi Fa* (Di 2 Ban) [*Modern Corporation Law* (2nd edn)]. Beijing: Law Press China.

Liu, Lanfang (ed) (2009). *Xin Gongsifa Yinan Anli Panjie* [*Understanding the Difficult Cases under the New Company Law*]. Beijing: Falv Chubanshe [Law Press China].

Liu, Qiao (2006). 'Corporate Governance in China: Current Practices, Economic Effects and Institutional Determinants.' (2006) 52:2 *CESifo Economic Studies* 415–53.

Jiang, Fei, Liu Caiping and Yue Yue (2015). 'How Beijing Intervened to Save China's Stocks'. english. www.caijing.com (last accessed 4 June 2016).

McGregor, Richard (2010). *The Party: The Secret World of China's Communist Rulers.* New York: HarperCollins.

Naughton, Barry (2003). 'The State Asset Commission: A Powerful New Government Body'. *China Leadership Monitor,* No 8. Stanford: Hoover Institution.

OECD (2011). Corporate Governance of Listed Companies in China – Self-Assessment by the China Securities Regulatory Commission. Paris, OECD Publishing, http://www.oecd.org/corporate/ca/corporategovernanceprinciples/48444985.pdf (last accessed 8 August 2016).

Peerenboom, Randy (2002). *China's Long March Toward Rule of Law.* Cambridge: Cambridge University Press.

Peng, Xue (2015). *Corporate Governance of Chinese Privately Owned Enterprises Listed in Hong Kong: An Empirical Study of Three Levels of Agency Problems.* PhD Thesis, The University of Hong Kong, in The HKU Scholars Hub http://hdl.handle.net/10722/216295 (last accessed 4 June 2016).

Roe, Mark J. (2003). *Political Determinants of Corporate Governance: Political Context, Corporate Impact.* Oxford: Oxford University Press.

SASAC (State-owned Assets Supervision and Administration Commission) (2013a). 'Zhuyao Zhize' ['Main Responsibilities'] www.sasac.gov.cn (last accessed 4 June 2016).

Schneider, Hannes and Heidenhain, Martin (1996). *The German Stock Corporation Act.* The Hague: Kluwer Law International.

Siems, Mathias (2008). *Convergence in Shareholder Law.* Cambridge: Cambridge University Press.

Smith, Roy C. and Walter, Ingo (2006). *Governing the Modern Corporation: Capital Markets, Corporate Control, and Economic Performance*. Oxford: Oxford University Press.

SSE (Shanghai Stock Exchange Research Centre) (2003). *Zhongguo Gongsi Zhili Baogao (2003 nian)* [*China Corporate Governance Report 2003*]. Shanghai: Fudan University Press.

SSE (Shanghai Stock Exchange Research Centre) (2004). *Zhongguo Gongsi Zhili Baogao (2004 nian)* [*China Corporate Governance Report 2004*]. Shanghai: Fudan University Press.

Standard and Poor's (2003). 'Corporate Governance in China'. November 2003.

Tan, Lay-Hong and Wang, Jiangyu (2007). 'Modelling an Effective Corporate Governance System for China's Listed State-owned Enterprises: Issues and Challenges in a Transitional Economy', (2007) 7:1 *Journal of Corporate Law Studies*.

Tenev, Stoyan and Chunlin Zhang (with Loup Brefort) (2002). *Corporate Governance and Enterprise Reform in China: Building the Institutions of Modern Markets*. Washington D.C.: World Bank and the International Finance Corporation.

Wang, Liming (ed.) (2010). *Minfa (Di Wu Ban)* [*Civil Law* (5th edn)]. Beijing: Renmin University Press.

Wang, Jiangyu (2004). 'The Rule of Law in China: A Realistic View of the Jurisprudence, the Impact of the WTO, and the Prospects for Future Development', (2004) *Singapore Journal of Legal Studies* 347–89.

_____ (2014a). *Company Law in China: Regulation of Business Organizations in a Socialist Market Economy*. Cheltenham, UK: Edward Elgar.

_____ (2014b). 'The Political Logic of Corporate Governance in China's State-owned Enterprises', in 47:3 *Cornell International Law Journal* 631–69.

Wu, Jinglian (2005). *Understanding and Interpreting Chinese Economic Reform*. Mason, Ohio: Thomson Higher Education.

Xie, Ye and Belinda Cao (2015). 'China Bans Stock Sales by Major Shareholders for Six Months'. Bloomberg Business (8 July 2015) www.bloombergcom (last accessed 4 June 2016).

Zhang, Wei (2015). 民企外企为何都要建党委？《北京青年报》 (6 July 2015) A4 http://epaper.ynet.com/html/2015-07/06/content_141902.htm (last accessed 4 June 2016).

Zheng Yongnian (2010). *The Chinese Communist Party as Organizational Emperor: Culture, Reproduction and Transformation*. London and New York: Routledge.

12

Contemporary company law reforms in India

Harpreet Kaur

In 2013, India replaced its old Companies Act 1956 with the new Companies Act 2013, which has already undergone first amendment in 2015. The Companies Act 2013 has 29 chapters, 470 sections and 7 schedules. The new Act has been brought with the objective of better governance of companies with more powers in the hands of the shareholders. Some highlights of the Act include defined roles and duties of directors, more disclosures and strict auditing of companies with fewer government approvals with more self-regulation. The Act has provisions for synchronising it with the regulations of the Securities and Exchange Board of India. The Companies Act 2013 brought in some changes that are still being debated and to date it has not been possible to enforce all the provisions of the new Act. In this chapter, only the important contemporary reforms and thematic developments will be discussed, highlighting their need and challenges related to them.

New definitions

The first development is in the form of introducing new types of companies, together with certain other new definitions. Three types of companies are brought into existence by the Act, namely small companies, associate companies and one-person companies. Of these, the one-person company (OPC) is the most important company since it gives sole proprietors the opportunity to incorporate into an OPC. The structure provides for more flexibility with less compliance. Even though OPC is not a new term for rest of the world, in India, although the provision has been welcomed, it has raised concerns in view of increasing fraud by companies, since this would give the opportunity to an individual to limit his liability.

The J J Irani committee suggested that, in view of the changing business and economic environment of the country, it is necessary that entrepreneurial capabilities of the people are given an outlet for participation in economic activity, which may take place through the creation of an economic person in the form of a company.[1] The scope of misuse of the OPC

---

1 Irani, J.J. (2005), *Report on Company Law* http://www.primedirectors.com/pdf/JJ%20Irani%20 Report-MCA.pdf (last accessed 5 June 2016).

is very high when there is a lack of ability to prohibit corporate frauds by companies that are incorporated by associations of persons. It is hoped that this may not lead to further rises in the phenomenon of vanishing companies in India that has already increased exponentially.[2]

An associate company, in relation to another company, means a company in which that other company has a significant influence, but which is not a subsidiary company of the company having such influence and includes a joint venture company. Significant influence here means the control of at least 20 per cent of total share capital or of business decisions under an agreement with an associate company. This definition was probably necessitated to overcome complications in identifying the relations between the companies in order to apply provisions of different laws. It has been observed that group companies have complicated relationships, which are not simple relationships of holding and subsidiary companies.

A small company is a company other than a public company whose paid-up share capital or turnover does not exceed INR 50 lakh (5 million) or INR 2 crore (20 million), respectively. Paid-up share capital and turnover have been limited to of INR 5 crore (50 million) and INR 2 crore (20 million), respectively for small companies. However, this clause is not applicable to holding, subsidiary or charitable companies, or a company or body corporate governed by any special Act.

The next important definition is that of the term 'promoter'. The term 'promoter' was not defined in the erstwhile Companies Act 1956 and dependence was placed upon common law until 2009. In 2009, the Securities and Exchange Board of India defined the term 'promoter' under the SEBI (Issue of Capital and Disclosure Requirements) Regulations 2009 for the purposes of identifying promoters in order to fix liabilities relating to public funds raised by companies promoted by them.

The definition brought in by section 2(69) of the Companies Act 2013 provides that 'promoter' means a person in the first category, either named as promoter or identified by the company as a promoter in the prospectus or annual returns filed by the company. The second category includes a person who has control over the affairs of the company, directly or indirectly, whether as a shareholder, director or otherwise. The third category includes any person as a promoter who may not necessarily be a shareholder or a director of a company but has control over the board of directors of the company. He may be a promoter *simpliciter* who, after incorporating the company, moves out of the company but controls from outside. In view of the fact that Indian companies are promoter-dominated companies and manipulations by promoters are increasing, it was necessary to provide the definition of the term 'promoter'. Otherwise, until 2009, common law was heavily relied upon to identify a person as a promoter in a company.

In 2009, the term was defined by Securities and Exchange Board of India (Issue of Capital and Disclosure Requirements) Regulations 2009. If one refers to some recent statistics about promoters and their involvement in securities, according to the Bombay Stock Exchange 4578 promoters of different listed companies have been debarred by SEBI either from accessing the securities market or buying, selling or dealing in any particular security since 2007.[3] Promoters have been banned from accessing securities markets owing to their inability to maintain mandated minimum public shareholdings in listed companies, misuse of IPO

2 'Investigations against 122 vanishing companies are being carried out' http://www.mca.gov.in/MinistryV2/vanishing.html (last accessed 5 June 2016); http://www.mca.gov.in/Ministry/pdf/Updated_status_vanishing_companies_20jan2010.pdf (last accessed 5 June 2016).

3 Report on debarred promoters http://www.bseindia.com/investors/debent.aspx?expandable=4 (last accessed 5 June 2016).

proceeds,[4] manipulations in share prices before and after the preferential allotment of securities and generating fictitious long-term capital gains.[5] SEBI is now working on a standard operation procedure to handle such regulatory violations by promoters, proposing that promoters must first face penal action to safeguard the interests of investors, and that any action relating to securities will only be taken as a last resort.[6]

Another definition is that of 'key managerial personnel', which comprises five categories. The first category includes the chief executive officer or managing director or manager of a company. The second, third and fourth categories have only a company secretary, a full-time director or a chief financial officer, respectively. In the fifth category, the provision that any other officer may be prescribed by the central government has been kept. Every listed company and every other public company having a minimum prescribed paid-up share capital is required to appoint full-time key managerial personnel. These key managerial personnel play a significant role in the conduct of affairs of companies through execution of policies made by the board of directors of companies. Therefore, it was thought that their role, liability and accountability should be recognised in law itself.

Directors

The second contemporary development is in the area of the board of directors. Although all powers of management and administration as usual have remained with the board of directors, it is proposed to make their governing abilities of a very high quality and standard. In order to make the board more sharp, powerful and effective, some institutional changes have been brought in.

In the first place, the concept of independent directors has been introduced. This concept is not new for Indian companies; the term 'independent director' was not defined by the old Companies Act but defined under clause 49 of the listing agreement under the Securities Contracts Regulation Act 1956. It must be mentioned that India has witnessed corporate scams even when boards of directors of companies had independent directors.

The Act has tried to bring in strict provisions relating to independent directors. It has mandated listed companies to have one-third of directors to be independent directors on their boards. The Act provides for the definition, their manner of selection, their entitlement to payments and profit-related commissions and limits on their liability. The conditions for appointment as an independent director require that the director himself should not be a promoter, should be a person of integrity, relevant expertise and experience in the opinion of the board, should have no relationship with the promoters or directors, no pecuniary relationship, no relationship of having any employment or holding a position of key managerial personnel in the company in the last three financial years, should not have more than 2 per cent voting power and should not be related to audit firms or legal firms associated with the company in the last three financial years.

Few such conditions of eligibility operate even if any relative of the proposed independent director has transactions, employment or voting power in the company. Although the

---

4 http://articles.economictimes.indiatimes.com/2011/dec/01 (last accessed 5 June 2016).
5 http://articles.economictimes.indiatimes.com/2014-12 20/news/57257601_1_securities-market-artificial-volume-rajeev-kumar-agarwal (last accessed 5 June 2016).
6 'Promoters, not investors should first feel the pinch', *Business Standard* (9 August 2015) http://www.business-standard.com/article/pti-stories/promoters-not-investors-should-first-feel-the-pinch-sebi-115080900315_1.html (last accessed 5 June 2016).

definition of independent directors has restricted pecuniary relationships with companies at the time of appointment of independent directors, the Act has nonetheless given them the right to take profit-related commissions with the approval of the shareholders.

Another important aspect is limiting their liability. The Act has limited the liability of independent directors and non-executive directors who are not promoters or key managerial personnel of the company only for acts of commission or omission by a company, which occurred with their knowledge, or were attributable through board processes or with their consent, connivance or where they had not acted diligently. They can have a tenure of five years and are eligible for reappointment by special resolution. After two consecutive terms there is a requirement for a mandatory cooling-off period, during which they can neither be appointed in any other capacity in the company nor can they be associated with the company directly or indirectly.

The Act has provided for the code of conduct for independent directors in Schedule IV, which prescribes guidelines for professional conduct, role, functions, duties, appointment, resignation and an evaluation mechanism etc. Under the evaluation mechanism, it provides that the entire board – excluding the director who is being evaluated – shall undertake a performance evaluation of the independent directors. Another notable provision of the schedule is that it requires independent directors to hold at least one separate meeting a year without the attendance of non-independent directors and members of management. The meeting will review the performance of non-independent directors and the board as a whole; it will also review the performance of the chairperson of the company, taking into account the views of executive and non-executive directors and assess the quality, quantity and timeliness of flow of information between the board and the company management.

These two provisions of the schedule raise serious issues of independent and non-independent directors evaluating each other and are contrary to the scheme of independence sought by the Act. For the selection of independent directors, a data bank containing details of eligible and willing persons will be maintained by an association or institution that is notified by the central government. The companies are required to exercise due diligence when selecting a person from the data bank of independent directors. It will be necessary to examine who will operate the data bank as they will not be liable for breaches by selected persons. It is important to mention here that board independence has not led to improved corporate success or prevented mismanagement or fraud, and many such examples are already present in India.[7]

Putting reliance on what other countries including the USA and Great Britain have been following, it is submitted that India needs to consider the special characteristics of Indian companies, where not only every company matter is promoter-driven but some matters are only in the knowledge of promoters. There is no doubt that such provisions relating to independent directors would work in improving corporate governance in companies.

The second important institutional change is that of appointment of at least one female director in prescribed companies. The erstwhile Companies Act was silent on this point. The reform is in consonance with global practice of having gender diversity on boards. The sheer presence of a woman director has the effect of making others present act with considerably greater amounts of self-control and self-restraint. The enabling presence of women ensures that people put up more decent behaviour and conduct. Apart from that, there are likely to

---

7 D.C. Clarke, 'Three Concepts of the Independent Director' http://scholarship.law.gwu.edu/cgi/viewcontent.cgi?article=1045&context=faculty_publications (last accessed 5 June 2016).

be other quality benefits that are also attributable to gender diversity. Boards with a diverse perspective will definitely have balanced decision-making and will become more innovative and risk-bearing. This requirement was mandated for listed companies, although some companies still flout this rule.[8]

The third institutional change is that companies have to constitute a directors' nomination and remuneration committee, to consist of three or more non-executive directors out of which not less than half should be independent directors. The chairman of the company can be a member of such a committee but he cannot chair the committee. The committee has to identify persons qualified to become directors and who may be appointed at senior management positions. It has to formulate criteria for determining qualifications, positive attributes, recommend to the board their appointment, removal, evaluation of performance and remuneration policy for directors, key managerial personnel and other employees. One can see that a great deal of power has been given to such committees.

Remuneration paid to directors including independent directors has been a cause of concern after the Satyam scam, whereby in spite of high executive rewards, directors did not act responsibly, even though the provision for such a committee is made with the belief that it will control the tendency towards high executive rewards. However, it must be submitted here that since section 178 provides guidance to the committee that remuneration should be sufficient to attract, retain and motivate directors to run the company successfully, it may opt for high executive rewards.

The fourth important institutional contribution of the Companies Act 2013 is the statutory codification of directors' duties. This has happened for the first time in the history of company legislation in India. Earlier, directors' duties were a part of the evolution of common law on companies. Directors are now statutorily bound to act in accordance with the articles of association of the company, in good faith and in order to promote the objects of the company for the benefit of its members as a whole, as well as in the best interests of the company, employees, community and for the protection of the environment, to take due and reasonable care, skill and diligence and to exercise independent judgment. They have to avoid conflicts of interest with the company, either directly or indirectly, and should not achieve or even attempt to obtain any undue gain or advantage either to themselves or relatives etc and are not authorised to assign their office.

It is believed that this formulation of duties will bring about a greater degree in directors' working as people of probity, integrity, transparency and responsibility. These four concepts are not new to company law literature. Whilst probity and integrity are concerned with the moral aspects of directors' working, transparency is assured by disclosure. More disclosure requirements have been prescribed. Section 184(1) of the Companies Act 2013 provides that:

> Every director shall at the first meeting of the Board in which he participates as a director and thereafter at the first meeting of the Board in every financial year or whenever there is any change in the disclosures already made, then at the first Board meeting held after such change, disclose his concern or interest in any company or companies or bodies corporate, firms, or other association of individuals which shall include the shareholding, in such manner as may be prescribed.

---

8 '247 NSE firms miss Sebi deadline for appointing women directors', *Live Mint*, E paper (5 October 2015) http://www.livemint.com/Companies/FJAChH3O4hfWp47trh4CgN/Last-minute-dash-for-women-directors-as-India-enforces-deadl.html (last accessed 5 June 2016).

The Act requires that any director who is interested in a party with which the company is entering into a contract needs to specify his interest or concern explicitly. The scope of such a disclosure has been limited to the body corporate in which the director, individually or with other directors, holds more than 2 per cent shareholding of the body corporate or is a promoter, manager, chief executive officer of that body corporate or he is interested in a contract with a firm or entity in which such director is a partner, owner or member.

So far as the responsibility aspect is concerned, it is provided as a part of the contents of financial statement, that directors must make a statement of the way in which directors have fulfilled their responsibility. Financial statements have to give greater amount of disclosure than those contained earlier in the profit and loss account and balance sheet.

Section 195 of the Companies Act 2013 prohibits insider trading by any person, including any director or key managerial personnel of a company. Contravention is punishable under the section. The earlier Companies Act had no provision for controlling insider trading and such offences were referred under the Securities and Exchange Board of India (Insider Trading) Regulations 1992. Insider trading is a very common phenomenon in the Indian securities market[9] and, in order to curb such a tendency, the Insider Trading Regulations 2015 have been enforced, which along with provisions of the Companies Act 2013 may prove fruitful in this context.

Another important prohibition on directors and key managerial personnel of companies brought in by the new Companies Act is prohibition on forward dealings in securities of companies. A director or any of the key managerial personnel is prohibited to buy in the company or its holding, subsidiary or associate company a right to call for delivery or right to make delivery of a specified number of relevant shares or amount of relevant debentures at a specified price within a specified time. They are also prohibited to buy a right, as they may elect, to call for delivery or right to make delivery of a specified number of relevant shares or amount of relevant debentures at a specified price within a specified time. Contravention of this provision is punishable and securities acquired in contravention will have to be surrendered by the director or key managerial personnel concerned. Although such provisions are welcome, it is not clear just how much benefit they will accrue; these will have to be time-tested.

It is also necessary here to discuss that the scope of the expression 'officer who is in default' has been widened by the new Act. An officer of the company who is in default is liable to any penalty or punishment by way of imprisonment, fine or otherwise. An 'officer who is in default' includes not only full-time directors but also key managerial personnel, the chief financial officer, and directors aware of default through participation in board meetings or receiving minutes of the meeting are also included. Companies generally have been granting ceremonial positions to persons who are not actually much concerned with the affairs of companies.

The previous Companies Act also used the expression 'officer who is in default' for serious defaults. The purpose of such a provision has been to make liable those persons who fall under the expression 'officer who is in default' without any further enquiry. It has been the experience that in actual practice it is very difficult to find the person in charge of an act in

9 K. Machado (2014), 'Why It's Hard to Catch India's Insider Trading' (21 April 2014) http:// blogs.wsj.com/indiarealtime/2014/04/21/why-is-it-tough-to-catch-insider-trading-in-india/ (last accessed 5 June 2016).

respect of which the default is being committed.[10] Therefore, widening the scope and bringing more persons under the expression will, it seems, be beneficial.

Disclosures

The third important development is about different disclosures that a company will have to make. The new Act registers a change in philosophy from a control-based regime to a disclosure-based regime.[11] First, we will discuss the most important provision, which is about disclosure of related party transactions (RPTs). A 'related party' for a company means a director, a key managerial person or their relatives, a firm in which a director, a manager or his relative is a partner or a director or a private company in which a director or manager is director or manager, a public company in which a director or manager is a director or holds more than 2 per cent of its paid-up share capital with his relatives, any body corporate whose board or managing director or manager is accustomed to act according to the advice, instructions or directions of the director or manager.

In addition to them, any person on whose advice, directions or instructions a director or manager is accustomed to act, any holding, subsidiary or an associate company of such company along with a subsidiary of a holding company to which it is also a subsidiary and other prescribed persons also fall under the definition of related party. Consent of the board by a resolution is required for related party transactions and section 188 of the Companies Act 2013 includes the following contracts or arrangements:

- sale, purchase or supply of any goods or materials
- selling or otherwise disposing of, or buying, property of any kind
- leasing of property of any kind
- availing or rendering of any services
- appointment of any agent for purchase or sale of goods, materials, services or property
- such related party's appointment to any office or place of profit in the company, its subsidiary company or associate company and
- underwriting the subscription of any securities or derivatives of the company.

The network of contractual arrangements has been widened by the Act as it now includes arrangements such as leasing, selling or otherwise disposing of property. The Companies Act 1956 did not use the term related party transactions (RPTs) but section 297 of the earlier Act has been considered as a precursor to the present section. It is obvious that the definition of RPTs is provided to control and regulate such transactions and to protect the interest of investors. Under the new Act there is no requirement of obtaining central government's approval. By the Companies (Amendment) Act of 2015, the requirement of prior approval by special resolution of the company for RPTs has also been changed to ordinary resolution of the company owing to the difficulties faced by the companies in passing a special resolution for all such transactions.

---

10 A. Singh (2014), *Introduction to Company Law* (11th edn, Eastern Book Company) 114–115.
11 PWC Report (2013), 'Enhancing Governance with Companies Act 2013' http://www.pwc.in/
en_IN/in/assets/pdfs/forensic-news-alerts/news-alert-enhancing-governance-with-companies-act-2013.pdf (last accessed 5 June 2016).

Now only an ordinary resolution of the company is required for approval of RPTs. However, the consent of the board and the requirement for a resolution is not required in cases where the transaction entered into by the company is in the ordinary course of business of the company and is on an arm's length basis. Severe consequences of non-compliance have been provided by the Act. Every RPT has to be disclosed to shareholders in the board's report and accounts, along with the justification of such contract or arrangement.

It is believed that widening the network contractual arrangements will help in improving financial statements of companies and offer a clear indication of actual profit and loss for a company. However, concerns have been raised about the possibility of subjectivity in defining arm's length transactions and consumption of extra time in the entire process of approval. It is necessary to mention here that terms of reference of audit committees, which every listed and other prescribed companies have to constitute, include approval or any subsequent modification of transactions of the company with related parties. In addition to this, independent directors are also duty bound by Schedule IV to pay sufficient attention and ensure that adequate deliberations are held before approving related party transactions and assure themselves that the same are in the interests of the company.

These two provisions, along with section 188 and the narrowed down definition of 'relative', may prove to be helpful in improving corporate governance in companies. It should also be mentioned here that directors in addition to RPTs are also duty bound to disclose their interest to the board in transactions in which they are personally interested under section 166 of the Companies Act 2013. This was a common law duty and directors were held liable where they did not disclose their interest under the earlier Companies Act following common law.

Other important disclosures that are required to be made include disclosure of shareholding pattern of the company in the annual returns filed by the company under section 92 of the Companies Act 2013. Every prospectus issued by the company should disclose in the statement of the board of directors the unutilised public money, i.e. money raised in previous issues, if any, which has not been used by the company and the sources of promoters' contribution in the current issue under section 26 of the Companies Act 2013. A financial statement is required to disclose compulsory consolidation of accounts, along with summary statements of subsidiary companies, associate companies and joint ventures, if any, under section 129 of the Companies Act 2013. Along with the financial statement, a report of the board of directors is required to be attached under section 134 of the Companies Act 2013.

This report, along with routine matters, should also disclose material changes and commitments in the financial position of the company, development and implementation of the risk management policy, policy for corporate social responsibility during the year and the manner in which formal annual evaluation by the board of its performance and that of its committees and individual directors. The report of board with enhanced disclosures will surely work towards making boards more responsible towards shareholders. The new Companies Act has laid emphasis on proper risk management policy to be in place and charged directors for its disclosure.

Additionally, it has imposed a duty on independent directors under Schedule IV to help in bringing an independent judgment to bear on the board's deliberations, especially on certain issues including risk management. Similarly, the audit committee has to satisfy itself not only on the integrity of financial information but to see that financial control and the systems of risk management are robust and defensible under section 177. This is indeed a step towards improving corporate governance, with more transparency and checks.

An important part of the board's report of listed companies is the directors' responsibility statement, which should state what internal financial controls had been followed by the company and whether such controls are adequate and operating effectively. Internal financial controls are the policies and procedures adopted by the company for ensuring orderly and efficient conduct of business, including adherence to the company's policies, safeguarding its assets, prevention and detection of fraud and errors, accuracy and completeness of accounting records and timely preparation of reliable financial information. The scope of the expression 'internal financial controls' has been expanded by the new Act. It now covers all aspects of operations of a company. In addition to all this, the responsibility system also has to report whether the proper system for ensuring compliance of all laws has been devised and inform on its adequacy and effectiveness.

This is an additional disclosure as the earlier Companies Act did not include such disclosures in the directors' responsibility statement. In order to make the process effective, auditors and the audit committee have been involved in the process. The audit committee to be constituted under section 177 is mandated to evaluate internal financial controls and risk management systems. The auditors under section 144 have to report to shareholders in general meeting whether the company has adequate internal financial controls systems in place and also on the operating effectiveness of such controls. This is a step towards more transparency, which may be effective in improving governance of companies by their directors.

Audit of companies

The fourth contemporary development is related to audit of companies. Section 138 of the Companies Act 2013 provides that prescribed classes of companies have to appoint an internal auditor who will conduct an internal audit of functions and activities of the company and provide a report to the board of directors of the company. Section 139 provides for the appointment of auditors. An auditor can be an individual or a firm. A listed company and other prescribed companies cannot appoint or reappoint an individual as an auditor for more than one term of five consecutive years and a firm of auditors for more than two terms of five consecutive years. An individual auditor who has completed his one term of five years is not eligible for reappointment in the same company for five years from the completion of his term.

The same disqualification applies to an audit firm which has a common partner or partners with another audit firm whose tenure has expired. Therefore, mandatory rotation of auditors has been provided for listed and prescribed classes of companies. Section 144 of the Companies Act 2013 has placed restrictions on the rendering of specified non-audit services by an auditor to the company in which he is appointed as an auditor. The auditor will provide only such other services in addition to the core function of auditing that are approved by the board or the audit committee. Excluded services include accounting and book-keeping services, internal audit, design and implementation of any financial information system, actuarial services, investment advisory and banking services, the rendering of outsourced financial services, management services and other prescribed services.

Such a provision has been added to ensure independence and accountability of the auditors. Such provisions ensuring independence of auditors and restrictions on tenure of auditors were absent in the earlier Act. Auditors were appointed by the company on the recommendation of the board of directors and their working for the company on instructions of the board can be best exemplified by the famous Satyam scam in India.[12]

Section 177 of the Companies Act 2013 mandates the constitution of an audit committee for all listed and prescribed companies which shall consist of a minimum of three directors with independent directors forming a majority. Special provisions relating to an audit committee include calling for the comments of auditors about internal control systems and the scope of audit including observations of auditors and a review of the financial statement. Much reliance has been placed on audit committees by the new Companies Act. It must be noted such committees were also required to be constituted under the earlier Companies Act for prescribed companies but their performance has not been successful in putting expected checks in place.

Under section 292A of the Companies Act 1956, the audit committees were required to have discussions with the auditors periodically about internal control systems, the scope of audit including the observations of the auditors and to review the half yearly and annual financial statements before submission to the board and also ensure compliance of internal control systems. The recommendations of the audit committee on any matter relating to financial management including the audit report were binding on the board. If the board did not accept any of its recommendations, it had to record the reasons for not accepting any recommendation and was mandated to communicate such reasons to the shareholders. The only important change in the new Companies Act is that terms of reference for audit committees have now been provided by section 177(4), which include the following:

(i)   the recommendation for appointment, remuneration and terms of appointment of auditors of the company
(ii) review and monitor the auditor's independence and performance, and effectiveness of audit process
(iii) examination of the financial statement and the auditors' report thereon
(iv) approval of any subsequent modification of transactions of the company with related parties
(v)   scrutiny of inter-corporate loans and investments
(vi) valuation of undertakings or assets of the company, wherever it is necessary
(vii) evaluation of internal financial controls and risk management systems
(viii) monitoring the end use of funds raised through public offers and related matters.

All important areas have been brought within the terms of reference for audit companies, which should lead to greater reliability under the Companies Act of audit committees.

The same section further provides that every listed and prescribed company should lead to greater vigilance on the part of directors and employees in leading them to report genuine concerns. This mechanism will provide adequate safeguards against victimisation of persons who use the so-called "vigil" mechanism for reporting and will make provision for direct access to the chairperson of the audit committee in appropriate and exceptional cases. This is a new provision and it has to be seen whether such a mechanism will actually be workable in family-run companies in India.

12 H. Kaur (2012), 'Corporate Fraud: Auditors' and Managerial Liability' in K.T. Caliyurt and S.O. Idowu, *Emerging Fraud: Fraud Cases from Emerging Economies* (Berlin: Springer, 2012) 115.

Section 132 of the Companies Act 2013 provides for establishment of the National Financial Regulatory Authority (NFRA) to provide for auditing and accounting standards. This will be established by the central government and will make recommendations to it on the formulation and accounting and auditing policies for companies and their auditors. It is necessary to mention here that the Institute of Chartered Accountants of India is the authority which has been the regulatory body for the auditing profession in India. There has been a debate as to the need of such a new institution as it will lead to overlapping of roles performed by it with the already existing institution with regard to disciplinary matters. It is recommended that such an institution should be established to function as an oversight body without any jurisdictional conflict or overlap.[13]

Corporate social responsibility

The fifth new development relates to corporate social responsibility of companies. India became the first country to mandate companies for spending towards corporate social responsibility after debates for years. Under section 135 of the Companies Act 2013, every company having a net worth of INR 500 crore (5 billion) or more, or turnover of INR 1000 crore (10 billion) or more, or a net profit of INR 5 crore (50 million) or more is required to constitute a corporate social responsibility committee (CSR committee). This committee will consist of three or more directors, at least one of whom should be an independent director. The committee will formulate and recommend to the board the CSR policy to indicate the activities to be undertaken by the company and the amount of expenditure to be involved and it will also monitor the policy.

The board of every such company has to ensure that the company spends at least 3 per cent of the average net profits of the company made during three immediately preceding financial years. In seeking to enhance disclosure to shareholders, under the CSR policy, the board is required to specify the reasons in its report for not spending the recommended amount of CSR expenditure in case the company was unable to spend the whole amount. It is necessary for the company to give preference for the local area and areas around the place where it operates for spending the earmarked CSR amount. It was the expectation that companies would spend about 15,000 crore towards CSR in the first year. However, initial reports indicate that about half of this amount may actually be spent.[14]

It is reported that nearly two-thirds of the top listed companies have failed to spend the minimum 2 per cent of profits on social responsibility activities in the first year.[15] It has been reported that out of 50 listed companies of Nifty Index 48 companies spent a combined amount of INR 4252, which is 1.6 per cent of the stand-alone net profit for the financial year 2015.[16]

13 'Constitution of National Financial Reporting Authority, Significant Development Concerning Profession' http://www.icai.org/new_post.html?post_id=11583 (last accessed 5 June 2016).

14 R. Arora (2015), 'Panel on corporate social responsibility assessment to submit report next month', ET Bureau, *The Economic Times* (5 June 2015) http://economictimes.indiatimes.com/news/economy/policy/panel-on-corporate social-responsibility-assessment-to-submit-report-next-month/articleshow/47548287.cms (last accessed 5 June 2016).

15 'CSR regime begins on disappointing note; two-third companies miss target', *The Economic Times* (2015) http://articles.economictimes.indiatimes.com/2015-07-12/news/64333921_1_csr-committee-annual-csr-report-csr-work (last accessed 5 June 2016).

16 K.K. Somvanshi (2015), 'India Inc beats Mr Scrooge hands down in art of giving', *The Economic Times* (30 September 2015) http://epaperbeta.timesofindia.com/Article.aspx?eid=31818&articlexml=India-Inc-Beats-Mr-Scrooge-Hands-Down-in-30092015001072 (last accessed 5 June 2016).

The Indian Government has set up a panel for improved monitoring of social welfare activities undertaken by companies through mandated CSR spending.

Loans and investments

The sixth thematic development is in the area of loans and investments. Companies have been freed from the shackles of control of central government for inter-corporate loans and investments. No approval of the central government is required now; only an internal control mechanism is applicable. Boards have been authorised to invest or advance up to 60 per cent of paid-up share capital, free reserves and securities premium account or 100 per cent of their free reserves and securities premium account, whichever is more, with their own decision and beyond that they need approval of shareholders through a special resolution. The following transactions are covered under section 186(2) of the Companies Act 2013:

(a) loans to any person or other body corporate
(b) guarantee or security in connection with loans to any other body corporate or person and
(c) acquiring securities of any body corporate by subscription, purchase or otherwise.

The new provision provides that, unless otherwise prescribed, a company has to make investments through not more than two layers of investment companies to increase corporate transparency. Under the erstwhile Companies Act, companies were allowed to make investments through multiple layers of investment companies in multiple sectors. Now it will not be possible through the means of investment companies. This requirement will not affect a company from acquiring any other company incorporated outside India if such other company has investment subsidiaries beyond two layers in accordance with the law of its country. It will also not affect a subsidiary company from having any investment subsidiary for the purposes of meeting the requirements under any law or rules or regulations framed under any law for the time being in force.

The new provision is applicable to both public and private companies. The erstwhile Companies Act under section 372A restricted loans to any other body corporate, whereas section 186 of the new Act restricts loans to any person or other body corporate. Therefore, loans even to individuals are restricted. The company is required to disclose all such loans, investments, guarantees or security in the financial statement to shareholders.

It further provides that any company which is registered under section 12 of the Securities and Exchange Board of India Act 1992 and covered under a prescribed class or classes is not authorised to take inter-corporate loans or deposits exceeding the prescribed limit. Such a company will have to furnish in its financial statement the details of the loan or deposits. No loan is to be given at a rate of interest lower than the prevailing yield of one year, three year, five year or ten year government security closest to the tenor of the loan. Any company who has defaulted in repayment or payment of interest is not allowed to give any loan or guarantee, provide security or make any acquisition whilst such default subsists.

When it comes to loans to directors etc, section 185(1) of the Companies Act 2013 provides that a company can neither advance any loan (including a loan represented by a book debt) nor give any security in connection with the loan to a director or person in whom a director is interested. Lending of money by a company to its directors has been strictly regulated by the section. Loans to directors are not allowed in the following cases:

(a) loans to the directors of the company or to those of its holding company or to any partner or relative of the director
(b) loans to any firm in which such director or his relative is a partner
(c) loans to any private company of which any such director is a director or member
(d) loans to a body corporate at whose general meeting any such director or directors control 25 per cent of voting power
(e) loans to a body corporate whose board of directors, managing director or manager is accustomed to act in accordance with the instructions or directions of the board or any director of the lending company.

An exception is carved out in favour of managing or full-time directors, such that the restriction will not be applicable if the loan is given either as a part of service conditions extended to all employees of the company or under any scheme approved by the members by a special resolution. This provision does not apply to a company which in the ordinary course of its business provides loans, guarantees or securities for due repayment of any loan at an interest rate not less than the bank rate declared by the Reserve Bank of India.

Another noteworthy provision is under section 67 of the new Companies Act, read with section 232, which prohibits companies from creating and keeping treasury stocks in any form, either by creating trusts or buying shares in their own name. During amalgamations companies are now restricted from having treasury stocks. Only fully paid-up shares can be purchased by a company for the benefit of its employees through the means of a trust. The old Companies Act allowed companies to create such treasury stocks, which carried voting rights and generally were controlled by promoters of companies.

Investor protection

The seventh important development is meant for investor protection. The first major development is the right to have class action suits under section 245 of the Companies Act 2013, which has filled the existing procedural lacunae. This was a much-awaited development as shareholders who suffered corporate scams did not have the right to file class action suits. Class action suits may be filed by the requisite number of members and depositors or any class of them if, in their opinion, the management or the affairs of the company is being conducted in a manner prejudicial to the interests of the company or its members or depositors. The application can be filed before the National Company Law Tribunal (NCLT) and can include a claim for damages, compensation or any suitable action against the company, directors, auditors, any expert, adviser or consultant.

A few other rights in the form of exit options are given to shareholders by the new Companies Act. Such opportunities add to shareholders' democracy and freedom. Section 13 of the Companies Act 2013, which provides for alteration of the memorandum makes a special provision for dissenting shareholders. It provides that a company that still has un-utilised funds from the amount raised from the public through the issue of prospectus shall not change its objects for which the money was raised from the public unless a special resolution is passed. If some shareholders do not agree to such a change they should be given an opportunity to exit the company. Dissenting shareholders should be provided this opportunity by the promoters and shareholders having control over the company in accordance with regulations to be specified by the Securities and Exchange Board of India.

Section 27 of the Companies Act 2013 provides an exit opportunity for dissenting shareholders when a variation in terms of contract or objects in the prospectus is proposed by the company. A company can vary the terms of a contract referred to in the prospectus or objects for which the prospectus was issued with a special resolution in general meeting. Dissenting shareholders are required to be provided an exit offer by promoters or controlling shareholders at the exit price, in a manner and with conditions specified by the Securities and Exchange Board of India by regulation.

The purchase of minority shareholdings in cases involving mergers and acquisitions is delayed by section 236 of the Companies Act 2013. It provides that any acquirer becoming the registered holder of 90 per cent or more of the issued equity share capital of a company or a person who holds 90 per cent of the issued share capital of a company may notify the company of his intention to buy the remaining equity shares. The acquirer may hold a shareholding of 90 per cent with persons acting in concert with him or there may be a person or group of persons involved. The offer should be made at a price determined on the basis of valuation undertaken by a registered valuer in accordance with the rules. Minority shareholders may also offer their shares to majority shareholders to purchase their shares at the price determined on the basis of valuation undertaken by a registered valuer in accordance with the rules.

In order to follow best global practices, shareholder participation in decision-making is being increased by the new Companies Act to strengthen corporate accountability by providing more information in the financial statements.

Establishment of new tribunals

The eighth thematic development is in the form of provision for the establishment of institutions such as the National Company Law Tribunal (NCLT), the National Company Appellate Tribunal (NCLAT) and special courts. Special courts can try offences punishable under the Companies Act 2013 with imprisonment for two years or more after the amendments by the Companies (Amendment) Act 2015. The Amending Act provides that all other offences are to be tried by a metropolitan magistrate or a judicial magistrate of first class, which is the lowest Indian court.

The Act has also provided for the establishment of a serious fraud investigation office, which will consist of experts from different fields and the central government by order will assign it to investigate the affairs of any company. The NCLT and NCLAT have been constituted by the Central Government with effect from 1 June 2016. All corporate disputes will now be filed before the NCLT and appeals will lie with NCLAT. Before the constitution of NCLT, disputes were raised before the Company Law Board constituted under the old Companies Act and appeals went to High Courts designated for dealing with company matters. The Company Law Board has now been dissolved. The Indian Government took a great deal of time in constituting the NCLT and NCLAT. It must also be mentioned here that the old Companies Act also provided for the constitution of NCLT but the constitutionality of such an institution had been under challenge.

Mergers and acquisitions

The ninth thematic development relates to mergers, especially cross-border mergers. Under section 234 of the Companies Act 2013, a foreign company may with the prior approval of the Reserve Bank of India merge into a company registered under the Companies Act 2013, or vice versa. A fast-track mechanism exists for mergers or amalgamations between two or more small companies or between a holding and its wholly-owned subsidiary companies and other prescribed classes of companies. Provisions relating to mergers and acquisitions have not been enforced to date as there has been no clarity as to the role of the Reserve Bank of India in the process. The old Companies Act provided for mergers of an Indian company with a foreign company only.

There are certain miscellaneous provisions worth noting, namely the insertion of a chapter on revival and rehabilitation of sick companies in the Act, new definitions for matters relating to raising of funds by companies, procedures for board meetings including participation through video-conferencing or audio visual methods. In cases where no independent director is present in a board meeting, decisions taken at the meeting must be circulated to all directors and only become final on ratification by at least one independent director.

The Companies (Amendment) Act 2015 has done away with the minimum paid-up capital requirements for incorporating private as well as public companies in India and the use of the common seal has also been made optional. All documents which required affixing the common seal can now be signed by two directors or one director and a company secretary of the company. No documents for commencement of business are required to be filed with the registrar of companies.

The new Companies Act 2013 has been the subject of much debate since the day it entered into force. It was expected to improve corporate governance, enhance accountability on the part of companies, directors and auditors, and to provide more protection to investors by increasing transparency through disclosures. More importantly, it was expected to be a business-friendly piece of legislation, although this does not seem to be wholly the case. There are many provisions that are not workable. There is more control now with the central government and penalty provisions have been added in almost every section. However, the Act seems to be more of a penal statute rather than a business-friendly one.

The counter-argument has been that penalties have a deterrent effect and that companies will now be more law-abiding and compliance-oriented. It is submitted here that Indian companies are characterised by family-run businesses and concentrated ownership. Companies are family-managed, family-run and are under family supervision and governance. Effective corporate governance is only possible with provisions that can work in companies with such special characteristics.

Bibliography

Analysis of Companies Act 2013, Wolters Kluwer (India) Pvt Ltd.

Arora, R. (2015) 'Panel on CSR Assessment to submit Report next month', *The Economic Times* (5 June 2015).

Kaur, H., 'Promoters, Corporate Governance and the Companies Act 2013', working paper presented at Corporate Law Teachers' Association (CLTA) Annual Conference in Melbourne Law School, University of Melbourne (February 2015).

Kaur, H. (2012), 'Corporate Fraud: Auditors' and Managerial Liability' in K.T. Caliyurt and S.O. Idowu, *Emerging Fraud: Fraud Cases from Emerging Economies* (Berlin: Springer, 2012) 115.

'Lok Sabha passes amendments to Companies Act to improve business climate' (17 December 2014) http://www.businesstoday.in/current/policy/lok-sabha-approves-passes-amendments-to-companies-act/story/213616.html.

'Rajya Sabha passes changes in Companies Act' (13 May 2015) *The Hindu* http://www.thehindu.com/news/national/rajya-sabha-passes-changes-in-companies-act/article7201967.ece (last accessed 5 June 2016).

'Remaking of Companies Act 2013', *The Economic Times* (4 June 2015).

Singh, A. (2014) *Company Law* (11th edn, Eastern Book Company).

Zachariah, R. (2014) 'Sebi mulls five – Board cap for Independent directors', *The Economic Times* (10 January 2014).

Websites

http://www.mca.gov.in/MinistryV2/companiesact.html (last accessed 5 June 2016).

http://www.mca.gov.in/Ministry/pdf/CompaniesAct2013.pdf (last accessed 5 June 2016).

13

Company law and corporate governance in Malaysia

Harmonisation of *Shariah* and the common law

Aiman Nariman Mohd-Sulaiman and Shanthy Rachagan

1 Introduction

The last two decades have seen prolific company law reform and corporate governance transformation internationally. The changes have been attributed to various factors ranging from changes to shareholding demographics, the growth and impact of technology on corporate law and practice to new business and investment models. An added dimension to corporate law and governance reform is the growth of Islamic capital markets and the Islamic financial services industry. This development has intensified interest about *Shariah* principles in commerce, particularly its interaction with conventional company law and practice.

This chapter analyses how and to what extent *Shariah* principles in commerce are considered in modern company law within a common law jurisdiction. The analysis is posited within the legal and regulatory framework of Malaysia, which has a strong common law tradition but has developed Islamic commercial law in parallel with the common law as exemplified in its Islamic capital market and Islamic financial services sector.

Malaysia is a prime example of a jurisdiction that has successfully applied *Shariah* principles alongside conventional common law in relation to the capital market. The market capitalisation of *Shariah*-compliant securities in 2014 stood at RM1.01 trillion or 61.3 per cent of total market capitalisation of the stock exchange, which was worth RM1.65 trillion (Securities Commission 2014). Similar to the equity market, Malaysia's bond market also comprises conventional and *sukuk* or *Shariah*-compliant bonds. The *sukuk* market consists of Islamic debt securities which are structured to comply with *Shariah* principles of which a primary principle is prohibiting the charging of *riba'* or usury.[1]

---

1 *Sukuk* are certificates of equal value that represent an undivided interest (proportional to the investor's interest) in the ownership of an underlying asset (both tangible and intangible), usufruct, services or investments in particular projects or special investment activities.

Malaysia's bond market, which accounted for 58.5 per cent of total corporate financing, is increasingly popular as an alternative to bank borrowings (International Monetary Fund 2013a). Internationally, Malaysia has the largest *sukuk* market in the world for 2013, accounting for 58.8 per cent of global *sukuk* outstanding and 69 per cent of *sukuk* issuances, with a value of US$148 billion worth of *sukuk* outstanding as at Q3 2012 (Securities Commission 2013). In 2014, corporate *sukuk* issuances represented 76.1 per cent of total private debt securities issuances, whilst corporate *sukuk* outstanding accounted for 70.4 per cent of total private debt securities outstanding (Securities Commission 2014).

The chapter also includes some discussion regarding the Islamic financial services sector in Malaysia, which has been developed alongside the Islamic capital market. The Islamic financial services industry is currently estimated to be worth about US$1.1 trillion (Ernst & Young 2012). Whilst this is less than 1 per cent of global financial assets, the industry has expanded at an average rate of 14.1 per cent per annum over the past decade, and is expected to grow further to US$1.8 trillion by 2016.

The growth and progress of these two sectors are interconnected. The Islamic financial sector, particularly Islamic banking, has been a precursor to the establishment of a robust Islamic capital market, which also owes its depth and liquidity to the comprehensive and wide range of Islamic finance products. Demand for new or alternative products is spurred by the growth of the capital market, particularly from asset and fund management companies, as well as pension funds looking for alternative products to diversify their investment portfolios.

The total Islamic financial assets in Malaysia, which stood at US$272.5 billion as at the end of 2011, comprised *sukuk* (outstanding US$107 billion), Islamic banking assets (US$105.5 billion), Islamic fund assets (US$11.8 billion) and *Takaful* assets (US$5.3 billion) (Mahmood, 2013). The financial sector is the main issuer of conventional bonds and bonds issued by financial institutions accounted for 33 per cent of the total RM335.7 billion of corporate bonds (conventional and *sukuk*) issues (International Monetary Fund, 2013b).[2]

The rise of more ethical investment and socially responsible investing has also contributed to the growth of investments in shariah-compliant or Islamic-compliant investments. Islamic-compliant investments operate on the basis of a value-based system that primarily aims at ensuring moral and material well-being of the individual and society as a whole (Siddiqi 2000). This seems to resonate with ethical investors who are very concerned that their investments are channelled into ethical investments of which *Shariah*-compliant securities is a sub-set. From the governance perspective, much of the *Shariah* governance reform occurs within the Islamic financial services industry. Owing to the financial institutions being corporate bodies, the transformation has several implications for company law.

2 Legal landscape and institutional structure

The primary laws for the capital market in Malaysia are the Companies Act 1965 and the Capital Markets and Services Act 2007 (CMSA 2007). The Companies Act 1965 was the result of recommendations and review conducted by a committee established by the

---

2 Ibrahim M. and Wong, A. in 'The corporate bond market in Malaysia' www.bis.org/publ/bppdf/bispap26p.pdf (last accessed 5 June 2016), where they stated that: 'In 2004, companies from the construction and utilities sectors were the main PDS issuers, raising 31.5% and 28.0% of total funds, respectively. Issuers from these sectors are the country's major infrastructure developers, water authorities and independent power producers, all of whom require long-term and flexible financing'.

Ministry of Commerce and Industry in October 1963. The committee's recommendations were primarily based on the UK Companies Act 1948, the Australian Uniform Companies Act 1961 and law reform reports of the UK Cohen Committee 1945, Jenkins Committee 1962 and the Gower Report 1961. Prior to 1965, the applicable company legislation was the various laws applied to the Straits Settlements, the Federated Malay States and the Unfederated Malay States, with their respective company laws. These were also largely based on the development of English company law.

Owing to the historical origin of the Companies Act 1965, decisions from the UK courts and Australian courts have been either binding or highly influential in interpreting the corresponding Malaysian statutory provisions. The Companies Act 1965 is therefore deeply rooted in the common law. In 2015, the government introduced the Companies Bill 2015, intended to replace the Companies Act 1965. The Bill was passed by Parliament in mid-2016. The new Companies Act 2016 retains the present deference to the common law.

The Capital Markets and Services Act 2007 (CMSA 2007) applies to capital raising activities of a public company and contains provisions dealing with market misconduct offences and enforcement mechanisms, including investor protection provisions.[3] These two main corporate and capital market laws are administered by two regulatory authorities. The Malaysian Companies Act 1965 falls within the purview of the Companies Commission of Malaysia (CCM), whilst the CMSA 2007 is administered and enforced by the Securities Commission (SC). The SC's regulatory and supervisory functions include the supervision of market institutions such as exchanges, clearing houses and central depositories, the issue of securities, takeovers and mergers, unit trust schemes, the designation of futures markets and the registration of market participants.[4]

As the single regulatory body for the capital market, it had the responsibility to promote the development of the capital market, to streamline the regulation of the securities market and to facilitate the processing and approval of corporate transactions. However, some aspects of the rule-making power is shared by the SC with Bank Negara Malaysia (BNM), i.e. the Central Bank, particularly in relation to debt securities.

At first glance, these capital market laws do not contain any statutory provisions referring to *Shariah* principles and practices. However, the regulatory approach in general is to rely less on *legislative* intervention and more on industry-driven and practice-based reform. In the initial stages of the Islamic capital market's development, there were steps taken to identify points of convergence and divergence between the Companies Act 1965 with *Shariah* principles. At this point, reliance was placed on expert groups to consider the harmonisation of *Shariah* law within the conventional legal system.

These consultative meetings and deliberations were conducted by BNM and the SC. Whilst BNM considered a wide range of laws to ascertain their compatibility with the *Shariah*, the Securities Commission took a more concentrated approach by considering

---

3 The CMSA 2007 was introduced for the purpose of replacing and consolidating various laws that were then used to regulate the capital market. These were the Securities Industry Act 1983 (SIA 1983) and Futures Industry Act 1993 (FIA 1993). The CMSA 2007 consolidates the Securities Industry Act 1983, Futures Industry Act 1993 and Pt IV of the Securities Commission Act 1993, which deals with fundraising activities. It is enforced by the main capital market regulator, i.e., the Securities Commission.

4 The SC, which absorbed the functions of the Capital Issue Committee (CIC), the Panel on Takeovers and Mergers (TOP) and some of the previous functions of the ROC, began operating on 1 March 1993 and is accountable to the Minister of Finance.

the compatibility of company law and capital market law with Islamic commercial law. However, the approach of BNM and the SC was largely similar and that was to move away from mere academic discussion and enable a functioning Islamic capital market where investors can trade *Shariah*-compliant securities and avail themselves of the same level of investor protection found in the conventional capital market. In 2010, the Law Harmonisation Committee was established under the auspices of BNM to formalise harmonisation initiatives.[5]

A major concern then was the relative inexperience of regulators to deal with the Islamic commercial law concepts and practices and the Islamic law experts' lack of exposure to sophisticated market operations and needs. The shariah-compliant nature of Islamic products and business operations is the cornerstone of the Islamic capital market and Islamic financial services sector (Chapra and Ahmed 2002). Theoretically, the risk of fraud or excessive risk-taking should be minimised in an environment where accountability to a higher order is the norm, as in the case of the Islamic capital market and Islamic financial services sector. However, the reality is that Islamic norms which had become internalized within Muslim society during the early period of Islam may not be apparent or observed in today's society (Chapra 2007).

There is also the risk of human error, owing to directors' incompetence and lack of skill, particularly in an environment where financial and capital market products become more complex and the business environment becomes more competitive. Opinions on what structures and products are and are not shariah-compliant can also diverge (Hainsworth 2007). This may lead to 'expert shopping' and to 'forum shopping'. Issuers may choose to offer products in markets with less strict regulations, enabling the institutions to exert leverage on products or investments, which would otherwise be considered less shariah-compliant or even divert funds into non-shariah-compliant investments. The behaviour of experts advising on *Shariah* matters can also change from rather restrictive in an effort to maintain the origins and uniqueness of Islamic finance to more permissive, more focused on the demand side and motivated by the need to ensure better returns to shareholders (Alman 2013).

During the initial stages, industry consultations and continuous engagement between the regulators, expert groups and industry practitioners were instrumental in resolving these concerns and other legal and regulatory issues. A significant outcome of these efforts was the establishment of the Shariah Advisory Council (SAC) in 1996 by the SC, in the exercise of its power under section 18 of the Securities Commission Act 1993. The SAC's establishment was primarily to advise the SC on *Shariah*-related matters in the Islamic capital market and to provide guidance on various transactions and activities in the Islamic capital market. On the Islamic finance side, the Shariah Advisory Council of BNM was established in 1997 as an advisory council. The Central Bank of Malaysia Act 1958 was amended in 2003 to enhance the role of the SAC, where the SAC of BNM shall be the authority for the ascertainment of Islamic law for the purposes of Islamic banking business, *Takaful* business, Islamic financial business.

The establishment of the respective SACs by the SC and BNM enables the regulators to deal with concerns regarding reputational risks and moral hazard. However, the fact that there are two SACs has been identified as a cause for concern, particularly since there is a need to ensure consistency in *Shariah* resolutions (Thani and others 2010: 357). Nonetheless,

---

5 The Law Harmonisation Committee Report 2013 http://www.bnm.gov.my/documents/2013/ BNM_LHC_Report_2013.pdf (last accessed 5 June 2016).

the risk of conflicting opinions is minimised because a majority of the members of the SAC of SC are also members of the SAC of BNM. This may not be the optimal solution and has led to a recommendation to consolidate these two SACs (ibid: 376).

Owing to the continuous efforts to harmonise the common law with *Shariah* in the area of commerce, as noted earlier, regulators were clearly aware that some arrangements and transactions in the capital market were incompatible with *Shariah* principles in commerce. To address compatibility concerns, SAC of the SC identified criteria for shariah-compliant securities, i.e. shares and *sukuk* or Islamic bonds, which comply with *Shariah* principles in terms of the company's primary business and investment activities. Shares that were traded on the stock market were then appraised against these criteria before being designated as such. The list of *Shariah*-compliant securities has since then been issued and published by the SAC and reviewed periodically, enabling investors to make their investment decisions based on the list.

The latest updated list, which took effect on 28 November 2014, featured a total of 673 *Shariah*-compliant securities. The list included 40 newly classified *Shariah*-compliant securities and excluded 30 from the previous list issued in May 2014 (Securities Commission 2014). In Malaysia, the screening method is centralised at the SAC level and is conducted twice yearly. The SAC also conducts *Shariah* review for securities to be listed on the stock exchange. Apart from the general *Shariah* principles (discussed below), the SAC adopts a two-tier quantitative approach, which applies the business activity benchmarks and financial ratio benchmarks.

Malaysia has also taken a bold step to standardise the criteria of *Shariah*-compliant products, which can be viewed as an attempt to codify Islamic commercial contracts. This is being conducted by BNM by issuing guidelines identifying types of Islamic financial contracts or transactions and the criteria that these transactions must fulfil for these 'contracts' to be *Shariah*-compliant. As of 2015, five of these have now been adopted: *Murabahah*, *Mudharabah*, *Musyarakah*, *Tawarruq* and *Istisna*, whilst several others are under discussion.

These efforts enabled the regulators to deal with the rising demand for Islamic products and investments. Existing conventional products were evaluated and then modified and any prohibited elements were removed if they were incompatible with *Shariah*. New products were benchmarked against various *Shariah* principles to facilitate new product development (OICD-IOISCO 2004). It could be said that regulators were perceptive that, as the Islamic capital market becomes more developed, the appraisal of product compatibility will need to be made quickly, for which the legislative process is ill-suited.

Malaysia's approach was also to utilise existing institutional structure in so far as these do not clearly contradict *Shariah* principles. During the early stages of the Islamic capital market's development, Malaysia already had in place a fully functioning and relatively well developed stock exchange with the facilities for listing and trading of securities and price settlement mechanisms and payment facilities. During this initial stage, the basic infrastructure of the stock exchange in facilitating listing and trading of securities was evaluated and considered suitable for shariah-compliant securities. The stock market henceforth enabled the listing of shariah-compliant securities.

In 2007, the FTSE Bursa Malaysia Hijrah Shariah Index and the FTSE Bursa Malaysia EMAS Shariah Index were launched, with the FTSE Bursa Malaysia Small Cap Shariah Index being launched subsequently. At the end of December 2014, *Shariah*-compliant securities constituted 74.3 per cent of the 906 listed securities on the Bursa Malaysia, making it the world's largest exchange in terms of *Shariah*-compliant equities. (Bursa Malaysia 2014; Securities Commission 2014).

Malaysia also relied on the existing court system to resolve conflicts regarding Islamic commercial transactions, as the legal framework places Islamic banking matter under the jurisdiction of the civil court. The judiciary took administrative action to set up a special High Court in the Commercial Division known as the *Muamalah* bench through Practice Direction No 1/2003; this court will only hear cases on Islamic banking. However, this approach resulted in several instances where the civil courts took it upon themselves to decide on the validity of Islamic commercial transactions without any guidance from *Shariah* experts, hence causing several products and transactions to be declared as non-shariah-compliant, despite their wide use.

Affin Bank Bhd v Zulkifli Abdullah,[6] *Bank Muamalat Malaysia Bhd v Suhaimi Md Hashim*[7] and *Malayan Banking Bhd v Marilyn Ho Silk Lin*[8] were decisions where the court did not refer to the SAC of BNM, despite the power to do so being made available under the Central Bank of Malaysia Act 1958, as this would be an abdication of the court's judicial functions (Thani and others 2010: 370–75)

In contrast, the Court of Appeal in *Bank Islam Malaysia Bhd v Lim Kok Hoe*[9] reversed the decision of the lower court in *Arab Malaysian Finance Bhd v Taman Ihsan Jaya Sdn Bhd*,[10] which held that there was no need for referral as the decision of SAC of BNM was not binding on the court; in *Bank Islam Malaysia Bhd*, the Court of Appeal held that, given the legal infrastructure providing for the setting up of an internal *Shariah* supervisory committee and the SAC of BNM, the court should have regard to their resolutions in deciding on Islamic commercial transactions.

This view was affirmed in *Bank Kerjasama Rakyat Malaysia Bhd v Sea Oil Mill (1979) Sdn Bhd*,[11] a decision of the apex court in Malaysia (Thani and others 2010: 370–75). The reason for the conflicting views was that, prior to 2009, the decisions of the SAC of BNM were binding only on other *Shariah* bodies or committees constituted in Malaysia and prevailed over any other contradictory decisions of these *Shariah* bodies or committees but not the courts in Malaysia. However, the inclusion of a statutory provision in the Central Bank of Malaysia Act 2009 (replacing the Central Bank Act 1958) providing that the decision of the SAC shall also be binding on the court should resolve this uncertainty.[12]

For the Islamic capital market, the legal framework has made use of existing legislation and there is no separate legislation for corporations that may want to operate based on *Shariah* principles. The legal framework for the capital market was also quite advanced with the Companies Act 1965 and the Capital Markets and Services Act 2007 (CMSA 2007). However, the approach is different in relation to Islamic financial services. Specific laws have been enacted to cater to Islamic financial institutions.

In the past, several laws were enacted such as the Islamic Banking Act 1983 (IBA) and the Takaful Act 1984, which relate to *Shariah*-compliant insurance. These are now superseded by the Islamic Financial Services Act 2013 (IFSA), which streamlines and consolidates various

---

6 [2006] 1 CLJ 438.
7 [2006] 7 CLJ 321.
8 [2006] 3 CLJ 796.
9 [2009] 6 CLJ 22.
10 [2009] 1 CLJ 419.
11 [2010] 1 CLJ 793.
12 Internationally, there have been judicial decisions where the choice of law clause has been interpreted to mean civil/common law and not *Shariah* law: see further Hassan and Kyaw 2012; Hasan 2010; Junius 2007. This issue remains unresolved.

laws concerning the Islamic financial services sector.[13] The IFSA contains, amongst others, rules for the establishment of Islamic financial institutions including the board's role, functions, duties, rights and responsibilities, as well as rules relating to the supervision and licensing of the Islamic financial institutions and other market participants by BNM. The main purpose relates to the promotion of financial stability and compliance with the *Shariah*.

3 Islamic commercial law and company law compared

The *Shariah* comprises the set of rules that guides all forms of behaviour: spiritual, mental and physical (Abdal-Haqq 1996; Laldin 2006). As a term it is more than the law, and includes faith and practices as well as personal behaviour, ethical, legal and social transactions. The *Shariah* is composed of three basic elements: *aqidah*, which concerns faith and belief held by a muslim in *Allah* his Creator and His will; *fiqh*, which governs relationships between man and his Creator and between fellow men; and *akhlaq*, which covers all aspects of a muslim's behaviour, attitudes and work ethics with which he performs his actions. *Fiqh* is divided into *ibadah*, regulating the practicalities of human worship of *Allah* and *muamalat*, which regulates man-to-man relationship.

Whilst injunctions relating to *aqidah, ibadah* and *akhlaq* are fixed and unchangeable, injunctions regulating relationships between fellow men change with changes in circumstance, custom, time and place (Haron 1997; Laldin 2006). The sources of *Shariah* law are the *Quran*, the *Sunnah* of the Prophet Muhammad, *Ijma'* and *Qiyas*.[14] The purpose of law-making are to achieve the following goals (*maqasid al-Shariah*). These are the preservation of: (1) Religion Faith (*din*); (2) Life (*nafs*); (3)Lineage/Progeny (*nasl*); (4) Intellect ('*aql*); and (5) Property/Wealth (*mal*).

Shariah principles in commerce, which is a subset of *fiqh muamalat*, are based on prohibiting Riba' (usury or interest),[15] *Gharar* (uncertainty) and *Jahala* (Ignorance), *Qimar* and *Maysir* (gambling and speculation) (Al-Qaradawi 1994; Al-Zuhayli 2003). Business requires profit and loss sharing (equity-based) backed by real assets and the business must involve assets

---

13 Banking and Financial Institutions Act 1989, Exchange Control Act 1953, Insurance Act 1996, Islamic Banking Act 1983, Payment Systems Act 2003 and Takaful Act 1984.

14 The *Quran* is the original and eternal source of *Shariah* law. It constitutes messages that Allah inspired the Prophet to relay for the guidance of mankind. These messages are universal, eternal and fundamental. It is the first source of *Shariah* and it is referred to first to find guidelines relating to any issue. The *Hadith*, the second foundation of *Shariah*, is next in importance to the *Quran*. It is an account, narrative or story that represents a record of the *Sunnah* (way of life) of the Prophet Mohammad, which has been handed down from generation to generation and has become the rules of faith and practice of Muslims. The *Sunnah* (pl. *sunan*) signifies the custom, habit, or usage of the Prophet Mohammad. It designates his behaviour, mode of action, his sayings and declarations under a variety of circumstances in life. *Ijma'* is a consensus of the Muslim jurists of a particular era on a question of law. *Qiyas* is the process of reasoning by analogy of the scholars with regard to certain difficult and doubtful questions of doctrine or practice. The process involves finding the *illah* or ratio decidendi of cases already settled by the authority of the *Quran* and *Sunnah* and then applying and comparing them with new cases to arrive at a solution: see Laldin (2006).

15 Although *Riba'* is categorically prohibited through both the *Quran* (see *Surah* (Ch) 30: v 39; *Surah* 4: v 161; *Surah* 3: v 130–32; *Surah* 2: v 275–81) and the *Sunnah* of the Prophet Mohammad, the distinction between interest and usury was highlighted by a few scholars in Islam where the view is that what is prohibited is usury and not interest: see further Wayne and McIntosh (1998); Visser (2009: 31–48) gives an account of the scholars' differing views regarding the prohibition of *Riba'*, *Gharar* and *Maysir* and their application in the modern context.

classified as *halal*, which in general is not prohibited (*haram*); examples of prohibited assets include gambling, alcohol, prostitution, pork or those that are *haram* owing to their harmfulness or impurity (Al-Qaradawi 1994). These also include pornography, conventional financial services and insurance, weapons and certain businesses such as the hotel or entertainment industries, depending on the element of *haram* and prohibited practices in that business.

This part explains several significant features of company law with a view to ascertaining the application of these principles within the Islamic capital market.

Capital rules, limited liability and decision-making

The Islamic capital market envisages the listing and trading of securities that are shariah-compliant. The types of securities listed and traded on the stock exchange comprise shares and debenture stock. The equivalent forms of securities in the Islamic capital market are shares and *sukuk*.

Under the Companies Act 1965 framework, the initial capital of a company is normally provided by the shareholders, i.e. the subscribers, either by providing cash or property. In return, the subscribers or original shareholders obtain shares. Shares represent a shareholder's interest in the company. In *Borland's Trustee v Steel Bros & Co Ltd*,[16] a share was described as the interest of a shareholder in the company measured by a sum of money, for the purpose of liability in the first place and of interest in the second. Being a shareholder means that the shareholder has certain 'interests' in the company. These are normally *control rights* which refer to the entitlement to participate in certain decision-making processes through exercising voting rights.

In addition, a shareholder has *financial rights*, i.e., entitlement to share in the profits of the company through dividends or a return of capital, whilst the company is still carrying on business or upon winding up. The shareholder also owes certain 'liabilities', although this is limited to the number of shares that he has agreed to take but has not paid for. In a company limited by shares, these rights are given to a member who must be a shareholder. In contrast, a company limited by guarantee would not have any shares and a member of this type of company is not a shareholder.

The most common types of shares issued are *ordinary shares* and *preference shares*. Section 4 of the Companies Act defines a *preference share* as a share by whatever name called, which does not entitle the holder thereof to the right to vote at a general meeting or to any right to participate beyond a specified amount in any distribution whether by way of dividend or on redemption in a winding up or otherwise. For preference shares the memorandum or articles of association must contain the terms of issue of new preference shares relating to the following: to repayment of capital, participation in surplus assets or profits, cumulative and non-cumulative dividends, voting and priority of payment of capital and dividends in relation to other shares or classes of preference shares, must be contained in the memorandum or articles: section 66(1). Whilst there is no precise definition of ordinary shares, these are shares that are not preference shares and would normally have the following rights: the right to vote at general meeting and the right to participate beyond a specified amount in any distribution, whether by way of dividend or on redemption in a winding up or otherwise.

16 [1901] 1 Ch 279.

Islamic commercial law considers investment in a business venture as being made up of a series of contracts. Under Islamic commercial law, investment in a business venture, where parties agree to share in profit and loss through a contribution of property and/or skill and credit worthiness, can arise out of a *musharakah* contract. In a *musharakah* contract, the participants themselves may be involved in trading. Alternatively, where parties agree to share profits only and one side contributes assets in terms of money or money's worth, while the other provides skill, this gives rise to a *mudharabah* contract. In a *mudharabah* relationship, profit is shared between the parties but only the capital contributor bears the loss.

In ascertaining whether the investment agreement is a *musharakah* or a *mudharabah* contract, the actual terms and the rights given to the parties are crucial (Mohd-Sulaiman 2005). Parties may agree on the terms of the contract and the rights to be exercised by the investors, so long as the terms are not against the *Shariah*. In modern terms, the word 'share' reflects the Arabic word *sharaka*, which is used to refer to an arrangement for participation or sharing in contribution of capital and out of this contribution, participation in profit and/or loss. A share therefore is a term to represent the capital used in the business divided into documents (*sukuk*) of equal value and acceptable for exchange by way of trade and something that defines the rights of an investor by his contributing to the capital. These rights are exercisable by the investor, especially in relation to entitlement to profit (Abu Zayd 1983: 108).

Conceptually, this means that the modern share is compatible in principle with *Shariah*. However, there are specific rights attached to shares in the modern corporations which may not be *Shariah*-compliant, resulting in the share itself being against the *Shariah*. Several substantive issues are highlighted below.

Arrangements regarding dividends entitlement

Under the Companies Act 1965, dividend entitlement reflects the sharing of profits from the investment. Dividends may be cumulative or non-cumulative. The common law considers that preference shares are presumed to confer a right to cumulative dividends, unless the terms of issue of the shares or the constitution of the company expressly state otherwise. The holder of *cumulative* preference shares carries forward the entitlement to a dividend to the next year if no dividend is declared for that year.

Under the *Shariah*, agreements that a participant will not share in the profit or loss, or is prevented from participating in profit, or that only some will bear the loss or that some are protected from bearing any loss are against the *Shariah*. In a *mudharabah* arrangement, the capital contributor cannot be guaranteed profit. If preference shares are issued with cumulative dividends rights, the arrangement means that the profit is guaranteed and is therefore against the *Shariah* (Mohd-Sulaiman 2005).

There are also other types of dividend arrangements such as discretionary dividend types where, even if profits are available, the dividend is discretionary on the directors to pay, or where the dividend is mandatory if the profit reaches a certain quantity (Cox, Hazen and O'Neal 1997: 502). Such arrangements must also be benchmarked against the *Shariah* principles. The SAC of SC, at its 20th meeting on 14 July 1999, resolved that *cumulative* preference shares are not *Shariah*-compliant.

Fixed dividends for preferred shares where their entitled share in the profits is predetermined

Islamic jurists agree that profit must be determined as a proportionate share and not a fixed amount. Thus, a ratio most be agreed upon; for example a third or a fourth (or in the modern context by a percentage) but it cannot be a fixed amount of the profit (for example 50 cents) (Al-Kasani 1910: 59; Siddiqi 1985: 22).

Priority in payment of dividends and payment of capital in relation to other shares

The priority here means that before any payment is made to other shareholders, the obligation to the preferred shares must be satisfied. There are differences of opinion regarding the *Shariah*-compliant nature of validity of priority (Ibrahim 2010). However, the SCA of Securities Commission (SC) at its 20th meeting on 14 July 1999 decided that the priority given to basic preference share (non-cumulative) is permissible, based on the Tanazul concept. Tanazul refers to surrendering the rights to a share of the profits based on partnership, by giving priority to preference shareholders (Ibrahim 2010).

Time for payment of dividends

According to traditional Islamic jurists, division of actual profit and loss is to be made at the termination of the business and not whilst the business is ongoing, although parties may agree otherwise (Siddiqi 1985: 32). However, modern Islamic jurists argue that the modern corporation has existed for a long time and to postpone the calculation and division of profit and loss at the termination of business will deprive investors of enjoying a return on their investment (Al-Khayyat: 157). The modern practice of relying on financial statements prepared periodically enables profits and losses to be calculated during that cycle, so that a shareholder who wants to terminate his *musharakah* or *mudharabah* arrangement will be able to ascertain the value, based on the financial statements.

Two distinct characteristics of a company under the Companies Act 1965 is the separate legal personality and limited liability. It has often been said that these two concepts are the total antithesis of business under Islamic commercial law principles. This is because an important feature of investment is that, where the business suffers losses, it is compulsory that the loss is borne in proportion to capital contributions (Ibn Qudamah 1972: 140). The Shari'ah Standard No 12 of Accounting and Auditing Organization for Islamic Financial Institutional (AAOIFI)[17] (2003) provides that:

> It is a requirement that the proportions of losses borne by partners be commensurate with the proportions of their contributions to the *sharika* capital. It is not permitted, therefore, to agree on holding one partner or a group of partners liable for the entire loss or liable for a percentage of loss that does not match their share of ownership in the partnership. It is, however, valid that one partner takes, without any prior condition, the responsibility of bearing the loss at the time of the loss.

The view amongst orientalists (Schacht 1964) is that limited liability is arguably not *Shariah*-compliant because it restricts the loss to be borne by the capital contributors. Contemporary Islamic scholars, however, view juristic personality and limited liability of capital contributors

---

17 AAOIFI is the body that sets *Shariah* standards for reporting of financial information in general and functions in a similar manner as international standard setters. In addition, AAOIFI also issue *Shariah* resolution for Islamic financial institutions.

as not against *Shariah* because the *musharakah* and *mudharabah* arrangement allows for limitation of loss by the capital contributors (Zahraa 1995).

Reliance has also been placed on historical practices of juristic personality such as the state treasury (Bait-ul-Mal) and Waqf, where the institutions are fully liable to their creditors. By and large, countries professing to have Islamic law as the law of the land have also accepted juristic personality and limited liability of shareholders. The concern within the common law scholarships regarding creditors' interests seems to be shared by those reviewing limited liability from the Islamic perspective. However, it is worth noting that limited liability is a creation of statute and, even under the conventional or common law system, limited liability is not absolute.

Other aspects of the company's operations must comply with the general principles of *Shariah*. This includes issues regarding liability of the director/manager, which is recognised under the *musharakah* and *mudharabah* transaction. The scope of power of director/managers may be loosely compared with *wakalah* contracts, where there is delegation of power and authority and with it the corollary liability where the 'agent' or authorised representative exceeds his authority and causes loss or harm to the capital contributors. However, the range of remedies and types of breach of directors' duties under Islamic commercial law do not seem to be as detailed or as nuanced as the principles under conventional company law. This could be because *muamalat* practices during the early Islamic period were not as developed or as sophisticated as present day practices. Generally, the concept of damages and compensation are embedded within *fiqh muamalat* but the extent to which the remedies framework under company law is compatible with *Shariah* has not been widely discussed.[18]

Corporate governance framework

In terms of board structure, the governance framework for a financial institution's board, i.e. in relation to its role, functions, duties, rights and responsibilities, is set out in the FSA 2013 and the IFSA 2013 for Islamic financial institutions. Where the financial institutions establish an Islamic banking business with the approval of Bank Negara Malaysia (BNM) i.e., the Central Bank, the FSA 2013 requires that certain provisions of the IFSA 2013 must be complied with by the financial institutions. For financial institutions, the guidelines issued by BNM relating to corporate governance apply.

These are the Guidelines on Corporate Governance for Licensed Institutions (CG Guidelines) and the Guidelines on Corporate Governance for Licensed Islamic Bank (CG IFI Guidelines). These set out the minimum requirements for sound corporate governance to be implemented or practised by Islamic financial institutions and institutions carrying out Islamic banking business. Financial institutions are also required to disclose in the annual report, any non-observance of the Guidelines and provide explanations and alternative measures taken to comply with the principles of the Guidelines.[19]

Both the CG Guidelines and the CG IFI Guidelines expressly state that their rules and standards are aligned with those of the Malaysian Code on Corporate Governance (MCCG),

---

18 For some discussion see Abdul-Hamid Oba Yusuf, *The Directors, Shareholders and Stakeholders Dimension in Corporate Governance: An analysis of the law in Nigeria* (unpublished PHD thesis, International Islamic University, Malaysia, 2012).

19 These guidelines were issued under ss 56, 57 and 126 of the BAFIA, which has been superseded by the FSA 2013. The guidelines for IFIs were issued under s 53 of the Islamic Banking Act, which has been superseded by the IFSA 2013.

the Bank of International Settlement Guidelines on Enhancing Corporate Governance for Banking Organisations and other international best practices on corporate governance. In addition, for IFIs, the Islamic Financial Services Board Guiding Principles on Corporate Governance for Institutions Offering Only Islamic Financial Services (Excluding Islamic Insurance (Takaful) Institutions and Islamic Mutual Funds) is also applicable.

The Guidelines refer to the Malaysian Code on Corporate Governance (MCCG), which was primarily intended for and adopted by non-financial listed companies.[20] Listed companies are required by the listing rules of the stock exchange, i.e. the Bursa Malaysia Listing Requirements (BMLR) to comply with the recommendations of the MCCG or explain to what extent they have not and alternative governance strategies. However, according to the Guidelines, even if the financial institution is not a listed company, the MCCG recommendations are applicable. This brings up the question regarding the suitability of corporate governance reforms for non-financial firms to deal with the governance concerns of financial firms. In addition, for Malaysia, the question of compatibility with *Shariah* also arises.

For a financial institution which is a listed entity, the Bursa Malaysia Listing Requirements (BMLR) is also applicable. The BMLR contains rules to enhance governance of the governing body. Chapter 15 of the BMLR discusses the following governance issues for the governing body of a listed entity:

- composition of the board, including whether the chairperson and other directors are executive or non-executive directors as well as the board having independent non-executive directors
- procedure for selection of new directors, and criteria for board membership
- access of directors to independent advice at the company's expense
- arrangements for setting and reviewing remuneration of directors
- arrangements relating to selection of the auditor, reviewing audit arrangements, establishment of audit committee and rights of an audit committee
- procedures for identifying and managing business risk.

In addition, the rules under the CA 1965 (or the prospective new Companies Bill 2015 once it comes into force) are also applicable. These rules are relevant, particularly in clarifying the duties of directors and the interface between the various committees of the board to the board and the interaction amongst the board members.

In contrast, there is no specific governance framework for the non-financial listed companies whose securities are *Shariah*-compliant. However, owing to the attraction and benefits of being designated as *Shariah*-compliant securities, the listed companies would more likely have a system of internally ensuring that their securities continue to abide by the *Shariah*-compliant criteria, particularly in view of the IFSA 2013.

Reform regarding directors' qualifications has included gradual changes from focusing on independence of directors to requiring independence *and* expertise. The Malaysian Code on Corporate Governance (MCCG) in 2000 initially focused on independence, but its revision in 2007 resulted in, amongst other things, the shift to competence through the

---

20 The MCCG was first promulgated in 2000 as a result of the recommendations of the Malaysian Finance Committee on Corporate Governance (1999). The MCCG was reviewed in 2007 and more recently in 2012. It provides guidelines on key aspects of the internal governance of a company, including board structure and composition and the interaction with shareholders, particularly institutional shareholders.

introduction of 'financial literacy' for audit committee members. Much earlier, in 2001, Bursa Malaysia introduced the requirement that at least one audit committee member must be an expert. For the Islamic capital market, an additional and crucial development for the capital market is the Shariah Supervisory Committee.

The Shariah Supervisory Committee is required under the IFSA 2013. For non-Islamic financial institutions that establish Islamic banking business, the Financial Services Act 2013 (FSA 2013) requires that certain provisions of the IFSA 2013 must be complied with by the financial institutions, including the *Shariah* governance framework. The main role of this committee is to ensure that the IFI's operations and products comply with the *Shariah*. Under the predecessor legislation, the Shariah Supervisory Committee was a statutory licensing requirement for all banks that offer Islamic banking products or a requirement for being registered to carry on *Takaful* business. Conventional financial institutions providing Islamic banking business or Islamic financial business are also statutorily required to establish a Shariah Supervisory Committee to advise the bank relating to these matters. The *Shariah* committee is now the norm for IFIs.

Directors and boards of financial institutions must comply with the 'fit and proper' criteria. This has been part of the regulatory environment in line with the Basel Committee's recommendations. The FSA 2013 and the IFSA 2013 reiterate this power found in predecessor legislation, which confers on BNM authority to set the criteria. The 'fit and proper' criteria includes a minimum criteria of (a) probity, personal integrity and reputation; (b) competency and capability; and (c) financial integrity. BNM has the final say as to what 'fit and proper' encompass. The power of BNM under the FSA 2013 and the IFSA 2013 to determine board composition is further enhanced with the guidelines relating to 'fit and proper' qualifications for key responsible persons in the banking and financial institutions in March 2011.

Similar guidelines were issued in relation to the Shariah Governance Framework for Islamic Financial Institutions issued by Bank Negara Malaysia (which took effect in June 2011). Both the CG Guidelines and the IFI CG Guidelines list several factors that need to be considered by the board for developing formal policies defining 'fit and proper' standards for directors and senior management of the financial institutions and IFIs. These guidelines need to ensure that the fit and proper test must cover technical and professional skills, including those relating to risk. This *Shariah* literacy is also crucial for audit committees where the institution provides Islamic financials services, given that there are different reporting and auditing standards for Islamic transactions.

This is also of significant concern for Islamic financial institutions, particularly in relation to their ability to comply with regulatory requirements. Listed Islamic financial institutions must ensure compliance with BMLR, which requires a listed company to ensure that each of its directors, chief executive officer or chief financial officer has the character, experience, integrity, competence and time effectively to discharge his role as a director, chief executive officer or chief financial officer.

In addition, the IFSA 2013 allows BNM to remove a director or the chief executive officer of financial institution if it is of the opinion that he/she no longer fulfils the fit and proper requirements as specified by BNM. The IFSA 2013 also confers power of removal to BNM where a director or CEO has failed to comply with a direction of BNM or an enforceable undertaking accepted by BNM. There is also power to remove the director or CEO if he has, by action or negligence, contributed to the breach or contravention of any provisions of the Act(s). The 'fit and proper' criteria must incorporate a skill set that reflects competence and capability about *Shariah* in general, and Islamic commercial law in particular. Skill set and competency requirements contribute to corporate governance as it provides a facility for the investors to evaluate the stewardship of those who manage or supervise the management of companies (Villiers 2006). Reliability depends to a certain extent on the competency of directors and directors' competence should be able to provide some degree of assurance to investors.

Islamic financial institutions could face a real challenge in fulfilling the 'fit and proper' criteria leading to a reduction in the talent pool of directors willing to serve on boards, unless measures are taken to widen the pool of qualified candidates.[21] There could also be the possibility that the quality of the pool of candidates could be affected. Enforcement by the regulators is therefore very much needed to ensure compliance with the fit and proper criteria.

The establishment of the Shariah Supervisory Committee also has a significant impact on company law principles, particularly in relation to directors' duties. Traditional governance structure and company law operate on the basis that committees to the board must report to the board and make recommendations to the board, with the board retaining the authority to make the final decision. Company law also allows the board to delegate decision-making power to a committee or other persons but the board must ensure that this is not an abdication of responsibility or power. Whilst the IFSA 2013 provides that the shariah committee must be established to *provide advice* to the IFIs, the IFI Guidelines state that the board *must follow* the recommendations of the Shariah Committee. Paragraph 55 of IFSB's Guiding Principles for Corporate Governance for Institutions Offering only Islamic Financial Services (Excluding Islamic Insurance Institutions and Islamic Mutual Funds) (the ISFB Guidelines) state that Islamic financial institutions 'shall comply with the rules and principles issued by their *Shariah* scholars'.

The IFSA 2013 specifically deals with the conflict between the Guidelines and the traditional company law and governance. It provides that the Companies Act 1965 applies in addition to the IFSA 2013 but, where the conflict may not be reconciled, the IFSA 2013 will prevail. However, the IFI Guidelines and the IFSB's Guiding Principles created a conundrum. The amendment to the Companies Act 1965 in 2007 has provided a way to reconcile this dichotomy. This apparent conflict may be resolved by relying on section 132(1C) and (1D) of the Companies Act 1965, which allows the board to rely on information provided by certain persons, including experts and other directors in a committee of the board in the performance of a director's role and responsibilities.

Shareholder primacy versus stakeholder primacy

The traditional common law position is that a company must be managed primarily in the best interests of the general body of members. This view, i.e. the shareholder primacy, means that the law considers that the directors' obligation is to promote the company's interests as represented by what the benefit is that can be conferred on or obtained by the shareholders as a whole. In its strict form, shareholder primacy mandates directors only to consider the members' interests and to make decisions that maximise profit for members. However, it is widely acknowledged that a company typically has many stakeholders, i.e.

---

21 There is empirical evidence from 2010 on domestic banks in Malaysia which showed that 68% of directors of local banking groups and 44% of the directors felt that there is an insufficient talent pool of FI directors in Malaysia. See PriceWaterhouseCoopers, *Performance Pays: Directors' Remuneration Survey* (2010) Bank Negara Malaysia and Perbadanan Insurans Deposit Malaysia, Kuala Lumpur.

persons who have an impact on the company's operations and business and who are also affected by the company's operations and business. In reality, decisions made by the board of directors will have an impact not only on shareholders but also on other persons.

Because of the impact that a company has on its stakeholders, there is a view that the directors must also consider how their decisions will affect the interests of stakeholders. This view, i.e. the stakeholder primacy, argues that directors are not in breach of their duties to the company if they make decisions that take into consideration other stakeholders' interests. In its widest form, the stakeholder primacy view argues that preference should be given to the stakeholders even if it is not beneficial to the members.

Whilst these two views seems to be at opposite ends, a more conciliatory approach is the 'enlightened shareholder value', which suggests that directors *should* promote the success of the company for the benefit of its shareholders and, in doing so, *may* take into consideration the impact that the company's decision will have on stakeholders. There is, however, a big difference in the law allowing directors to take into consideration stakeholders' interest and the law making it an obligation to do so. Modern company law is still grappling with this issue, although development seems to be in favour of a more expansive view of what a 'company' means through the exhortation of corporate social responsibility and corporate sustainability.

The *Shariah* may be able to provide an alternative view to this debate. In Islam, ownership of property is not an absolute right. Man has certain obligations in the use of his property which includes promoting public good and public interest. The achievement of the *maqasid al-Shariah* and distributive justice are the fundamental theoretical foundations for the promotion and maintenance of human relations and interaction. Thus, any institutions that claim to be *Shariah*-compliant must operate under the concept of accountability to the promotion of Islamic values and principles.

The application of this view can be seen in the Islamic financial institutions. A unique feature of financial institutions is the position of depositors and, for IFIS specifically, the investment of account holders. Investment account holders under the IFI are capital providers but do not have control rights exercisable by shareholders. In this situation, there is an obvious separation of control and cash flow rights. The funds are managed by the managers and, owing to the nature of the contract under the *Shariah*, the capital providers (IAH) bear the risk of financial loss, unless this was as a result of the misconduct or negligence of the manager. This is not the case for depositors in conventional financial institutions. This is exacerbated by the fact that their 'agents', i.e. the managers of their funds, are appointed and monitored by the shareholders and shareholders' and depositors' interests do diverge (Safieddine 2009).

Both the FSA 2013 and the IFSA 2013 contain an express provision stating that the directors must consider the interests of depositors or investment account holders.[22] However, there is no further clarification of how this is to be achieved. Reform relating to this issue has suggested the establishment of a board with investment holders' representation, or by way of representation in the audit committee (Safieddine 2009). Better protection of investment holders may be addressed by a holistic reform of investors' rights and protection supplemented by rigorous enforcement.

---

22 Section 56(3) of the FSA and s 65(3)(a) of the IFSA. This is similar in concept to the enlightened shareholder value in s 172 of the UK CA 2006.

4 Conclusion

Malaysia has been able to harmonise *Shariah* principles in commerce with the common law as exemplified by its fully functioning Islamic capital market, complemented by its Islamic financial services sector. For the most part, the common law principles relating to the operations of a modern corporation share similarities with Islamic commercial law principles. Significant differences have been addressed through legal and extra-legal measures. However, this does not indicate an end to harmonisation efforts.

Because Islamic commercial law practices are evolving owing to market demands and are doing so in a business environment that may involve the conventional system, an assessment of the compatibility between Islamic commercial law and the common law is needed. New company law rules need to take into consideration whether these are compatible with Islamic commercial law principles and existing regulatory frameworks. Islamic capital market products and operations must also navigate within a common law ecosystem. This interaction is likely to provide new challenges to regulators, practitioners and investors alike.

Bibliography

Abdal-Haqq, I. (1996) 'Islamic Law: An Overview of Origin and Elements', *Journal of Islamic Law,* 1: 1–60.

Abu Zayd, R. (1983) *Sharikah al-Musahamah*, Qahirah: Dar al-Fikr.

Accounting and Auditing Organization for Islamic Financial Institutional (AAOIFI) (2003) *Shari'a Standards* 1424–5 H/2003–4, Bahrain.

Alman, M. (2013) 'Shariah Supervisory Board Composition Effects on Islamic Banks' Risk-Taking Behavior' http://www.efmaefm.org/0EFMAMEETINGS/EFMA%20ANNUAL%20MEETINGS/2013-Reading/papers/EFMA2013_0082_fullpaper.pdf (last accessed 5 June 2016).

Al-Kasani, A.B.M. (1910) *Bada'i al'Sana'i fiTtartib al'Shara'i*, Egypt: Matba'ah Jamaliyah.

Al-Khayyat, A.A. (1994) *Al-Sharikat Fil Shariah al-Islamiyyah*, Beirut: Mu'assasah al-Risalat.

Al-Qaradawi, Y. (1994) *The Lawful and the Prohibited in Islam (al-Halal Wal Haram Fil Islam)*; trans. El-Helbawy, K., Siddiqui, M.M. and Shukry, S. (1999) Indianapolis: American Trust Publications.

Al-Zuhayli, W. (2003) *Financial Transactions in Islamic Jurisprudence Vol 1*, Damascus: Dar al-Fikr.

Bank Negara Malaysia (2013) 'Exposure Drafts on Islamic Financial Contracts' (Shariah Requirements and Optional Practices) http://www.bnm.gov.my (last accessed 5 June 2016).

Basel Committee on Banking Supervision (1999) *Fit and Proper Principles*, Bank for International Settlements.

Basel Committee on Banking Supervision, (2010) *Principles for Enhancing Corporate Governance*, Bank for International Settlements.

Bursa Malaysia, 2014, *Annual Report 2014*.

Chapra, M.U. (2007) *Challenges Facing the Islamic Financial Industry*, in Hassan, M.K. and M.K. Lewis (eds), *Handbook of Islamic Banking*, Edward Elgar Publishing Limited, Cheltenham, UK338–57.

Chapra, M.U. and Ahmed, H. (2002) *Corporate Governance in Islamic Financial Institutions, Islamic Development Bank: Periodical Document No. 6*, Islamic Research and Training Institute.

Cohen Committee (1945) *Report of the Committee on Company Law Amendment*, Cmd. 6659, London: HMSO.

Cox, J.D., Hazen, T.L. and O'Neal, F.H. (1997) *Corporations*, New York: Aspen Law & Business.

Ernst & Young (2012) *The World Islamic Banking Competitiveness Report: A Brave New World of Sustainable Growth 2011–2012.*

Gower, L.C.B. (1961) *Final Report of the Commission of Enquiry into the Working and Administration of the Present Company Law of Ghana*, Accra: Government Printing Department.

Hainsworth, A. (2007) 'Governance Rules for Islamic Financial Institutions: The New Frontier?' *Butterworths Journal of International Banking and Financial Law*, 22: 515–20

Haron, S (1997) *Islamic Banking, Rules and Regulations,* Petaling Jaya: Pelanduk Publications.

Hasan, Z. (2010) 'Regulatory Framework of *Shari'ah* Governance System in Malaysia, GCC Countries and the UK', *Kyoto Bulletin of Islamic Area Studies*, 3(2): 82–115.

Hassan, A.A. (1997) *Sales and Contracts in Early Islamic Law*, New Delhi: Kitab Bhavan.

Hassan, A. and Kyaw, H.W. (2012) 'The Application of Choice of Law and Choice of Forum Clauses to Islamic Banking and Financial Cross-Border Transactions', *Australian Journal of Basic and Applied Sciences*, 6(11): 370–80.

Ibn Qudamah, A.M.A. (1972) *Al-Mughni Wa Yalihi al-Sharh al-Kabir*, Vol 5, Beirut: Darul Kitab al-Arabi.

Ibrahim, A.B. (2010) 'Islamic Preference Shares: An Analysis in Light of the Principles of Musharakah and Tanazul', paper presented in International Conference on Islamic Banking & Finance: Cross-border Practices & Litigation (15–16 June 2010).

International Monetary Fund (2013a) *Malaysia: Publication of Financial Sector Assessment Program Documentation: Detailed Assessment of Implementation of IOSCO Objectives and Principles of Securities Regulation: IMF Country Report No 13/59*, International Monetary Fund, Washington.

International Monetary Fund (2013b) *Malaysia: Financial Sector Stability Assessment: IMF Country Report No. 13/52*, International Monetary Fund, Washington.

Jenkins Committee (1962) *Report of the Company Law Committee*, Cmd 1749, London: HMSO).

Junius, A. (2007) 'Islamic Finance-Issues Surrounding Islamic Law as a Choice of Law under German Conflict of Laws Principles', *Chicago Journal of International Law*, 7(2): 537–50.

Laldin, M.A. (2006) *Introduction to Shariah and Islamic Jurisprudence*, Kuala Lumpur: Cert Publications.

Mahmood, N.K. (2013) 'Developing a Platform For Consumer Protection in the Islamic Financial Services Industry', presentation at Sixth Islamic Financial Stability Forum *Promoting Resilience and Stability of the Islamic Financial Services Industry: Strengthening Consumer Protection and Business Conduct* (12 December 2012) Jeddah: Islamic Financial Services Board http:// www.ifsb.org (last accessed 5 June 2016).

Mohd-Sulaiman, A.N. (2005) 'Shares in the Modern Corporation: A Comparison Between Malaysian Companies Act 1965 and the Islamic Perspective', *IIUM Law Journal*, 13: 1–25.

Mohd-Sulaiman, A.N. (2006) 'Payment for Company's Shares' *IIUM Law Journal*, 14(2): 271–86.

Naqvi, S.N.H. (1982), *Ethics and Economics: An Islamic Synthesis*, Leicester: The Islamic Foundation.

OICD-IOISCO (2004) *Malaysia's Capital Market*, Securities Commission Malaysia, Kuala Lumpur. *Islamic Capital Market Fact Finding Report: Report of the Islamic Capital Market Task Force of the International Organization of Securities Commissions* http://www.sc.com.my (last accessed 5 June 2016).

PriceWaterhouseCoopers (2010), *Performance Pays: Directors' Remuneration Survey*, Kuala Lumpur: Bank Negara Malaysia and Perbadanan Insurans Deposit Malaysia.

Rahman, F. (1964) 'Riba and Interest', *Islamic Studies* (Karachi), 3(1): 1–43.

Safieddine, A. (2009) 'Islamic Financial Institutions and Corporate Governance: New Insights for Agency Theory', *Corporate Governance: An International Review*, 17(2): 142–58.

Schacht, J. (1964) *An Introduction to Islamic Law*, Oxford: Clarendon Press.

Securities Commission (2007: 2nd ed) *Resolutions of the Securities Commission Shari'ah Advisory Council*, Kuala Lumpur: Securities Commission.

Securities Commission (2011) *Malaysia's Capital Market*, Kuala Lumpur: Securities Commission.

Securities Commission, (2013), *Annual Report 2013*, Kuala Lumpur: Securities Commission.

Securities Commission (2014) *Annual Report 2014*, Kuala Lumpur: Securities Commission.

Siddiqi, M.N. (1985) *Partnerships and Profit Sharing in Islamic Law*, Leicester: The Islamic Foundation.

Siddiqi, M.N. (2000) 'Evolution of Islamic Banking and Insurance as System Rooted in Ethics', Proceedings of the Takaful Forum (April 2000), New York.

Thani, N.N, Abdullah, M.R and Hassan, M.H (2010) *Law and Practice of Islamic Banking and Finance, 2nd ed*, Malaysia, Sweet & Maxwell Asia.

Villiers, C (2006) *Corporate Reporting and Company Law*, Cambridge: Cambridge University Press.

Visser, H (2009) *Islamic Finance Principles and Practice*, Cheltenham: Edward Elgar Publishing Ltd.

Wayne, V. and McIntosh, A. (1998) 'A Short Review of the Historical Critique of Usury', *Accounting, Business & Financial History*, 8(2): 175–89.

Zahraa, M. (1995) 'Legal Personality in Islamic Law', *Arab Law Quarterly*, 193–206.

14

Chinese family companies in Hong Kong

Governance, predicaments and regulatory challenges[1]

Angus Young and Alex Lau

Introduction

Family companies are one of the most common forms of business structure around the world and several studies have found that many outperformed non-family businesses in terms of profitability and growth (International Financial Corporation 2011). This is due to a number of factors, including strong commitment of the family to the business, knowledge continuity from one generation to another and having a reputation for being reliable, and family members taking pride in the company's accomplishments. There are, however, a number of weaknesses. They include complexities arising from family emotions, different levels of participation of family members, and informality in governance, as family members usually have very little interest in setting clearly articulated business practices and procedures. In addition, these businesses have a general lack of discipline on key strategic areas, such as succession planning and family members being employed in the company (International Financial Corporation 2011).

More importantly, a source of problems in governing family companies is the blurring between work and family matters (Cadbury 2000), in particular, personal relationships between family members, because 'those involved cannot stand back and look at business issues separately from family issues' (ibid: 7). Given that it is common for the owners, board and management in family companies to be the same individuals, relationships amongst members of the family are more likely to be more significant in influencing the company's governance than what the law prescribes. As such, the governance of family companies is more likely to deviate from international best practices (Arcot and Bruno 2012).

Whilst research and interests about governance of family companies had flourished in the last decade (Poutziouris, Smyrnios and Goel 2013), the focus of this chapter is on the

---

1 Note that the chapter draws from Angus Young's PhD thesis on the corporate governance of Chinese family companies in Hong Kong.

intricacies of regulating the governance of Chinese family companies in Hong Kong. The appeal to examine Hong Kong's family companies is owing to the unique regulatory challenge arising from what the laws regulate and what the norms obligate. Like many Asian countries where many of the laws were transplanted from developed Western economies, the values espoused from the imported rules into Hong Kong might remain alien to many because the norms and culture are different.

At a glance, Hong Kong is a modern cosmopolitan international city like New York or London. On closer inspection, it is in fact a Chinese society that is steeped in traditional Chinese customs on the one hand and, on the other hand, it has a Westernised population with many citizens educated in Western countries, as well as foreigners from all over the world living and working in a densely populated city. The same could be said about other types of companies in the territory. Whilst company laws transplanted from the UK since the colonial era work well for many businesses in Hong Kong, in contrast, Chinese family companies founded by heads of families decades ago had always looked towards Confucian ideals as the benchmark for the governance of their firms.

Some point to the fact that since there has not been a massive corporate failure or crisis in Hong Kong, this has indicated that there is no need to reconsider the regulation and governance of Chinese family companies in Hong Kong. Furthermore, Young (2014: 12) has argued that: 'Critics might label directors of Chinese family companies in Hong Kong who disregard their legal duties as rogues or crony capitalists. However, this would be a crude and presumptuous observation as these commentators cast their judgment of Chinese values and norms against Western standards and benchmarks'. Because there are about half a million Chinese family companies in Hong Kong (Young 2014), the subject-matter is anything but trivial.

This chapter is divided into five sections. Following this introduction, an analysis of laws regulating directors will examine Hong Kong courts' decisions about directors' duties. This goes to the heart of corporate governance in Hong Kong and asks the question – do the courts take into consideration the family dimensions and cultural attributes of Chinese family companies? The next section explores how Chinese family companies are governed; this is critical because it will reveal not only how these companies are governed, but also whether the laws that regulate directors in these types of companies are apt. The ensuing section will examine the cases brought forward by members of Chinese family companies claiming unfair prejudice or even seeking their winding up. These cases reveal that the operation of the law as it stands is incongruent with how these companies are governed. In addition, this discussion will illustrate the problems associated with regulating the governance of Chinese family companies. The conclusions to this chapter will discuss possible solutions and the challenges facing family companies.

It is important to note at the outset that the phrase 'Chinese family company' refers to entities that are wholly-owned and operated by Chinese family members, with no outside shareholders. As such, the shareholders are often the directors of the company, so agency problems do not apply. Another matter worth mentioning is that this work is not concerned with the debate about the choice of alternative models of governance, whether Anglo–American, Continental stakeholder or Chinese family-centred is better. The discussion that follows is concerned with the law as it stands; this helps us to appreciate how these companies are governed, and why legal recourse failed to address the problems associated with the governance of Chinese family companies in Hong Kong.

An analysis of the laws regulating corporate governance in Hong Kong

In 1978, Lord Denning observed in a speech that directors are a self-perpetuating oligarchy; as such they have the ability to exploit their powers for self-interest and at the shareholders' expense (Denning 1978). Holding these individuals accountable to shareholders for their decisions and behaviour is the foundation of good governance (Solomon and Solomon 2004: 14). Du Plessis, McConvill and Bagaric (2005: 8) explained that: 'individuals or groups in a company who make decisions and take actions on specific issues need to be accountable for their decisions and actions. Mechanisms must exist and be effective to allow for accountability. These provide investors with the means to query and assess the actions of the board and its committees'.

Furthermore, it has been argued that transparency is a mechanism for reinforcing accountability (Young 2014). Solomon and Solomon (2004: 119) have noted that: 'Transparency is an essential element of a well-functioning system of corporate governance'. This is crucial to good governance, as it is important that directors disclose any material personal interest in a transaction or contract. The reason for this is simple: personal interests of directors could have a direct or indirect bearing on the decisions made by them on behalf of the company (Farrar 2008).

The legal regulation of directors in Hong Kong has been developed by the courts and draws upon cases from the United Kingdom since 1795. These legal duties are seen as core regulatory mechanisms to monitor and discipline directors. However, directors are in a somewhat unique category as they are not trustees per se nor are they agents. In some respects their function is similar to that of a trustee and, as they stand in a fiduciary relationship with their principal, the company (Austin, Ford and Ramsay 2005; Smith and Keenan 1970). Thus, the legal characterisation of directors could be said to bear elements of both trustee and agency.

As an agent, directors take on a monitoring role to ensure that professional managers act in the interests of shareholders (Lan and Heracleous 2010). Shareholders have the power to appoint or remove directors; however, shareholders cede control over the company to directors. Furthermore, shareholders have the power to authorise, or consent to depart from, the exclusive benefit principle (Brudney 1997), thereby treating owners and controllers as separate parties. This structural and functional separation enhances the status of directors as being in a fiduciary position in relation to the company (Yorston and Brown 1962).

Fiduciary relationships arise when there is trust and confidence or confidential relations between parties, as they involve the exercise of a power or discretion affecting the interests of another person in a legal capacity or practical sense (Meagher, Heydon and Leeming 2002: 157). Redmond (2009: 343) stated that a good director is a person who 'brings to the office an ethic of self-denial or disinterested service'. Also, directors are bound to exercise their powers in good faith for the benefit of the company, and not to benefit themselves unless this is done with full disclosure (transparency) and with the assent of the company (accountability) (Yorston and Brown 1962). These duties stipulate what directors should do, as well as what they cannot do (Van 2006).

Another duty incidental to the fiduciary relationship is the duty of care (Kwan 2006). If directors act within their powers then they are required to act with such care in good faith for the benefit of the company (Davies 2003). This means that a director should acquire and maintain sufficient knowledge about the affairs of the company. In addition, he/she is required to exhibit in the performance of his/her duties such a degree of skill as would be expected from a person of his/her knowledge and experience. This duty also arises out of contracts and tort law (Austin, Ford and Ramsay 2005: 211). Directors' duties can thus be further divided into two broad categories. First, there is the duty to act in good faith, for a proper purpose in the interest of the company with no conflict of interest; these may be described as fiduciary duties. Second, directors have a duty to exercise care and diligence.

The cases decided in Hong Kong courts have shown that the courts have often followed decisions of English courts when considering directors' duties. These fiduciary duties include: the duty to act *bona fide* for the benefit of the company; the duty to exercise powers for a proper purpose; the duty to avoid a conflict of interests and the duty not to make secret profits; in addition, there is the general duty of care that applies to directors. It is interesting to note that in Hong Kong, litigation for breach of directors' duties has mainly involved former employees (for example see *Kishimoto Sangyo Co Ltd and Anor v Akihiro Oba and Ors* [1995] HKCFI 382, HCA000396/1995), or business partners (for example see *Kao Lee and Yip v Donald Koo Hoi Yan and Ors*),[2] with the exception of one case where the familial relationship between two of the directors was relevant in a first instance judgment (*Law Wai Duen v B. F. Construction Co Ltd and Ors*).[3]

In *Law Wai Duen v B. F. Construction Co Ltd and Ors*,[4] the plaintiff sought to enforce her rights as a director to inspect a company's accounts under general law and section 121 of the then Companies Ordinance (cap 32). Mr Yip, the defendant, claimed that he had been appointed director of a family company (the other board members were the husband, wife and daughter) because of his technical expertise. As such, he considered himself to be an employee, having nothing to do with the accounting or the keeping of those records. Mr Chan, who was the major shareholder and director, commenced divorce proceeding against his wife, Madam Law, the other major shareholder and director of this family company, who was also the plaintiff in this case (Mr Yip's employer). Mr Chan claimed that his wife was undermining his position and interests in the company out of spite because she suspected that he was having an extra-marital affair. The wife alleged instead that there were irregularities in the company accounts, and claimed that Mr Yip and her husband had denied her the right to inspect the accounts.

In the court of first instance, Chu J held that: 'the court should not overlook the fact that the parties, except for Mr Yip, are family members and also the family dimension of the matter'.[5] The company books were not in Mr Yip's possession, even though he was a board member; he had no controlling or beneficial interest in the company and was a mere employee. Her honour furthermore noted that: 'It cannot be realistically suggested that he can on his own volition and decision, make the documents available to the Wife and/or the Daughter without regard to the views of the Husband. It is therefore immaterial that he is on the board of directors'[6] and that: '. . . it must be plain that the dispute or disagreement over inspection of corporate books and records is very much a dispute between the husband and the wife. There is little purpose to be served by joining Mr Yip, who evidently has no role to play in resolving the dispute'. However, on appeal the first instance judgment was overturned as the appeal court did not believe that it should take into consideration the family dimensions raised by Chu J.

2 [2003] HKCFI 850, HCA008847B/1993.
3 HKCFI 926, HCMP000703/2001.
4 Ibid.
5 Ibid 37.
6 Ibid 50, 51.

This decision highlights a contrast with the assumptions of modern company law as corporate governance has been said to evolve with the growth of disperse shareholdings in companies in the United States, where the control of a company is in the hands of managers and the board and not the shareholders (Berle and Means 1932: 66, 69). Moreover, over time, corporate governance had evolved alongside economic modernisation and public participation in capital pooling (Frankel 1983). Whilst the courts have acknowledged that companies owned and operated by individuals with personal relationships involving mutual confidence could be deemed to be quasi-partnerships,[7] the courts and the law in Hong Kong did not include or even contemplate the relevance of Chinese cultural factors to the governance of Chinese family companies.

For many years business research had examined cultural influences upon the way in which companies in different parts of the world are governed (Tricker 2009). However, this has not been reflected in corporate law principles. Legal scholars have looked at the importance of the path dependency model in relation to corporate law, with scholars arguing that corporate structures and regulations are different in many countries because of historical, cultural and political factors (Bebchuk and Roe 1999). This is in contrast to the high profile convergence model in regard to corporate governance (Hansmann and Kraakman 2004). Only a limited number of scholars have considered the impact of cultural influences on corporate laws transplanted from one jurisdiction to another; in many cases, such transplanted norms read like an alien set of rules to those who receive the transplanted norms (Young 2014: 192).

The corporate governance paradigm in Chinese family companies

It has been strongly argued that culture shapes corporate governance because cultural orientations are often deeply ingrained in the functioning of major societal institutions (Licht, Goldschmidt and Schwartz 2007). Widespread practices, reflected in symbols and traditions, shape the values of individuals. Hofstede, a widely respected scholar concerned with cross-cultural business issues has shown how national culture affects the values of individuals in the workplace (Mead 2005). Hofstede's research findings were based on surveys of over 116,000 employees in IBM branches spanning across 50 countries (Hofstede 1994). From the data generated, he came up with four (and later added a fifth) value dimension to profile the cultural and behavioural differences that exist between countries. Given that many of the laws regulating companies in Hong Kong are essentially derived from the United Kingdom, value differences arise between the two jurisdictions. From the results of Hofstede's five value dimensions, Hong Kong illustrates noticeable differences in three of the value dimensions (power distance, individualism versus collectivism and long versus short-term orientation) (Hofstede 1994).

Cultural diversities translate into startling differences in the work place between those in Hong Kong when compared with Western countries such as the United Kingdom. Employees in Hong Kong tend not to disagree with their bosses and these bosses are seen as autocratic or paternalistic (Hofstede 1994). The ideal boss is seen as a benevolent autocrat, which means that subordinates are expected to do what they are told. As such, leaders possess wide discretionary power with few checks and balances over an entire company, is common for CEOs in Hong Kong. They are most likely to be the chairperson and with this greater

---

7 *Ebrahimi v Westbourne Galleries Ltd* [1973] AC 360.

stature, also the CEO, both of whom have political influence over the board (Li and Harrison 2008).

Hence, a CEO rules over the affairs of the company with almost absolute discretion, which contrasts with the structured, process-oriented and rule-based governance found in the West (Redding 2004). Furthermore, in societies with collectivist values such as Hong Kong, interpersonal relationships and group affiliations are much more highly valued than in Western countries including the United Kingdom (Hofstede 1994: 53). Hofstede found that, in Hong Kong, the maintenance of harmony amongst people having an acute sense of shame, the importance of face, and voluntary compliance with social norms are key social attributes (Hofstede 1994).

Another interesting value dimension is the long-term orientation of individuals; a group of researchers in Hong Kong led by Bond, identified certain Chinese values that were not addressed in Hofstede's earlier work (The Chinese Culture Connection 1987). Bond and his team found that Confucian work dynamism did not correlate with Hofstede's four value dimensions. This was later adapted by Hofstede as the fifth value dimension, consisting of: 'values of persistency; ordering relationships by status and observing this order; thrift; and having a sense of shame' (Mead 2005: 47). Hong Kong ranked in second place out of 23 jurisdictions for this value dimension. This indicated that Confucian doctrines have considerable influence on the population in Hong Kong (Hofstede and Bond 1988: 17).

Cross-cultural studies are relevant to corporate governance laws because laws are value-laden. The assumption that directors' duties norms derived from the United Kingdom will work for all types of companies in Hong Kong is a highly doubtful proposition. Cultural value disparity leads to different mindsets, and thus the measurement of what is appropriate or ideal in the West may be viewed as unacceptable in jurisdictions where the culture of Confucian traditions dominates (Miles 2007: 858–60). More importantly, value differences translate into distinct models of corporate governance.

Chinese family and Anglo–American governance models in Table 14.1 below summarise the key differences between these two types of companies. This table is collated from the literature on business and related disciplines (Clarke 2007; Tricker 2009; Solomon and Solomon 2004; Jensen and Meckling 1976; Tong 2009; Chen 2001; Li, Park and Li 2004; Mallin 2010; Redding 1990; Hamilton 2006). It identifies key values, norms and practices that shape the governance practices in the two cultures.

The term 'Anglo–American model' is a label commonly used to identify systems of corporate governance in public companies in the US and Britain (Clarke 2007: 129). Such a model of governance is also adopted in Hong Kong, in terms of the laws that regulate corporate governance. However, Table 14.1 illustrates that the governance of Chinese family companies in Hong Kong does not resemble the Anglo–American model, in particular paternalism and harmonious relationships are uniquely Chinese cultural attributes. Hence, there is a 'disconnect' between what the transplanted laws from the United Kingdom seek to regulate, as the legal duties were shaped by the Anglo–American model, and the practices amongst Chinese family-centred model companies, where Confucian influences are evident.

Redding found, from the interviews with a number of chairs/CEOs of Chinese family companies in Hong Kong, that the family patriarch or matriarch governs these companies with total control and discretion. This approach to governance is characterised by Redding as 'paternalistic' (Redding 1990: 156–69). There is no exact equivalent to paternalistic governance in the West, although closely held family companies in the West may sometimes delegate all authority to a 'governing director'; this may also be the case in one-person companies that have been permitted to be formed in Western legal systems.

Table 14.1

Anglo–American Model	Chinese Family-centred Model
Separation between ownership and control	Owners are in control of the company.
Outsider system (where large firms are controlled by their managers but owned by outside shareholders)	Insider system (owned predominantly by insider shareholders, who also wield control over management)
Company managed by professional managers	Company managed by family members or relatives
Rule rather than relationship-based governance system	Relationships and trusts are more important than formal legal safeguards
Disperse shareholdings	100 per cent or block shareholdings held by family members
Emphasis on independent non-executive directors to bring independent judgment to the board – transparency	Paternalistic governance and decision-making with the head of the family dominating and no clear separation between the interests of the family and the company
Power is linked to the appointment and responsibilities conferred by the board	Power is conferred by status within the family hierarchy – legitimacy
Interests of the shareholders as a whole is paramount	Interests of the family is often not separated from the interest of the company
Sense of duty and legal obligations is important – therefore the focus is accountability	Sense of loyalty and family obligations comes first – the focus here is on harmonious relationship

Source: Young (2014)

Westwood remarked that, in paternalistic governance, patriarchal authority is bound by reciprocal obligations (Westwood 1997). Empirical research on Chinese family companies across Singapore, Hong Kong and Taiwan identified two common features: the first is order and compliance, and the second is harmony (Westwood 1997: 453). The first feature exhibits the following attributes: patriarchy, large power distance (Hofstede's value dimension), hierarchical structure and 'filial piety', much of which is a family-centred value-system based on Confucian teachings (Westwood 1997: 456–7). The second requirement for harmony is a distinctive feature of collectivism: reciprocity, moral leadership, propriety, virtue and face sensitivity (*mianzi*), where harmony is the end goal (Young 2014: 124).

For Hong Kong Chinese, the cohesiveness of a family is maintained through a strong sense of responsibility and obligation towards one another (Ward and Lin 2010: 669). This means that an individual's interest is subordinated in favour of the family's, so as to achieve harmony (Smith 2010: 702–3). A key undertaking of a paternalistic leader is to foster harmony and stability amongst family members (Westwood 1997: 454). Furthermore, the strong sense of responsibility amongst family members (and even employees) creates an obligation to acquiesce for the sake of harmony to the instructions of the head of the company, even if they disagree on a personal level (Redding 1990: 144–5, 156–7). As such, harmonious relations in this context are extensions of paternalism.

It is helpful to appreciate certain advantages to the Chinese family model of governance so as to explore various regulatory options in subsequent sections of this chapter. First, since power is usually vested with one person in family companies, decisions can be made relatively quickly (Redding 1990: 144–5, 156–7). Second, internal organisational efficiency is said to be achieved through vertical control (Redding 1990: 208–12). Third, it is not uncommon for members of a Chinese family to help out for little or no remuneration or provide loans at no interest charged for a family business out of a sense of loyalty and personal obligation (Mead 2005: 281–3). Finally, given that Confucian ethics encourage cooperation and avoidance of conflict, it lends support to the argument that the Chinese family model of governance has been relatively successful in terms of corporate performance (Kahal 2001: 134; Redding 1990: 156; Yeung 2004: 80).

However, there are disadvantages in this model. First, the heads of Chinese family companies often do not distinguish between company and personal assets (Wong 2001: 60–61). Second, decisions of a paternalistic leader tend to be based on their own values and personal experiences. Third, the focus on familial loyalty tends to repress professional talent (Chen 2001: 76). Fourth, nepotism appears to be common in Chinese family companies, where privileges and resources are given to those deemed by the head (patriarch) of the company as favourites (Erben and Guneser 2008: 957). Finally, Chinese family companies are often disadvantaged when it comes to access to capital, because they rely on personal savings or loans from family members and extended-family relatives to fund their enterprise (Mead 2005: 282–3).

In sum, the governance of the Chinese family-centred company differs considerably from the Anglo–American model upon which the corporate laws regulating directors in Hong Kong are based. Whilst the aim of this chapter is not to evaluate which model of governance is better or superior, the analysis does reveal some vulnerabilities of the Chinese family-centred model. Such peculiarities, which emphasise paternalism and harmonious relationships, do, however, denote that the law as it stands does not effectively regulate the governance of Chinese family companies in Hong Kong. This could explain why, when governance in this type of companies break down, disgruntled Chinese family company members sue the company for unfairly prejudicial conduct or seek to wind up the company.

Critics might point out that this gap in corporate governance regulation has not created upheavals in the Hong Kong business community, massive dislocation or corporate collapse. However, the regulatory incongruence that exists had not been trouble-free, as a growing body of case law has shown that this regulatory gap has adversely affected the workings of those companies when tensions within families emerge and, in the worst case scenario, *fen jia* (division of assets leading to liquidation) is realised. Given that Hong Kong has an estimated half a million family companies (Young 2014), this lacuna or gap in regulation could trigger more corporate woes if left unaddressed.

Problems with legal recourse through unfairly prejudicial and winding-up actions

In one study, Lawton (2007) examined 275 minority shareholder petitions from 1980 to 1995 to the court of first instance in Hong Kong. Out of these cases, only 26.9 per cent involved Chinese family companies. However, in many of the cases the courts did not see minority shareholder protection in the same way as the litigants in Chinese family companies. The risk of *fen jia* meant that a break-down in governance could lead to winding up action in the courts.

In *Re Shiu Fook Company Ltd*,[8] the plaintiff applied to the courts to wind up the company under section 180 (1A) and unfair prejudice under section 168A of the Companies Ordinance

---

8 [1989] HKCFI 259, HCCW000185/1988.

(cap 32). The petitioner was the concubine of the founder of the company.[9] She alleged that a deadlock with the other family members (who were also directors and shareholders), arose following an extraordinary general meeting about the assets of the company. Madam Wong (the petitioner) contended that there was a long history of family disputes between her side of the family and the siblings of the first wife. However, the court held that many of her allegations concerning the family dispute had no relevance to the winding up action.

Wong Tin Chee Tiny and Ors v Wong To Yick and Ors concerned a series of family disputes that had spilt over into the family company.[10] The father (first respondent) founded the family company in 1988, and the company manufactured and sold a Chinese medicated ointment. It was first made and sold as early as the 1960s. The incorporation of the company was the result of the children (the first, second and third petitioners) of the first respondent (the father) becoming involved in the business. The petitioners (the three children) alleged that a general meeting was held without their knowledge in December 1999. They also claimed that as directors and shareholders, they did not have access to various documents and that information was withheld from them, so that they were unable to assess the value of the family company. Finally, they also claimed that the father and the new directors had conducted the affairs of the family company in such a way that it was unjust and inequitable to require the petitioners either to continue as members or to leave on unjust terms.

Her honour rejected the petitioners' application on the grounds that: '. . . it is plain and obvious that a court would not make a winding-up order but would grant the alternative relief sought, and that the court would hold the Petitioners to be unreasonable should they insist on the winding-up order' (at 31–32, 34).[11] The petitioners were not satisfied with the judgment and took further legal action. This time the litigation was about the goodwill of the family company, together with its related trademarks and businesses.

In this subsequent case, Lam J stated, in his opening remarks, that: 'This is a sad case'. His honour then went on to say that:

> There is no scope for coming up with any other solution even though the answer provided by the law may not deal with all the problems. It is not possible for a court of law to mend the relationship between the parties . . . A lot of parents would gladly pass the family business to their children hoping that they could carry on the same trade after the parents' retirement. But there are exceptions. In the present case, the 2nd Plaintiff is almost 90 years old. He claims that the children had misappropriated his (or the 1st Plaintiff's) rights in the goodwill of the Ointment and seeks relief from this court against them. The evidence shows that at one stage, the Ointment business was run by the children and the family had had happier days. It is therefore quite distressing for this court to observe that when they gave evidence, both the father and the son harboured bitterness towards each other. The father was particularly vocal in expressing his animosity.[12]

From the facts of this case there were two key issues that led to the demise of the family company. The first was the alleged reneging of the father about letting his son take over the

---

9 In Hong Kong if a concubine was wedded to a married man before 1971, the courts will recognize the union under Chinese customary marriages; see Marriage Reform Ordinance (cap 178).

10 [2001] HKCFI 1290, [2001] 2 HKRLD 683, HCCW668/2000.

11 ibid 31–32, 34.

12 *Wong To Yick Wood Lock Ointment Ltd and Anor v Wong Tin Chee Tinley and Ors* [2007] HKCFI 221, HCA 7984/2000 (15 March 2007) 4–5.

business. The second was the father's extra-marital affair that led the children to side with their mother against the father. The father's affair also had implication on the governance of the family company as his honour noted that: 'the mother and the children were concerned about the possibility of Kwan's [father's mistress] intervention into the Ointment business through the shareholding of the father in the Company'.[13] Whilst the judge found in favour of the father's petition, he stated in his concluding remarks that:

> Based on my key findings, no matter how the other issues raised in these actions are to be decided, there would not be a final resolution of the disputes between the parties . . . No judgment in these actions can change the reality that unless they agree on the way ahead for the Company, there will be no end to their fighting. That would not be good for business and I do not see how it could be in the interest of any one of them. It is high time that the family members should sincerely attempt to make peace with each other. Even though previous attempts have failed, I think it is worthwhile for them to try again in the light of this judgment. There are alternative ways of resolving conflicts and litigation may not always produce the most satisfactory outcome.[14]

It is evident that the judge knew that the law could not mend family relationships and Chinese cultural norms.

Another recent case, *Kam Kwan Sing v Kwam Kwan Lai and Ors*,[15] concerned one of Hong Kong's popular Chinese restaurants and tourist eateries, Yung Kee, established in 1947. The dispute involved the second-generation leadership between the two brothers who took over the business after their father's death. The elder brother petitioned the court to wind up the company under section 327(3)(c) and unfair prejudice under section 168A of Companies Ordinance (cap 32). The judge held that: 'I do not find the respondents [including Kam Kwan-lai, the younger brother] have been able to establish any grounds put forth in support of this application [to strike out the winding up move]'.[16]

However, two years after the first attempt had failed, another legal action was launched in January 2012.[17] This time the petition failed again, but it was on different grounds. The verdict was handed down on the 31 October, about three weeks after the petitioner died. In essence, the application failed because the company in question (holding all the business assets and ownership of the restaurant), was incorporated outside of Hong Kong. On appeal, the judges noted that the judge at first instance did not make findings on the allegations of exclusion from management and the mutual understanding in that regard. They also found that the petitioner had not demonstrated any unfairly prejudicial conduct in relation to the payment of dividends. In conclusion, they 'agreed with the judge that the court's jurisdiction under section 327(3)(c) should not be exercised, and that the conditions necessary for jurisdiction to arise under section 168A are not satisfied. The petition was therefore rightly dismissed on this basis'.[18]

---

13 ibid 93.
14 ibid 237–38.
15 [2010] HKCFI 629, HCCW000154/2010.
16 ibid 29.
17 *Kam Leung Sui Kwan, Personal Representative of the Estate of Kam Kwan Sing, the Deceased v Kam Kwan Lai and Ors* [2015] HKCFA 6, FAMV 49/2014.
18 ibid 152.

Clearly, the family feud had not been resolved either by the death of the petitioner or by losing two court battles.

The cases demonstrate that when governance breaks down in Chinese family companies, shareholders of the companies, who might also be directors, would petition the courts for unfair prejudice under section 168A or for winding up of the company on just and equitable grounds under section 177(1)(f) of Companies Ordinance (cap 32). This is closely linked to the way they are governed, where paternalism and harmonious relationships are central to governance of companies. This adds to the argument that the notion of fiduciary duties does not resonate with directors of this type of company.

A second observation from the cases discussed above is that, for both the plaintiffs and defendants, it appears that justice was not about holding directors accountable in the fiduciary sense; rather, it had more to do with the breakdown of paternalistic control and absence of harmonious order (Young 2014). This leads to the fact that prevailing laws and courts as dispute resolution fora were not intended or apt to regulate directors of Chinese family companies in Hong Kong. However, the solution is far from clear.

Conclusions and commentaries

Hong Kong was a British colony for more than a century. Its laws, even after the return to Chinese rule, are essentially based on the British model. This chapter has argued that legal expectations of directors, and the norms that prevail in Chinese family companies, are incongruent. This is because fiduciary duties and the duty of care are premised on the notion that directors have trustee and agency-like obligations towards the company. However, it is evident from the directors of Chinese family companies that they do not see themselves in this way. Instead, heads of Chinese family companies equate paternalistic order with good governance. This view is a product of traditional cultural values originating from Confucianism.

Interestingly, another element of good governance is to achieve and maintain harmonious relationships; this is an extension of a paternalistic approach. Harmony is said to be realised when order is present. What is clear thus far is that the transplanted laws from the UK and the norms emerging from traditional Chinese cultural values cannot easily be reconciled. This is not to say that Chinese family companies are unregulated, as norms do form the basis of their governance, but these norms are different from those found in the Hong Kong Companies Ordinance.

Hong Kong's brand of entrepreneurialism is based on networks of family companies. This is built upon interpersonal bonds between the heads of Chinese family companies matters; these bonds enable them to pool resources together and collaborate on larger business projects, something that has been referred to as the 'Bamboo Network' (Yeung 2004). Underpinning this shared belief is Confucianism (Hamilton 1996). These entrepreneurs rely more on trust (*xingyong*) than contracts when conducting their business. Hong Kong's business networks are clearly regulated through communal norms and relationships so as to build trust, allowing social instead of legal norms to dominate (Young 2014).

This regulatory phenomenon is nothing new; it is a polycentric regulatory regime in which the state is not the locus of authority and in which the state plays a minimalist role (Wright and Head 2009). Its effectiveness is the dependent key actor, tying together the various strands into an effective web of control (Freiberg 2010). This control is effective where violators can be sanctioned directly or indirectly. Even if the sanctions are informal and non-punitive, violators can suffer reputational damage. Since trust between the heads of these companies hinges on relationships, these norms possess normative characteristics.

However, without associations or bodies to institutionalise them or at least to create a forum in which Chinese values are applied as codes of conduct, aggrieved parties have nowhere to turn to when governance breaks down. Unfortunately, at present, no Chinese business associations or bodies are capable of taking on a regulatory role or creating a dispute resolution forum for these companies. Without such mechanisms, as noted in this chapter, *fen jia* (division of assets leading to liquidation) might be the end result when the governance in these companies breaks down.

This chapter has also noted that, in many disputes within Chinese family companies, the plaintiffs (family members) end up petitioning the courts for relief under sections 168A and 177(1)(f) of Companies Ordinance (cap 32). Claims of unfair prejudice made under section 168A perhaps best reflect the fact that relationships in Chinese family companies have broken down. But judges had repeatedly remarked that it is not the function of the courts to examine family disputes in litigation concerning those statutory duties. Whilst this chapter has focused on Hong Kong's family companies, the issues for company laws are the distinctiveness in how Chinese family companies are governed. Whether the same problems are found in family companies in other parts of Asia calls for future research to address. If the answer is in the affirmative, there are implications concerning the effectiveness of prevailing regulations of governance in Asian family companies, as the laws that regulate these entities are also transplanted from developed Western economies.

Nevertheless, since 1 January 2010, Hong Kong's Court Practice Direction 3.3 has allowed voluntary mediation for petitions arising under section 168A of the Companies Ordinance (cap 32), provided that there are no allegations of insolvency concerning the company in question. However, mediation in Hong Kong is modelled upon Western countries, such as Denmark, the UK, Australia, Austria, France, Germany, Italy, the Netherlands, New Zealand, Switzerland and the US (Young 2014). In contrast, traditional Chinese notions of mediation, according to Goh (2002), differ substantially from those in the West. This is because Chinese mediation is vertically structured, where cultural values play a pivotal role in bringing about compromise.

In lieu of a palatable regulatory solution, mediation under Practice Direction 3.3 for section 168A of the Companies Ordinance (cap 32) could work if the mediator is trained or at least well versed in traditional Chinese mediation techniques. Whilst mediation might not resolve the underlying problems in the governance of Chinese family companies, it could help the parties (family members) to mend their relationships. The idea here is, if harmonious relationships could be gradually restored, order will hopefully ensue. Then, governance in Chinese family companies could be trouble-free. Therefore, the government or mediation centres in Hong Kong should consider having mediators to be trained in traditional Chinese mediation techniques. Even if this is not a complete solution to the problem, it is a step in the right direction.

Bibliography

Arcot S. and Bruno V. (2012) 'Do Standard Corporate Governance Practices Matter in Family Firms?' *Financial Markets Group Discussion Paper 710*, September 2012: London School of Economics.

Austin R., Ford H. and Ramsay I. (2005) *Company Directors: Principles of Law and Corporate Governance*, Australia: LexisNexis.

Bebchuk L. and Roe M. (1999) 'A Theory of Path Dependence in Corporate Ownership and Governance' 52 *Stanford Law Review*, 127.

Berle A. and Means G. (1932) *The Modern Corporation and Private Property*, San Diego, CA: Harcourt.

Brudney V. (1997) 'Contract and Fiduciary Duty in Corporate Law' 38 *Boston College Law Review*, 595.

Cadbury A. (2000) *Family Firms and their Governance Creating Tomorrow's Company from Today's*, London: Egon Zehnder International.

Chen M. J. (2001) *Inside Chinese Business: A Guide for Managers Worldwide*, Watertown, MA: Harvard Business School Press.

Clarke T. (2007) *International Corporate Governance: A Comparative Approach*, London: Routledge.

Davies P. (2003) *Gower and Davies' Principles of Modern Company Law*, 7th edn, London: Sweet & Maxwell.

Denning A. (1978) 'Restraining the Misuse of Power', Speech delivered at the Holdsworth Club Presidential Address, Birmingham, 3 March 1978.

Du Plessis J., McConvill J. and Bagaric M. (2005) *Principles of Contemporary Corporate Governance*, New York: Cambridge University Press.

Ebrahimi v Westbourne Galleries Ltd [1973] AC 360.

Erben G. and Guneser A. (2008) 'The Relationship Between Paternalistic Leadership and Organizational Commitment: Investigating the Role of Climate Regarding Ethics' 82 *Journal of Business Ethics*, 955.

Farrar J. (2008) *Corporate Governance in Australia and New Zealand*, 3rd edn, New York, NY: Oxford University Press.

Frankel T., (1983) 'Fiduciary Law' 71 *California Law Review*, 795.

Freiberg A. (2010) *The Tools of Regulation*, Australia: The Federation Press.

Goh B. C. (2002) *Law Without Lawyers, Justice Without Courts: On Traditional Chinese Mediation*, Surrey: Ashgate.

Hamilton G. (1996) 'The Theoretical Significance of Asian Business Networks' in Gary Hamilton (ed), *Asian Business Networks*, Berlin: Walter de Gruyter.

Hamilton G. (2006) *Commerce and Capitalism in Chinese Societies*, London: Routledge.

Hansmann H. and Kraakman R. (2004) 'The End of History for Corporate Law' in Jeffrey Gordon and Mark Roe (eds) *Convergence and Persistence in Corporate Governance*, 33, 45–48, Cambridge: Cambridge University Press.

Hofstede G. and Bond M. (1988) 'The Confucius Connection: From Cultural Roots to Economic Growth' 16 *Organizational Dynamics*, 5.

Hofstede G. (1994) *Cultures and Organizations, Software of the mind: Intercultural cooperation and its importance for survival*, London: Profile Books.

International Financial Corporation (2011) *IFC Family Business Governance Handbook*, Washington: International Financial Corporation.

Jensen M. and Meckling W. (1976) 'The Theory of a Firm: Managerial Behavior, Agency Costs and Ownership Structure' 3 *Journal of Financial Economics*, 305–60.

Kahal S. E. (2001) *Business in Asia Pacific: Text and Cases*, New York, NY: Oxford University Press.

Kam Kwan Sing v Kwam Kwan Lai and Ors [2010] HKCFI 629, HCCW000154/2010.

Kam Kwan Sing v Kam Kwan Lai and Ors [2012] HKCFI 1672, [2012] 6 HKC 246, HCCW154/201.

Kam Leung Sui Kwan, Personal Representative of the Estate of Kam Kwan Sing, the Deceased v Kam Kwan Lai and Ors [2015] HKCFA 6, FAMV 49/2014.

Kao Lee and Yip v Donald Koo Hoi Yan and Ors [2003] HKCFI 850, HCA008847B/1993.

Kishimoto Sangyo Co Ltd and Anor v Akihiro Oba and Ors [1995] HKCFI 382, HCA000396/1995.

Kwan P. (2006) *Hong Kong Corporate Law*, Australia: LexisNexis.

Lan L. L. and Heracleous L. (2010) 'Rethinking Agency Theory: The View from Law' 35 *Academy of Management Review*, 294.

Lawton P. (2007) 'Modeling the Chinese Family Firm and Minority Shareholder Protection: The Hong Kong Experience 1980–1995' 49 *Managerial Law*, 249.

Law Wai Duen v B. F. Construction Co Ltd and Ors [2001] HKCFI 926, HCMP000703/2001.

Licht A., Goldschmidt C. and Schwartz S. (2007) 'Culture Rules: The Foundations of the Rule of Law and Other Norms of Governance' 35 *Journal of Comparative Economics*, 659, 682.

Li J. and Harrison J. R. (2008) 'National Culture and the Composition and Leadership Structure of Boards of Directors' 16 *Corporate Governance: An International Review*, 375.

Li S., Park S. H. and Li S. (2004) 'The Great Leap Forward: The Transition from Relation-Based Governance to Rule-Based Governance' 33 *Organizational Dynamics*, 63.

Mallin C. (2010) *Corporate Governance*, 3rd edn, New York: Oxford University Press.

Mead R. (2005) *International Management: Cross-Cultural Dimensions*, 3rd edn, Chichester: Blackwell.

Meagher R., Heydon D. and Leeming M. (2002) *Meagher, Gummow and Lehane's Equity: Doctrines and Remedies*, 4th edn, Australia: LexisNexis.

Miles L. (2007) 'The Cultural Aspects of Corporate Governance Reform in South Korea' 51 *Journal of Business Law*, 851, 858–60.

Poutziouris P., Smyrnios K. and Goel S. (eds) (2013) *Handbook of Research on Family Business*, Cheltenham: Edward Elgar Publishing.

Redding G. (1990) *The Spirit of Chinese Capitalism*, Berlin: Walter de Gruyter.

Redding G. (2004) 'The Conditional Relevance of Corporate Governance Advice in the Context of Asian Business Systems' 10 *Asia-Pacific Business Review*, 272.

Redmond P. (2009) *Companies and Securities Law: Commentary and Materials*, 5th edn, Australia: Thomson.

Re Shiu Fook Company Ltd [1989] HKCFI 259, HCCW000185/1988.

Smith K. and Keenan D. (1970) *Company Law*, 2nd edn, London: Pitman Publishing.

Smith P. (2010) 'On the Distinctiveness of Chinese Psychology; or: Are We all Chinese?' in Michael Bond (ed), *The Oxford Handbook of Chinese Psychology*, 699, New York, NY: Oxford University Press.

Solomon J. and Solomon A. (2004) *Corporate Governance and Accountability*, New York: John Wiley & Sons.

The Chinese Culture Connection (1987) 'Chinese Values and the Search for Culture-Free Dimensions of Culture' 18 *Journal of Cross-Cultural Psychology*, 143.

Tong F. S. (2009) *Dynamics of Family Business: The Chinese Way*, Singapore: Cengage.

Tricker B. (2009) *Corporate Governance: Principles, Policies, and Practices*, New York, NY: Oxford University Press.

Van V. (2006) 'Causation and Breach of Fiduciary Duty' *Singapore Journal of Legal Studies*, 86.

Ward C. and Lin E. Y. (2010) 'There are Homes at the Four Corners of the Seas: Acculturation and Adaptation of Overseas Chinese' in Michael Bond (ed), *The Oxford Handbook of Chinese Psychology*, 657, 669, New York, NY: Oxford University Press.

Westwood R. (1997) 'Harmony and Patriarchy: The Cultural Basis for 'Paternalistic Headship' Among the Overseas Chinese' 18 *Organization Studies*, 155.

Wong Tin Chee Tiny and Ors v Wong To Yick and Ors [2001] HKCFI 1290, [2001] 2 HKRLD 683, HCCW668/2000.

Wong W. K. (2001) *A Study of Corporate Governance Amongst Listed Chinese Family Enterprise in Hong Kong*, PhD Thesis, University of Hong Kong.

Wright J. and Head B. (2009) 'Reconsidering Regulation and Governance Theory: A Learning Approach' 31 *Law and Policy*, 192.

Yeung H. (2004) *Chinese Capitalism in a Global Era: Towards a Hybrid Capitalism*, London: Routledge.

Yorston R. and Brown S. (1962) *Company Law*, London: Pitman Publishing.

Young A. (2014) *Family Business and Corporate Governance in Hong Kong*, Hong Kong: Wolters Kluwer.

15

Piercing the corporate veil in Latin America

Jose Maria Lezcano Navarro

The corporate entity is a pillar of contemporary economies. The existence of a fiction that can contract, own assets, be held liable and offer limited liability to its members, has definitely been a boost for economic development. However, the corporate entity has also been an instrument used to avoid obligations and, in some circumstances, to engage in fraudulent schemes. Therefore, the piercing of the corporate veil is a remedy against the abuse of the corporate entity. Nonetheless, the application of this remedy has been in some circumstances controversial. The existence of the corporate entity is full of uncertainties; for example, no one can determine the real reasons for a group of investors to operate under the cover of a corporate entity. A creditor that has not been paid may argue that the existence of the entity is to defraud but how can one prove that?

Anglo–American courts have faced this situation throughout the twentieth century. On the one hand, US courts have directly tackled this issue by creating methods such as the instrumentality doctrine and the alter ego doctrine. On the other hand, English courts have ignored corporate entity issues and opted for a 'backdoor alternative' in order to establish liability of the individuals behind the corporate entity. Consequently, these two jurisdictions have been the main cases of study for corporate law researchers on corporate entity issues.

The objective of this chapter is not to repeat an Anglo–American study on corporate entity issues but to refresh this subject by focusing attention on Latin American countries. The impact of piercing the corporate veil in Latin American company law is a subject that has received little attention. Certainly, there are reasons for this, such as Latin America's slow development. Whilst Europe and the USA were experiencing industrialisation and its benefits, Latin American countries were young republics that had to face political and economic issues. However, during the last three decades, Latin America has enjoyed political stability and consequently there has been a boost to Latin American economies.

The availability of corporate personality has played a role in Latin American development. Indeed, as part of a contemporary, capitalist world, Latin American countries have used the corporate entity as a means to motivate investment. Nonetheless, the use of the corporate entity can also produce negative 'secondary effects'. Therefore, the following questions arise: how have Latin American countries dealt with corporate personality issues? What impact has piercing the corporate veil had on Latin American company law?

In order to develop this subject and answer the aforementioned questions, this chapter focuses on three main case studies: Argentina, Brazil and Colombia. These countries have been chosen because of their advances in the study of corporate personality issues. In order to study the subject and each case study, the following structure will be use. First, the legal tradition in each country and its influence on piercing the corporate veil will be discussed. The legal tradition is the pillar of each legal system and consequently influences the way that corporate personality issues are handled. Second, piercing the corporate veil in Latin America will be addressed. This section presents each of the case studies (Argentina, Brazil and Colombia) individually. Third, some comparisons and general comments will be made.

1 The Latin American civil law tradition: effects on corporate entity issues

Latin America is a region that follows the civil law tradition largely due to the Spanish influence. Indeed, most Latin American countries were Spanish colonies. Consequently, language, culture and law, amongst other things, can be considered to have a Spanish heritage. The adoption of the civil law tradition also included the rituals and formalisms that are part of this legal tradition. This creates a complicated environment in which to apply remedies such as piercing the corporate veil because such remedies are based on a judge's ability to use critical thinking (something generally reserved for common law systems).

The use of critical thinking to apply the piercing of the corporate veil doctrine is characteristic of common law systems such as Anglo–American jurisdictions. There are deep and complex differences between the common law and the civil law legal traditions. However, this chapter will focus on one key aspect of this tradition, which can be considered as vital when dealing with corporate personality issues: this is the flexibility to apply critical thinking and positive law.

On the one hand, the common law tradition is flexible with regard to the application of law. The common law judge is not obliged to adhere to positive law. Judges can go beyond the scope of the law in order to provide a 'coherent' and 'equitable' judgment (Perdomo and Marryman 2007). Moreover, in the common law tradition the judge has the status of a virtual law-maker. This fact makes case law a primary source of law in common law countries.

With regard to corporate personality issues, this has had an impact; for example, in England there is no written law that directly allows the piercing of the corporate veil in a commercial context. Therefore, English judges have had to study the circumstances of each case in order to decide whether to adhere to the positive rule that supports the corporate entity, or instead to create an exception to this rule in their decision. The best example of this is the case of *Salomon v A Salomon & Co*, a case in which the English Court of Appeal decided to ignore the corporate entity on grounds that Mr Aron Salomon used the corporate entity in an inappropriate manner.[1] This decision was famously overturned by the House of Lords, where it was held that there is nothing in the Companies Act that prohibited what Mr Salomon had done.

On the other hand, the civil law tradition is stricter regarding the application of the law. The civil law judges are required to adhere to positive law. They cannot decide outside of the scope of positive law (Perdomo and Marryman 2007). The civil law judge is merely a means of applying the law. This has definitely influenced the way that corporate entity

---

1 [1897] AC 22.

issues have been handled in Latin American jurisdictions. The corporate entity is abstract and contemporary society has accepted its existence throughout law. Indeed, the availability of the corporate entity boosts investment and consequently benefits society. However, since its creation, an exception to its existence has not existed; it can be compared to a building without an emergency exit.

In Anglo–American countries, as precursors of the contemporary corporate entity, judges have used their ingenuity and developed remedies such as the US alter ego doctrine or the English sham approach. Latin American judges do not enjoy the same freedom, owing to the formalism of the civil law tradition. However, this has not been an obstacle to developing a means of dealing with corporate entity issues. In order to deal with corporate personality issues, the Latin American judge has relied on traditional legal concepts, derived from the civil law tradition.

Although each Latin American country has a different legal system, they share common principles and concepts of their legal tradition. In this context, the following legal concepts are most commonly used to address corporate entity issues:

- *Fraude a la ley*: (Fraud on the law): the use of alternative legal means to achieve a result intended by another law or laws to be prohibited (Becerra 1999). For example, an individual who is restricted from contracting with the state owing to administrative faults avoids this restriction by using a legally incorporated company to contract with the state.
- *Simulación*: this is a concept based on the use of legal means to avoid obligations. In civil law there are two types of simulated acts, *simulación absoluta* and *simulación relativa*. *Simulación absoluta* refers to an act, which assumes an appearance not corresponding to reality, and is usually the result of two or more persons who attempt to accomplish an unlawful purpose. For example, X transfers his property to Y. In reality X continues to own the property but, by simulating the transfer, X avoids the enforcement of Z's credit over X's property. *Simulación relativa* refers to an act that is made to conceal the true character of the purpose sought by the parties and therefore once discovered the true act or transaction is made retroactively effective for all purposes (Becerra 1999). For example, X sells his property to Y for £100,000, but in the contract, it is stated that the price is £50,000. The purpose here is to conceal the original price so as to avoid taxation. The remedy provided by *simulación* reveals the scheme.
- *Abuso del derecho*: (Abuse of rights): this is the intentional exercise of rights by a person that causes harm to another with no benefit to the person, and which entails an indemnity obligation, provided it is proven that such right was exercised for the sole purpose of causing damage or harming the other person (Becerra 1999). For example, individuals have the right to associate and use the benefits of the corporate personality. However, if the right to use and benefit from the use of the corporate form is employed to defraud third parties, there is an abuse.
- *Acción pauliana*: the *acción pauliana* is a legal device which has been used to deal with corporate veil issues. The *acción pauliana* is a legal remedy to facilitate the enforcement of contractual obligations. This remedy is applied when one of the contracting parties performs other legal acts in order to avoid their obligations to the other party. The affected party may request this remedy in order to nullify the acts made by the other party (De la Cuesta 1984) so as to enforce the contract.

These concepts were not originally conceived to deal with corporate entity issues. However, they are useful because they are applicable to the situations derived from the use of the corporate entity. Certainly, this evidences the ingenuity of the Latin American policy-makers, but it also points out that the Latin American approach is not doctrinal. As previously mentioned, judges in Latin America do not participate in the law-making process; rather, they see themselves as an instrument for applying the law. Consequently, the judge cannot use their initiative to develop a doctrinal method in the same way as a judge in the Anglo–American countries can do.

It is appropriate to ask how these concepts have been implemented. As soon as the corporate entity proved to be a potential issue, reforms to core laws were made and exceptions to corporate personality were included. These legal reforms were not made spontaneously as Latin American countries that have created an exception to corporate personality have done so only on the basis of strict necessity.

2 Piercing the corporate veil in Latin America: the cases of Argentina, Brazil and Colombia

This section addresses three Latin American countries: Argentina, Brazil and Colombia. These three jurisdictions have been chosen because, first, these jurisdictions have shown the greatest development regarding methods of dealing with corporate personality issues and, second, each of these jurisdictions has included an exception in its statutes that provides the basis for corporate personality.

Concerning the first of the reasons given above, dealing with corporate personality issues has developed so as to fill a gap in the law. Latin America has experienced substantial economic growth throughout the last three decades. Corporate personality has been a pillar of economic growth as a result of the advantages and benefits that it has provided. Argentina, Brazil and Colombia can be considered as jurisdictions that have not only used the corporate entity, but have also been aware of the potential damage that this instrument can produce. Hence, these jurisdictions have engaged in developing a remedy to counteract potential corporate personality abuses. As a result, the approaches developed by these countries can be regarded as the most advanced in the region.

With regard to the second reason mentioned above, each jurisdiction has developed its own law in response to its own needs. Therefore, the way corporate personality issues are handled has varied in each jurisdiction. Certainly, the Latin American jurisdictions that are the subject of study have included an exception in core statutes that are the pillar of corporate personality in their countries. However, as will be explained in more detail below, each of these jurisdictions has introduced a statute satisfying a need or gap in the law without affecting the existing legal framework for companies.

The approach developed by each jurisdiction, as well as the effects it has produced, will now be addressed in more detail.

The piercing of the corporate veil in Argentina

With the implementation of a statutory rule that directly addresses the disregard of the legal entity, Argentina is most definitely the jurisdiction that has pioneered the piercing of the corporate veil in Latin America (Hurtado 2008). In 1983, Law 22.903 modified the Ley of Sociedades Comerciales of 1972-Ley No 19,550, the current regulation of the different forms of business associations in Argentina, by adding Article 54. That Article provides that:

> The liabilities of a corporation used to seek a purpose beyond the corporate goals, as a
> mere instrument to defraud the law, the public policy or the good faith, or to frustrate

rights of third persons, will be imputed directly to its shareholders or to the controlling persons who facilitated such activities'.[2]

Argentinian academics and judges have addressed the rule contained in Article 54 as '*inoponibilidad de la persona jurídica*'; the trigger for this remedy is based on acts beyond the corporation's goals, combined with a fraudulent intention. In the context of corporate personality, the concept of *inoponibilidad* has been used as part of a mechanism to hinder the effectiveness of illicit acts performed through a corporate entity (Crispo 2005).

Inoponibilidad de la persona juridica

As in other jurisdictions, corporate personality is sometimes used, when considered necessary, in order to achieve an objective; for example, the creation of an automobile manufacturing company that requires a considerable amount of capital. In order to gather the necessary capital, two or more investors would associate and protect their investment using the mechanism of corporate personality. In this example, the corporate entity would be conceived as a manufacturer of cars, which would receive finance, contract with its workforce and be held liable for its acts. However, if the investors deviated from the company's original goal, i.e. the manufacture of cars, then the existence of that corporate entity would be in jeopardy.

Certainly, this last statement is a little extreme because in modern economies the corporate entity may be used for an objective different from that stated in the memorandum of association. Nonetheless, there are circumstances where the deviation from the original corporate goal may affect third parties. Therefore, in some jurisdictions measures have to be taken to deal with this problem.

Argentina is a jurisdiction that has taken this approach to deal with the deviation from stated corporate goals. Moreover, it has focused on the essence of the Argentinean corporate entity. The Argentinean judiciary and academia consider that the corporate personality has its essence in a contractual relationship (Bomchil 2011). In other words, it is the product of a contract. This is supported by the fact that the corporate personality originates from the agreement between two or more (natural or juridical) persons, which in turn generates obligations amongst the parties.

Certainly, this is arguable, but this is the general position in regard to the nature of the corporate personality in this jurisdiction (Oliveira and Rodriguez 2015). Consequently, it is the basis on which a remedy such as *inoponibilidad de la persona juridica* has been developed. The contractual essence of corporate personality definitely gives room for the application of the *inoponibilidad de la persona juridica* owing to the degree of similarity between the corporate entity and an ordinary contract. For example, a contract needs to have a legal objective. If the objective is not legal, the contract is considered as *viciado* (not legal). Consequently, it would be *inoponible* amongst the parties and the third parties affected by the contract.

---

2 Article 54: '*El daño ocurrido a la sociedad por dolo o culpa de los socios o de quienes no siéndolo la controlen, constituye a sus autores en la obligación solidaria de indemnizar, sin que puedan alegar compensación con el lucro que su actuación haya proporcionado en otros negocios. El socio contratante que aplicare los fondos a efectos de la sociedad a uso o negocio de cuenta propia o de tercero está obligado a traer a la sociedad las ganancias resultantes, siendo perdida de su cuenta exclusiva. La actuación de la sociedad que encubra la consecución de fines extrasocietarios, constituya un mero recurso para violar la ley, el orden publico o la buena fe o para frustrar derecho de terceros, se imputará directamente a los socios o a los controlantes que la hicieron posible, quienes responderan solidaria e ilimitadamente por los perjuicios causados*'.

In the case of the corporate personality, the *inoponibilidad* works as a means of rendering the acts of the corporate personality void, as long as the corporate personality has been used against the objective established in the original contract. Returning to the example, if the automobile manufacturing company was used as a means to lure investors and accordingly gather capital that was not used to manufacture motor cars but was actually used for other purposes that were against the interest of the investors, *inoponibilidad* would hold the shareholders and not the company liable.

Consequence derived from the *inoponibilidad de la persona juridica*

The mechanism of the *inoponibilidad de la persona juridica* can be applied to any type of business association. This is an interesting characteristic of this particular remedy because in other jurisdictions piercing of the corporate veil is limited only to a specific type of business association. The *inoponibilidad de la persona juridica* has a wide scope of application. Furthermore, it is contained in the Argentinean core regulation regarding company law, the Ley de Sociedades Mercantiles de 1972, a regulation that establishes the parameters that have to be followed for the creation, management and dissolution of different types of business associations recognised by the Argentinean framework for companies (Kerr 2012).

Like the piercing of the corporate veil, the *inoponibilidad de la persona jurídica* addresses the wrongdoers behind the corporate entity. First, it renders ineffective the acts carried out by the corporate personality that have affected the claimant party. Second, the wrongdoers must answer for any damage resulting from their acts. It is of upmost importance to observe that the corporate personality will not cease to exist and only the illegal acts will become invalid and the shareholder will therefore be held liable. This is attributable to the fact that the *inoponibilidad de la persona juridica* was not developed as a means to eradicate the corporate personality; rather, it simply renders the illegal acts made through the corporate entity ineffective and holds wrongdoers liable. Accordingly, the rights of innocent shareholders and the interest of good faith creditors are protected.

Some Argentine academics argues that *inoponibilidad de la persona juridica* is different from piercing the corporate veil (Alonso and Giatti 2015). They support their view by arguing that the effect that this remedy has over the corporate personality is the annulment of the acts performed by the entity to achieve the wrongdoers' fraudulent objective, and not the annulment of the corporate entity. However, this argument is debatable. In this chapter, the *inoponibilidad de la persona juridica* is not regarded as different to piercing the corporate veil. The piercing of the corporate veil is a remedy applied according to the particular needs of each jurisdiction. Therefore, the remedy should not be addressed as a remedy that has simply been borrowed from the US but should be seen as unique to each jurisdiction.

The piercing of the corporate veil is not a subject that has been developed uniformly. Each jurisdiction has developed a 'personalised version' that differs from the original US doctrine, yet still achieves the same result. Thus, the *inoponibilidad de la persona juridical* must be regarded as the Argentinean mechanism for dealing with corporate personality issues. Additionally, it must be noted that it has been created not only in accord with the Argentinean framework for companies, but it is also in accord with the essence of the Argentinean idea of corporate personality.

Certainly, the following question may arise: if this remedy does not affect the corporate personality, why does it need criteria for its application? Any remedy or legal phenomena that affects the structure of the corporate entity in any way should be applied in a systematic manner. Should it not be applied in such manner, the foundations of the concept of corporate entity and its attributes of legal personality and limited liability could be undermined.

Criteria to apply the *inoponibilidad de la persona juridica*

The *inoponibilidad de la persona jurídica* cannot be considered as something limited to one statutory rule contained in the Argentinean regulation for companies. A statutory rule requires certain elements to be established in order to boost its application. For this reason, the Argentinean judiciary has supplemented this statutory exception with a parameter for its application. Indeed, in order to apply the *inoponibilidad de la persona juridica*, Argentinean jurisprudence has considered the concurrence of two necessary elements:

- the existence of *vicio* or an illegal act and
- the concurrence of circumstances such as the *simulación, realización del negocio en fraude a terceros, abuso de derechos, actos en contra de la moral y las buenas costumbres.*

The first of these, 'the existence of an illegal act', is a key factor because it is the rationale upon which this remedy has been developed (the prevention and punishment of the misuse of the corporate entity). The circumstances mentioned in the second of the above elements are the means through which the illegal act is to be identified. Clearly, the concept of an illegal act cannot be left alone because it will offer room for vague arguments. Consequently, the concurrence of the above two requirements were needed as part of the criteria for the application of this remedy. It should be mentioned that these circumstances were not created by Argentinean authorities and are established in the Argentinean Civil Code as circumstances that may produce the nullity of a contract.

As has been pointed out previously, corporate personality in Argentina is considered as the product of a contract. Therefore, the Argentinean authorities have adapted elements of contract law as a supplement to the *inoponibilidad de la persona juridica*. The rationale behind this addition is to establish a parameter for the application of this remedy. The corporate entity is important for the Argentinean economy and thus a remedy that upsets its structure cannot be applied in an uncontrolled manner.

Who can summon the *inoponibilidad de la persona juridica*?

The *inoponibilidad de la persona juridica* remedy represents Argentina's willingness to deal with corporate personality issues. However, it is not a remedy that can be easily utilised. Not only does this remedy require the concurrence of special circumstances, but it can be summoned only by specific parties. As a means of controlling the application of this remedy, the Argentinean judiciary has demanded that only specific parties be able to summon the *inoponibilidad de la persona juridical*. They are as follows:

- *Third parties*: a person (natural or juridical) who has been affected by the corporate entity can summon this remedy. However, the party that has been affected has to prove the damage resulting from an illegal act was performed through the corporate personality. Additionally, the argument under one of the circumstances that triggers the application of this remedy has to be developed.
- *Shareholders*: A shareholder (or group of shareholders) can summon the *inoponibilidad de la persona juridica* if the actions of the shareholders who have majority control over the

company threaten the existence of the corporate entity and the interests of minority shareholders and stakeholders (Oliveira and Rodriguez 2015).

Furthermore, with regard to corporate groups, this remedy can be summoned by the subsidiary that was controlled and abused by the parent company, or by a shareholder (or group of shareholders) that has been affected by the actions of the controlling company (Manovil 1998).

The influence of the ultra vires doctrine on the Argentinean approach

From Article 54, it can be considered that Argentinean policy-makers have used the concept of ultra vires as a basis for their approach to dealing with corporate personality issues (Greenberg 2012). Certainly, there is no direct mention of the ultra vires doctrine but the phrase 'an act beyond the corporate goals' can be interpreted as an act that is made against the objective of the corporate entity presented in the memorandum of association. Through the registration of the memorandum of association, the corporate entity comes into existence. In this document, one of the requirements is to state the objective of the company. This is one of the conditions that should be met in order for the law to recognise the existence of the corporate entity.

If a company acts against this objective, it should be considered as having acted beyond what was authorised by law. Certainly, in practice, companies may be allowed to act beyond their original objective, since changing this objective may involve a burdensome process. However, this omission of formalities goes with a tacit condition, 'as long as it is not against the public order'. Therefore, an act beyond corporate goals in this context should be interpreted as the use of the company as a tool for achieving fraud.

Comment

It is important to emphasise that the existence of a statutory rule, in addition to the willingness of the Argentinean judiciary to apply this remedy, has not meant that the disregard of the legal entity is a frequent practice in this jurisdiction. The Argentinean judiciary emphasises the exceptional application of the rule contained in Article 54, based on the premise that the uncontrolled application of this remedy may affect legal certainty and undermine the benefits of the corporate personality. In the case of *Pardini v Fredel SRL y Otros*, the Argentinean judiciary drew attention to the fact that a remedy such as *inoponibilidad de la persona juridica* 'must be applied when it is proved that there has been a fraudulent use of the corporate entity and there is no other remedy available'.

The piercing of the corporate veil in Brazil

The piercing of the corporate veil in Brazil is interesting because the corporate personality is likely to be ignored in this jurisdiction owing to 'pro-social' policies. Whilst corporate personality is a pillar of the economy in Brazil, since the 1940s Brazilian authorities have adopted a labour law policy to punish the wrongful use of the corporate personality. In this area of law there has been a tendency to protect workers' rights because the corporate structure provides ample opportunity to avoid legal obligations. In the context of labour, the corporate personality tends to be used as a means to hide things; for example, assets can be transferred from one company to another and thus hidden. Therefore, the lack of assets to fulfil obligations regarding employees is considered by authorities to be the main trigger for disregarding corporate personality; for example, if the company does not have capital, the shareholders will automatically answer for the debts. Indeed, in the labour law context, the public interest has overcome corporate entity.

For some 20 years after the 1970s, Brazilian authorities were considering the development of a formal mechanism that could be widely applied to ignore the corporate personality. It was not until the 1990s that these considerations were implemented in Brazilian positive law. Initially, exceptions to the corporate personality were introduced in specific statutes aimed at dealing with specific circumstances, but gradually its scope of application expanded and was introduced into a core regulation, the Brazilian Civil Code.

The Brazilian author Bruno Saloma considers that the position of Brazilian authorities towards corporate personality has given room to a 'regime of unlimited liability' (Saloma 2012). The opinion of Saloma is strong and he has grounds on which to support his argument; these reflect the policies aimed at preventing and punishing the misuse of the corporate personality in Brazil. Examples of such policies include, first, the labour law policy against the corporate personality and, second, the gradual development of an exception that can be applied in any area of law. However, the strength of an exception to the corporate personality principle is not the same in all branches of law. Moreover, although there is a 'pro-social' policy on this subject, Brazilian authorities have retained this exceptional remedy to be used as a last resource.

The origins of the Brazilian exception to corporate personality

The exception to the implications of corporate personality in Brazil can be traced back to the 1940s, when the country was subject to major social and legal reforms.[3] Reforms in the context of labour law can be considered as a breakthrough regarding corporate personality matters. These reforms established that shareholders and companies were both liable for obligations to workers. Nowadays, academics and practitioners may regard such policies as dangerous. However, they are limited to labour issues and were honorably created to prevent and punish abuses by employers towards employees. In the context of labour, the existing inequalities between employer and employee were a relevant issue in shaping public policies.

In early Brazilian labour law policy against the corporate entity, there was no mention of disregarding the corporate personality or of piercing the corporate veil. However, the establishment of joint liability created a precedent for later exceptions to the corporate entity. Indeed, it provided room for reflection on the extent that the corporate personality should be preserved.

It was not until the 1970s that the metaphor of piercing the corporate veil started to be used amongst Brazilian academics and the judiciary. It should be pointed out that Brazil only imported the metaphor and not the American doctrine. Policy-makers developed their own mechanism for dealing with corporate personality issues by reference to Brazil's own legal framework and needs. However, although the piercing of the corporate veil became a subject of interest in Brazil, early formal exceptions to the corporate personality were limited to

---

3 One of the key factors in the development of the Brazilian policy towards the corporate personality was the 1930s revolution. This revolution together with the rise to power of the leader Getulio Vargas brought a political shift in Brazil. The changes were aimed at developing laws in accordance with the needs of the poor and individuals who are susceptible to abuse.

specific circumstances, in specific statutes such as the Brazilian Consumer Protection Law and the regulation for the protection of economic order and environmental law. Certainly, the use of this remedy was limited but it was used in accordance with Brazilian 'pro-social policies'.

In this chapter, the concept of 'pro-social policies' refers to the policies implemented to protect the public interest, including those protected by Brazilian labour laws enacted during the 1940s. Brazilian authorities adopted a position against the use of the corporate entity to defeat regulations aimed at the protection of workers' rights, which are of course *a public interest*. These statutes clearly have a public interest, such as consumer rights, economic order and the preservation of the environment. Indeed, the development of an exception in these three areas shows the Brazilian tendency for a pro-social policy, rather than a capitalist policy. This factor had an influence over the later introduction of an exception to corporate personality in the Brazilian Civil Code.

Brazilian authorities did not introduce an equivalent to the piercing of the corporate veil until 2002, when reforms to the Brazilian civil code were made. The introduction of an exception in a core regulation such as the Civil Code created a uniform approach to dealing with corporate personality issues. The Civil Code is now the pillar of the corporate personality concept. Consequently, the rules contained in this code have an impact on any area of law where the corporate personality has been challenged.

Brazilian statutory exceptions can be considered a breakthrough. However, it should be noted that the piercing of the corporate veil has been present in Brazilian case law since the 1970s. Family law, labour law (Reali 2003) and tax law are some of the areas where case law has catalysed a debate regarding the extent to which corporate personality should be preserved. Some statutes, including the Labour Law, had already extended a company's liabilities to shareholders.[4] However, these statutes did not explicitly prescribe the piercing of the corporate veil. Therefore, Brazilian courts were not legally authorised to apply this remedy.

The origins of the current Brazilian approach took place in the early 1990s with the enactment of the Consumer Protection Law and subsequent regulations. Thus, it was at this point of Brazilian legal history that authorities received express authorisation to disregard corporate personality. Certainly, the previous statutory exceptions and reflections contained in Brazilian case law influenced the current mechanism. However, it is only since the 1990s that Brazilian authorities have formalised this subject.

Lei No 8.078 de 11 de septembro de 1990 (Consumer Protection Code)

The Lei No 8.078 de 11 de septembro de 1990 (Consumer Protection Code) was the first Brazilian statutory regulation that directly addressed the piercing of the corporate veil. In Article 28, it is established that a judge can disregard the corporations' legal personality if it

---

4 The Lei No 4.137 of September 1962 art 9 established that directors and managers will be personally liable for the company's debts if they have carried out illegal acts during the course of their administrative duties. See http://www.planalto.gov.br/ccivil_03/decreto/1950-1969/D52025. htm (last accessed 7 June 2016). Also, the Lei 4.729 of 1965, in art 1, established that courts were allowed to impose criminal sanctions on directors and members of corporations that dishonestly concealed taxes. See http://www.planalto.gov.br/ccivil_03/leis/1950-1969/L4729.htm (last accessed 7 June 2016).

has been used to the detriment of a consumer's rights.[5] The enactment of this rule is derived from a constitutional initiative. The Constituição Federal of 1988 in its Articles 5, 48 and 170 establishes the defence of the consumer as one of the commitments of the state.[6] Indeed, the authorities considered that corporate personality had the potential to affect a consumer's rights. Therefore, in the law enacted to deal with this subject a means to combat the misuse of corporate personality was included. The constitution not only motivated the inclusion of an exception to corporate personality, but also gave weight to this remedy owing to the superior status of the constitution in the Brazilian legal framework.

It should be pointed out that the constitutional rule regarding the protection of consumers was not a legislative whim; rather, it was a matter of principle. The judiciary and academia considered that the consumer could be at a disadvantage when confronted with the fraudulent acts performed by a merchant. Moreover, the potential of the corporate entity to affect consumers was not ignored. Therefore, the rationale for giving the judge the authority to disregard the legal entity has been the protection of the weaker party (the consumer) against the abuses of a stronger party (the enterprise). Definitely, this reflects a pro-social tendency of the Brazilian authorities in the enactment of this rule.

Although Article 28 addresses the issue only in a consumer–merchant relationship, this rule has also established the template on which later statutory exceptions to the corporate personality were drafted.

Lei No 9.605 of 12 February 1998 (Environmental law)

The Lei No 9.605 of 12 February 1998 (Environmental law), in section 4, established that the corporation's legal personality will be disregarded when the environment has been damaged and the corporation frustrates any efforts to recover any damage to the environment.[7] This exception to corporate personality has its foundation in a policy aimed at the protection of the environment. As such, this is a policy based on the public interest. Indeed, environmental law has gradually gained strength to such a point that it overrides the economic policy and supports corporate personality. In addition to the public interest contained in environmental

---

5 Article 28:' *O juiz poderá desconsiderar a personalidade jurídica da sociedade quando, em detrimento do consumidor, houver abuso de direito, excesso de poder, infração da lei, fato ou ato ilícito ou violação dos estatutos ou contrato social. A desconsideração também será efetivada quando houver falência, estado de insolvência, encerramento ou inatividade da pessoa jurídica provocados por má administração.*

§ 1° (Vetado).
§ 2° As sociedades integrantes dos grupos societários e as sociedades controladas, são subsidiariamente responsáveis pelas obrigações decorrentes deste código.
§ 3° As sociedades consorciadas são solidariamente responsáveis pelas obrigações decorrentes deste código.
§ 4° As sociedades coligadas só responderão por culpa.
§ 5° Também poderá ser desconsiderada a pessoa jurídica sempre que sua personalidade for, de alguma forma, obstáculo ao ressarcimento de prejuízos causados aos consumidores.

6 *A constituição Federal de 1988 no seu artigo 5.° inciso XXXII, determina que o Estado promoverá, na forma da lei, a defesa do consumidor. No artigo 170 inciso V, preceitua que um dos princípios da ordem econômica, fundada na valorização do trabalho humano e na livre iniciativa, é a defesa do consumidor. E finalmente, no artigo 48 no Ato das Disposições Constitucionais Transitórias, determina que seja elaborado o Código de Defesa do Consumidor'.*

7 Article 4: '*Poderá ser desconsiderada a pessoa jurídica sempre que sua personalidade for obstáculo ao ressarcimento de prejuízos causados à qualidade do meio ambiente. Lei No 9.605 de 12 de fevereiro de 1998 Dispõe sobre as sanções penais e administrativas derivadas de condutas e atividades lesivas ao meio ambiente, e dá outras providências'.*

law, the Brazilian pro-social tendency also gives strength to the environmental law exception to corporate personality.

It should be acknowledged that this exception to corporate personality is limited to circumstances where the activities of the corporate personality have damaged the environment. Therefore, the disregard of the corporate personality in this context should not be a dramatic concern. The idea of corporate personality is not aimed at aiding investors to avoid liability derived from environmental damages; rather, it aims to stimulate economic growth by the limitation of liability in a commercial context.

This statement is subject to discussion because some academics may consider that the limitation of liability should extend to environmental disasters. However, the limitation of liability should not be allowed on grounds of environmental matters. If limited liability allows shareholders to override environmental regulation, it is likely that because of the lack of a sanction, entrepreneurs will not take the necessary steps to prevent environmental damage. The Brazilian exception to corporate personality in environmental law regulation can be regarded as an initiative aimed at pushing entrepreneurs to take the necessary measures to prevent environmental disasters.

Brazilian Civil Code

Limiting the power to disregard a corporation's legal personality to specific circumstances can be considered as a gradual introduction of a formal mechanism for dealing with corporate personality issues in the Brazilian legal framework. In 2002, the enactment of the new Brazilian Civil Code included a rule that allows the legal entity to be disregarded when it is used for fraudulent purposes. Most notably, this remedy steadily expanded from specific laws into a whole body of law such as the Civil Code.

The exception contained in the Brazilian Civil Code now empowers the judge to consider the disregard of the legal entity throughout any area of Brazilian private law. Article 50 of this code establishes that:

> In the case of abuse of the corporate form characterised by acts against a company's purpose or commingling of assets, a judge may decide, at the petition of the plaintiff or the State Department, if it has the right to intervene, that liability for certain obligations be extended to the personal property or assets of the managers or partners of an entity.[8]

The phrase 'In the case of abuse . . .' clearly allows for an exception to corporate personality based on the concept of abuse; but what can be considered *abuse* in this context? The use of the word 'abuse' by itself is vague; for example, the mere action of incorporating a business so as to reduce liability may be considered by a creditor to be an abuse. Therefore, Brazilian authorities have structured this exception to corporate personality with the concept of *abuso del derecho* (abuse of rights). As previously noted, the concept of *abuso del derecho* establishes that a right is a benefit that is conferred by the law and this benefit can be confiscated if used improperly.

---

8 Article 50: '*Em caso de abuso da personalidade juridica, caracterizado pelo desvio de finalidade, ou pela conflisio patrimonial, pode o juiz decidir, a requerimento da parte, ou do Ministrrio Publico quando the couber intervir no processo, que os efeitos de certas e determinadas relagoes de obrigagdes sejam estendidos aos bens particulares dos administradores ou socios da pessoa juridica*'.

In the context of the corporate personality, Brazilian law regards corporate personality and limited liability as rights and, as such, they must be exercised without affecting other parties' rights. *Abuso del derecho* is the core feature of this exception because it established the misuse of a right as the foundation of an argument based on the concept of abuse. Moreover, in order to ensure certainty, this article has also described the type of behaviour that can be considered as *abuso del derecho* in this context:

- the use of the company against its original purpose
- and commingling of assets.

Highlighting these two circumstances creates greater certainty because it prevents the concurrence of vague arguments. To determine whether the company has been used against its originally intended purpose, or whether there has been a commingling of assets, is not a simple process. Evidence and reflection over the claim are required in order to decide whether there has been a disregard of corporate personality. However, the existence of this rule gives guidance for applying this remedy.

It should also be noted that Article 50 does not mention fraud. Certainly, fraud is a rationale for piercing the corporate veil. However, Brazilian authorities have not limited this remedy to the occurrence of fraud. Clearly, the commingling of assets and the inadequate use of the corporate entity are situations that may not necessarily involve fraudulent behaviour, but are likely to affect third parties. The fact that this exception can be applied in circumstances that may not involve fraudulent behaviour shows the 'pro-social policy' that is followed by the authorities in the context of piercing the corporate veil. Indeed, Brazilian authorities have introduced a remedy that compensates for the inequalities produced by the corporate entity.

Comment

The judiciary and academia have gradually introduced a mechanism for dealing with corporate personality issues in the Brazilian legal system. It can be considered that this remedy has been widely accepted owing to its enactment in a core regulation (the Civil Code). However, its application has not been common. Indeed, the judiciary has emphasised the exceptional application of this remedy. In a 1997 sentence, a Brazilian court held that: 'The legal existence of a corporation may, in certain cases, be disregarded. However, substantial evidence of abuse of rights has to be produced'. Although the piercing of the corporate veil was introduced as a measure to counter the abuse of the entity doctrine, the Brazilian judiciary has been aware of the vital role that corporate personality has had in the development of the nation's economy. Consequently, jurisprudence has emphasised the fact that the corporate veil may be pierced only when the abuse of the corporate form has been proven. The civil law principle of *abuso del derecho* can be considered as a way of reaching the degree of certainty demanded by Brazilian jurisprudence on this subject.

In Brazil, as in other jurisdictions, the piercing of the corporate veil has been the product of a legal need. However, besides the need for a law to deal with corporate personality issues, it can be argued there was a need for equity. Corporate personality tends to produce inequalities in situations where, for example, the environment has been damaged because of negligence and where those responsible try to evade liability. The consumer protection law and environmental law are an example of Brazilian attempts to combat inequalities produced by corporate personality. As has been emphasised above, the Brazilian mechanisms for dealing with corporate personality issues have had their foundations in pro-social policy.

Piercing the corporate veil in Colombia

In Colombia, corporate personality issues have been present since the corporate entity became commonly used. However, piercing the corporate veil is a relatively recent subject. As in other Latin American countries, the creation of an equivalent remedy to piercing the corporate veil in Colombia has been the product of the country's recent economic dynamism. Certainly, remedies such as the *acción pauliana* and exceptions to the corporate personality in insolvency law were used in the past. However, the express use of an exception to corporate personality is relatively recent, a fact that can be attributed to the need for a more effective remedy. Colombia is a particularly interesting case study because it has developed an exception to the corporate personality in order to deal with specific types of business entities. Moreover, the exceptions used have been developed in such a way that there is not a direct attack on the business entity, but on the acts made through it.

This remedy was derived from the need of business entities to have light regulation. This need is the product of tight regulation over the Colombian joint stock corporation, known as *sociedad anonima*. This type of business association is popular because of the attributes of legal personality and limited liability. However, its tight regulation presents a burden rather than an advantage for small entrepreneurs. For that reason, Colombian policy-makers created the one-man company (*sociedad unipersonal*) and the *sociedad por acciónes simplificadas* as an alternative for small entrepreneurs. These legal entities have flexible regulations, which makes them susceptible to be used for fraudulent or illicit purposes. Therefore, exceptions equivalent to the piercing of the corporate veil were included in the regulation of these legal entities.

It should be noted that in Colombia other means have been employed in order to deal with corporate personality issues; for example, bankruptcy law and labour law contain regulations that have, as an indirect effect, disregarded the legal entity. However, this section is aimed at the one-man company and *sociedad por acciónes simplificadas*. The core of the Colombian mechanism for dealing with corporate personality issues is the concept of *abuso del derecho*. The exceptions to the corporate personality contained in these regulations have been structured around this concept. Moreover, other regulations that have indirectly dealt with corporate personality issues have employed this concept as a point of reference.

The Ley 222 of 1995, which creates the *empresa unipersonal* (one-man company)

This law modified the Code of Commerce and the regulation of companies. One of the most relevant aspects was the creation of the *empresa unipersonal*. Small businessmen have been interested in acquiring the benefits of the corporate entity for individual enterprises. However, the creation of a joint stock corporation or a limited liability company requires the compliance of a series of formalities, which are a burden rather than an advantage, for small entrepreneurs. Therefore, the Colombian legislator made a breakthrough with the introduction of the *empresa unipersonal*, a device for commerce that provides the advantages of the corporate entity to a sole entrepreneur. Traditional company law requires a company to have at least a minimum of two members; the lack of the required membership may invalidate the company. However, the *empresa unipersonal* is not subject to this membership requirement because it is an entity designed to function with a sole member, benefited by the attributes of limited liability and legal personality.

The objective of the *empresa unipersonal* is to allow a natural or legal person to develop a personal business and enjoy the benefits of separate legal personality and limited liability.[9] This is certainly a device that encourages entrepreneurs. However, when drafting this law, the potential of this device to be used for practising illicit and fraudulent purposes was also considered. Therefore, in the same law that created this entity (Article 71), the policy-makers included an exception: 'if this form of enterprise is used for fraudulent purposes or to affect third parties, the entrepreneur shall answer together with the entity for its debts'.[10]

The exception to the one-man company was a proposal made by the Colombian *Superintendencia de Sociedades*.[11] However, the proposal was not only aimed at the one-man company but at every type of business entity recognised by the Colombian legal framework for companies. The policy-makers evaluated the proposal but decided to limit the exception to the one-man company. This decision can be attributed to two factors. First, to disregard the corporate personality is a delicate subject and to allow its free application can undermine the concept of corporate personality. Second, this remedy was not needed for dealing with other business entities owing to the strict regulations to which other business entities are subjected. However, although the exception included in the regulation of the one-man company was considered an equivalent to piercing the corporate veil, this exception has a different effect.

The remedy does not establish the disregard of the legal entity; rather, it makes the wrongdoer liable by nullifying all the fraudulent acts made through the business entity. Accordingly, the business entity is kept alive to safeguard the interests of third parties. Other parties may have contracted in good faith with the business entity and, should it be dissolved, these other parties may be affected.

Besides the exception to the *empresa unipersonal* legal personality, this law also included a rule that addressed the disregard of the corporate entity in the context of corporate groups. In Article 148 (derogated by the Ley 1116 of 2006),[12] the law established that a parent company may be held liable for the subsidiary's insolvency if the situation of the latter is the

---

9 Ley 222 of 1995, art 71: '*Mediante la empresa unipersonal una persona natural o juridical que reúna las cualidades requeridas para ejercer el comercio, podrá destinar parte de sus activos para la realización de una o varias actividades de carácter mercantil. La empresa unipersonal, una vez inscrita en el registro mercantile, forma una persona juridical*'.

10 ibid, art 71, para: '*Cuando se utilice la empresa unipersonal en fraude a la ley o en perjuicio de terceros el titular de las cuotas de capital y los administradores que hubieren realizado, participado o facilitado los actos defraudatorios responderan solidariamente por las obligaciones nacidas de tales actos y por los perjuicios causados*'.

11 The *Superintendencia de Sociedades* (Superintendence of Corporations) is a technical body, ascribed to the Ministry of Commerce, Industry (in some jurisdictions to the ministry of Tourism). This legal entity has juridical personhood, administrative autonomy and its own assets through which the President of the Republic exercises the inspection, surveillance and control of commercial companies, as well as the faculties appointed by law in relation to other entities, legal persons and natural persons. Example of a country with a *Superintendencia de Sociedades* is Colombia. See http://www.supersociedades.gov.co/English/OurOrganization/WhoWeAre/Pages/default.aspx (last accessed 7 June 2016).

12 The Ley 1116 of 2006 established the Entrepreneurial Insolvency Regimen in Colombia. The art 61 of the Ley 1116 of 2006 addressed some aspects that were not covered by the art 148. First, the art 61 more extensively developed the concept of parent company. It established that a parent company could be a holding or could be a group of companies controlling the subsidiary. Additionally, the art 62 established the expiration of the action, which is 4 years. This was not addressed in the Ley 222 of 1995. The Ley 1116 of 2006 also established that the *Superintendencia de Sociedades* is the competent authority to address liquidation proceedings in this context.

product of the excessive control of the former and if there are decisions made against the interest of the subsidiary. This rule is founded on the dominance of the parent over the subsidiaries, which in some cases is so strong that it leaves the subsidiary with a level of dependence. However, an argument against a parent company on grounds of this rule may be refuted if the parent proves that the subsidiary's insolvency is a product of other circumstances. The Constitutional Court held in the *Sentencia* C–510/97 that: '. . . if the defendant can prove that its decisions and management was not the cause for the subsidiary's insolvency, the separation of personality and liabilities will be held'.[13]

The reforms introduced in the Ley 222 of 1995 definitely supplemented the Colombian commercial legislation and brought innovation. First, a legal entity that encourages entrepreneurship was introduced. Additionally, an exception to deter its misuse was established. Second, a parent company's liability in a case of insolvency was addressed. The Colombian judiciary, based on the concept of control, developed an exception to separate corporate personality – something of a breakthrough during that period.

The Ley 1258 of 2008, the regulation for the *sociedad por acciónes simplificadas*

This law creates the *sociedad por acciónes simplificada*. The *sociedad anónima* (Colombian joint stock company) is subject to regulations that make its creation a burdensome process for small entrepreneurs. Consequently, the *sociedad por acciónes simplificada* was created as an alternative. The law that regulates this business entity is flexible in terms of the requirements for its constitution. Moreover, this form of business association has the attributes of legal personality and limited liability. This business entity has the potential to be used for fraudulent purposes, owing to its flexible regulation. Therefore, policy-makers developed an exception to the legal personality of this form of business association. In Article 42 the following is established: 'If the *sociedad por acciónes simplificadas* has been used for fraudulent purposes and against third parties, the shareholders and directors that participated in the fraud shall be held liable'.[14]

The exception to the *sociedad por acciónes simplificadas* personality seems to be a tool against the corporate entity. However, this remedy does not dissolve this business entity; rather, it nullifies the fraudulent or illicit acts made through this business entity. It renders the fraudulent shareholder(s) liable without affecting the interests of innocent shareholders and third parties.

The exception to the corporate personality contained in this regulation did not cause an impact because a direct mechanism against the corporate personality already existed in a commercial law context, in the regulation for the one-man company. However, the remarkable aspect of the exception to the *sociedad por acciónes simplificadas* personality is in its

---

13 '*Se trata, entonces, de una presunción Iuris Tantum, que puede ser desvirtuada por la matriz controlante, o por sus vinculadas, demostrando que sus decisiones no han causado la desestabilización económica de la filial o subsidiaria, sino que esta procede de motivos distintos*'. Constitutional Court *Sentencia* C-510 of 9 October 1997.

14 Ley 1258 of 2008 art 42: '*Cuando se utilice la sociedad por acciones simplificada en fraude a la ley o en perjuicio de terceros, los accionistas y los administradores que hubieren realizado, participado o facilitado los actos defraudatorios, responderán solidariamente por las obligaciones nacidas de tales actos y por los perjuicios causados.*
La declaratoria de nulidad de los actos defraudatorios se adelantará ante la Superintendencia de Sociedades, mediante el procedimiento verbal sumario.
La acción indemnizatoria a que haya lugar por los posibles perjuicios que se deriven de los actos defraudatorios será de competencia, a prevención, de la Superintendencia de Sociedades o de los jueces civiles del circuito especializados, y a falta de estos, por los civiles del circuito del domicilio del demandante, mediante el trámite del proceso verbal sumario'.

result. This exception was drafted in a way so as not undermine the concept of corporate personality. Like its predecessor, the exception to the *sociedad por acciónes simplificadas* was crafted to punish wrongdoers on grounds of abusive behaviour. Certainly, even if both statutory rules are observed, they are short and do not detail what can be considered fraud and the circumstances that must concur in order to trigger an exception. However, it should be pointed out that these exceptions have their foundation in a basic civil law tradition concept. This in turn allows the judiciary to apply these exceptions free of vague arguments. This concept is *abuso del derecho*.

The foundation of the Colombian approach to corporate personality issues

The Colombian equivalent to the piercing of the corporate veil has been developed on solid grounds. Indeed, as a country of civil law tradition, this remedy cannot be structured on vague principles or doctrines. As with the Argentinean jurisprudence, in Colombia the corporate entity is considered to be the product of a contract. As an entity born from the agreement between two or more parties, the corporate entity is subjected to the principles and concepts governing the contractual relationship (Paucar 2010). Consequently, in order to deal with corporate personality issues, the Colombian authorities have relied on the concept of *abuso del derecho*.

The *abuso del derecho* refers to abuse committed under the exercise of a right; for example, the corporation is based on the right to associate and thus also based on this right the corporate entity is developed to boost commerce and limit shareholders liability. It is not to cover abusive or fraudulent conduct and consequently the exception to the corporate personality will be triggered if the parties that benefit from this right to associate have been used in an abusive way such as to defraud other parties.

The concept of *abuso del derecho* is contained in Article 830 of the Colombian Code of Commerce. This concept is not aimed at the corporate personality. Nonetheless, authorities can rely on it owing to the contractual nature of the corporate personality. Moreover, the judiciary has relied on *abuso del derecho* to the point that the statutory exceptions to the corporate personality are based on this concept.

In addition to *abuso del derecho*, in the exception to the *sociedad por acciónes simplificadas* the concept of *fraude a la ley* is summoned. The concept of *fraude a la ley* differs from the concept of *abuso del derecho*, but both concepts are triggered by the same circumstance; i.e., the harm to third parties through the commission of an illicit act. The concept of *fraude a la ley* can be considered supplementary to the exception to the corporate entity because it expands the exception to circumstances where the corporate entity has been used to defraud the law. It can be considered that *abuso del derecho* can also cover this type of inappropriate use of the corporate entity. Nonetheless, the concept of *fraude a la ley* frees *abuso del derecho* from this burden and brings more certainty by providing specific grounds for the application of the remedy. Consequently, it can be regarded as the Colombian equivalent to the piercing of the corporate veil and has its foundations in the concepts of *abuso del derecho* and *fraude a la ley*.

Controversy between statutory exceptions to the corporate personality and the Colombian Constitution

The piercing of the corporate veil has been a controversial subject in every jurisdiction and has been challenged on different grounds. In the case of Colombia, the Colombian statutory exceptions to corporate personality have been challenged at a constitutional level. In Colombia, the case law concerning the piercing of the corporate veil is mainly based on decisions from the Colombian Constitutional Court, rather than decisions from regular courts (Garnica and others 2007). The exception to the corporate entity has clashed with rights such as the preservation of the economic order (Article 2),[15] as well as the freedom to associate for any legal purpose (Article 38).[16]

Freedom of association and the preservation of the economic order are key for the existence of steady economic development and thus for the existence of the corporate personality. On the one hand, the right to associate allows people to join and achieve a common objective, often commercial. The use of this right for commercial purposes gave rise to the business entity. Consequently, this right is a factor that contributes to the creation of wealth in contemporary capitalist society. Moreover, it aids a country's development. On the other hand, the state has the duty to create stability for its citizens; for example, citizens have the right to a steady environment for the exchange of goods and services. In other words, they have the right to the existence of an economic order. These rights are at a constitutional level, yet in the constitution there are no exceptions to these rights. Consequently, can the statutory exceptions to the corporate personality undermine constitutional rights? If so, to what extent can congress legislation override constitutional rights and duties?

The *Sentencia* C–865 of 2004 is a relevant precedent in which the Constitutional Court has reflected over this controversy.[17] In this precedent, the Constitutional Court emphasised that the rationale for ignoring the corporate personality is the prevention and punishment of fraud. The court established that 'the shareholders will be liable when the good faith is affected and limited liability is used to achieve an objective that is against the purpose of constitutional rights and defrauds third parties'. Indeed, the Constitutional Court approached this dilemma taking into account the concept of *abuso del derecho* (abuse of rights). According to this concept, a right cannot be preserved if it is used to affect other parties' rights. It was established that an exception to the constitutional right of association is to be granted when it is used for an illegal purpose. Additionally, in this precedent the fact that the Congress has the authority to regulate the use and limitations of the corporate personality was clarified. Regarding this last point, part of the dilemma over the exceptions to the corporate personality was the power of the congress to enact a law that challenged constitutional rights.

The final decision did not nullify the statutory exceptions to the corporate personality. Although Congress cannot challenge a constitutional right such as the right of association, it can be considered that the Constitutional Court is inclined to maintain the exception to the corporate personality because it is part of the mechanism for deterring and controlling the misuse of constitutional rights. This inclination can be attributed to the fact that an introduction of an exception to constitutional rights in the constitution involves a controversial

---

15 Article 2. '*Son fines esenciales del Estado: servir a la comunidad, promover la prosperidad general y garantizar la efectividad de los principios, derechos y deberes consagrados en la Constitución; facilitar la participación de todos en las decisiones que los afectan y en la vida económica, política, administrativa y cultural de la Nación; defender la independencia nacional, mantener la integridad territorial y asegurar la convivencia pacífica y la vigencia de un orden justo.*'

16 Article 38. '*Se garantiza el derecho de libre asociación para el desarrollo de las distintas actividades que las personas realizan en sociedad. Constitución Política de Colombia 1991. Título II, de los derechos, las garantías y los deberes*'.

17 Constitutional Court *Sentencia* C-865 of 7 September 2004 http://www.corteconstitucional.gov. co/relatoria/2004/C-865-04.htm (last accessed 7 June 2016).

and long process. Therefore, the creation of a law by the congress can be regarded as more 'practical'.

It should also be pointed out that the Constitutional Court clarified that the exception to the corporate entity only applies if it has been used to commit wrongdoings and under extraordinary circumstances. In summary, the Constitutional Court can be seen to be following the trend regarding the development of a mechanism to deal with corporate personality issues. However, the Colombian authorities have done it in accordance with their framework for companies.

Comment

The Colombian equivalent to the piercing of the corporate veil is not aimed at the business entity itself; rather, it is aimed at the acts committed through the business entity. This is supported in the rationale for the development of this approach, which rests on the policy of seeking to protect the corporate entity. Certainly, the existence of exceptions to the business entity in Colombian positive law shows a willingness to deal with corporate entity issues. However, this does not mean that the Colombian authorities do not protect the business entity. Colombia, as any other developing economy, depends on the business entity. Consequently, this cannot be undermined. For that reason, the exceptions contained in the regulation for one-man company and *sociedades por acciónes simplificadas* do not attack the business entity. Moreover, they are only applied in exceptional circumstances.

3 The impact of piercing the corporate veil in Latin American jurisdictions

The piercing of the corporate veil certainly influences the legal framework for companies in each jurisdiction that implements a method for dealing with corporate entity issues. It has been a difficult process for Anglo–American jurisdictions because of constant debates over the issue throughout the twentieth century. In Latin America, the methods for dealing with corporate entity issues are relatively new. Moreover, policy-makers have continued debating during the development and introduction of exceptions in statutory law. However, this does not mean that the introduction of an exception to the corporate personality doctrine has not had an impact. Has this fact deterred investment?

The answer to this question is difficult to reach because statistics are hard to come by. However, investment has not been hindered. The exceptions to the doctrine are limited to specific circumstances and a criterion has to be met in order for this remedy to be applied. Additionally, this exception has created an awareness of the issues. In Brazil, for example, there is an exception focusing on environmental issues. This creates an awareness amongst investors and encourages them to take the necessary precautions to prevent environmental disasters.

Conclusion

In conclusion, despite being in its early stages, the exception to the corporate entity influences Latin American company law.

Latin American and Anglo–American approaches to lifting the veil of incorporation can be contrasted. It can be considered that the Latin American approach offers more certainty because it establishes the circumstances where the corporate entity can be disregarded. Although Anglo–American case law reflects a tendency to preserve the corporate entity, there is no certainty regarding the judge's decision over a matter related to corporate entity issues. However, although the Latin American statutory approach offers a degree of certainty, it cannot be considered superior to the Anglo–American approach. Exceptions to the corporate personality are the product of a need within each legal system. Each jurisdiction adapts a remedy in accordance with its own systems and needs, owing to the impact remedy on the framework for the operation of the corporate entity.

Bibliography

Books and articles

Alonso, J. and Giatti, G. (2015) *Aspectos Procesales de la Aplicacion de la Teoria de la Inponibilidad de la Personalidad Juridica* http://www.rivera.com.ar/sites/default/files/alonsogiatti_aspectos_procesales_de_la_aplicacion_de_la_teoria_de_la_inoponibilidad_de_la_personalidad_juridica2.pdf (last accessed 7 June 2016).

Becerra, F. (1999) *Diccionario de Terminología Jurídica Mexicana (español/Inglés)*. Mexico: Escuela Libre de Derecho.

Bomchil, M. (2011) *La Inoponibilidad de la Persona Juridica Societaria y el art. 54, Tercer Párrafo, de la Ley 19.550 de Sociedades Comerciales* www.bomchil.com.ar (last accessed 7 June 2016).

Camargo, A. (2003) 'Three Essential Aspects of Corporate Law: A Brief Overview of Brazilian and American Approaches' *Southwestern Journal of Law & Trade in the Americas*. Volume 9, No 1. 89–108.

Crispo, D. (2005) *Inoponibilidad de la Persona Juridica* http://www.iprofesional.com/adjuntos/documentos/09/0000929.pdf (last accessed 7 June 2016).

De la Cuesta, J. M. (1984) *La Acción Pauliana*. Madrid.

Garnica, C and others (2007) *Corte Constitucional Linea Jurisprudencial 1997–2007, Levantamiento del Velo Corporativo*. Universidad Sergio Arboleda.

Greenberg, D. (2012) *Stroud's Judicial Dictionary of Words and Phrases* (8th edition). London: Sweet & Maxwell.

Hurtado, J. (2008) *La Doctrina del Levantamiento del Velo Societario en España e Hispanoamérica*. España. Atelier.

Kerr, I. (2012) '*La Teoria de Inoponibilidad de la Personalidad y su Aplicación al Arbitraje. Posibilidad de Extenderla Clausula Arbitral a Partes no Signatarias*' *Revista Argentina de Derecho Empresario*. Available at http://ijeditores.com.ar/articulos.php?idarticulo=65067&print=2#indice_4 (last accessed 7 June 2016).

Manovil, R. (1998) *Grupos de Sociedades*. Argentina, Abeledo-Perrot.

Olivera, N. and Rodriguez, C. (2015) *Inoponibilidad de la Persona Juridica*. http://www.derechocomercial.edu.uy/RespInop.htm (last accessed 7 June 2016).

Paucar, J. (2010) *El Levantamiento del Velo Corporativo en Colombia* in Franco, A. *El Levantamiento del Velo Corporativo, panorama y perspectivas. El caso colombiano*. Colombia, Editorial Universidad del Rosario.

Perdomo, R. and Marryman, J. (2007) *The Civil Law Tradition: An Introduction to the Legal Systems of Europe and Latin America* (3rd edition) California. Stanford University Press.

Reali, R. (2003) *Desconsideração da Personalidade Jurídica no Direito Positivo Brasileiro*. Universidad Regional de Blumenau http://www.boletimjuridico.com.br/doutrina/texto.asp?id=327 (last accessed 7 June 2016).

Saloma, B. (2012) 'The End of Limited Liability in Brazil' http//works.69bpress.com/Bruno_mayerhof_Salama/69 (last accessed 30 October 2015).

Cases

*   English
    Salomon v A Salomon & Co [1897] AC 22
*   Argentinean
    Pardini v Fredel SRL y otros 2006

- Colombian
  Corte Constitucional, Sentencia C–510 del 9 de octubre de 1997
  Corte Constitucional, Sentencia C–865 del 7 de septiembre de 2004

Legislation

- Argentina
  Ley de Sociedades Comerciales of 1972-Ley No 19,550
- Brazilian
  Brazilian Civil Code
  Lei No 8.078 of 11 September 1990, Código de Defesa do Consumidor
  Lei No 9.605 of 12 February 1998, Lei de Crimes Ambientais
- Colombia
  Colombian Constitution
  Ley 222 of 1995 por la cual se Reforma el Codigo de Comercio
  Ley 1258 of 2008 sobre Sociedades por Acciones Simplificadas

Index

For Product Safety Concerns and Information please contact our EU
representative GPSR@taylorandfrancis.com
Taylor & Francis Verlag GmbH, Kaufingerstraße 24, 80331 München, Germany

www.ingramcontent.com/pod-product-compliance
Ingram Content Group UK Ltd.
Pitfield, Milton Keynes, MK11 3LW, UK
UKHW011454240425
457818UK00021B/820